Day Hikes in the Santa Fe Area

Founded in 1892, the Sierra Club works in the United States and other countries to restore the quality of the natural environment and to maintain the integrity of ecosystems. Educating the public to understand and support these objectives is a basic part of the Club's program. All are invited to participate in its activities, which include programs to study, explore and enjoy wildlands.

DAY HIKES
IN THE
SANTA FE AREA

SIXTH EDITION
EXPANDED AND REVISED

BY THE NORTHERN NEW MEXICO GROUP
OF THE SIERRA CLUB

Published by
The Northern New Mexico Group of the Sierra Club
802 Early Street
Santa Fe, NM 87505

RioGrande.SierraClub.org/SantaFe/

First edition - 1981
First edition, second printing - 1982
Second edition - 1986
Third edition - 1990
Fourth edition - 1995
Fifth edition - 1999
Sixth edition - 2007

ISBN: 978-0-9616458-4-7

Printed in U.S.A.

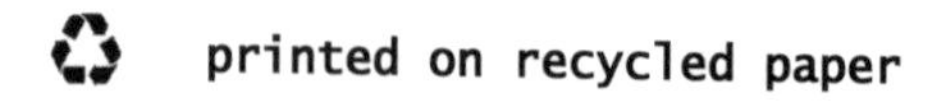

TABLE OF CONTENTS

Santa Fe - Immediate Area

East of Santa Fe

West of Santa Fe

Northwest of Santa Fe

South of Santa Fe

North of Santa Fe

In memory of Ken Adam, Bill Chudd,
and Arnold & Carolyn Keskulla,
all of whom were
long term Sierra Club members,
passionate hikers,
local hike leaders,
and contributors to this book.

ACKNOWLEDGMENTS

The idea of a trail guide for the Santa Fe area was first promoted by Ann Young. She, Betsy Fuller, Bill Chudd, Ingrid Vollnhofer and Linda Zwick put out the first edition. Many others were driving forces behind succeeding editions. This 6th Edition would not exist without their earlier labors of love.

From the first edition in 1981, "Day Hikes in the Santa Fe Area" has been a volunteer team effort by outing leaders and hiking enthusiasts in the Northern Group. Credit is still given to the original authors, even though each new edition has involved revisions based on the changing conditions of roads and trails.

Many thanks are due to the following contributors to this edition:

Editorial Committee - Dan Rusthoi, Norbert Sperlich, Jonni Pool, Laura Hamilton, and Norma McCallan

New Hikes - Norbert Sperlich, Norma McCallan, Steve Markowitz, Eliza Schmid and Lionel Soracco

Hike Reviews - Norbert Sperlich, Tobin Oruch, Norma McCallan, Voitek Byszewski, Lionel Soracco, Laura Hamilton, Gail Bryant, John Buchser, Pam Bell, Michael di Rosa, Art Judd, Les Drapela, Marcia Skillman, Donna Wilson, Keith Grover, Dan Rusthoi, and others

Cover Art - Dorothy Grossman

Photographs - Mostly by Norbert Sperlich, and also Robert Reifel (p.29), Robert McKee (pps. 41, 179, 201), Marcia Skillman (pps. 288, 289), Stephen Markowitz (p. 218), and anonymous (pps. 119, 139).

Line Drawings - Robin Bond

Summary Chart - Tobin Oruch

Maps - A very special thank you to Greg Ohlsen, owner of the Travel Bug, a popular book and map store in Santa Fe, who volunteered to produce these great new maps

Production - Kudos to Bill Baxter, a local historian, editor and author, who offered to handle all production tasks, adding a significant level of professionalism to this edition.

Pecos High Country

Background of Sierra Club Outings

by Ken Adam

In 1892, a group of concerned and dedicated people met in San Francisco to form an organization, the Sierra Club, of those interested in mountain exploration. The first president was John Muir, and there were 182 charter members. The club's purposes included the publication of information about the mountains and the enlistment of support and cooperation by the public and government in preserving the forests and natural features of the Sierra Nevada. Almost immediately, it took the lead in the successful battle to preserve Yosemite Valley and its high country as a National Park. The club held its first outing in 1901.

The Rio Grande Chapter came into being in 1963 with 52 members, and initially included not only New Mexico, but all of Texas and the eastern part of Arizona. Shortly thereafter, Texas and Arizona formed their own chapters. The Rio Grande Chapter now consists of the state of New Mexico and the El Paso area of Texas. In the early 1970s, the Santa Fe Group (now called the Northern Group) was formed, and soon had an active outings program. This outing program continues, with well over a hundred hikes each year.

Every weekend, visitors to Santa Fe, as well as newly arrived and long-time residents, take advantage of our local Sierra Club hikes, car camps, snowshoe or cross-country ski trips, which are open to the public without charge. For a complete list of Sierra Club outings and public meetings throughout New Mexico and El Paso, pick up a copy of the bimonthly Rio Grande Sierran in a box outside our office at 802 Early Street or call us at 505-983-2703. Easier yet, go to the Rio Grande Chapter website to see the electronic copy of the newsletter at http://riogrande.sierraclub.org. And better yet, become a Sierra Club member and receive all local and national mailings. There is a membership application at the end of the book, or you can sign on directly through the Northern Group's website at riogrande.sierraclub.org/santafe/.

INTRODUCTION

by Betsy Fuller

The area around Santa Fe contains a wealth of varied hikes perhaps unequaled by any other in the state. Access to the 12,000-ft peaks of the Sangre de Cristo Mountains is within an hour's drive of the plaza. Winter walks at elevations of 7,000 ft or less are easily accessible when the mountains are too deep in snow to be walked. There are several nationally designated wilderness areas nearby, and the Santa Fe National Forest contains over a million and a half acres of land. Within an hour's drive of Santa Fe you can find five of the seven life zones.

The Northern Group of the Sierra Club has felt the need for a guide to this wealth of wilderness, and this volume describes some of the typical walks that are so close, as well as those further away, but still within a day's time. We have included walks that are classed as easy as well as more difficult ones, and we have tried to give fair representation to the many varied types of terrain that are within reasonable driving distance of Santa Fe. For further hikes in the Santa Fe area, as well as relevant reference materials, we refer you to the publications listed in the "Additional Reading" section at the back of this book.

The fifth edition of this guide has sold out, as have all previous editions. All hikes carried forward from that edition have been re-hiked and revised. Two of the old hikes have been dropped; others have been changed. Ten new hikes have been added. Each of our 60 hikes has an accompanying map.

The money earned from the sale of earlier editions of this book has been used in a variety of environmental campaigns including efforts to save old timber stands from logging, to save pristine wilderness areas from mining operations, to protect the foothills east of the city and the National Forest near the ski basin from development, to have the East Fork of the Jemez declared a National Recreation Area, to dedicate the Baca Ranch (Valles Caldera) to public ownership, to pass New Mexico's hard rock mining bill, and to help publish the mining manual, "Avoiding the Shaft," a guide on how to use the new mining law in reclamation issues. Because of the rising threat of global warming, we have initiated a multi-layered "Cool Cities" campaign in Santa Fe, working with the Mayor, City Council and neighborhoods to take actions that reduce heat trapping emissions, lower energy bills, cut our dependence on oil, encourage the use of renewable energy resources and make our city more liveable.

After an intense three year battle, the Sierra Club, as part of the Valle Vidal Coalition, just won a big victory in the passage of legislation protecting the beautiful Valle Vidal in the Carson National Forest by withdrawing that special area permanently from mineral leasing. Currently, along with Navajo living in the affected area, the Sierra Club, church groups, and many others are working to make sure that the proposed Desert Rock, a huge new power plant, is not built in the Four Corners area, where its polluting emissions and huge output of CO_2 gas would only add to the already degraded air quality caused by the two existing coal-fired plants located in that northwestern corner of the state.

We have also contributed to the support of many other local environmental groups furthering complementary aims. Little of this would be possible were it not for "Day Hikes in the Santa Fe Area."

Hikes Locator Map

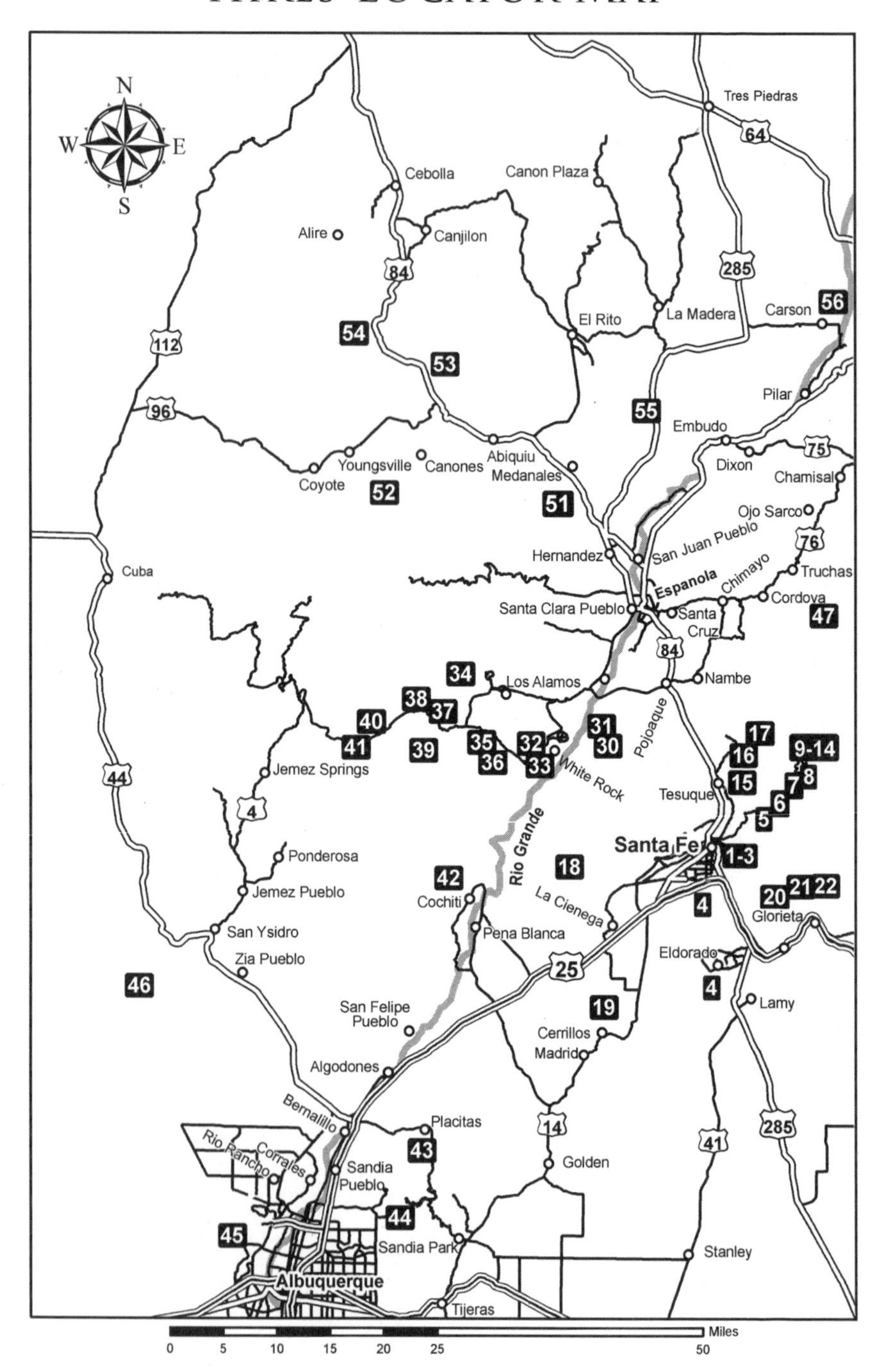

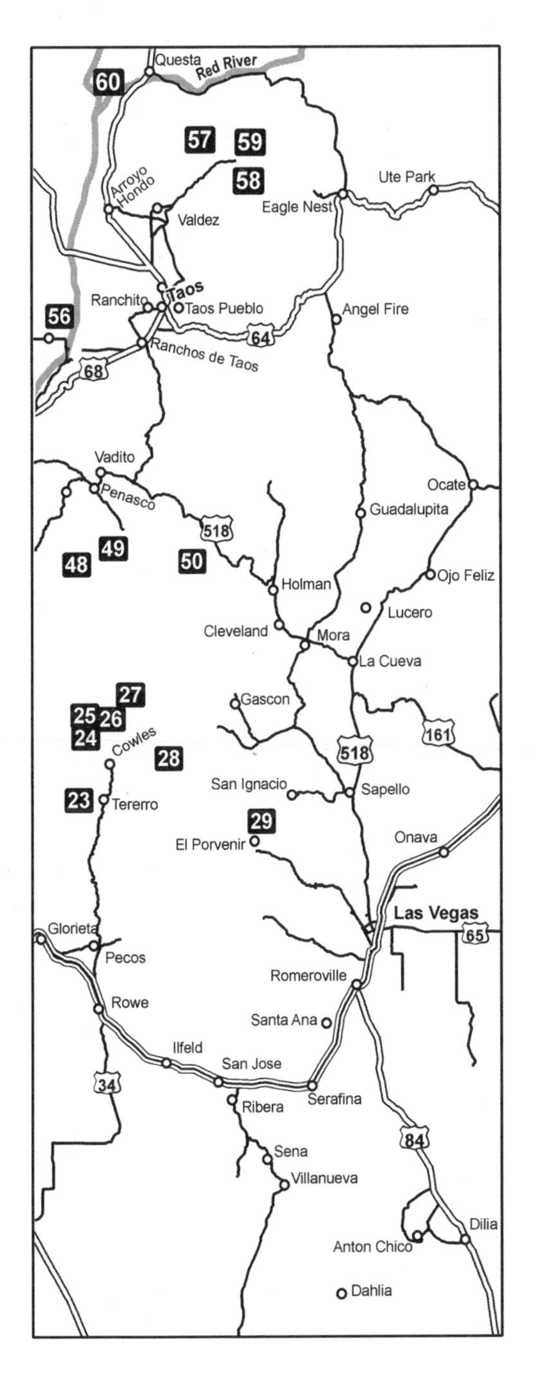

Hikes

1 - Dale Ball Trails
2 - Dorothy Stewart Trail
3 - Atalaya
4 - Rail Trail
5 - Hyde Park Circle
6 - Chamisa Trail
7 - Borrego / Bear Wallow
8 - Aspen Vista
9 - Rio Nambé
10 - Deception, Lake & Penitente Pks
11 - Nambé Lake
12 - La Vega
13 - Lake Katherine
14 - Santa Fe Baldy
15 - Tesuque Creek
16 - Rio en Medio / La Junta
17 - Rancho Viejo
18 - Tetilla Peak
19 - Cerrillos Hills

East of Santa Fe

20 - Apache Canyon / Glorieta Baldy
21 - Glorieta Baldy
22 - Glorieta Ghost Town
23 - Holy Ghost / Spirit Lake
24 - Stewart Lake
25 - Dockwiller Trail
26 - Cave Creek / Horsethief
27 - Pecos Baldy Lake / Pecos Baldy
28 - Beatty's Cabin / Pecos Falls
29 - Hermit Peak

West of Santa Fe

30 - Diablo Canyon
31 - Buckman Mesa

Northwest of Santa Fe

32 - Blue Dot / Red Dot Trails
33 - Ancho Rapids
34 - Caballo Peak
35 - Upper Crossing Loop
36 - Stone Lions
37 - Cerro Grande
38 - Valle Grande / Coyote Call Trails
39 - Painted Cave
40 - East Fork Jemez River
41 - Los Griegos Ridge

South of Santa Fe

42 - Tent Rocks
43 - Tunnel Spring
44 - La Luz
45 - Petroglyph National Monument
46 - Ojito Wilderness

North of Santa Fe

47 - Brazos Cabin
48 - Trampas Lakes
49 - Santa Barbara West Fork
50 - Jicarita Peak
51 - Window Rock
52 - Pedernal
53 - Kitchen Mesa
54 - Rim Vista / Salazar Trails
55 - Ojo Caliente
56 - West Rim Trail
57 - Lobo Peak
58 - Wheeler Peak
59 - Gold Hill
60 - Wild Rivers

How to Use This Book

By Betsy Fuller

The hikes in this book are arranged and numbered according to location beginning with the ones closest to Santa Fe. The map on pages xiv-xv shows the approximate location of the hikes. At the beginning of each hike description is a table that indicates approximate roundtrip hike distance (**RT Distance**), approximate hike time (**Time**), **Elevation Range** (with elevation gain shown), **Rating**, roundtrip driving distance and time from Santa Fe (**RT Drive**), seasonal conditions and suggestions (**Seasons**), and suggested maps to use. Fees, if applicable, are also indicated in the table, as are the GPS coordinates for the trailhead. Before you start the hike, read through the preliminary material and the hiking instructions to be sure that it's the kind of outing you have in mind. Consider taking a camera, binoculars, and wildflower or bird field guides along.

RT Distance – Hiking distances given in the table at the beginning of each hike are approximations rounded up to the next ½ mile. Distances appearing on the hike maps are based on measurements made on a flat map. They don't take into account the ups and downs of a trail and might be a bit shorter than the distances given in the table.

Elevation Range – The term "gain" under "Elevation Range" in each hike description is the estimated cumulative total number of feet you must walk uphill during that hike. Merely subtracting the lowest elevation point from the highest does not accurately describe a trail that involves a great deal of up and down hiking.

Rating – Hikes are rated as "easy," "moderate," and "strenuous." These terms are used somewhat loosely and can mean different things to different hikers. It would be wise for a hiker new to the area to attempt one of the shorter hikes first to see how his or her rating compares with the editors'. In general, a hike is described as easy if it is less than 6 miles in length and involves relatively little elevation change. "Easy to moderate" would indicate that a hike has an easy but rewarding first part, but would be considered moderate if completed. A moderate hike is usually between 6–10 miles, involves more uphill climbing, and may use trails that are not well maintained. A strenuous hike is over 10 miles in length, usually involves substantial changes in elevation, is often at high elevations and can be on very rough trails. Additional descriptions may be used if applicable, such as "short and steep." Some hike descriptions explain two or more related hikes and can also include alternative loops or return routes. Of course, any hike can be partially completed, reducing the time and difficulty while still providing a rewarding experience.

Seasons - This section includes our recommendation concerning the time of year the hike will be most enjoyable. Some hikes can be uncomfortably hot in the summer, and some can be treacherous in the winter. Other important information is included in this section, such as necessity of 4-wheel drive or a high-clearance vehicle.

Maps - The map at the beginning of each hike description gives a general idea of the length, direction and "shape" of the walk. The primary route for the hike is shown in a heavy dashed line, while secondary and alternate routes may be indicated by dotted lines. (*Note that the map may not be oriented with the direction "North" pointing to the top of the page. "North" may be oriented to the side to provide the best display.)* We list the appropriate USGS topo maps and other relevant maps at the beginning of every hike. However, the trail itself may not always be shown on the topo. Highly recommended maps are Drake's *Map of the Mountains of Santa Fe*, Sky Terrain Trail Maps' *Santa Fe, Bandelier & Los Alamos*, the FS *Pecos Wilderness*, FS *Latir Peak and Wheeler Peak Wildernesses*, and the FS *Sandia Mountain Wilderness* maps. Dharma Maps (www.DHARMAmaps.com) is planning a series of maps featuring popular hiking areas of Northern New Mexico. Check them out. In addition to the above maps, you may wish to obtain maps of the Santa Fe, Carson, and Cibola National Forests, where most of these hikes are located.

All maps are available in Santa Fe at the Travel Bug, 839 Paseo de Peralta, Santa Fe, NM 87501 (505-992-0418). Other FS, BLM and commercial maps (but no USGS topo maps), plus useful information about local trails, State Parks, forest closures, hunting and fishing regulations, can be found at the Public Lands Information Center in the BLM Office, 1474 Rodeo Road (505-983-7542). Learn how to use topo maps. A topo map, a compass, and a GPS unit (plus the skills in using them) might save the day if you get lost or disoriented. The last section of the table shows the GPS coordinates for the trailhead of the hike.

Additional Help - In the back of this book you will find further useful information, including safety tips for hiking, instructions on using GPS, useful addresses and phone numbers, a listing of relevant books and publications, and a discussion of New Mexico's drought, heat and dead trees, in addition to a glossary, index, table of abbreviations, and a Sierra Club Application form. Most useful is a table in the back of this book, summarizing the 60 hikes with key data, designed to help you decide at a glance what hikes might be most appropriate or desirable for a particular time or purpose.

We have undertaken to make the directions, both driving and hiking, easy to understand. However, this book should not be considered a step-by-step, do-it-yourself hike book for beginners. Because of changes in the routes of trails, vandalism of signs, destruction of landmarks, as well as the possibility of human error, the accuracy of every detail cannot be guaranteed. Mileages given are necessarily approximate.

One Final Word – Wilderness is destructible, so when you are in it, respect it, love it and take care of it. Stay on the trails and don't take shortcuts. Pack out your trash to the last gum wrapper, and pack out others' trash when you can. Be careful with matches. Admire the flowers and rocks, but leave them there for the next passerby to admire as well. All archaeological artifacts, such as potsherds, must be left in place, and petroglyphs left untouched. And remember that you are only visiting where other animals live, so treat them and their environment with the respect you'd like to receive where you live.

Happy hiking!

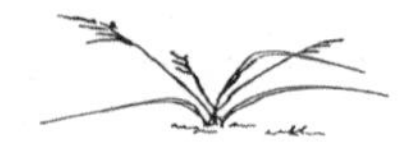

1 A DALE BALL TRAILS NORTH & CENTRAL

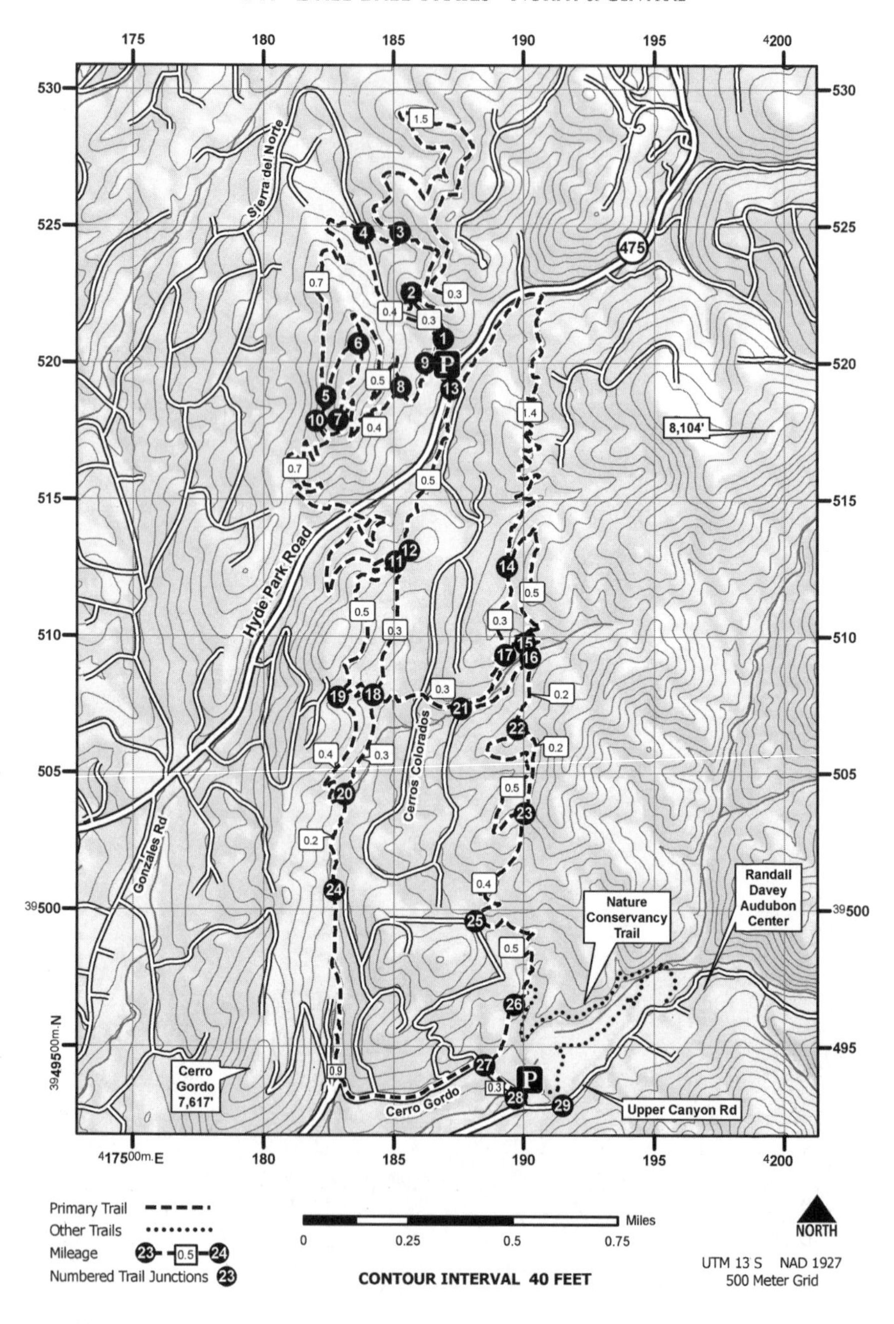

1 - DALE BALL TRAILS

by Lionel Soracco

A system of interconnected trails in the piñon-juniper foothills east of Santa Fe.

RT Distance: 2.3-4.4 miles (depending on route)

Time: 1½-3 hrs (depending on route)

Elevation Range: 7250-8577 ft; gain 250-1227 ft (depending on route)

Rating: Easy to moderate

RT Drive: 6-7 miles

Seasons: The trails can be hiked year round. North-facing slopes (particularly in the higher parts of the Southern Section) can be icy in winter; however, alternate routes are usually available in the network.

Maps: *Dale Ball Trails* by Santa Fe County and by Travel Bug. Sky Terrain's *Santa Fe, Bandelier & Los Alamos* is also recommended.

North TH: 418,710 mE 3,952,055 mN elev.7590'
South TH: 419,016 mE 3,949,327 mN elev.7320'

Summary

The Dale Ball Trail system contains over 22 miles of interconnected hiking and mountain biking trails spread across the foothills east of Santa Fe. All sections lie within piñon-juniper woodlands with occasional ponderosa, cactus, and yucca. We describe several hikes in areas referred to as the northern, central and southern areas. The northern area hikes begin off Hyde Park Road, and the central and southern area hikes begin off Upper Canyon Road. The trails form an elaborate web with multiple loops and a variety of possible hiking routes.

1 B DALE BALL TRAILS SOUTH

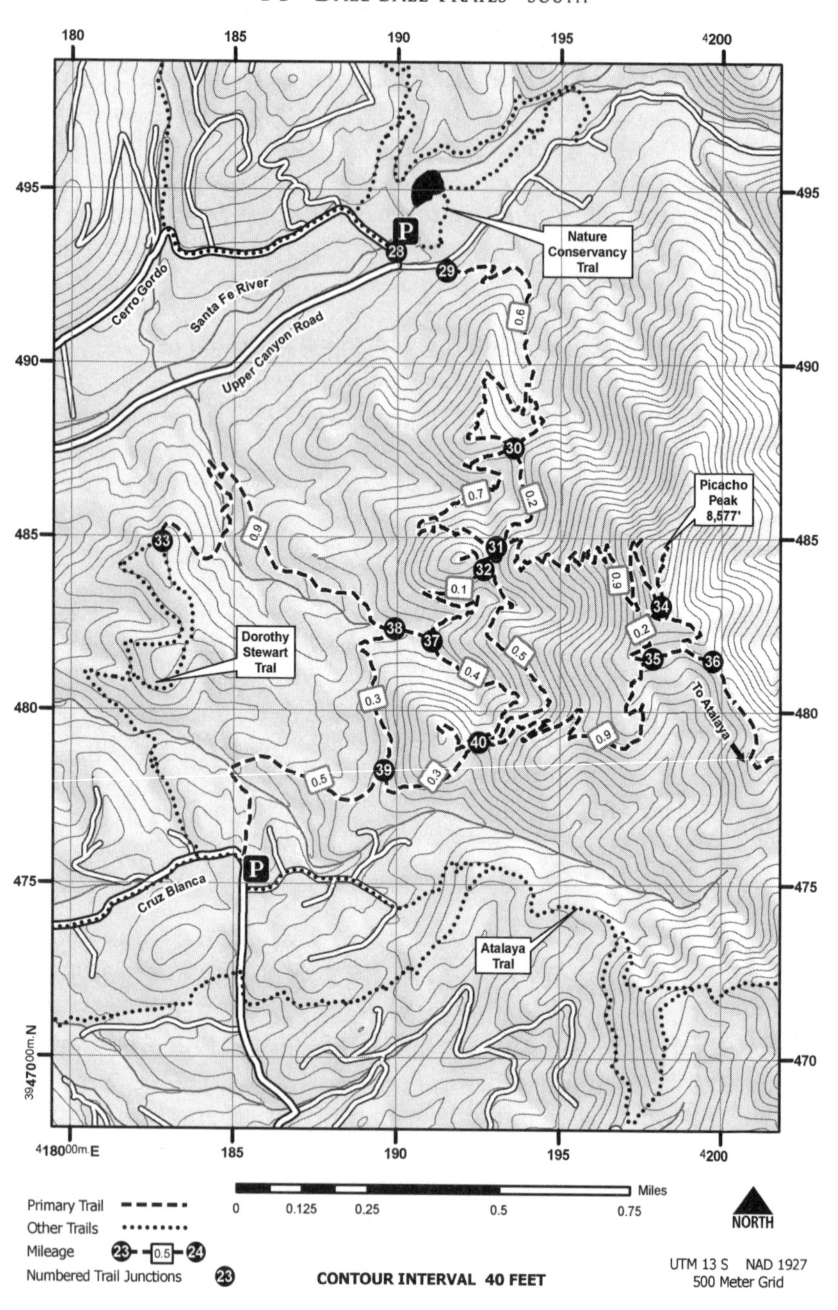

The system is well mapped and well marked. Every intersection is numbered in sequence and has a posted map of the entire section. The map also indicates the distances between adjacent junctions. The northern area is clearly marked with junctions on the trails. The central and southern areas are sometimes spotty on markers, but trails are clear and easy to follow. Occasionally, there are trails that do not appear on the map and you may find your correct trail through some trial and error. The system was constructed within strict guidelines and there are no extreme grades (but there are ups and downs).

An attractive feature of the Dale Ball Trails is that you can select a route as long or as short as you want, depending on your time, energy and desire. Elevations are between 7,000-8,000 ft with gains of less than 500 ft, with the exception of a hike to Picacho Peak in the southern area, rising to 8,500 ft. This narrative will describe a number of suggested routes, all of which are identified by the sequence of numbered junctions.

Bikes and leashed dogs are allowed on the trails. Pick up after your dog. Across from the Hyde Park-Sierra del Norte parking lot, there is a large, fenced dog-run area.

Many thanks are due to Dale Ball who advocated the creation of the trails. The network was not only Dale Ball's idea, but he also secured funding and directed the construction.

Driving Directions

Northern Area Hikes - Drive up Artist Road (the road to Hyde State Park and the Santa Fe Ski Basin). Measure your mileage from the start of Artist Road, and drive 2.7 miles to Sierra del Norte. Turn left onto Sierra del Norte and after a hundred yards or so, turn right into the parking lot.

Central and Southern Area Hikes - Drive east on Alameda until it veers right (south) and becomes Camino Cabra. Continue south on Camino Cabra to the first stop sign (Cristo Rey to the right and Upper Canyon to the left). Turn left onto Upper Canyon and travel 1.3 miles to Cerro Gordo. Turn left onto Cerro Gordo and almost immediately turn right into the parking area.

Hiking Instructions (Northern Area)

Option A (2.3 miles) – Exit the parking lot and follow the trail into the trees. The trailhead is the junction marked 1. Follow 1-2-3 (take the shorter route from 2 to 3). 3-4 takes you down to and across Sierra del Norte. 4-5 is uphill, then level, affording nice views of the Sandia Mountains, Santa Fe, and the Jemez Mountains to the west. 5-6-7 takes you to the high point at the top of the hill you began climbing at 4. 7-8-9 is downhill to Sierra del Norte, opposite the parking lot.

Option B (2.3 miles) – Follow 1-2 and take the right fork trail to 3 and then back to 2-1.

Option C (~3 miles) – Begin at 9 and cross Hyde Park Road to 13-12-11, looping back across Hyde Park Road to 10 where you have additional options at 5 (left) or 7 (right) to loop back to the parking lot.

Option D (3 miles) – Starting from 13, proceed to the trailhead on the trail that parallels Hyde Park Road toward the Ski Basin. After a while, the trail departs from Hyde Park Road and heads uphill. About halfway to 14, you pass the high point, and then go down to 14. Head for 21. There are several options; the shortest is 14-17-21.

At 21, you come to Cerros Colorados Road. Turn right onto the road, walk about 200 yards to the next road (which is a continuation of Cerros Colorados) and walk straight across to find the continuation of the trail. Follow the trail downhill and across an arroyo to 18-12-13. Between 12 and 13 there is a fork to the left, heading down a gulley. Don't take it. Stay on the main trail, which is the right fork. From 13, cross Hyde Park Road and return to the parking lot.

Hiking Instructions (Central Area)

Option E (3.3 miles) – Leave the parking lot and turn right onto Cerro Gordo Road. Walk about 200 yards to 27. 27-26-25 is uphill on an old, rutted dirt road. The right fork option at 26 is 400 yards longer but more pleasant, because it's a trail, not a road. 25-

23 is uphill. 23 is the high point of the hike. At 23, take the right fork to 22-16-21.

At 21, you come to Cerros Colorados Road. Turn right onto the road, walk about 200 yards to the next road (which is a continuation of Cerros Colorados) and walk straight across to find the continuation of the trail. Follow the trail downhill and across an arroyo to 18-20-24.

You may find a trickle of water in the arroyo just before 24. As you continue down the arroyo, occasionally switching sides, you will encounter two abandoned vehicles. Just before the second of these wrecks, the trail seems to turn right and ascend to a road. Don't follow this: continue down the arroyo past the vehicle and soon you'll be at Cerro Gordo Road.

At Cerro Gordo Road, there is a small parking area and a map of the trail system. (You could park your car here and do the loop in reverse order). Turn left onto Cerro Gordo and follow it to 27 and on to the parking lot.

Hiking Instructions (Southern Area)

Option F, including Picacho Peak (4.4 miles) – Exit the parking lot at the east end (away from the road) through a gate, then follow the trail across the Santa Fe River streambed and up to Upper Canyon Road. Cross the road to the green gate (this is 29; however, the sign on the post faces away from you). The trail leads uphill (and is fairly steep for the first 50 ft or so), then follows an old acequia.

Just before you enter the forest look up for a view of Picacho Peak. It rises to the south over the nearby hills. The forest is mainly piñon-juniper, with the addition of ponderosa at higher elevations.

After a while, the trail splits at an arrow pointing to the left. Follow the arrow. After a few hundred yards in an arroyo, the trail climbs again to 30. At 30, there are four trails splitting off but the map only shows three, and two of them go to 31. While facing the posted map at 30, take the trail to 31 (for Picacho Peak) to your right. If you do not plan to go to Picacho Peak, skip down to Option G.

At 31, take the left fork to begin the ascent towards Picacho Peak. About 400 yards up, you'll come to an excellent rest stop offering plenty of rock seats and an unobstructed view of Santa Fe as well as the mountains and beyond.

Continuing beyond the rest stop, you'll traverse over a dozen switchbacks, which finally bring you to 34 atop the ridge leading to Picacho. At this point, the trail splits. Take the left fork and follow the trail up the ridge about 200 yards to the peak. Enjoy a well-deserved sense of exhilaration at reaching the highest point on the Dale Ball Trails, and enjoy the 360° views.

On returning from the peak, when you reach the fork at 34, keep to the left side and follow the trail downhill to 35. At 35, take the right fork and begin the long descent to 40. 40 is on a saddle between two hills, one on the Picacho ridge and the other beyond. Just before you would begin climbing this first hill (it's ~25 ft high), the trail makes an abrupt right turn. Unfortunately, the Dale Ball Trail also appears to continue up and over the hill, so it's easy to miss the turn. At this writing, there is a large cairn at the turning point, but there's no guarantee it will be there when you arrive. Make the turn and after a few long switchbacks, you'll be at 40.

If you miss the turn, don't despair. If you continue straight ahead, you'll pass over the hill to Lookout Rock (aka Castle Rock), then downhill around the right side of the rock and down the ridge to 40. This way is actually shorter than the switch-backed official way. Also, in the winter, the switchbacks can be icy (they're on the north side of the ridge). This "unofficial" way is mostly on the sunny side and less prone to ice.

At 40, follow the trail to 32-31-30-29 and the parking lot.

Option G (3.4 miles) – Follow the directions for the Picacho Peak route until you reach 31. At 31, continue on to 40 and return via the same route or make a loop through 37.

Note: You can also access the Southern Section of the Dale Ball Trails from the Ponderosa Ridge-Wilderness Gate parking area on Upper Camino Cruz Blanca (see ATALAYA MOUNTAIN Hike #3 for driving directions). At the northeast corner of the parking area there's a trail taking you to 39 in about 15 minutes. Be advised that this parking area only holds 7 cars and is often full.

You can also make an interesting (but rather strenuous) loop from the Ponderosa Ridge-Wilderness Gate parking area to Atalaya Peak via the Dale Ball Trail. Take the link to 39 (described above), and turn right to 40. At 40 take the rightmost fork to 35, then the right fork to 36 and onward to 41 across a long saddle to the north side of Atalaya. Follow the trail eastwards a short distance across the north side of Atalaya. Turn right on an unmarked trail just before the Santa Fe watershed "keep out" sign and climb steeply upwards to the peak. Return to the parking area on the Atalaya Trail.

2 Dorothy Stewart Trail

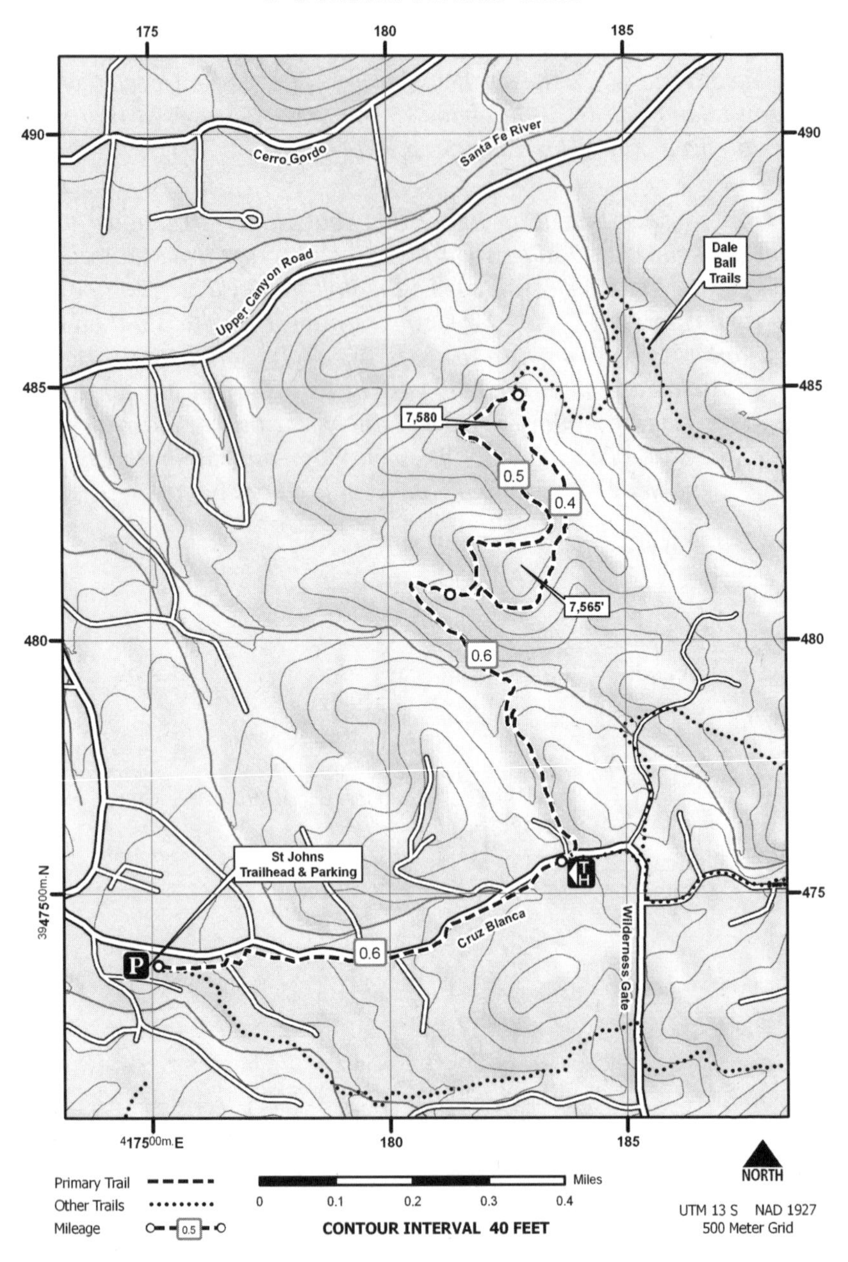

2 - DOROTHY STEWART TRAIL

by Lionel Soracco

A short, easily accessible and very pleasant hike on the east side that affords great views of the Santa Fe landscape.

RT Distance:	2.5 miles (from Camino Cruz Blanca TH) 3.5 miles (from St. John's parking lot)
Time:	1 hr (from Camino Cruz Blanca TH) 2 hrs (from St. John's parking lot)
Elevation Range:	7320-7550 ft; total gain 440 ft
Rating:	Easy
RT Drive:	5 miles
Seasons:	Can be hiked year round. A few inches of snow could be on the ground in winter.
Maps:	USGS Santa Fe - 7.5' series. Drake's *Map of the Mountains of Santa Fe* and Sky Terrain's *Santa Fe, Bandelier & Los Alamos* are recommended
Cruz Blanca TH:	418,388 mE 3,947,604 mN elev.7522'
St. Johns TH:	417,513 mE 3,947,357 mN elev.7372'

History

The Dorothy Stewart Trail is named for an artist who lived in Santa Fe from 1925 to 1955, and was known for her New Mexico subjects, both mystical and whimsical, in styles from realist to abstract.

Summary

The hike described in this section is within Santa Fe and easily accessible. It takes no more than 1-2 hours, is easy, leads you out of development, and affords great views of the Santa Fe landscape.

However, drought conditions and bark beetles have taken their toll on the piñons.

Driving Directions

Drive east on Alameda until it veers right (south) and becomes Camino Cabra. Continue south on Camino Cabra past the Cristo Rey Church on the right and the Los Miradores condominium development on the left. Turn left onto Camino Cruz Blanca at the St. John's College sign.

Continue 0.7 miles further on Camino Cruz Blanca to reach the trailhead and a 4-car parking area on your left. No street parking is allowed, so if the parking spaces are filled, go back to the St. John's entrance, turn left into the college visitor parking lot and park at the far (east) end.

Hiking Instructions

If you were lucky to get one of the four parking places, you're at the trailhead. If you parked in the college parking lot, the next paragraph guides you to the trailhead.

The trailhead is on Camino Cruz Blanca, 0.7 miles east of St. John's. Walk to the east end of the parking lot. Check the large trail map showing all trails in the immediate vicinity. Continue 80 yards to a fork. Take the left fork towards the Dorothy Stewart Trail. After 0.1 miles, the trail parallels Camino Cruz Blanca. You're on an excellent dirt sidewalk provided by the residents of Upper Camino Cruz Blanca to keep you safely off the street. Continue another 0.6 miles until you find a sign indicating the Dorothy Stewart Trailhead is across the street. Cross over and enter the trail.

The trail leads northward along the east edge of an arroyo on an easement donated to the Forest Trust by Irene von Horvath. This easement serves to provide access to otherwise inaccessible city property. You are soon beyond any homes and into the characteristic piñon-juniper woodland.

After ¼ mile, you descend on a few switchbacks before reaching Arroyo Mora. A trail sign announces "Dorothy Stewart Trail" with due credits to the Forest Trust which built the trail.

Continue north past this sign about 70 yards to reach a streambed, and in about 20 yards further, a trail leading off to the left. Don't take this trail, but continue north. After rising slowly for 250 yards, the trail turns right and starts uphill. Hiking about 100 yards more brings you to a fork. You are about to enter a loop around the hill you're on. We prefer the clockwise route, so turn left. After a pleasant and fairly level half-hour walk, you'll return to this point.

After a 10-minute walk northward, the trail turns toward the east. At this point you'll find a rustic bench just off the trail to your left, where you can rest and get a great view of the Santa Fe river valley, Cerro Gordo (the hill bordering it on the north), and to the west across the Rio Grande valley, the Jemez Mountains and Los Alamos.

Continuing eastward on the loop, the trail climbs, and finally turns south where it meets Junction 33 of the Dale Ball Trails. The trail to the left (down) is a link to a network of trails on Picacho Peak (the southern section of the Dale Ball Trails – see DALE BALL TRAILS Hike #1).

You'll take the right fork, continuing to the south. Soon you'll come to a second bench. This one offers views of nearby Picacho Peak due east, and, to the northwest, the distant Tesuque Peak, top of the Santa Fe Ski Area. A bit further, and the trail moves to the south side of the hill, bringing you back to the start of the loop. Retrace your steps down the hill, turn left and follow the trail south to Camino Cruz Blanca. If you parked at St. John's, cross Camino Cruz Blanca, turn right (west) onto the dirt sidewalk and continue 0.7 miles to the lot where you parked your vehicle.

3 Atalaya

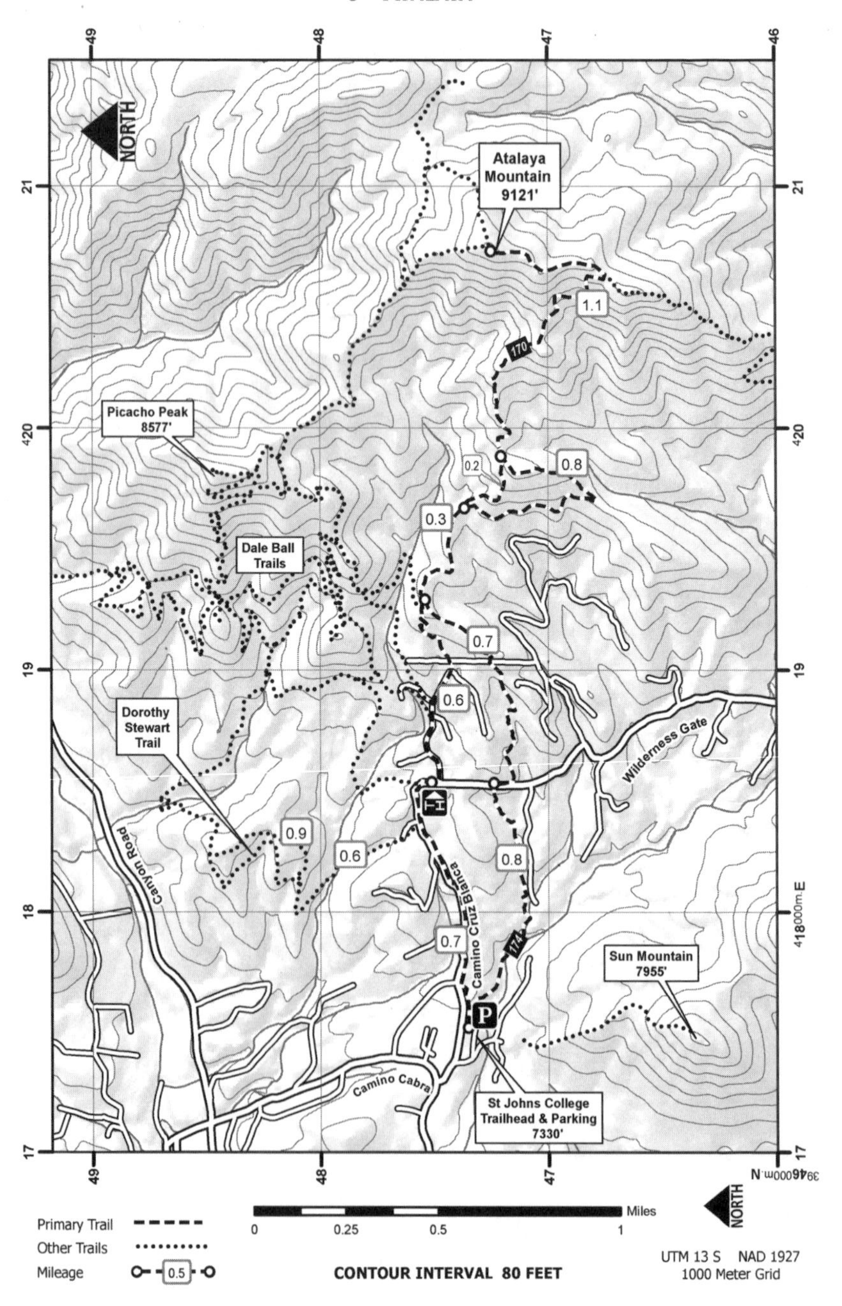

NORTH
Atalaya Mountain
9121'
Picacho Peak
8577'
Dale Ball Trails
Dorothy Stewart Trail
Canyon Road
Camino Cruz Blanca
Wilderness Gate
Camino Cabra
Sun Mountain
7955'
St Johns College Trailhead & Parking
7330'
170
174
1.1
0.8
0.2
0.3
0.7
0.6
0.9
0.6
0.8
0.7
49
48
47
46
21
420
19
18
17
418000m.E
3946000m.N
Miles
0
0.25
0.5
1
Primary Trail
Other Trails
Mileage
0.5
CONTOUR INTERVAL 80 FEET
UTM 13 S NAD 1927
1000 Meter Grid

3 - ATALAYA

by Lionel Soracco

Two short, easily accessible but steep trails, shaded by a forest of piñons, junipers and ponderosas, providing an expansive view of Santa Fe and the surrounding area.

RT Distance:	~7 miles (from St. John's Parking lot) ~5.5 miles (from Ponderosa Ridge parking)
Time:	4+ hrs (from St. John's) 3+ hrs (from Ponderosa Ridge parking)
Elevation Range:	7340-9121 ft; gain 1781 ft (St. John's) 7540-9121 ft; gain 1581 ft (Ponderosa)
Rating:	Moderate (short but steep)
RT Drive:	5 miles (to St. John's) 6.5 miles (to Ponderosa Ridge TH)
Seasons:	Can be hiked all year, but likely hot in summer. Snow possible in winter (several inches at higher elevations - a foot or more at the top), although the trail is usually accessible.
Maps:	USGS Santa Fe - 7.5' series. Drake's *Map of the Mountains of Santa Fe* and Sky Terrain's *Santa Fe, Bandelier & Los Alamos* are recommended.
St. Johns TH:	417,513 mE 3,947,357 mN elev.7372'
Ponderosa TH:	418,533 mE 3,947,602 mN elev.7536'

Summary

Atalaya (Spanish for "watchtower" or "height") is the ridge that rises just east of Santa Fe. This popular destination can be reached from two trailheads, one on Camino Cruz Blanca at the Ponderosa Ridge development, the other at St. John's College. The trail is mostly shaded and uphill through a forest, which changes from piñon-juniper to ponderosa and Douglas fir and some white fir as you climb. At the top you'll have a broad view of Santa Fe and the surrounding area.

Driving Directions

Drive east on Alameda until it veers right (south) and becomes Camino Cabra. Continue south on Camino Cabra past the Cristo Rey Church on the right and the Los Miradores condominium development on the left. Turn left onto Camino Cruz Blanca at the St. John's College sign. If you start the hike at St. John's College (Trail 174), turn right off Camino Cruz Blanca into the college visitor parking lot. The trailhead is at the far (east) end of the lot.

If you start at the Ponderosa Ridge residential development (Trail 170), continue eastward on Camino Cruz Blanca 0.8 miles to where the road turns right (south). After turning, you'll be facing the entry gate to the Ponderosa Ridge-Wilderness Gate residential development. To your left is a 7-car parking area with a large sign showing all trails in the area. Park here, and not along the roadside. If the lot is full, park at St. John's College and begin the hike there.

Hiking Instructions

Trail 174 (St. John's trailhead) and Trail 170 (Ponderosa Ridge trailhead) intersect a short way up the mountain; from there to the top, the trail is 170.

St. John's Trailhead (Trail 174) - Looking eastward from the St. John's parking lot, you'll see your destination, a long ridge rising gradually as it proceeds northwards. Starting at the far end of the parking lot, follow Trail 174 eastward about 50 yards where the trail splits. Take the right branch which quickly winds down to Arroyo de los Chamisos (dry except for a few weeks early in spring), crosses the arroyo, rises to traverse a field of chamisa bushes skirting St. John's new dormitory complex, re-crosses the arroyo, and starts eastward up a narrow creek bed. Signs will guide you.

After entering the small arroyo of the creek, you'll pass through a log maze built to discourage equestrians and cyclists. For the next ¼ mile, the trail follows the arroyo, with numerous "Stay on Trail" signs at creek crossings. A sign indicates where you leave the creek and head to the right and steeply upward to the Wilderness Gate Road.

Cross the road (be careful of occasional traffic here), climb the steps and continue another ¼ mile through woods to the log fence marking the entrance to the Santa Fe National Forest. Overhead are power lines running north-south across the foothills. A trail marker indicates that Atalaya is 2 miles distant. Climb up from the fence 40 yards, and then turn left to follow Trail 174 another ¼ mile to its intersection with Trail 170.

Ponderosa Ridge Trailhead (Trail 170) - Starting the hike at the Ponderosa Ridge parking area, you follow the wall south 50 yards to a gate. Turn left, through the gate, and continue uphill on the dirt road. You'll spot a house with a red metal roof. Just past that house the road veers right, but you continue straight ahead, passing under some power lines and climbing wooden steps which lead to a log fence marking the Santa Fe National Forest boundary. Passing through the gate, follow the trail as it winds steeply uphill to its intersection with Trail 174.

Note: Both Trail 174 and Trail 170, from trailheads to log fences, pass through private property. Rights-of-way were negotiated over a period of years by the Sierra Club, Friends of Atalaya, Forest Trust, representatives of the Santa Fe National Forest, and private landowners. Please respect this arrangement by keeping to the trails.

From the intersection to the top, you'll be on Trail 170. Some 10 minutes past the intersection, this trail forks at a trail sign. You have the option of going straight ahead and uphill on the steeper route, or going to the right and slightly downhill on the easier route. Both routes will come together in a while. The steeper route, steep indeed and with poor footing in some places, will shorten the hike by about ½ mile or 10 minutes.

The easier route is much more pleasant, offering great views along the way. It goes in a southerly direction for about 10 minutes, with little elevation gain. At a trail fork, marked by an "Atalaya Lookout Trail" sign, take the left branch. (The right branch crosses an old road and heads up a small peak to the south—the new Atalaya Lookout area.) In less than a minute, you will reach the top of a ridge and a trail junction at a Trail 170 sign. Turn left here (and remember to turn right at the sign on your way back).

The trail now follows the ridge uphill and in a northerly direction for about 10 minutes to an intersection where it meets the steeper route trail that is coming up on the left. After this merger, your trail goes east and uphill, toward the main ridge of Atalaya Mountain. As the terrain gets steeper, the trail forms a number of switchbacks. You will get great views to the south, toward the Sandia and Ortiz Mountains.

About ½ mile past the last intersection, your trail will top out on the main ridge of Atalaya and then sharply turn left at a Trail 170 sign. Follow the trail north and uphill along the ridge top, past an outcrop of quartz and mica, to a series of granite cliffs on the left. These cliffs offer stunning views of Santa Fe and the mountains to the west. For more vistas, follow the trail for a few minutes to the highest point of the ridge, where you get glimpses of Tesuque Peak to the north. It is around here where ravens like to hang out in some dead trees.

Return the way you came.

Among the Ponderosas

Arroyo Hondo Trestle along the Rail Trail ☞

4 Rail Trail

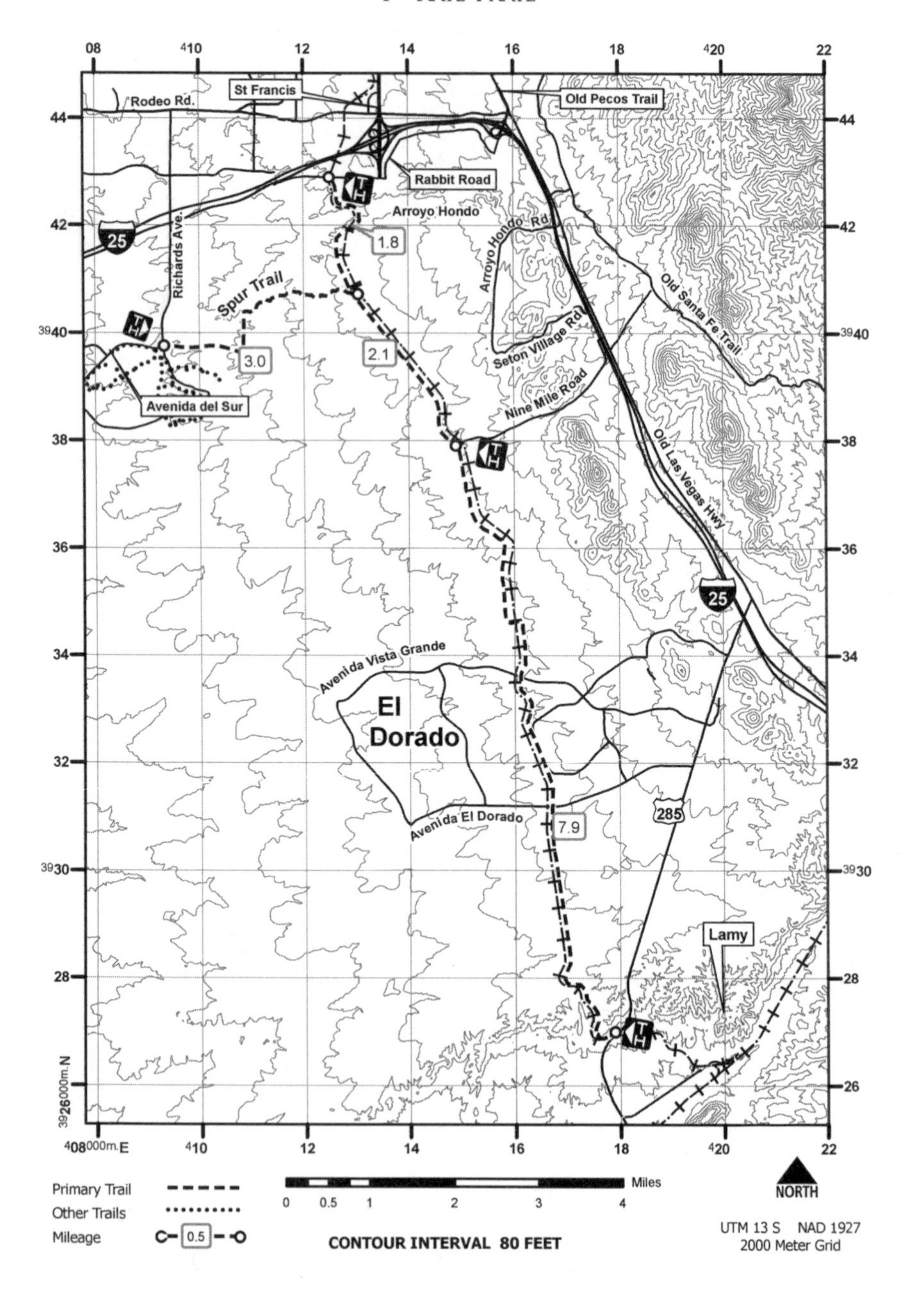

Rodeo Rd.
St Francis
Old Pecos Trail
Rabbit Road
Arroyo Hondo
Arroyo Hondo Rd
Richards Ave.
25
1.8
Spur Trail
Seton Village Rd
Old Santa Fe Trail
3.0
2.1
Avenida del Sur
Nine Mile Road
Old Las Vegas Hwy
25
Avenida Vista Grande
El Dorado
Avenida El Dorado
7.9
285
Lamy
Primary Trail
Other Trails
Mileage
0.5
Miles
0 0.5 1 2 3 4
CONTOUR INTERVAL 80 FEET
NORTH
UTM 13 S NAD 1927
2000 Meter Grid

4 - RAIL TRAIL

by Norma McCallan

Ideal for a short hike or walk close to town along an old historic railroad route with great vistas and the possibility of sighting a train.

RT Distance: 4 miles (Route #1 - Rabbit Rd)
4 miles (Route #2 TH - Nine Mile Rd North)
6 miles (Route #2 TH - Nine Mile Rd South)
7-10 miles (Route #3 - Hwy 285)
Note: Official length of Rail Trail is 11.5 miles one way, so we recommend hiking the described round trip segments.

Time: Depends on length traveled. Segments recommended are 2-3 hrs each.

Elevation Range: 6600-6880 ft; total gain 280 ft

Rating: Easy to moderate. Strenuous if you do the entire distance.

RT Drive: 13 miles for Route #1
19 miles for Route #2
31 miles for Route #3

Seasons: Best fall through spring. Hot in summer.

Maps: USGS Santa Fe, Seton Village and Galisteo - 7.5' series (maps not necessary, but the trail overlaps these three).

Rabbit Road TH: 412,544 mE 3,942,897 mN elev.6835'
Nine Mile TH: 415,033 mE 3,937,999 mN elev.6902'
285 TH: 417,865 mE 3,926,956 mN elev.6606'

Summary

Little driving, ideal for a short hike along an historic railroad route. Great vistas. Can be done in sections, with various options possible. Minimal elevation change. No water available. You are likely to see hikers, bicyclists and an occasional horse. Three routes are described, with starting points at the beginning of the trail, the end of the trail, and the midpoint at Nine Mile Road.

The Santa Fe Southern Railway is a working railroad, which is one of the charms of this hike. You are quite likely to see either the regular run or a chartered trip pass by. The train moves slowly and whistles a lot, but observe caution when crossing the tracks.

History

Soon after the Atchison, Topeka & Santa Fe established the first rail line in New Mexico, starting at Raton Pass in December 1878, it abandoned plans to route its main line through Santa Fe and ran the tracks from Las Vegas (NM) to Galisteo Junction (now Lamy) and on down through the Galisteo Basin to the Rio Grande and Albuquerque. A station was established at Lamy and a branch line completed to Santa Fe in February 1880. The AT&SF ran passenger service along this branch line until 1936 and continued freight service until March 1992, when the line was purchased by the Santa Fe Southern Railway.

Through a joint endeavor between the Santa Fe Conservation Trust and Santa Fe County, an easement was purchased from the Santa Fe Southern Railway to create a public trail next to the tracks between Rabbit Road and the intersection of the tracks and US 285. The Santa Fe Rail Trail Inaugural Celebration was held in June 1998.

Driving Directions

Route #1 Trailhead - Drive south on St. Francis Dr. to the end of the road. Turn right onto Rabbit Road and, just before the railroad tracks, turn left and park in the flat area.

Route #2 Trailhead - Drive to the intersection of Rodeo Road and Old Pecos Trail. Check your odometer at this intersection, and turn onto (or continue onto) Old Las Vegas Highway (a continuation of Rodeo Road), which parallels I-25. You will drive past two I-25 overpasses, Arroyo Hondo and Seton Village. At 2.8 miles, turn right onto the third overpass, CR 660, "Timberwick & Nine Mile Road." The road veers left after passing over the interstate. Stay on Nine Mile Road (Timberwick soon takes off to the right) as it ambles south.

At 5.9 miles, the pavement ends at a turnabout. Park here. Nine Mile Road accesses the 9-mile marker of the railroad tracks.

Route #3 Trailhead - Drive north on I-25 toward Las Vegas (NM), and take the exit to Clines Corners, US 285. After about 5 miles on US 285 and shortly before CR 33 heads left for Lamy, the railroad tracks cross the highway. Turn off to the right onto the dirt parking area just before the tracks and park.

Hiking Instructions

Note: Mileage numbers indicate RR mileposts ("milepost 13"), or a mile indicator painted on a trestle or tunnel ("mile 12.6"), not hiking miles traveled.

Route #1 - Rabbit Road - Proceed south along the tracks, past homes and backyards. At 0.1 miles in, you will pass milepost 13. At mile 12.6, the trail dips down to cross Arroyo Hondo, which is spanned by the longest trestle of the line. Arroyo Hondo is the site of a large Indian pueblo that was excavated in the 1970s and reburied by the School of American Research.

Once past the trestle, the hiking trail on the left of the tracks is joined by a trail on the right. The two trails continue for the remainder of the way. Houses are now very sparse and generally at some distance from the trail. Soon you pass a dirt road on the left that accesses the subdivision of Arroyo Hondo. Just before this intersection, high on the right bank is a small white wooden cross, a *descanso,* inscribed "en memoria de Conzalo Valdez de 1888 a 1966."

About 30 minutes into the hike and at milepost 12, you will reach an open area. Enjoy the vistas of the Sangre de Cristo Mountains to the east and the Jemez Mountains to the west. In the spring there are lots of wildflowers such as lupine and verbena among the grasses and the many large piñon and juniper trees. You may be lucky and see a flock of Mountain Bluebirds; you will probably be visited by noisy ravens that roost in the area.

Some 15-20 minutes past milepost 12 and after crossing a rutted dip, you will come to an unmarked trail intersection, where a dirt trail goes off to the right (west). This trail crosses a fence about 80 yards from the intersection. At that point, you will find wooden posts, a map and a trail sign marking the beginning of the Spur Trail. The Spur Trail continues for 3 miles to Richards Avenue just south of Santa Fe Community College. But let's go back to the Rail Trail!

The next landmark, shortly before milepost 11 (the end point for this section), is a large, dark-green water tank. Directions to reach the water tank going north from Route 2 are in the next section.

Route #2 - Nine Mile Road - This trailhead has an official sign, "Santa Fe Rail Trail, 11.5 miles unimproved trail" by the stile which gives you access through the fence and down to the tracks.

North Route - If you want to check out the 1.8 miles of track between here and the green water tank mentioned above, turn right (north). Note the fine stonework in the double culverts under the tracks at mile 9.5 and the trestle at milepost 10. Another culvert with a handsome arch (one so large you could walk through it) appears at mile 10.4, and makes a good spot for a break. A weathered old RR crossing sign marks an abandoned dirt road coming in from the east and a large trestle can be seen at mile 10.8. At milepost 11.0, you can see the water tank mentioned above.

South Route - To cover the next section of track, turn left (south) and almost immediately you will pass a trestle at mile 9.4. Note the two old windmills near the house on the left. To the southwest there are great views of the Ortiz, San Pedro, and Sandia Mountains as well as the closer Cerrillos Hills. To the south is the faint blue silhouette of the Manzano Mountains. At mile 8.1, a trestle is passed and at 7.4 there is a culvert with a handsome stone arch.

Soon the trail crosses to the east side of the tracks and you pass a low wooden trestle at milepost 7.1. Ahead you can see the many houses of the Eldorado subdivision. At milepost 6.7, there is a small electric substation on the east side. Shortly you come to a paved road, Vista Grande, one of the two main roads traversing this popular subdivision.

This intersection, approximately mile 6.5 on the tracks, is a good spot to turn around on this segment. On your way back you will enjoy views of Tetilla Peak to the west, the Jemez Mountains to the northwest, and the Sangre de Cristo Mountains to the east.

Route #3 - US 285 - There is no easement for the last 1.5 miles of tracks to Lamy east of the highway. The private landowners do not like hikers in that section. There is a sign at this southern end of the Rail Trail that says "End of Trail, Hazardous Conditions Beyond this Point - No Trespassing!" So, turn right (west) to hike.

There is a different feel to the southern end of the Rail Trail. Here you'll find sweeping vistas of the broad Galisteo Basin, San Pedro and Ortiz Mountains, Cerrillos Hills, and far to the south, the faint blue outline of the Manzano Mountains. Stop at milepost 2 to admire the view before the tracks turn northwards. There is a handsome wooden trestle over a small arroyo at mile 2.2, a good spot for a brief break. Now you start getting great views of the Jemez Mountains to the northwest, the Sangre de Cristo Mountains to the east and Glorieta Baldy and Thompson Peak prominent on the horizon. A dirt road appears at milepost 3 and a trestle at mile 3.2. Another dirt road at mile 3.3 has mailboxes. You pass a good-sized trestle at mile 3.9 and another at mile 4.8. Shortly you arrive at the paved Avenida Eldorado, the other major road through Eldorado. You can turn around here, where you are entering the most populous part of Eldorado, or continue on to the Vista Grande intersection at mile 6.5, where it was suggested that you turn around on the last segment.

Note: The City of Santa Fe has plans to extend the Rail Trail from Rabbit Road north to the railyards. Thus far only the section from Yucca & Zia north to Siringo Road is complete, while Siringo to St. Michael's Drive is in process.

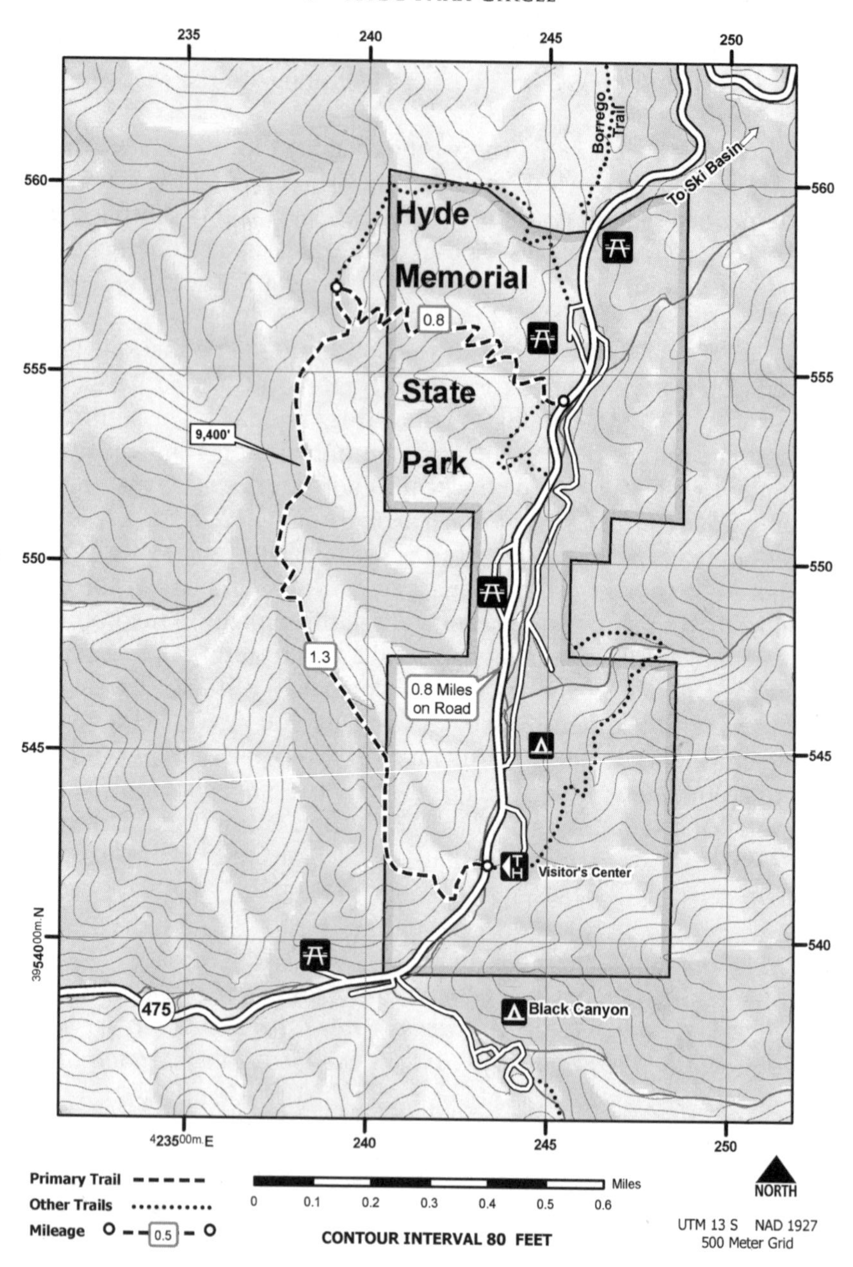
Hyde Memorial State Park
Borrego Trail
To Ski Basin
0.8
9,400'
1.3
0.8 Miles on Road
Visitor's Center
Black Canyon
475
235
240
245
250
560
555
550
545
540
3954000m.N
423500m.E
Primary Trail
Other Trails
Mileage
0.5
0
0.1
0.2
0.3
0.4
0.5
0.6
Miles
CONTOUR INTERVAL 80 FEET
NORTH
UTM 13 S NAD 1927
500 Meter Grid

5 - Hyde Park Circle

by John H. Muchmore

A beautiful mountain hike close to Santa Fe with excellent views.

RT Distance:	3.5 miles
Time:	~3 hrs (stops included)
Elevation Range:	8400-9400 ft; total gain 1100 ft
Rating:	Easy/moderate, with steep trails
RT Drive:	16 miles; ~45 min
Seasons:	Good year-round hike, unless heavily snowed in.
Maps:	USGS McClure Reservoir - 7.5' series; however, the trail described below is not shown on the map. Drake's *Map of the Mountains of Santa Fe* and Sky Terrain's *Santa Fe, Bandelier & Los Alamos* are recommended.
Fees:	Parking $5/day
Trailhead:	424,330 mE 3,954,180 mN elev.8391'

Summary

Short drive from Santa Fe over paved road. Gaining 1100 feet in elevation, this hike offers panoramic views of the Sangre de Cristo, Sandia, and Jemez Mountains. On the way, you will encounter stands of piñon, ponderosa, spruce, fir, Gambel oak, and wildflowers.

Driving Directions

Drive up Artist Road (the road to Hyde State Park and the Santa Fe Ski Basin). Measure your mileage from the start of Artist Road, and drive 7.4 miles to Hyde Memorial State Park Headquarters on your right. There are parking spaces in a large lot below the headquarters on the right-hand side of the road and in a smaller lot above the headquarters on the left side. Pay your fees at the self-service payment box. The trailhead is directly across the road from the Visitor Center and is marked by a "Hiking Trail" sign.

Hiking Instructions

The trail starts on the west side of the road, opposite the Visitor Center. It crosses Little Tesuque Creek on a stone bridge and turns left. Soon, it goes to the right and uphill, forming a series of switchbacks as it climbs steeply up a ridge where you are hiking on granite. Ten minutes into the hike you will pass a bench. In another ten minutes you will reach a second bench, with views toward the Santa Fe Ski Basin. As you continue climbing, Thompson Peak comes into view (to the southeast) above the Black Canyon notch. Later on, views toward the Sandia and Ortiz mountains unfold. About 1 hour into the hike, you will see the Jemez Mountains toward the west.

After reaching a high point on the ridge, the trail goes downhill for a few minutes, always following the ridge. The trail then goes up again, arriving at a high point about 1 hour and 15 minutes into the hike. There are two picnic tables here and a trail fork just before the second table. The trail that goes straight ahead past the second table was closed in 2006. The trail that goes down to the right, marked as Circle Trail, will enable you to complete the loop hike.

Time to take in the views. From the first table, you get views of Tesuque Peak toward the northeast, while the second table is the place to look toward the Jemez Mountains, Los Alamos, the Rio Grande Valley, and, closer to Santa Fe, the Santa Fe Opera and the Tesuque Flea Market.

Before moving on, consider the options. The most pleasant way to conclude the hike is to return the way you came. The other option is to continue on the circle trail to make a loop. This will save you a few minutes of hiking time, but you will spend almost ½ hour hiking close to the traffic on Hyde Park Road. If you decide to do the loop hike, look for the marked Circle Trail that goes downhill toward the southeast. This very steep trail takes you down on numerous switchbacks. In about 20 minutes, you will reach Hyde Park Road at the lower end of the RV campground. Turn right and follow the road down to the Visitor Center in about 25 minutes. Alternatively, to return to the Visitor Center, you can cross Hyde Park Road and hike along the dirt road through the camping area.

Hyde Park Trail Under a Dusting of Snow

6 Chamisa Trail

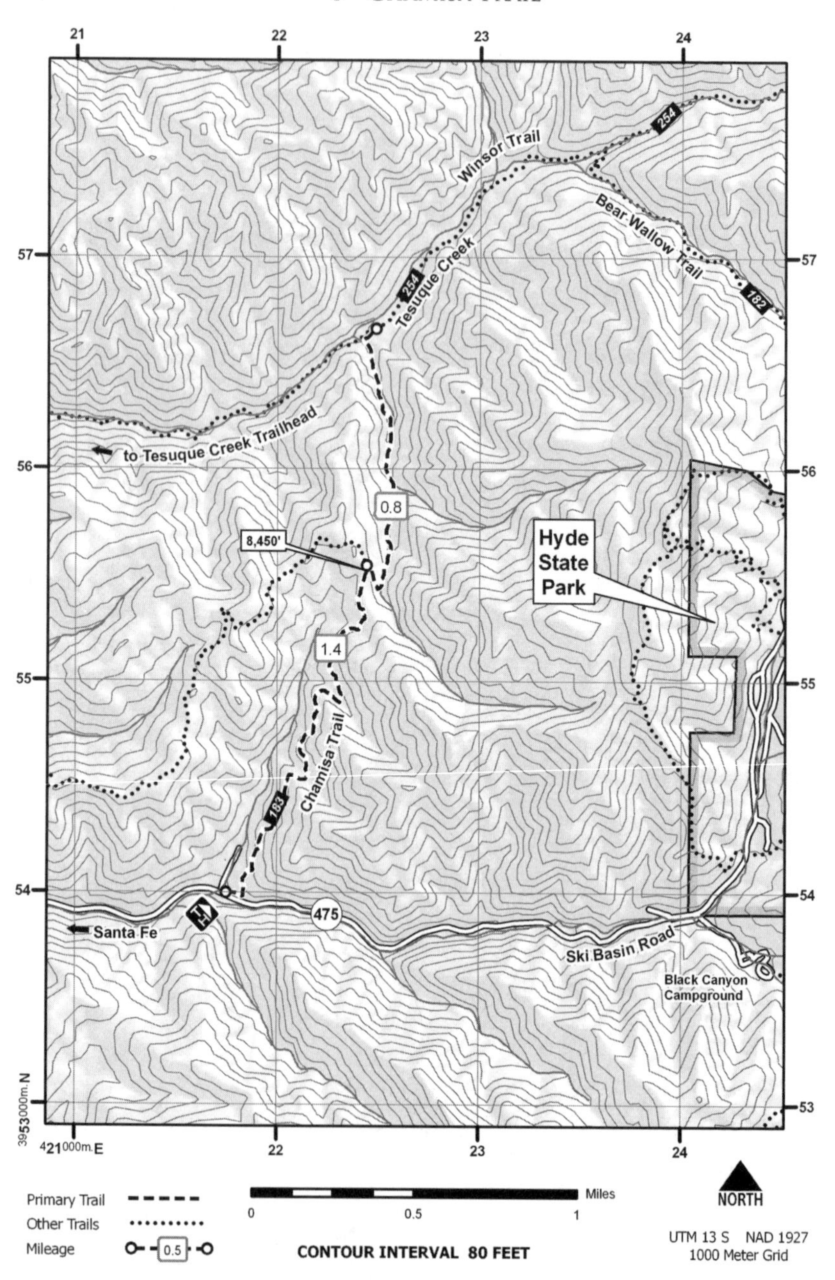

6 - CHAMISA TRAIL

by Bill Stone

A well-defined mountain trail close to Santa Fe, winding through an evergreen forest and ending at a beautiful grassy meadow beside the Tesuque Creek.

RT Distance:	5 miles
Time:	2½ -3 hrs
Elevation Range:	7950-8500 ft; total gain 1240 ft
Rating:	Easy
RT Drive:	12 miles; ~30 min
Seasons:	May be snowed-in and icy in midwinter.
Maps:	USGS McClure Reservoir and Aspen Basin - 7.5' series. Much of the trail has been re-routed and portions are no longer as shown on these maps. Drake's *Map of the Mountains of Santa Fe* and Sky Terrain's *Santa Fe, Bandelier & Los Alamos* are recommended.
Trailhead:	421,802 mE 3,953,981 mN elev.7853'

Summary

A well-defined mountain trail through evergreen forest, leading to a beautiful grassy meadow beside Tesuque Creek. Many wildflowers and birds in season. Close to Santa Fe.

Driving Directions

Drive up Artist Road (Hyde Park Road to the Santa Fe Ski Basin). Measure your mileage from the start of Artist Road, and drive 5.6 miles to where there is a wide canyon on the north (left) side of the road. Park on either side of the road. The trailhead is near the road on the north side. There is a US Forest Service sign saying "Chamisa Trail 183 - Tesuque Creek 2¼." This is the Chamisa Trail.

Hiking Instructions

The trail goes due east for a few hundred feet, climbing steeply, then turns due north. It is deeply forested, with piñon, two species of juniper, and ponderosa pine at the start. There are many switchbacks, and as you climb higher, there are views of the canyon and Hyde Park Road. Gambel oak and Douglas fir now appear. White (limber) pine and white fir appear at higher elevations. The trail is narrow and at some places proceeds along a steep dugway, with little room to pass another person. The footing here is loose and sandy.

After you have walked 1¼ miles and climbed 600 ft, you will come to the crest of the trail (altitude 8500 ft). A trail coming up the canyon from the left meets Trail 183 here. This is a good place for a break.

The trail now goes downhill. It turns sharply southeast, to your right, then, after a few hundred feet, toward the northeast (left) and continues in a northerly direction for the rest of the hike. It proceeds down a streambed (wet in spring). The footing is rocky in places. Aspen are found here as well as the trees already mentioned.

After another 1 mile, you come to a small grassy meadow. Continue about ¼ mile and you will see a signpost. This is the junction with the Winsor Trail (#254). See TESUQUE CREEK Hike #15, which ends at this intersection. The Chamisa Trail ends here. There is a grassy meadow with a large granite boulder in the middle, northeast (upstream) of the junction, and Tesuque Creek is on its western border. The meadow is a beautiful, quiet spot and a good place to have your lunch, while listening to the gentle flow of the water. The altitude is about 8,000 ft. This is the farthest point of the hike.

Return the way you came. Be sure to get back on the same trail (Chamisa), by turning left (south) at the trail signpost. Careful: if you miss the left turn and continue straight, you will be on the Winsor Trail which leads to Tesuque. The 540-ft climb back to the saddle is mostly moderate, but very steep in two places. On reaching the saddle again (8500 ft), the trail divides. The trail to the left, which is level here, is the trail you came up on. The other trail goes steeply down into the canyon and will eventually return you to the parking area. You can choose either trail.

Many wildflowers and plants may be seen along this trail. Among the predominant ones are Oregon grape, yucca, scarlet gilia, red penstemon, lupine (slopes near the crest are covered with its blooms in the late spring) and many Compositae. In addition, you may see mullein, yellow evening primrose, yarrow, wild iris, salsify and cone-flower in the meadows.

Forty-two species of birds have been seen along the Chamisa Trail. Among them were hawks, hummingbirds, woodpeckers, fly-catchers, swallows, jays, ravens, nuthatches, chickadees, thrushes, warblers, vireos and the sparrow types.

Tesuque Creek

7 Borrego / Bear Wallow Trails

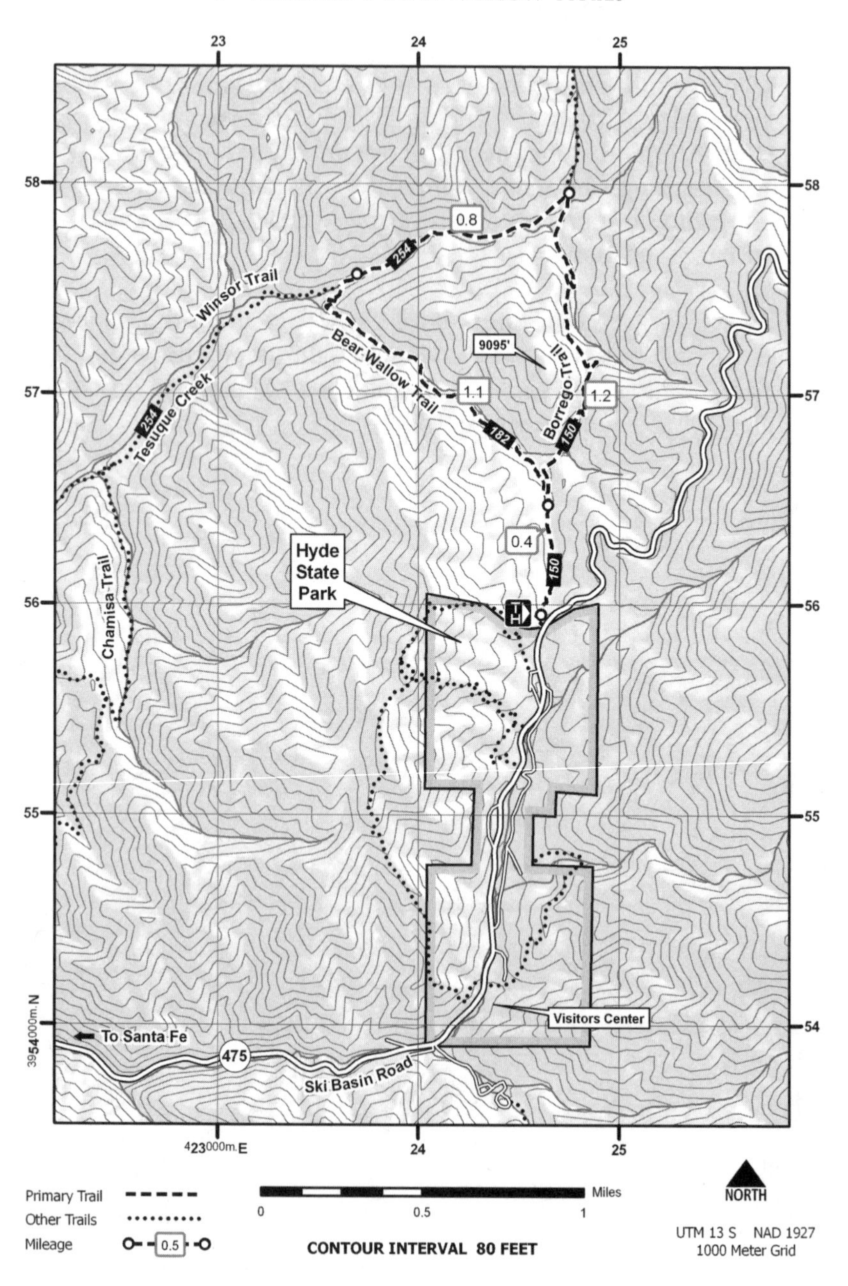

7 - BORROGO / BEAR WALLOW TRAILS

by Bill Chudd

An easily accessible short loop along good trails, partly stream-side, and through pleasant woods rife with seasonal wild-flowers.

RT Distance:	4 miles
Time:	2 hrs
Elevation Range:	8240–8880 ft; total gain 760 ft
Rating:	Easy
RT Drive:	~17 miles; 40 min
Seasons:	Usually snowed-in in mid-winter. Can be hot in mid-summer, but fairly well shaded.
Maps:	USGS Aspen Basin and (for the first ~500 yards) McClure Reservoir - 7.5' series. Drake's *Map of the Mountains of Santa Fe* and Sky Terrain's *Santa Fe, Bandelier & Los Alamos* are recommended.
Trailhead:	424,626 mE 3,955,911 mN elev.8881'

Summary

On this hike, you will make two stream crossings. If spring runoff is unusually high, the crossings can present some problems. On weekends you may encounter many hikers, bikers and dogs. If you are a seeker of solitude, this hike is probably not for you.

Driving Directions

Drive up Artist Road (Hyde Park Road to the Santa Fe Ski Basin). Measure your mileage from the start of Artist Rd, and drive a little over 8½ miles to the small paved parking area on the left side of the road. You will see an RV parking area at the left of the road 0.2 miles before the Borrego Trail parking area.

Hiking Instructions

The trail starts down from the far left corner of the parking lot. There is a sign identifying this as the Borrego Trail 150 and giving the distance to Trail 182 as ½ mile and the distance to Trail 254 as 1½ miles. After 4 or 5 twists, the trail becomes wide and easy to follow. You will enter a lovely forest of fir, aspen, and a few ponderosa pines. Later you see some shrubby Gambel oaks.

This is the Borrego Trail along which shepherds brought their flocks to market in Santa Fe from towns to the north, before modern roads and other developments made life easier and less interesting. In about ½ mile, the trail passes between two wooden signposts. If these remain intact, the left-hand one will point out the Bear Wallow Trail 182, with Tesuque Creek 1 mile away. The right-hand sign will show the Borrego Trail 150, with Tesuque Creek and the Winsor Trail 254 1¼ miles ahead. Take the left fork, the Bear Wallow Trail 182, which heads northwest. (You will return on the right fork.) After about 15 minutes, you will get glimpses ahead through the trees of a transverse ridge, indicating your approach to Tesuque Creek. Begin listening for the pleasant sound of its flow. Continue down the switchbacks to the stream bank, 1 mile from the Borrego Trail.

There are several small log crossings a bit downstream from the trail. Cross the creek here. The Winsor Trail 254, marked by a sign, parallels the stream. Your route will be upstream, a right turn after crossing the creek. If the season is right, look around for raspberries in this vicinity. Other berries you are apt to see are strawberries, edible thimbleberries, non-poisonous Oregon grape, kinnikinnick and poisonous baneberry.

Continue on the Winsor Trail, which at this point, is all upstream and uphill. After 1 mile, you will reach the junction of the Winsor and the Borrego trails, which is marked by a post with two signs. Turn right, southeast, through a small meadow, onto the Borrego Trail 150. You will shortly cross the Tesuque Creek. A huge fallen ponderosa over the creek will make your crossing easier. Soon thereafter you will cross a ridge by a switchback trail. After topping the ridge, the trail descends for a while, levels off, and returns to the junction with Bear Wallow Trail 182 which comes in from the right. You have now completed a triangle of the Bear Wallow, Winsor and Borrego Trails, each leg about 1 mile.

Continue up the Borrego Trail ½ mile to your car. Next time, take this circuit in the reverse direction. It will seem like a different walk.

Borrego / Bear Wallow

8 Aspen Vista

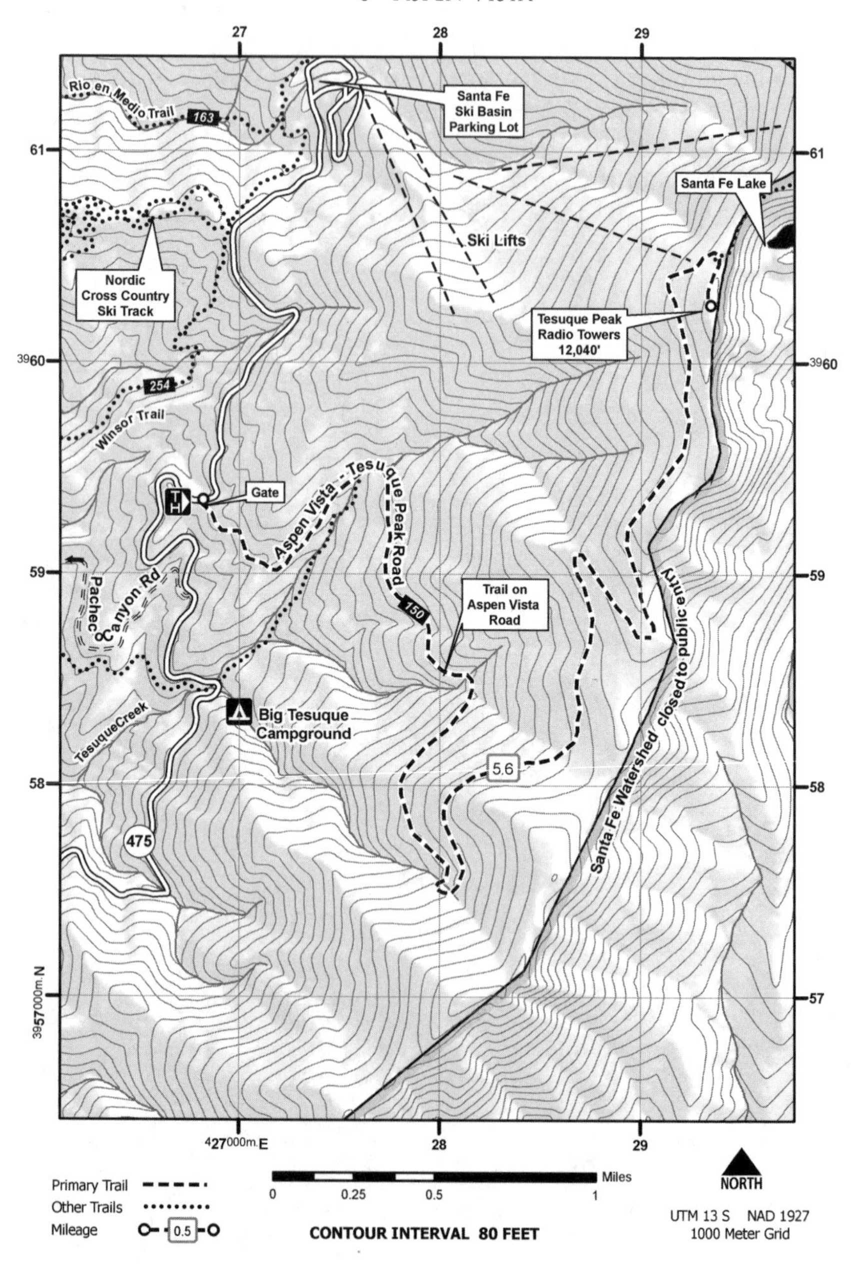

8 - ASPEN VISTA

by Walt Kunz

This hike has excellent views and is exceptionally beautiful in the fall when the aspen leaves have turned golden.

RT Distance: 11.5 miles

Time: 6 hrs

Elevation Range: 10,000-12,040 ft; total gain ~2040 ft

Rating: Easy to strenuous (depending on distance)

RT Drive: 27 miles; ~1 hr

Seasons: Usually snowed-in at higher altitudes in winter and spring; popular with x-country skiers in winter. Bring adequate clothing (can be cold at the top).

Maps: USGS: Aspen Basin - 7.5' series. Drake's *Map of the Mountains of Santa Fe* and Sky Terrain's *Santa Fe, Bandelier & Los Alamos* are recommended.

Trailhead: 426,811 mE 3,959,343 mN elev.9998'

Summary

Good stands of aspen, spruce and fir, clear streams, large open areas with excellent views. The trail is a gradual climb on a dirt road. This is a popular and often crowded area at the height of the aspen viewing season in late September and early October. This hike can be rewarding no matter how far you choose to go.

Driving Directions

Take Artist Road (Hyde Park Road) toward the Santa Fe Ski Basin. From the intersection where Artist Road begins, drive 12.6 miles, then turn right into a large parking lot marked by a large sign for Aspen Vista.

Hiking Instructions

There is a gated access road on the east side of the parking area, which is the start of the trail to Tesuque Peak. The "not for public use" sign refers to vehicles only; hiking (as well as x-country skiing) is permitted. This is the service road for the microwave relay station at the peak.

The first 2½ miles are through aspen (spectacular in the fall); the last 3½ miles are through fir and spruce alternating with large open areas. About ½ mile in, you can catch a glimpse of your destination, the bare peak with microwave towers straight ahead. At 0.8 miles, you cross the north fork of Tesuque Creek, at 1.6 miles, two more forks of the creek, and at 2.3 miles, the last fork. Water-loving flowers abound along the banks of the creeks. Late in the summer, the lower stretches of the road are lined with masses of yellow senecio and purple asters.

Just past the last creek crossing, the road makes a switchback to the north (left) and you will see fir and spruce. At 3.8 miles, the road traverses a large open area that affords good views of the Rio Grande valley north of Santa Fe. A bit farther along you get a panoramic view of Santa Fe. On your left you will see a large outcropping of rock that makes a good rest area and a turnaround point if you don't want to hike the entire distance.

At 5 miles, after a few more switchbacks, the road turns northeast and enters the trees again. At 5½ miles, the road enters another large open area. Below, to the northwest, you can see the top of a chair lift at the Santa Fe Ski Basin. The long fence straight ahead is a snow fence along one of the ski trails. Above, to the northeast, are the microwave towers on Tesuque Peak, about ½ mile away by road.

At the top, the terrain drops steeply to the east. If you stand at the eastern edge, you can see the well-hidden Santa Fe Lake, the source of the Santa Fe River. To the north are Deception Peak and Lake Peak (see DECEPTION, LAKE & PENITENTE PEAKS Hike #10), about 1 mile away.

Return by the same route.

Deception Peak as seen from Tesuque Peak,
on the Aspen Vista Trail

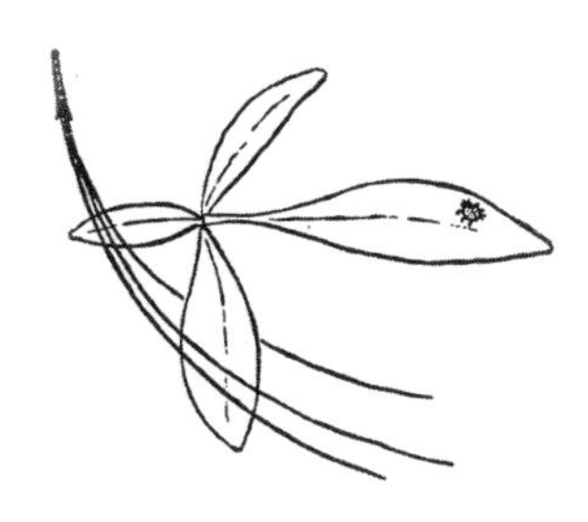

9 Rio Nambé

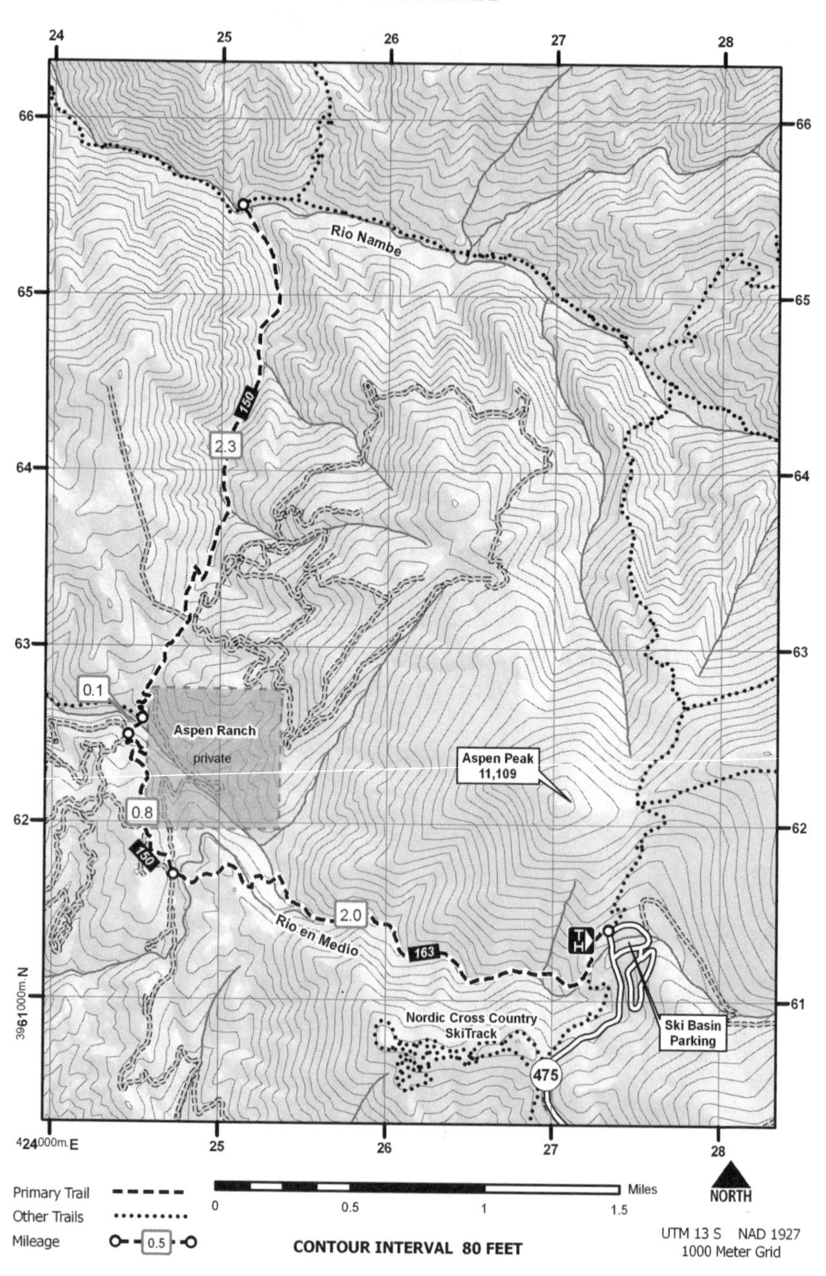

Rio Nambe
Aspen Ranch
private
Aspen Peak
11,109
Rio en Medio
Nordic Cross Country
SkiTrack
Ski Basin
Parking
475
150
163
2.3
0.1
0.8
2.0
424000m.E
3961000m.N
Primary Trail
Other Trails
Mileage
0.5
Miles
0
0.5
1
1.5
NORTH
CONTOUR INTERVAL 80 FEET
UTM 13 S NAD 1927
1000 Meter Grid

9 - RIO NAMBÉ

by Norma McCallan

A pleasant hike near the Santa Fe Ski Basin, with clear streams, lovely meadows, and abundant wildflowers in a deep forest of spruce, fir, ponderosa and aspen.

RT Distance:	10.5 miles
Time:	6 hrs
Elevation Range:	8187-10,250 ft; total gain 2600 ft
Rating:	Strenuous
RT Drive:	30 miles; 1 hr 20 min
Seasons:	Late spring, summer, and fall
Maps:	USGS Aspen Basin - 7.5' series. Drake's *Map of the Mountains of Santa Fe,* FS *Pecos Wilderness* and Sky Terrain's *Santa Fe, Bandelier & Los Alamos* are also recommended.
Trailhead:	427,338 mE 3,961,432 mN elev.10267'

Summary

This hike follows the little-travelled upper Rio en Medio, picks up the historic Borrego Trail near Aspen Ranch, and ends by the Rio Nambé. Unlike most routes from the Ski Basin, which gain altitude, this hike starts downhill and has most of its uphill climb on the return trip.

Driving Directions

Take Artist Road (Hyde Park Road) to the Santa Fe Ski Basin (~14 miles). As you approach the Ski Basin parking area, keep to the left and park in the lower lot. The trailhead for the Winsor Trail is located at the far western edge of the lower parking lot.

Hiking Instructions

From the trailhead, cross the small wooden bridge over the Rio en Medio and turn left, downhill, on Winsor Trail 254. In about 5 minutes, near a big pile of deadfall, the Winsor Trail makes a sharp left. Your unmarked trail (actually the upper end of the Rio en Medio Trail 163) continues straight, downhill, following Rio en Medio. About ½ hour from the start, the trail heads through a long narrow meadow lush with wildflowers. The trail gets less steep and rocky as it continues downhill and the stream widens. Further along, the trail makes a sharp left where a modest log barrier discourages you from continuing straight on an old trail which here enters private property. Your route, Trail 163, crosses the stream almost immediately, goes steeply uphill, crosses a ditch on an old log, and turns right, briefly paralleling the ditch, before veering left. After about 1 hour from the trailhead, the trail crosses a stile. It then heads down to the Aspen Ranch parking area on FR 412, used for access from Pacheco Canyon Road, whose current eroded condition discourages driving.

Walk about 100 yards farther along the road to the trailhead on the left side of the road. It is signed "Trail 163, Trail 150;" here the trails are combined. The trail goes uphill and winds through a mixed forest of ponderosa and occasional aspen. After about 15 minutes of uphill, the trail switchbacks downhill toward the Rio en Medio. Stay on the main trail - hikers have made many alternate ribbons of shortcuts. Cross the stream, veering left and up the opposite bank, where you will find a gouged-out sign marking the intersection of the Rio en Medio Trail 163 descending downstream, and the Borrego Trail 150 heading uphill. Ignore trail 163 which makes a sharp left, and follow the Borrego Trail (150) straight ahead.

Continue on the trail as it zigzags up the hill until it joins the old Lucky Star Mine Road. The sign here reads: "Borrego Trail 150, Rancho Viejo." Turn left here (noting this junction for your return). Follow the road uphill until you come to a saddle where the road turns sharply to the right. Leave the road here and look for a trail that starts leftwards and downhill to the north. There is a sign here: "Borrego Trail 150, Rio Nambé, Rancho Viejo, Aspen Ranch," with appropriate arrows.

Trail 150 is part of the historic Borrego Trail, which, as recently as the mid-20th century, was used to herd sheep from the high mountains east of Chimayo and Truchas to Santa Fe. As you walk down the small drainage, you'll be going through a dark forest of spruce and fir. In the summer, you may see the spectacular flowering green gentian, which sometimes grows as tall as 5 ft. If there is any water in the small drainage, watch for the one-sided pyrola in the wet dirt.

After about 1½ miles of steady descent through the forest, you will come to the Rio Nambé, which flows west to the Nambé Indian Pueblo 6 miles downstream. Just before the river, the trail forks. Your trail, the Borrego Trail 150, crosses the river, while the left fork, Trail 160, follows the Rio Nambé downstream. Use stepping stones or logs if you don't want wet feet. The trail continues, to the right and upstream, but your destination is the beautiful meadow in front of you. Wander around, find a comfortable grassy spot for your lunch, and enjoy the tranquility.

Return the way you came. If you come to a closed gate as you are walking down the old Lucky Star Mine Road, you have missed the place where your trail takes off to zigzag down to the Rio en Medio. Walk back up the road about 75 yards and you will see the trail you came in on.

Most wild animals get into the world and out of it without being noticed.

~ John Muir

10 Deception, Lake & Penitente Peaks

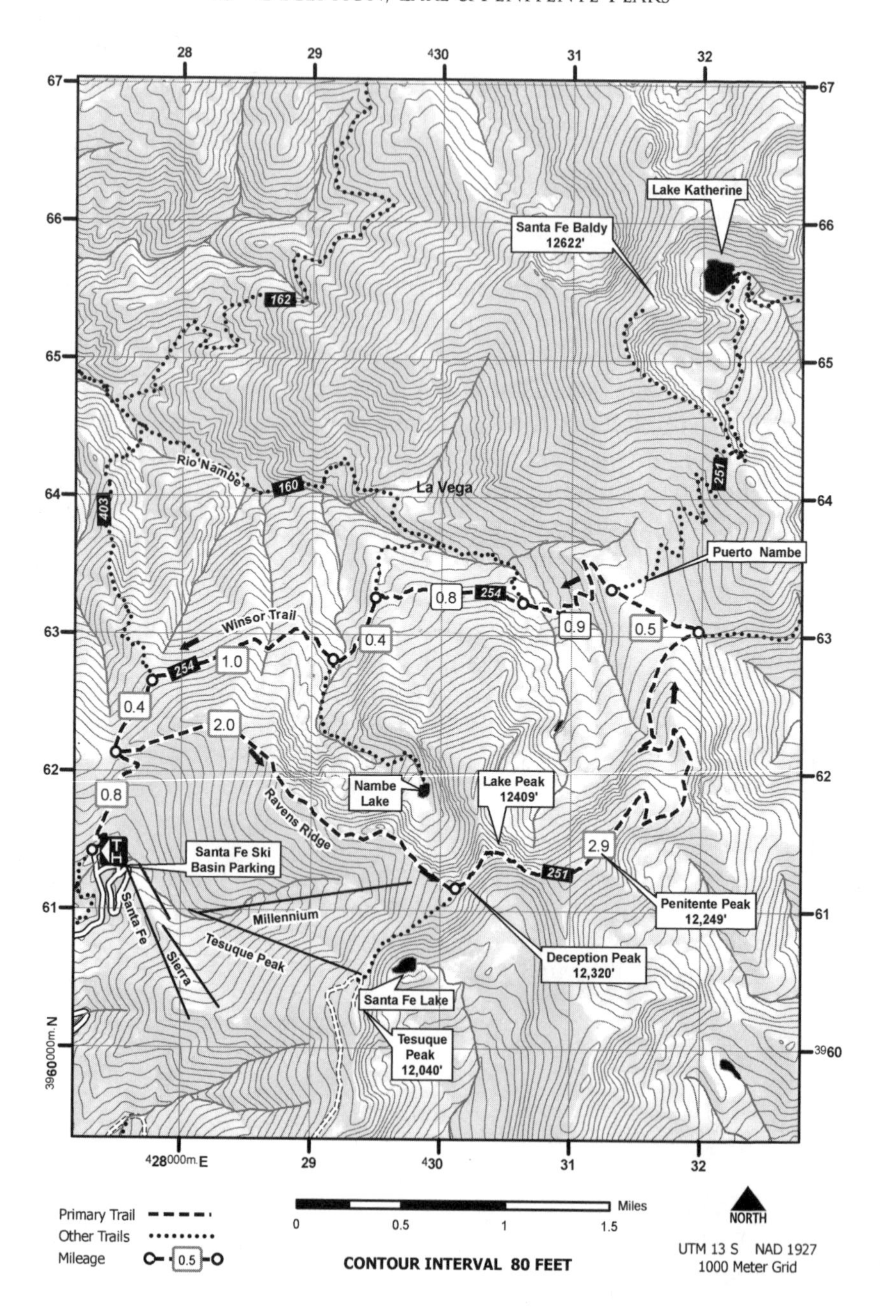

10 - DECEPTION, LAKE & PENITENTE PEAKS

by Norbert Sperlich

This hike up Raven's Ridge to Deception Peak is the shortest route from Santa Fe to reach the tundra above tree line, offering stunning views, beautiful alpine flowers, and additional trails.

RT Distance:	6 miles (Deception Pk only) 6.5 miles (Lake Pk extension) 11 miles (loop extension via Penitente Pk)
Time:	4+ hrs (Deception Pk only) 5+ hrs (Lake Pk extension) 7-8 hrs (loop extension via Penitente Pk)
Elevation Range:	10,250-12,409 ft Total gain ~2500 ft (Deception Pk) Total gain ~2600 ft (Lake Pk) Total gain ~3100 ft (loop via Penitente Pk)
Rating:	Strenuous
RT Drive:	30 miles; ~1 hr 20 min
Seasons:	June to October, snow conditions permitting. Snowdrifts tend to stay longer on north facing slopes between Penitente Peak and the Winsor Trail.
Maps:	USGS Tesuque, Aspen Basin - 7.5' series. Deception Pk, SW of Lake Pk, is not named on the topo map, nor is the trail up Raven's Ridge shown. Drake's *Map of the Mountains of Santa Fe* and Sky Terrain's *Santa Fe, Bandelier & Los Alamos* are recommended.
Trailhead:	427,338 mE 3,961,432 mN elev.10267'

Summary

The hike up Raven's Ridge to Deception Peak (12,320 ft) takes you above tree line and offers stunning views in all directions. Experienced hikers with route-finding skills might want to continue to

Lake Peak (12,409 ft). This requires navigating over rough terrain with poor footing, exposure, and marginal trails. Some scrambling is needed. Once you have arrived on Lake Peak, you can return the way you came, or go next to Penitente Peak (12,249 ft) and continue on to Puerto Nambé, returning on the Winsor Trail. If you do the loop hike, you will spend two hours or more above tree line. It does not get any better than this!

With high elevation come the dangers of lightning, rain or snow showers, hypothermia, and poor visibility if you end up in the clouds. Be equipped for the worst and turn back at any sign of thunderstorms. Start early and know your way down. Bring map, compass, and extra clothing!

Driving Directions

Drive up Artist Road (Hyde Park Road) to the Santa Fe Ski Basin (~14 miles). As you approach the Ski Basin parking area, keep to the left and park in the lower lot. The trailhead for the Winsor Trail is located at the far western edge of the lower parking lot.

Hiking Instructions

From the trailhead, you will cross a small stream and go up (right) on the Winsor Trail (Trail 254). After 30 minutes or so of steep climbing, you come to a fence marking the boundary of the Pecos Wilderness. A sign marks the Winsor Trail (which continues beyond the fence), and to the right (along the fence) the Raven's Ridge Trail. Leave the Winsor Trail and turn right onto the Raven's Ridge Trail that follows the fence uphill. This unmaintained trail follows Raven's Ridge all the way to Deception Peak. The ridge has several high and low points along the way, and the trail sometimes branches. Stay on the ridge top.

After following the fence line for about 20 minutes, you will pass a meadow on your left. Check out the wildflowers. Ten minutes later, the fence comes to an end at the edge of a steep drop. Great views of Santa Fe Baldy, Lake Peak, and the Nambé drainage below. The trail now follows the ridge to a boulder field. Stay to the left of the gneiss boulders. Soon you will reach a second boulder field. Stay on the left margin of the boulders. In a few minutes, the trail reaches a high point and goes left at a cairn. It descends briefly and goes up to a second high point, and then drops steeply down to a saddle, always following the ridgeline. The trail climbs to another high point, only to descend one more time. Look for Nambé Lake down below on your left (north). As you go up again, you will reach the tree line and a lone bristlecone pine.

The bare, rounded ridge ahead of you is Deception Peak. Follow the trail up to the ridge top. You may see a cairn. If you plan to come back the same way, the cairn will indicate where to leave Deception Peak and head back to Raven's Ridge. As for now, turn left toward the high point of Deception Peak. Time to take in the views! The nearby rocky pyramid to the northeast is Lake Peak, connected to Deception Peak by a narrow ridge. The rounded shape of Santa Fe Baldy appears further back, to the left of Lake Peak. To the west stretches the Rio Grande Valley, with the Jemez Mountains in the background. Tesuque Peak with its radio towers is within walking distance to the southwest; Glorieta Baldy and Thompson Peak are further away to the south. The Santa Fe Watershed, where the Santa Fe River originates, is down below to the southeast. The bare ridge of Penitente Peak is visible to the east. If Deception Peak is your final destination or if the weather looks dubious, turn around here.

Lake Peak Extension - To continue on to Lake Peak, follow the trail along the ridge top to the first low point. To the left and down, you will have a breathtaking view of Nambé Lake. Looking down on your right, you should see a faint trail parallel to the ridge some 60 ft below. Descend to that trail on a steep and rocky slope if you can. (If you can't, turn around. Lake Peak is not meant for you.) Follow the trail to a fork. The upper branch goes up toward some rocks, the lower branch goes a bit down and toward trees. Take the lower trail. Footing is poor here, and you will be glad you brought your hiking poles. At the next trail fork, stay on the upper branch. The trail now traverses a rocky, eroded slope and goes up toward the summit. Some 25 minutes or so after leaving Deception, you should be on Lake Peak. More views!

Loop Extension via Penitente - You will need another 30 minutes to reach Penitente, the bare, grassy ridge to the east. Go down in an easterly direction along the ridge that connects Lake Peak to Penitente. At a low point, the trail switches to the left side of the ridge, making a hairpin turn, but further along, it reverts to the right side again. Stunning views to the right (south) into the Santa Fe River drainage. When you arrive at the saddle below the grassy slope of Penitente, you have two choices to continue on the hike. The *preferred choice* is to leave the trail (which turns to the right and southeast) and head straight up (east) to the summit. It takes about 10 minutes (200 ft elevation gain) to reach the rock shelter on top. *Note: The next paragraph describes an alternative route.*

An *alternate choice* is to stay on the trail (Skyline Trail or Trail 251), which goes to the right and southeast. This trail stays below Penitente Peak—a welcome option in the event of thunderstorms or high winds. The trail, shown on Drake's and Sky Terrain's maps, contours around the south side of Penitente just above treeline and may be hard to find if the grass is tall. It makes a sharp left turn by a Trail 251 sign (people frequently get lost right around here), goes northeast and reaches Penitente Ridge near a large cairn. You are now back on the ridge route, about 20 minutes after you left it.

From the summit, follow the bare ridge toward the northeast. Awesome views! After about 6 minutes, you will come to a large cairn where a trail comes in from the right. This is the Skyline Trail, described in the previous paragraph. Continue northeast along the ridge on this trail for about 10 minutes. Look for a cairn and a second, larger cairn some 40 paces past the first cairn and close to the trees on your right. There might be a signpost here. At the cairn, the trail turns right, and so do you. The trail is level for a short distance, than it turns left and downwards into the big trees.

Some 20 minutes later, the trail makes a sharp left turn, marked by a cairn and a blaze on a tree. Look for blazes if the trail is hidden by snow. Another 25 minutes or so of hiking will get you to the marked T-junction with the Winsor Trail (Trail 254), where you take a left. From here, it is about 5 miles to the Ski Basin.

In about 10 minutes, you will reach Puerto Nambé, an open, grassy area marked by sign posts. Follow the Winsor Trail down switchbacks and across two streams that feed into the Rio Nambé. About one hour past Puerto Nambé, you will cross the main branch of the Rio Nambé. Rest up before continuing on the Winsor Trail. You have another hour of hiking ahead of you, including a long but gradual uphill climb that brings you back to the wilderness boundary, and the last downhill stretch to your car.

Note: When hiking toward Deception Peak, you are on National Forest land leased to the Santa Fe Ski Company. This part of the mountain is cherished by many hikers in search of solitude and has many sites sacred to people from nearby pueblos. Plans by the Ski Company to expand its operations met with resistance from the pueblos of Nambe and Tesuque, Santa Fe County, the Ski Area Containment Coalition, Sierra Club, and Forest Guardians as well as other groups and individuals. In spite of persistent opposition to further development and industrialization of the mountain, a mile-long ski lift to just below Deception Peak was built in 2005, and future development of Raven's Ridge may be possible.

Lake Peak

11 NAMBÉ LAKE

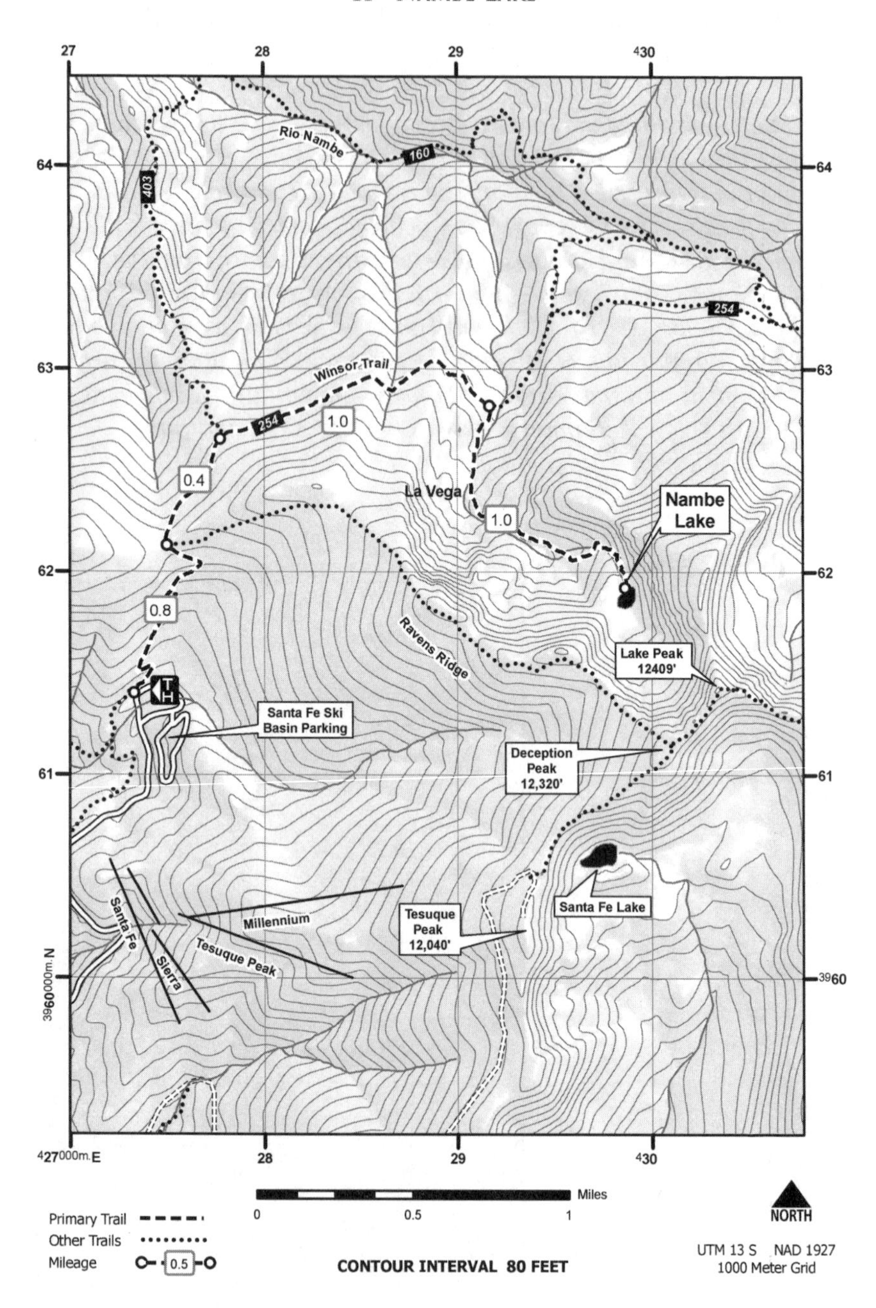

11 - NAMBÉ LAKE

by Carolyn Keskulla

The closest alpine lake to Santa Fe, Nambé Lake is nestled under the cliff face of Lake Peak, where flowers grow in profusion during summer along the stream and around the lake.

RT Distance:	7 miles
Time:	5 hrs (includes lunch, stroll around lake)
Elevation Range:	10,250-11,400 ft; total gain ~2100 ft
Rating:	Moderate (a few steep rocky climbs)
RT Drive:	30 miles; 1 hr 20 min
Seasons:	Generally accessible from mid-June to first heavy snow. During summer, the mosquitoes can be heavily concentrated along the river and lake, so bring repellent.
Maps:	USGS Aspen Basin - 7.5' series. This trail is not shown on the topo map but does appear on the Pecos Wilderness map. Drake's *Map of the Mountains of Santa Fe* and Sky Terrain's *Santa Fe, Bandelier & Los Alamos* are recommended.
Trailhead:	427,338 mE 3,961,432 mN elev.10267'

Summary

You will have the special treat of seeing Nambé Lake, which nestles under the cliff face of Lake Peak. Good hiking shoes are a necessity. The trail is very steep and rocky in places as it climbs alongside Nambé Creek.

Driving Directions

Drive up Artist Road (Hyde Park Road) to the Santa Fe Ski Basin (~14 miles). As you approach the Ski Basin parking area, keep to the left and park in the lower lot. The trailhead for the Winsor Trail is located at the far western edge of the lower parking lot.

Hiking Instructions

After crossing the small wooden bridge, turn right and start uphill on the well-used Winsor Trail (Trail 254). After ½ mile or more of steep climbing, you will be at the Pecos Wilderness boundary fence, 600 ft higher than the trailhead. Watch for the lovely wildflowers among the aspen and spruce. In June, you may see shooting star and fairy slipper orchids. After passing through the fence, the trail starts gently downhill. In about ¼ mile, you will come to a little noticed trail on the left, marked with the sign "Trail 403 Rio Nambé 1¾." This is a very steep trail to the Rio Nambé nicknamed the "elevator shaft." DON'T TAKE THIS TRAIL: it goes to the Rio Nambé, not the lake.

Continue past this junction another 1¼ miles or so. You will come to a clearing on your right. Ahead of you, the Winsor Trail drops down to cross the Nambé Lake Creek. A sign to the right of the main trail says "Nambé Lake." Look for a trail going up on the right (south), which will bring you alongside a lovely, cascading alpine stream. In places along the river, there are smaller paths that meander along the main path, but all will eventually lead you to the lake, which is hidden behind the high ridge to the southeast.

The trail consists of several steep ascents separated by level stretches. After the first ascent, keep to the left bank. The basic rule: keep the stream within earshot as the trail climbs steeply. The lake will eventually appear surrounded by spruce forest and talus slopes.

The shallow lake nestles under the cliff face of Lake Peak. Flowers grow in profusion in July along the stream and around the lake. Parry's primrose, mertensia and marsh marigold are spectacular in early July. Later there will be fireweed, yampa, monkshood and many others. You may also see marmots and pika scampering around the slopes.

Return by the same route.

On the way to Nambé Lake

I never saw a discontented tree.
~ John Muir

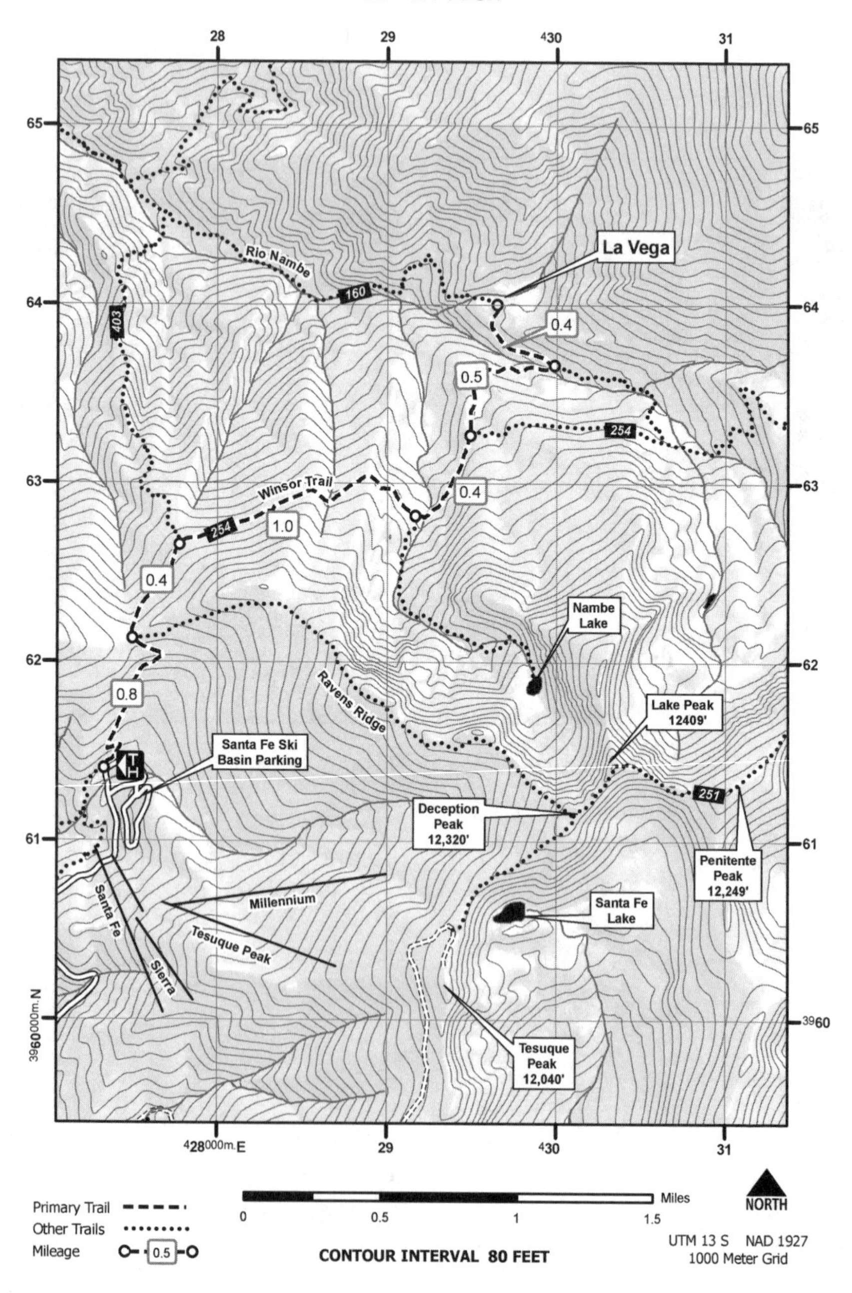
La Vega
Rio Nambe
160
403
0.4
0.5
254
Winsor Trail
0.4
1.0
254
0.4
Nambe Lake
0.8
Ravens Ridge
Lake Peak 12409'
Santa Fe Ski Basin Parking
251
Deception Peak 12,320'
Penitente Peak 12,249'
Millennium
Santa Fe Lake
Santa Fe
Tesuque Peak
Sierra
Tesuque Peak 12,040'
28
29
430
31
65
64
63
62
61
3960000m.N
3960
428000m.E
Primary Trail
Other Trails
Mileage
0.5
0
0.5
1
1.5
Miles
NORTH
CONTOUR INTERVAL 80 FEET
UTM 13 S NAD 1927
1000 Meter Grid

12 - LA VEGA

by Norbert Sperlich

A beautiful meadow at the foot of Santa Fe Baldy with many wildflowers in season.

RT Distance: 7 miles
Time: 3-4 hrs
Elevation Range: 10,000-10,840 ft; total gain ~1500 ft
Rating: Moderate
RT Drive: 30 miles; ~1 hr 20 min
Seasons: June until first heavy snow
Maps: USGS Tesuque, Aspen Basin - 7.5' series. *(Note: La Vega is not named on the topo map.)* Drake's *Map of the Mountains of Santa Fe* and Sky Terrain's *Santa Fe, Bandelier & Los Alamos* are recommended.
Trailhead: 427,338 mE 3,961,432 mN elev.10267'

Summary

This hike through aspen, fir and spruce takes you to an open meadow at the foot of Santa Fe Baldy. La Vega, Spanish for "meadow" or "pasture land," offers a beautiful setting away from the sometimes crowded Winsor Trail. Many wildflowers in season. Spectacular in late September and early October, when the aspens are golden.

Driving Directions

Drive up Artist Road (Hyde Park Road) to the Santa Fe Ski Basin (~14 miles). As you approach the Ski Basin parking area, keep to the left and park in the lower lot. The trailhead for the Winsor Trail is located at the far western edge of the lower parking lot. Look for a sign that says "WINSOR TRAIL."

Hiking Instructions

From the trailhead, you will cross a small stream and go up to the right on the Winsor Trail (Trail 254). The trail zigzags up through a forest of aspen, fir and spruce trees and crosses several small meadows. After half an hour or so of steep climbing you come to a meadow and the entrance gate to the Pecos Wilderness. You have reached the highest point of the hike (10,850 ft). Time to catch your breath and to feed the gray jays that are usually waiting here for handouts from hikers.

The trail now descends gradually through stands of conifers and aspens. After about 1 hour of hiking from the trailhead, you will see a smaller trail that goes off to the right to Nambé Lake (see NAMBÉ LAKE Hike #11) and then just afterwards, a clearing to the right with nice views of Santa Fe Baldy. You will continue straight ahead on the Winsor Trail which immediately crosses Rio Nambé. In about 5-10 minutes you will reach the turnoff to La Vega, a small trail that goes down to the left. Look for a sign on the right side of the trail. The sign says: "UPPER NAMBE TRAIL 101 - RIO NAMBE - LA VEGA."

For a while, the trail stays on top of a ridge, then it drops down into the valley to the right of the ridge. At the valley bottom, the trail enters a conifer forest and then comes to a stream (a tributary of Rio Nambé). At this point, you have hiked for about 15 minutes on the La Vega Trail. You have now reached the lowest point of the hike (~10,000 ft). Cross the stream on the log bridge.

The trail now turns left and goes up on the other side of the stream. About 30 yards away from the stream, your trail merges with Trail 160 (Rio Nambé Trail). The junction is marked by a sign-post with two signs. One of them points in the direction from which you came; the other sign, indicating the Rio Nambé Trail, says "Trail 160." Take the Rio Nambé Trail, Trail 160.

For a while, the trail descends slowly, with the stream on your left within earshot. After a few minutes, you will be going uphill again and the trail moves to the right, away from the stream. Some 10 minutes after passing the last sign (near the stream), the trail will take you up to a low ridge. Ahead of you is a clearing and a signpost. The sign, about chest high, will tell you: LA VEGA - RIO NAMBÉ TRAIL - BORREGO TRAIL 4 - ASPEN RANCH 7.

The trail is not clearly visible beyond this point. Walk 10 yards or so past the signpost and you will look down on La Vega, a large meadow (altitude ~10,100 ft) interspersed with spruce and fir, and patches of gooseberry bushes. Opposite you, to the north, the meadow is framed by two ridges that lead up to Santa Fe Baldy. (The top of Santa Fe Baldy is not visible from this point.) A little stream comes down the valley between the two ridges and meanders through the meadow, turning to the west to join Rio Nambé further down. If you are lucky, you might see deer bounding across the meadow. More likely, you will encounter a herd of grazing cattle.

Before you move on to explore La Vega or to relax at the side of the stream, memorize the location of the LA VEGA signpost. You will have to return to this post in order to find the trail. When exploring the meadow, watch out for swampy areas.

Start your return at the signpost and go back the way you came. After a few minutes of hiking you will hear the stream below you on the right. Once the stream comes into your view, watch for the turnoff to the right and the sign on the left side of the trail. Turn to the right and go down to the stream. Cross the stream and retrace your steps back to the Winsor Trail. When you reach the Winsor Trail, turn right and go back to the Ski Basin.

La Vega

13 Lake Katherine

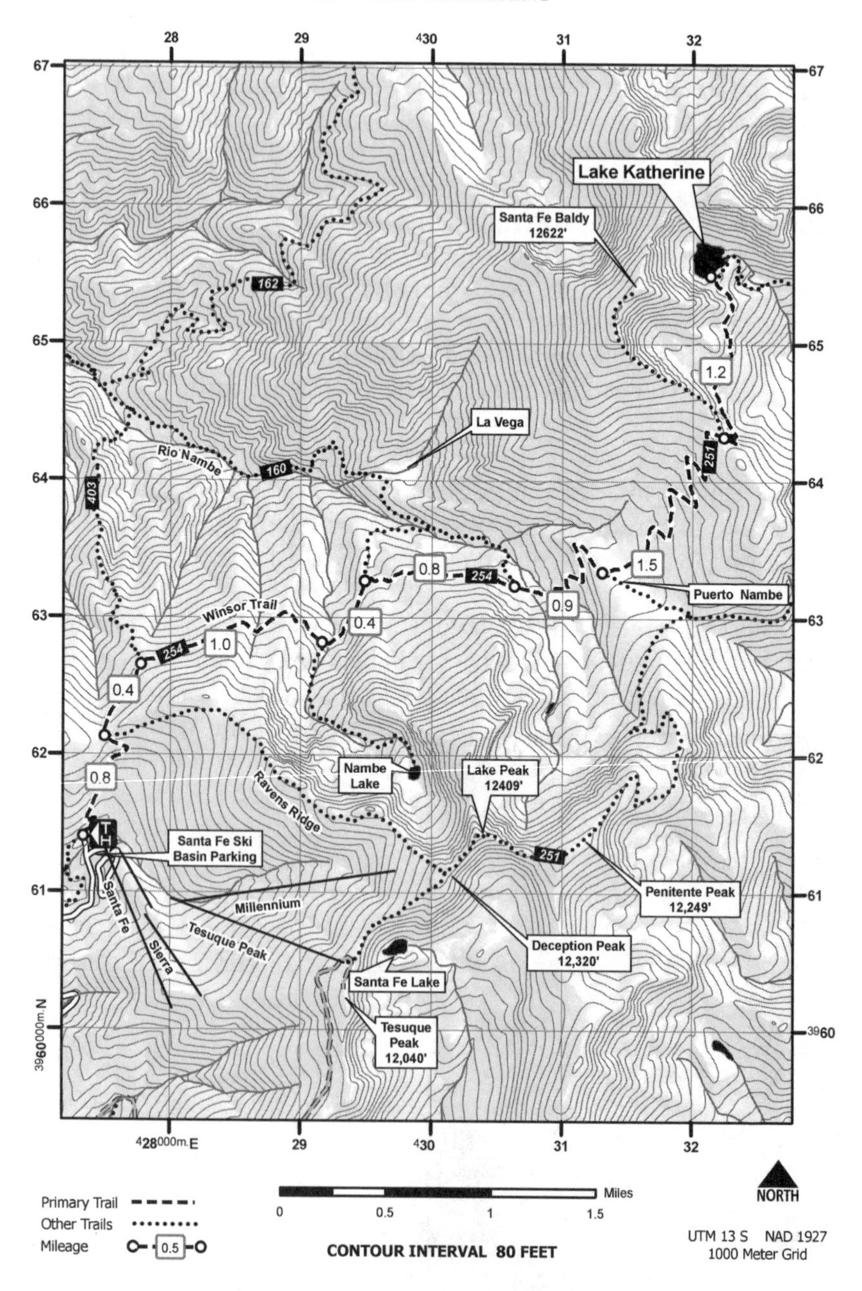

13 - LAKE KATHERINE

by Ken Adam

A high altitude hike over well-marked trails through aspen, fir and spruce, and high meadows, ending at a beautiful alpine lake.

RT Distance:	14.5 miles
Time:	8+ hrs
Elevation Range:	10,250-11,742 ft; total gain ~3300 ft
Rating:	Strenuous
RT Drive:	30 miles; ~1 hr 30 min
Seasons:	Generally accessible from mid-June to early October (until the first major snowfall).
Maps:	USGS Aspen Basin and Cowles - 7.5' series. Also, the FS *Pecos Wilderness* Map, Drakes's *Mountains of Santa Fe*, and Sky Terrain's *Santa Fe, Bandelier & Los Alamos* are recommended.
Trailhead:	427,338 mE 3,961,432 mN elev.10267'

Summary

Lake Katherine, east of Santa Fe Baldy, is the largest alpine lake in the Santa Fe area. The hike is over well-marked trails through aspen, fir and spruce forest, ending at a beautiful alpine lake in a spectacular setting. There are fine views of nearby peaks and distant valleys.

Driving Directions

Drive up Artist Road (Hyde Park Road) to the Santa Fe Ski Basin (~14 miles). As you approach the Ski Basin parking area, keep to the left and park in the lower lot. The trailhead for the Winsor Trail is located at the far western edge of the lower parking lot.

Hiking Instructions

After crossing the small wooden bridge, turn right and start uphill on the well-used Winsor Trail 254. The trail starts with the steepest climb of the day through mixed aspen and conifer forest (very spectacular in the fall). In about 30 minutes, after several switchbacks and a couple of small meadows (wild iris in season), you will arrive at the entrance gate of the Pecos Wilderness. This pass is between the watersheds of the Rio en Medio and Rio Nambé.

The trail now traverses the north slope of the divide. About 10-15 minutes after passing through the gate, you come to a fork in the trail. Trail 403, to Rio Nambé, goes to the left. You continue straight ahead on the Winsor Trail, gradually losing altitude for a little over 1 mile until you reach Rio Nambé. You will have walked about 1 hour to this point. Just before Rio Nambé, a fork leads upstream to Nambé Lake beneath Lake Peak (see NAMBÉ LAKE Hike #11), but you continue forward, crossing Rio Nambé on a log bridge.

The trail continues to traverse, without much altitude change, to the northeast. Keep to the main trail (Winsor Trail 254), now climbing slightly through aspen groves and small meadows. You will cross three minor streams and pass by two places where trails lead off to the left from the main trail. Stay on the main trail. The ¾-mile uphill stretch from the last stream to Puerto Nambé will seem more like a mile. After 20-25 minutes, you will reach a "Y" trail junction in a beautiful high meadow called Puerto Nambé. There are fine views of Santa Fe Baldy to the north and Lake Peak and Penitente Peak to the south and southeast. While you stop to rest at this junction, several gray jays will probably pester you for a hand-out. With just a little patience on your part, they will eat from your hand.

You now leave the Winsor Trail and take the Skyline Trail 251, the left trail at the "Y." The Winsor Trail is the trail to the right, which takes you across Puerto Nambé to Spirit Lake (See SPIRIT LAKE Hike #23). Trail 251 crosses the meadow and starts up a series of long switchbacks that finally bring you to a saddle at the divide between the Rio Nambé and Pecos watersheds. You will have been walking about 3 hours at this point. This is a wonderful resting spot with dramatic scenery in all directions: the upper Pecos basin to the east, the Rio Grande Valley and Jemez Mountains to the west, Santa Fe Baldy right next to you on the northwest, and Lake Peak and Penitente Peak to the south and southeast.

You are at the edge of a steep drop-off to the east and looking down you can see your trail zigzag down in a series of seven switchbacks. After dropping down these switchbacks, the trail starts climbing to the northwest across the upper edge of a large talus slope, then through open forest. Level stretches of trail are interrupted with short climbs up switchbacks. Look out for abrupt changes in trail direction. The trail leaves the forest and crosses an open talus-covered area. The trail is not well defined here, so keep a close eye on it. At the end of the talus area is a sign reading "Lake Basin closed to camping and fires." You cannot see the lake yet. A short walk through open forest brings you to the eastern shoreline of Lake Katherine at an elevation of 11,742 ft.

You are in a high alpine bowl, with Santa Fe Baldy directly above you to the southwest. The peak is so close that you may be tempted to climb it on your way home. This can be done by climbing the steep grassy slope above the west shore of the lake and following the ridge to the summit. It involves an extra 900 ft of climbing at high altitude. However, this detour is **not** recommended unless every member of your party is in excellent shape, you know your way down from the Santa Fe Baldy summit, and there is no threat of lightning.

Lake Katherine

The recommended return is by retracing your route in reverse. When leaving Lake Katherine, the trail can be difficult to find again. Hike to the southeastern shore of the lake and toward the southern wall surrounding the lake. Then head east and look for the no camping sign you saw on the way in.

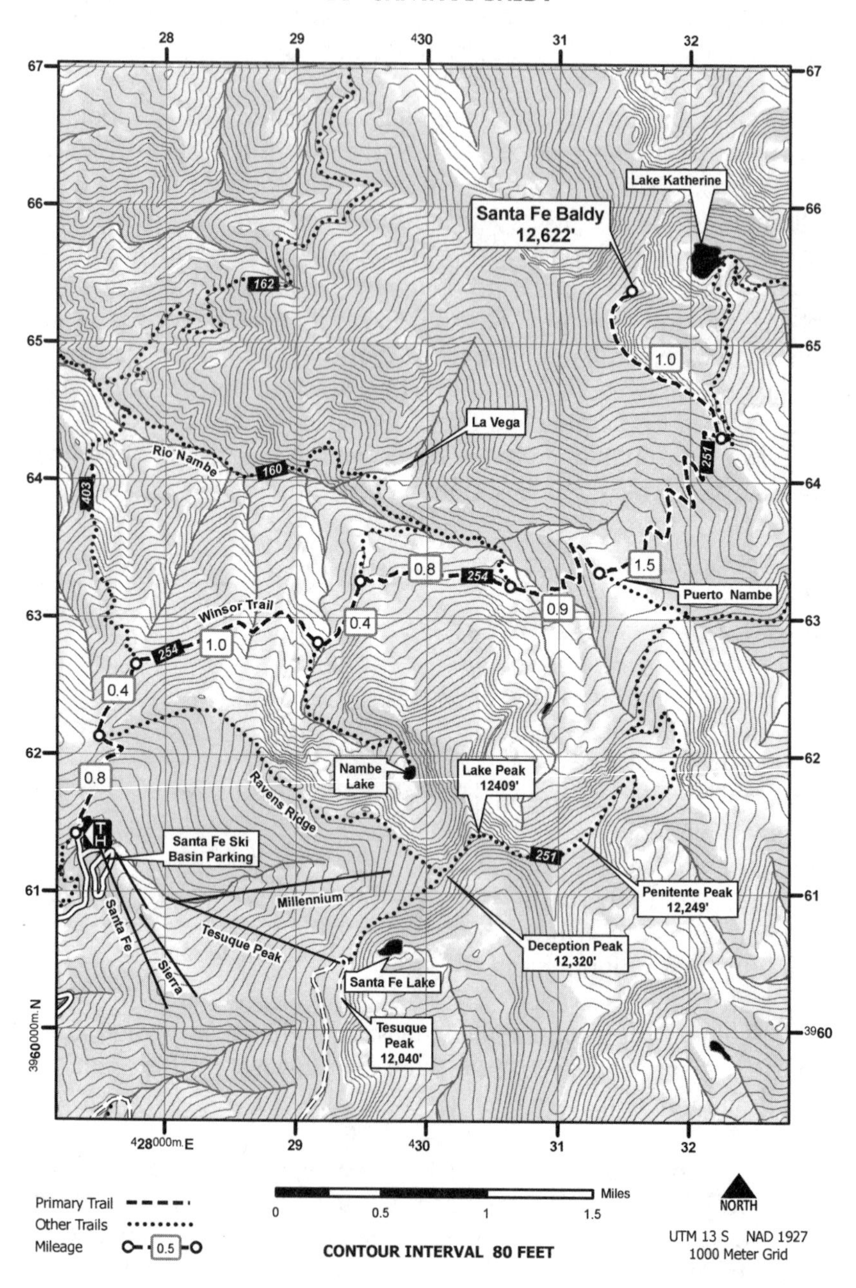
Santa Fe Baldy
12,622'
Lake Katherine
La Vega
Rio Nambe
Winsor Trail
Puerto Nambe
Nambe Lake
Lake Peak
12409'
Ravens Ridge
Santa Fe Ski
Basin Parking
Millennium
Tesuque Peak
Santa Fe
Sierra
Santa Fe Lake
Tesuque
Peak
12,040'
Deception Peak
12,320'
Penitente Peak
12,249'
162
160
403
254
251
1.0
0.8
0.9
1.5
0.4
Primary Trail
Other Trails
Mileage
Miles
0
0.5
1
1.5
CONTOUR INTERVAL 80 FEET
NORTH
UTM 13 S NAD 1927
1000 Meter Grid

14 - SANTA FE BALDY

by Arnold and Carolyn Keskulla

A strenuous but rewarding hike to the highest peak in the Santa Fe area with a 360° unsurpassed view, and prolific alpine flowers.

RT Distance:	~14 miles
Time:	8 hrs
Elevation Range:	10,250-12,622 ft; total gain ~3600 ft
Rating:	Strenuous
RT Drive:	30 miles; ~1 hr 30 min
Seasons:	Generally accessible from mid-June to early October. Best to check weather conditions before starting because of frequent thunderstorms.
Maps:	USGS Aspen Basin - 7.5' series. Drake's *Map of the Mountains of Santa Fe* and Sky Terrain's *Santa Fe, Bandelier & Los Alamos* are recommended.
Trailhead:	427,338 mE 3,961,432 mN elev.10267'

Summary

You will experience the satisfaction of achieving the summit of a beautiful mountain with unsurpassed views and lovely wildflowers. There are steep grades and high altitudes. Pick a clear day to make your climb and be well equipped with full canteen, poncho, lunch and energy. This is a strenuous hike and you should be in good shape. Start as early as you can in order to be off the peak before the usual summer afternoon thunderstorms begin. Marmots are prevalent at and near the peak.

Driving Directions

Drive up Artist Road (Hyde Park Road) to the Santa Fe Ski Basin (~14 miles). As you approach the Ski Basin parking area, keep to the left and park in the lower lot. The trailhead for the Winsor Trail is located at the far western edge of the lower parking lot.

Hiking Instructions

From the trailhead, cross the small wooden bridge over the Rio en Medio, turn right and start uphill on the well-used Winsor Trail 254. The first ½ mile is a steep climb, bringing you to the wilderness boundary fence, 600 ft higher than the trailhead. Watch for the lovely wildflowers among the aspen and spruce. In June you may see shooting star and fairy slipper orchids. From the fence, the trail starts gently downhill, passing in about ¼ mile a little-noticed trail on the left. This is a very steep trail to the Rio Nambé nicknamed the "elevator shaft." Continue past it for about 1 mile. Here a trail goes south up to lovely Nambé Lake beneath Lake Peak (see NAMBÉ LAKE Hike #11).

Continue straight ahead across the Rio Nambé along the Winsor Trail. After crossing two streams (which feed into the Rio Nambé), you start up several switchbacks that lead you to a trail junction at 11,000 ft, 4½ miles from the Ski Basin. The level grassy meadow here is referred to as Puerto Nambé. This junction is marked by signposts. The left branch is the Skyline Trail (Trail 251), which goes to Lake Katherine (see Hike #13) and beyond. The right branch (the Winsor Trail) goes to Spirit Lake (see Hike #23) and down into the Pecos Valley.

Take the Skyline Trail 251, which goes northeasterly up long switchbacks, and in about 1 hour or less, you'll reach the top of a saddle. From the saddle, leave the trail and strike for the summit up the ridge to your left (north) by line of sight. There is a rough trail near the edge of the ridge.

This is a steep ascent, so you may have to rest occasionally. Depending on your pace, the ascent may take anywhere from 45-90 minutes. There may be a few snow patches and marmots along the way as you approach the summit. At the large cairn marking the very top, enjoy the superb views along with your lunch. Don't miss looking down on Lake Katherine, which can be seen from the northeast edge of the summit. The tiny blue forget-me-nots, fairy primroses, sky pilots and other beautiful alpine flowers will be abundant early in the season. In late summer, bistorts, blue gentians, composites and others will appear. You have climbed to the summit of a 12,622-ft peak, a memorable experience!

Turn back at any sign of a thunderstorm. Before you leave the top, check your bearings by sight or compass so that you can reach Puerto Nambé and the trail back to the ski basin. Don't try to take a shortcut down; rather, return by the same route you ascended. Many hikers have gotten themselves lost by trying to take a shortcut back to the Winsor Trail.

Santa Fe Baldy

15 Tesuque Creek

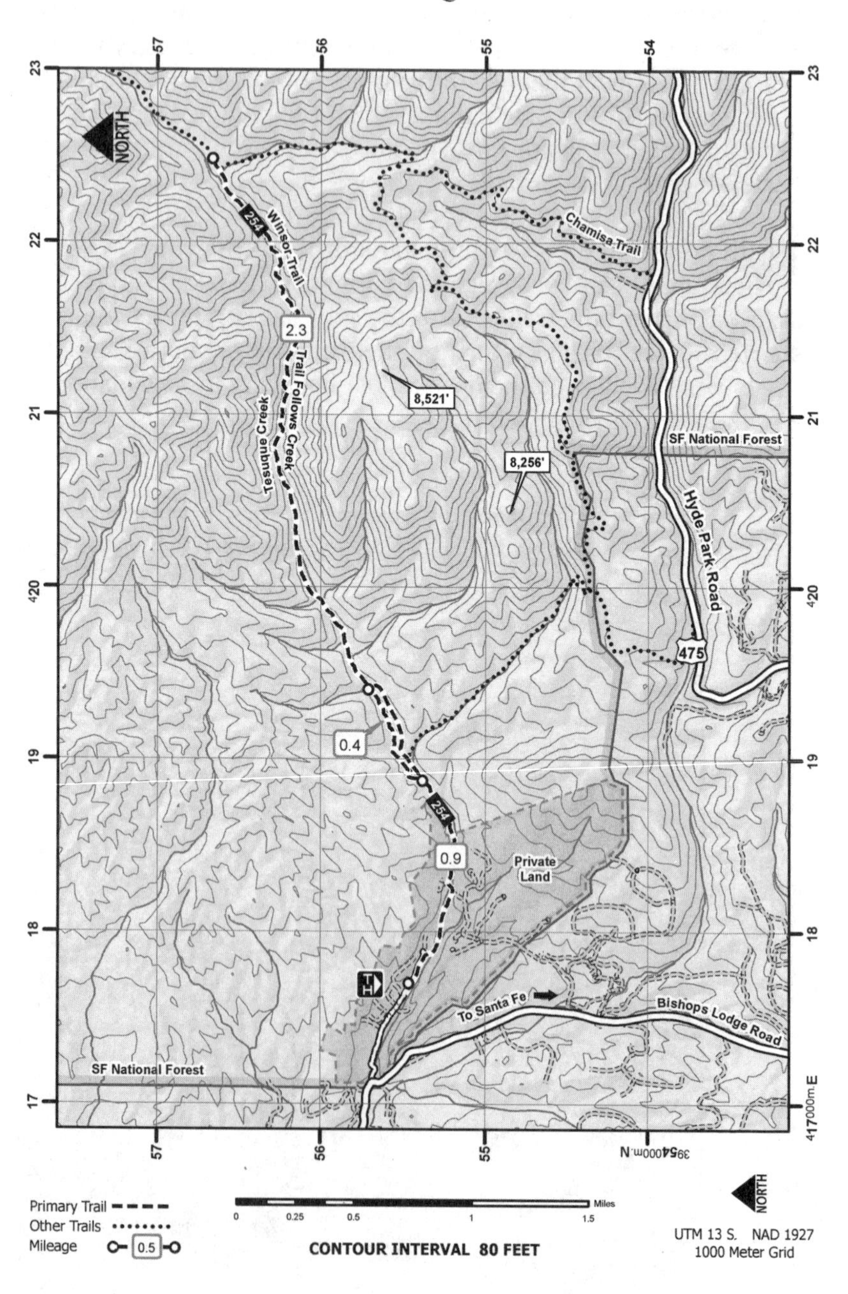

15 - Tesuque Creek

by Katie Parker and Elizabeth Altman

A pleasant walk near Santa Fe among ponderosa pine, piñon/ juniper and riparian woodlands along a lovely stream with several crossings.

RT Distance:	3 miles (easy option) 7.5 miles (RT to Chamisa Trail)
Time:	2 hrs (easy option) 4 hrs (RT to Chamisa Trail)
Elevation Range:	7100-7600 ft; gain 500 ft (easy option) 7100-7960 ft; gain 1000 ft (to Chamisa Tr)
Rating:	Easy to moderate
RT Drive:	8 miles; ~30 min
Seasons:	Passable for all but the snowiest months. During spring runoff, the creek may rise above logs and stones used for crossing and you may need to wade through the water. In winter, be prepared for snow on the creek's south side, and beware of crossing on icy logs; better to use rocks or get wet boots than risk a nasty fall.
Maps:	USGS Aspen Basin, McClure, and Santa Fe - 7.5' series. Drake's *Map of the Mountains of Santa Fe* and Sky Terrain's *Santa Fe, Bandelier & Los Alamos* are recommended.
Trailhead:	417,752 mE 3,955,536 mN elev.7117'

Summary

This walk near Santa Fe takes you along a lovely stream and through ponderosa pine, piñon, juniper and riparian woodlands. The stream is this trail's most significant feature.

Driving Directions

Drive north on Washington Ave / Bishop's Lodge Road past the entrance to Bishop's Lodge (~3½ miles from the Plaza). Almost exactly 1 mile beyond this entrance, the paved road takes a 90° turn to the left, marked by a large yellow highway sign with an arrow pointing left. Don't take this left turn. Instead, take the dirt road to the right, CR 72A, at the blue street sign that says "Big Tesuque Canyon." Drive a short distance down this road until you come to a parking space in one of the two areas on the right identified as trail parking. The second sign says "No Parking Beyond This Point." Please respect the admonition, for if hikers abuse the parking privilege, access to the trail along an easement over private land may be closed. If you are responsible for dogs, keep them under control and clean up after them.

Hiking Instructions

Walk a short way up the road to a rock pillar and three 5-ft wooden posts to your right. Pass through the posts. The trail begins immediately beyond the posts, although there is no sign. Stay on the trail to avoid encroaching on private land. You will immediately cross Big Tesuque Creek on a wooden bridge. The trail follows the river upstream and passes an old abandoned vineyard and orchard on your right. After about 5 minutes, you come out onto a dirt road. Note the sign on the left marking the trail back toward Tesuque that you just walked along. Go left over the car bridge and then turn right up the river, where a sign says "Winsor Trail." The Winsor Trail follows the fence line. Look for woodpeckers in the cottonwood trees along the river bottom here and for a little pond on the left, indicated by runoff crossing the trail.

In another 8-10 minutes, the fence ends and you will go through a Forest Service gate (more like an obstruction) to enter the Santa Fe National Forest. There is a sign here giving the distances to Tesuque, Hyde State Park and the Santa Fe Ski Basin. Be on the alert for bicyclists and equestrians along this popular trail. About 100 yards past the gate and just before reaching the stream, the trail forks. Keep to the right and follow Trail 254 (Winsor Trail) across the stream to the south side. You will be returning on the left fork.

As you climb upward along a trail that parallels the creek, you will see washes and trails leading off from the main trail. Keep to the main trail that leads upward to a rubble-covered hill where the trail splits. Take the left fork, where a sign will confirm that you are on the Winsor Trail. Continue along as the trail rises 20-50 ft above the creek. The trail here is quite wide, looking like an old road.

About 30 minutes into the hike, you will come to another stream crossing. This can be your turn-around point for an easy hike. To make a loop for an alternate return route, go back on the trail you came on for about 30 yards and you will notice a side trail heading down toward the river past a huge ponderosa pine. This is your return trail and involves another stream crossing. Cross to the north side of the creek and follow the trail back, until it joins the other trail at the fork near the Forest Service gate (mentioned earlier) to make a walk of about 3 miles, or about 2 hours of leisurely hiking.

Stop occasionally to look back up the canyon. At the highest point of the trail, where there are a few wooden steps to aid you in getting up and down, you will be able to see the radio towers above the Ski Basin. Notice the drier soils and sparser vegetation on this south-facing side of the creek. When you reach the large wooden bridge, cross the bridge and turn right onto the trail that you came in on. Remember to watch for the sign that points back to Tesuque.

If you want to go further to the Chamisa Trail intersection 2 miles up, continue on the main trail. It narrows and goes up and over a series of rises and 12 stream crossings. The forest is denser and the riparian vegetation thicker. You will see scrub oak, aspen, Western maples, ponderosa, spruce and fir, with the decaying trunks of fallen giants alongside the trail. In season, you will find wild roses, cow parsnips, bittercress, strawberries, columbine, meadow rue, and wild geraniums. The trail now moves away from the creek and the land opens up, with grassy patches and large ponderosa. Your destination is a sign saying Tesuque 3½ miles back, and the Ski Basin 6¼ miles further. The Chamisa Trail comes down the slope from your right (see CHAMISA TRAIL Hike #6). If you walk a few yards further you will find a pleasant spot for a break beside a large rock in the grassy meadow, near the creek. On your return, you will recognize the crossing that identifies the alternate return route described above. The stream makes a sharp right turn, and to the left you will see a large log that has fallen across the stream. Here you may return the way you came, or you may choose the alternate return route.

How glorious a greeting the sun gives the mountains! To behold this alone is worth the pains of any excursion a thousand times over. The highest peaks burned like islands in a sea of liquid shade. Then the lower peaks and spires caught the glow, and long lances of light, streaming through many a notch and pass, fell thick on the frozen meadows.

~ John Muir

Crossing Tesuque Creek

16 Rio en Medio / La Junta

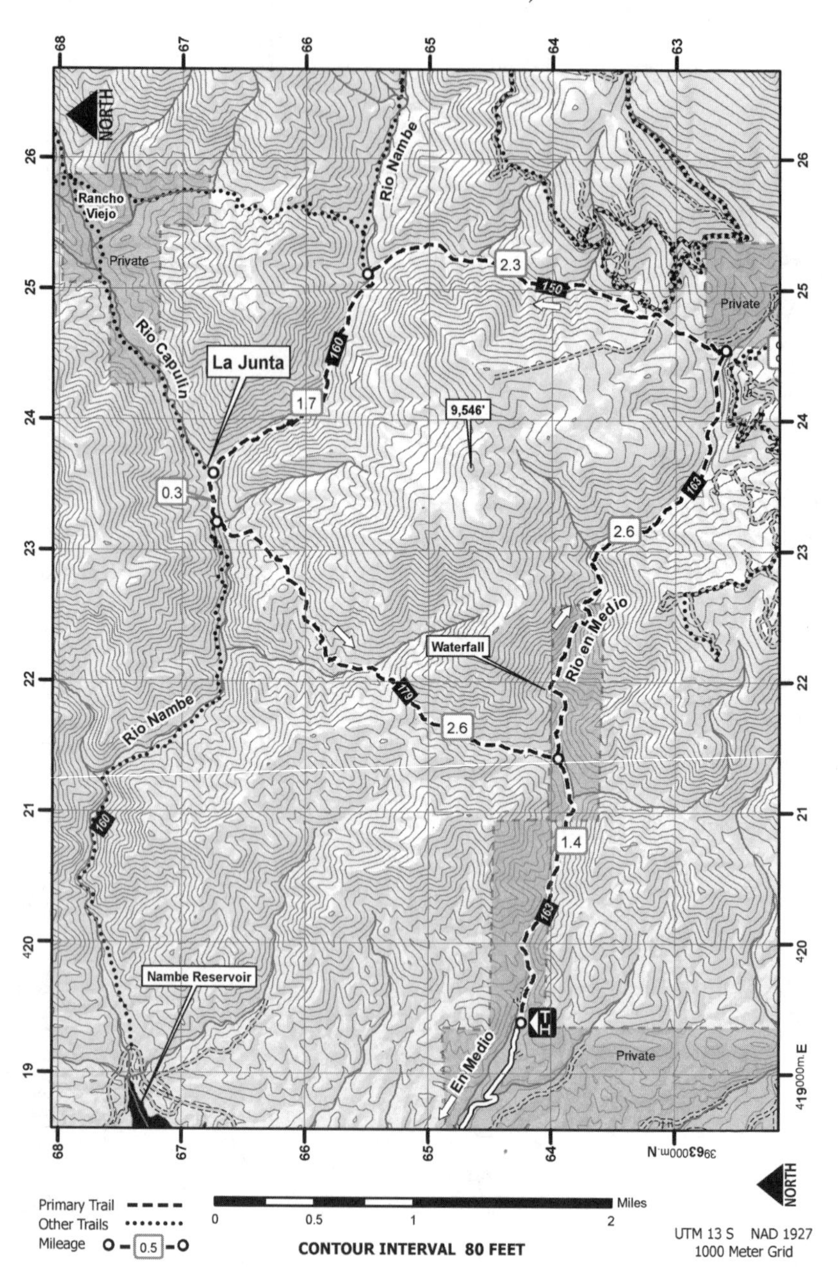

16 - RIO EN MEDIO / LA JUNTA

by Norbert Sperlich, Norma McCallan, Art Judd, E. J. Evangelos and John Jasper

Rio en Medio is a lovely streamside hike through lush vegetation to cascading waterfalls. The La Junta Circuit is a much longer loop which continues upriver, then crosses through deep forest and little visited terrain, before its return.

RT Distance:	5 miles (Rio en Medio) 13 miles (La Junta Circuit)
Time:	3-4 hrs (Rio en Medio) 8+ hrs (La Junta Circuit)
Elevation Range:	7200-8000 ft; gain 800 ft (Rio waterfalls) 7200-9200 ft; gain 2900 ft (La Junta Circuit)
Rating:	Easy to moderate (Rio en Medio) Strenuous (La Junta Circuit)
RT Drive:	30 miles; ~1 hr
Seasons:	Rio en Medio: possible all year, trail can be icy in winter. La Junta: late spring, summer, fall. Stream crossings may be difficult during spring runoff.
Maps:	USGS Aspen Basin - 7.5' series. The FS *Pecos Wilderness* map, Drake's *Map of the Mountains of Santa Fe* and Sky Terrain's *Santa Fe, Bandelier & Los Alamos* are recommended.
Trailhead:	419,345 mE 3,964,280 mN elev.7220'

Summary

The Rio en Medio hike follows along Rio en Medio beginning at En Medio village. La Junta circuit continues up Rio en Medio to the boundary of Aspen Ranch, turns onto the historic Borrego Trail, then the Rio Nambe Trail, to a little used trail, looping back to Rio en Medio. *Note: This is a revised route for the La Junta circuit hike which now starts at lower Rio en Medio instead of Aspen Ranch.*

Driving Directions

Take US 84/285 north past the Santa Fe Opera and Flea Market exits. Take exit 172, turn right and go toward Tesuque Village for about ¼ mile, then take a left onto NM 592. After 3½ miles, at the stop sign, turn left and continue driving on NM 592. Follow the winding road to the small village of En Medio. Here, the pavement ends and the road narrows. Follow the dirt road for about ¾ mile to a small parking area on your right with a Forest Service information board. Park here. Do not drive beyond this point. *Note: Do not park on private property as it upsets the residents.*

Hiking Instructions

Both Hikes - Hike along the road for a few minutes to a trail sign on the right, indicating the beginning of Trail 163. Take this trail and enter a thicket of oak trees and chokecherries. The trail crosses private property. A fence and Rio En Medio are on your left. In about 15 minutes, the trail crosses the stream and takes you to an open area, with cholla and prickly-pear cacti on your left and rose bushes and wildflowers on your right. After hiking for about an additional 10 minutes on the left of the stream, you will encounter three closely spaced crossings. You are now on the right bank again, surrounded by towering Douglas firs.

When you come to a marked trail junction, stay on the right side of the stream. Trail 179 goes off to the left, across the stream and towards the Nambé River. This trail (Trail 179) will be your return trail if you hike the La Junta circuit.

Your trail, Trail 163, continues along Rio En Medio. Some 15 minutes past the trail junction, cross the stream at a place where there is an upright section of a tree trunk in the water. A few minutes later, cross back to the right at a spot with three sections of a tree trunk in the water, and a huge peeled trunk on the right side of the stream. (If you miss the crossings described here, follow the stream on whatever trail you can find.)

After about 1 hour of hiking, the trail approaches a rocky slope, with a 20-ft high cliff directly on the right of the trail. About 10 yards further, the trail forks. The right fork goes up and away from the stream, and the left fork goes down to the stream. To reach the first and most dramatic of the waterfalls, go down to the stream, cross to the other side and follow the stream for about 2 minutes into a narrow gorge and to the waterfall. Some rock scrambling is required, and you will get your feet wet, but you won't want to miss this place. The water doesn't just fall, it arches in a graceful curve, forming a shimmering, gorgeous curtain.

To explore the other cascades and pools, return to the main trail and continue up over the rocky slope. After passing another waterfall on your left, the trail crosses to the left side of the stream. You will see more cascades tumbling into pools, before the trail crosses over to the right side again. Soon, a rock spire is towering on your left, and the trail crosses the stream two more times. Shortly after, you will reach a waterfall dropping into a beautiful pool with golden sand at the bottom. If cool water is all you need, go no further. For a view across the Rio Grande valley and to the Jemez Mountains, continue hiking for about 25 more minutes, gaining another 500 ft in elevation. The trail is steep and washed out and the footing is loose and rocky, but the view is rewarding at the end. The trail eventually moves away from the stream and takes you to a place where, looking back, you get a view to the west. What you see is Redondo Peak, located in the Valles Caldera. Also visible are white, tent-like structures of the Los Alamos National Laboratory on the Pajarito Plateau. Return via the same route if you are only hiking Rio en Medio.

La Junta Circuit – Continue up the Rio en Medio until you reach a gouged-out trail sign near the stream on the left. Here you leave Trail 163, and turn left onto the trail zigzagging up the steep bank. You are now on the Borrego Trail 150.

Very shortly the trail turns left, joining the old Lucky Star Mine Road. Follow the road uphill until you come to a saddle where the road turns sharply to the right. Leave the road here and look for a trail that starts downhill to the north. There is a sign "Borrego Trail

150, Rio Nambé, Rancho Viejo, Aspen Ranch," with appropriate arrows.

The trail makes a steep descent for about 1.7 miles to the Rio Nambé, through heavy forest. The Rio Nambé begins to make itself heard as you near the last quarter mile or so. Just before you get to the river, notice the huge moss-covered boulder on the left of the trail. In the spring, garlands of wildflowers bedeck this rock.

At the Rio Nambé, leave the Borrego Trail and take Trail 160 to the left, downstream for a few hundred yards and cross the river on rocks or logs. Continue on down the river for about ½ hour (a little over 1 mile) to the junction of the Rio Nambé with the Rio Capulin. This is La Junta, "the meeting point." You'll come to a fork in the trail when you get close to this junction. Take either one; they both lead to La Junta. The smaller Rio Capulin comes in from the right. Cross it and continue on downstream through several large meadows for several hundred yards to the junction of your Trail 160 with Trail 179. A sign marking this junction is tacked onto a large ponderosa, so watch for it. Trail 179 crosses the Rio Nambe here. Usually adequate deadfall bridges the river at this point. Cross with care, especially in early spring and on frosty mornings, as the tree trunks are often coated with ice and can be very slippery.

After crossing the river, veer right. Trail 179 climbs up a deeply scoured, steep and rocky arroyo. After about 45 minutes on this trail, you'll top out at a saddle — a good place for a rest and a snack. The trail now turns downhill, passes through another valley and then ascends to the top of another saddle. The power line crosses the trail at this saddle, which also makes a good spot for a break. You will now begin the 1-mile descent to Rio en Medio, a total of 3 miles from La Junta.

The trail follows an arroyo most of the way down, with mountain mahogany, tall piñon, lupine and asters. Shortly before reaching the Rio en Medio, a trail sign states "Rio Nambe 3 miles," pointing the way you have just come. Ignore the small trail here to the left and a second path to the left a few minutes later. Follow the main trail across Rio en Medio onto Trail 163, where a small sign notes "Trail 179" (noted at the beginning of the hike), pointing back the way you came. Turn right here and follow the river downstream. Enjoy the soothing sound of the flowing water, and the damp pungency of the heavy riparian vegetation on your last 1½ miles to the trailhead and your car.

Rio en Medio Waterfall in Winter

17 Rancho Viejo

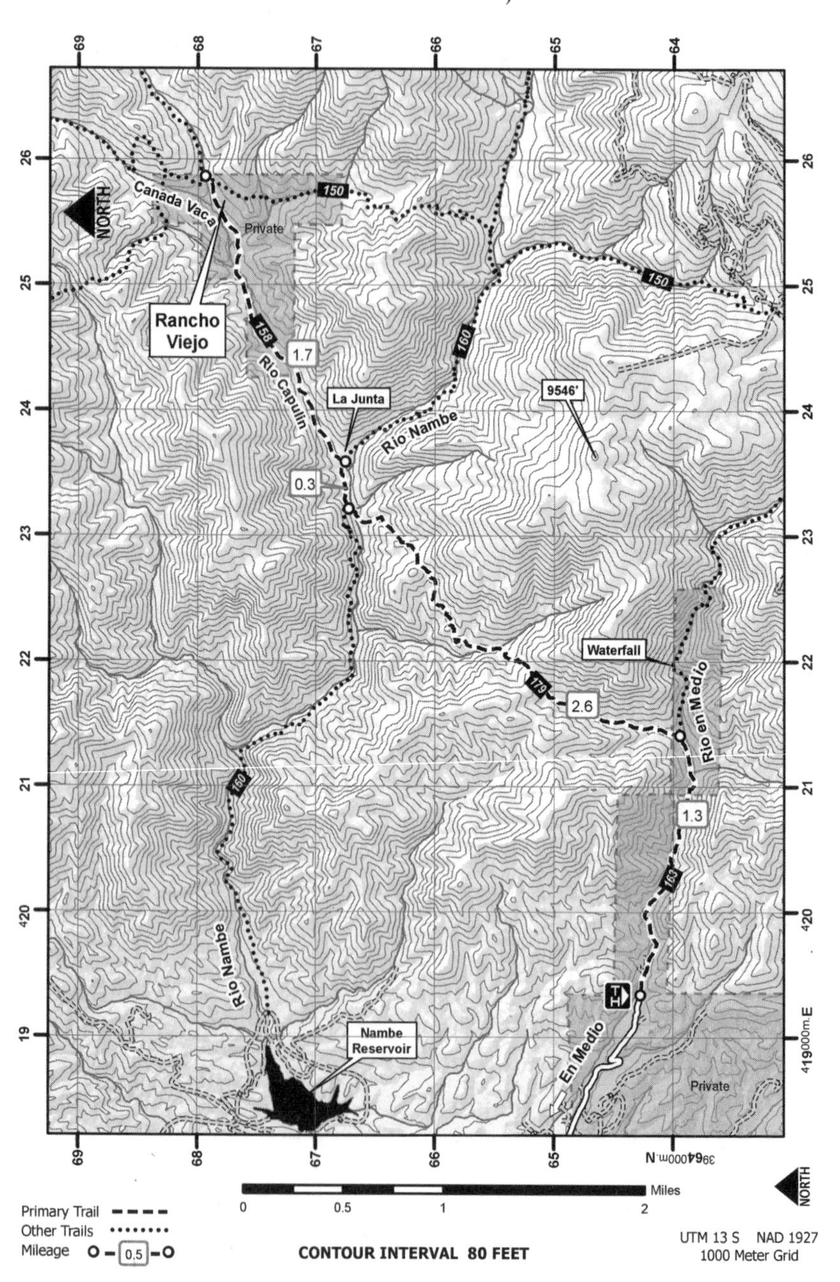

17 - RANCHO VIEJO

by Betsy Fuller and Norma McCallan

A pleasant hike in the Pecos Wilderness with clear streams, broad meadows, numerous wildflowers and deep forest.

RT Distance:	13 miles
Time:	7 hrs
Elevation Range:	7200-8200 ft; total gain 2800 ft
Rating:	Strenuous
RT Drive:	30 miles; 1 hr
Seasons:	Late spring, summer, fall. Stream crossings may be difficult during spring runoff.
Maps:	USGS Aspen Basin - 7.5' series. Also recommended are the FS *Pecos Wilderness* map, Drake's *Map of the Mountains of Santa Fe*, and Sky Terrain's *Santa Fe, Bandelier & Los Alamos.*
Trailhead:	419,345 mE 3,964,280 mN elev.7220'

Summary

This hike starts at the lower Rio en Medio trailhead. It follows Rio en Medio a short distance until it branches off onto a little-used trail which goes up and over two ridges before crossing Rio Nambé. It then follows Rio Capulin until it intersects the Borrego Trail at Rancho Viejo. This hike was re-routed because the original trailhead at Aspen Ranch became difficult to access due to poor road conditions.

Driving Directions

Take US 84/285 northbound past the Santa Fe Opera and Flea Market exits. Take exit 172, turn right and go toward Tesuque Village for about ¼ mile, then take a left onto NM 592. After 3½ miles and at a stop sign, turn left and continue driving on NM 592. Follow the winding road to the small village of En Medio. Here, the pavement ends and the road narrows. Follow the dirt road for about ¾ mile to a small parking area on your right with a Forest Service information board. Park here. Do not drive beyond this point. *Note: Do not park on private property as it upsets the residents.*

Hiking Instructions

Hike along the road a few minutes to a trail sign on the right, indicating the beginning of Trail 163. Take this trail and enter a thicket of oak trees and chokecherries as it crosses private property. A fence and Rio en Medio are on your left. In about 15 minutes, the trail crosses the stream and takes you to an open area, with cholla and prickly-pear cacti on your left and rose bushes and other wildflowers on your right. After hiking for about an additional 10 minutes on the left of the stream, you will encounter three closely spaced crossings.

You are now on the right bank again, surrounded by towering Douglas firs. When you come to a marked trail junction, turn left, crossing the stream onto Trail 179. The trail gradually veers away from the river. Stay straight at an intersection where a minor trail joins from the right. Very shortly, you will come to an intersection with a sign "Trail 179, Rio Nambé 3." Continue straight, on this trail. You will follow an arroyo up to a saddle.

The landscape changes from the lush vegetation of the stream banks to more open ponderosa, scrub oak, mountain mahogany, lupines, asters, and nodding onions. There is a small clearing on this 8200-ft saddle, good for a break. If you follow a short path on the left a few feet up, an opening in the trees affords a good vista of where you have come from.

Continue on the trail, now steeply downhill, through denser forest of spruce, fir and occasional aspen, with thimbleberries, wild rose, meadow rue, and barberry bushes. Shortly, you will ascend to a second saddle, which affords a new vista of the hills to the northwest. The trail descends steeply through an eroded and quite rocky arroyo until it reaches the wide Rio Nambé. You should be able to find sufficient logs and stones on which to cross. Just after the crossing, you will see a large sign nailed to a ponderosa, which points the way from which you have come, indicating "Rio en Medio 3, Trail 179." Continue on your trail as it wends through several meadows. You will come to an unmarked fork. Stay left on the fainter trail (Trail 158). If you turned right, you would see a downed sign by a post noting "Rio Nambé Trail 160, Aspen Ranch, Puerto Nambé, Lake Katherine." Do not take Trail 160, which crosses the small Rio Capulin.

Proceed on the unmarked trail (Trail 158) as it closely follows the Rio Capulin on the right. After ½ mile or more, it crosses the Rio Capulin, goes up a small embankment, and comes out into more open country, somewhat further from the stream. Continue through a series of broad, open meadows. You are now at Rancho Viejo. Please be advised that Rancho Viejo is private property. The owners are descendents of Ramón I. Ortiz, whose family settled here in the early 1940s, hence the name Rancho Viejo, "Old Ranch." While the owners have given Sierra Club hikers permission to use this segment of the Rio Capulin Trail, please understand that hikers must stay on the trail as it goes through the property so that this permission is not withdrawn.

Continue through the lush meadows until you reach the intersection with the Borrego Trail 150. This four-way intersection of Trails 158 and 150 is the destination of your hike. Just before this intersection you may see, to the left, the convergence of the Cañada Vaca with the Rio Capulin (~500 ft away). The Borrego Trail will follow this stream north for several miles. Drink in the beauty of the serene landscape, and return the way you came.

Note: If you choose the challenge of driving Pacheco Canyon and FR 412, you can still access Rancho Viejo via the old route. Park at the parking area on FR 412. From there, follow the directions described in RIO NAMBÉ Hike #9, and continue on the Borrego Trail 150 to the intersection with the Rio Capulin described above.

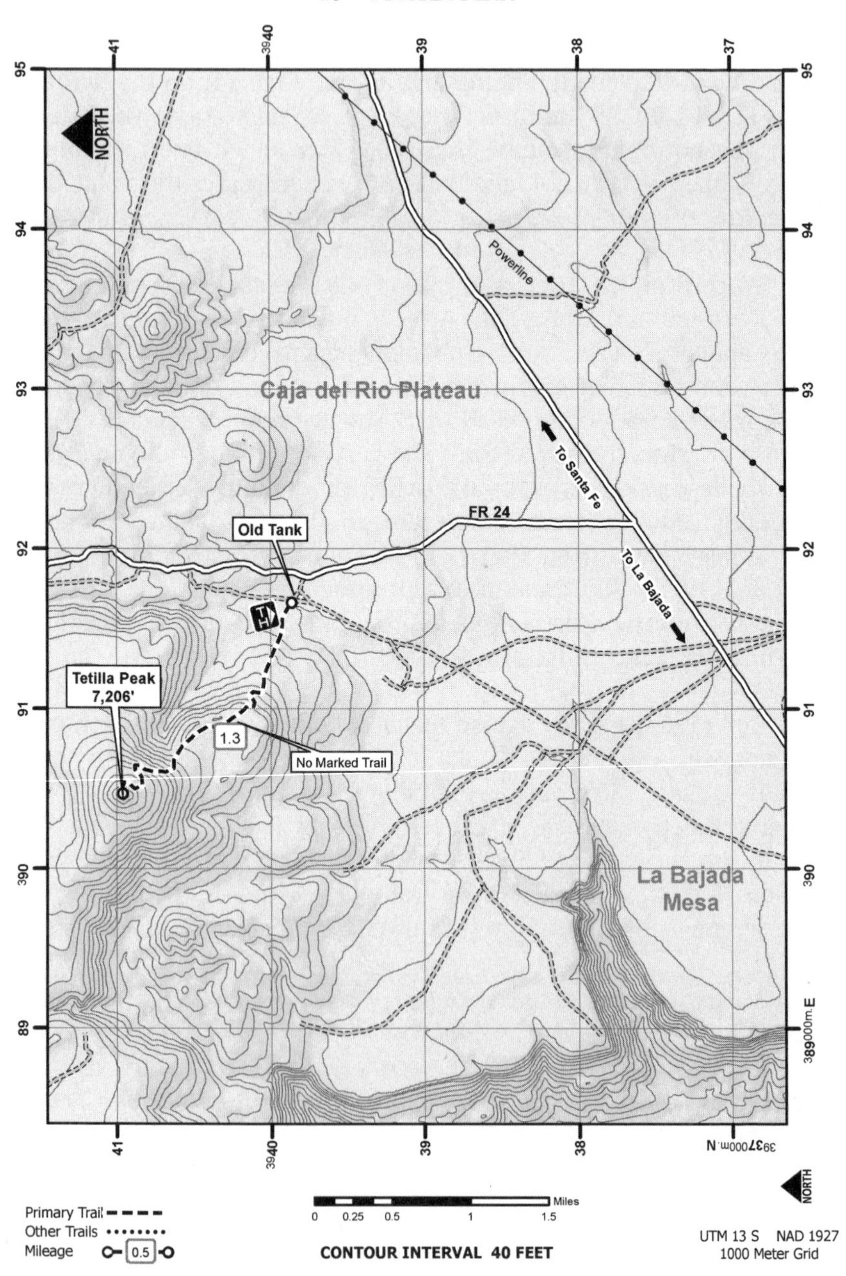
NORTH
Caja del Rio Plateau
Powerline
To Santa Fe
FR 24
Old Tank
To La Bajada
Tetilla Peak
7,206'
1.3
No Marked Trail
La Bajada
Mesa
Primary Trail
Other Trails
Mileage
0.5
Miles
0 0.25 0.5 1 1.5
CONTOUR INTERVAL 40 FEET
UTM 13 S NAD 1927
1000 Meter Grid

18 - TETILLA PEAK

by Ingrid Vollnhofer

A short but steep off-trail hike to a distinctive volcanic peak on the southwest side of the Santa Fe landscape.

RT Distance:	3 miles
Time:	2-2½ hrs
Elevation Range:	6260-7206 ft; total gain 946 ft
Rating:	Moderate; final portion steep
RT Drive:	30 miles; 1½ -2 hrs depending on road conditions
Seasons:	Year round, but very hot in summer. Road may be impassable after rain or snow.
Maps:	USGS Tetilla Peak - 7.5' series.
Trailhead:	391,683 mE 3,939,819 mN elev.6375'

Summary

Tetilla Peak is a prominent volcano on the Caja del Rio Plateau, a volcanic field formed some 2.6 million years ago. It is an open area with cholla cactus, juniper, and sparse grass. There is a wonderful panorama of Mount Taylor and the Jemez, Sangre de Cristo, Ortiz and Sandia Mountains from Tetilla Peak. Much of the access to the trailhead is very rough and rutted, and is impassable during or after wet weather. A vehicle with high clearance is highly recommended.

Driving Directions

Take Airport Rd west past NM 599 where Airport Rd soon becomes CR 56. Continue past the airport and the large tanks of the sewage treatment plant on the right. About 2 miles along CR 56, note a large red scoria boulder on your right and a sign for the Santa

Fe Horse Park. At 1.3 miles past this boulder, look for a large sign that points to NMARNG Camel Tracks Field Training Site and a dirt road coming in from the right, with a second Santa Fe Horse Park sign, and a small "CR 56C" sign. Turn right here. This graded dirt road crosses a filled-in cattle guard with an old "Entering Public Lands" sign, then climbs the plateau to the left. At the top (~1 mile in), where the road turns sharply to the right at a gated road to a gravel pit, drive straight ahead onto a rough, rutted, primitive road. Go straight on this road, ignoring roads that branch off to the sides. Use the right side parallel portion of the road as much as possible as it is less rutted. After a little more than 4 miles, you will cross a fence line. Immediately past the cattle guard is a sign that you are now on FR 24. Turn right (if you turn left, it would take you to the end of the mesa top), and drive another 1.6 miles on this somewhat smoother road to a small track or spur road going off to the left. Follow the spur road to a battered white tank (largely obscured by dirt) and park.

Hiking Instructions

There is no trail. Note what appear to be two large humps partially obscuring Tetilla Peak in front of you. The humps are actually the south flank of the peak, dissected by a draw in the middle. Avoid hiking in the draws that you see ahead of you, because they either get 'cliffy' or brushy and rocky. Instead, cross the draws in a straight west-northwest direction and hike up the second hump to the west. While climbing, look back and note the white tank, which will guide you on the way down. It is easier than you might believe to get off course in this open landscape. While catching your breath, once above the flank, look back to the south and enjoy the vista of the very flat Caja del Rio, ending abruptly at the steep basalt cliffs of La Bajada. At the very last stretch before the top, the way is quite steep (almost a scramble) around large volcanic outcroppings. Be patient, because the view at the top is magnificent! Take time there to enjoy your lunch or snack and savor the view of far-away Mount Taylor and the closer Jemez, Sangre de Cristo, Ortiz and Sandia Mountains, with Cochiti Lake below to the west. For variety, you may go back down by the other hump you didn't ascend. A small path leading north from the peak peters out very soon in the volcanic outcropping; you will need to scramble near the top if you are descending via the eastern hump.

You may drive back the way you came by heading back to FR 24 and turning right. Alternatively, instead of turning right, you may turn left on FR 24, which is a longer (20 miles of forest road from your parking spot) but a much more pleasant drive than the rutted road you came in on. It is rocky at first as it climbs around the base of Tetilla, but soon smooths out and affords pleasant vistas of the rolling terrain of the Caja del Rio. This forest road, which has a few isolated ruts and arroyos along the way, heads north, then east, and ends at the paved Caja del Rio Road by the Santa Fe City/County landfill. Turn right there, and you will end up back at NM 599, a couple of miles north of its intersection with Airport Road. Remember, no matter which route you take, neither dirt road is advisable for driving after rain or snow.

Tumbleweeds and the Road to Tetilla Peak

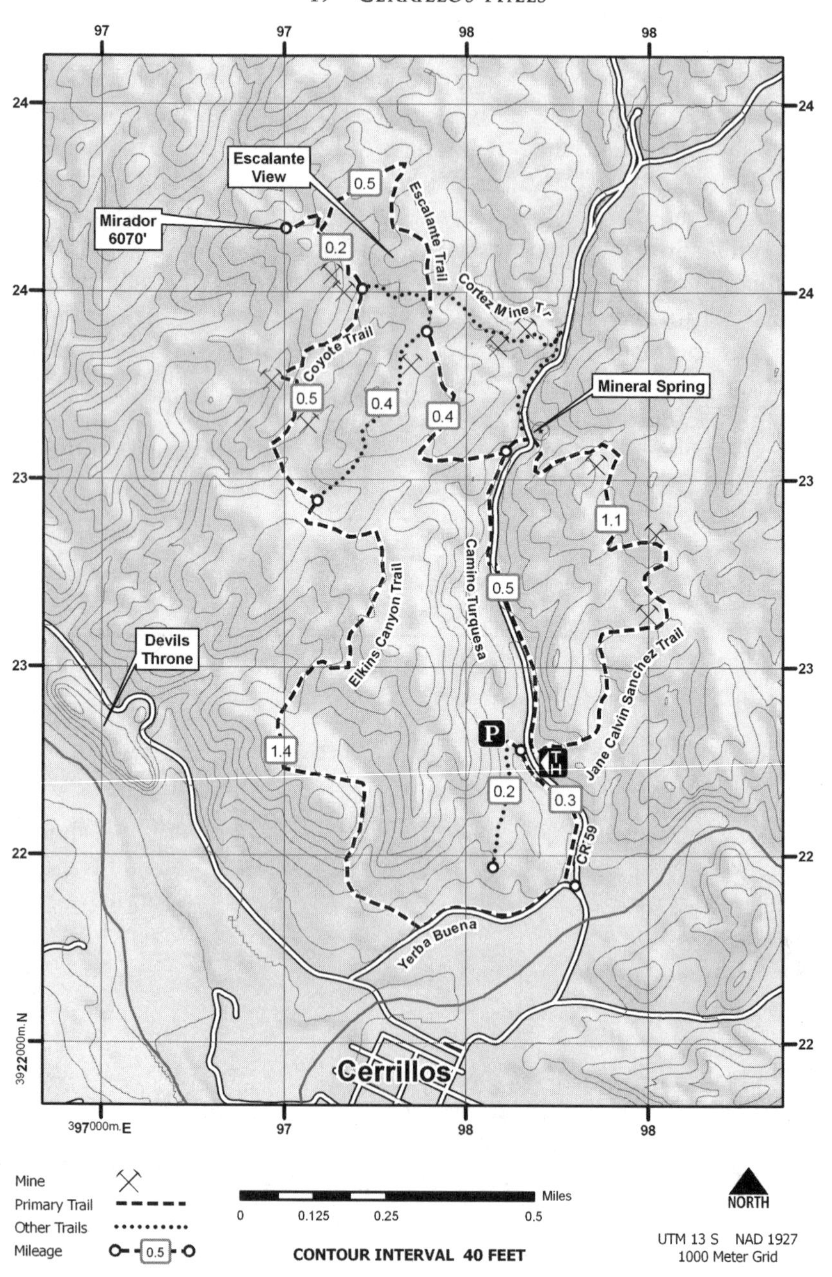

97
97
98
98
24
24
23
23
22
22
Escalante View
Mirador 6070'
0.5
0.2
Escalante Trail
Cortez Mine Tr
Coyote Trail
0.5
0.4
0.4
Mineral Spring
1.1
Camino Turquesa
0.5
Elkins Canyon Trail
Jane Calvin Sanchez Trail
Devils Throne
1.4
P
TH
0.2
0.3
CR 59
Yerba Buena
Cerrillos
3922000m.N
397000m.E
Mine
Primary Trail
Other Trails
Mileage
Miles
0
0.125
0.25
0.5
CONTOUR INTERVAL 40 FEET
NORTH
UTM 13 S NAD 1927
1000 Meter Grid

19 - Cerrillos Hills

by Norma McCallan

A series of short trails in an historic mining area recently designated as a Santa Fe County Park. The park offers 360° vistas and a sense of tranquility in an arid piñon-juniper landscape that is ideal for winter hiking.

RT Distance:	4.5 miles for full loop
Time:	2-3+ hrs (depending on pace)
Elevation Range:	5760-6123 ft; total gain 363 ft
Rating:	Easy
RT Drive:	50 miles; 1½ hrs
Seasons:	Best October through April, hot in summer
Maps:	USGS Picture Rock - 7.5' series; also, Cerrillos Hills Historic Park leaflet.
Trailhead:	398,316 mE 3,922,600 mN elev.5744'

Summary

Though man has left 'footprints' for many centuries, the landscape is serene and oddly beautiful. The park is full of abandoned mines. The hiking instructions will take you on a full loop around the park, although there are many possibilities for shortening your route along the way as described below.

History

The origin of the Cerrillos Hills goes back more than 30 million years, when magma (a hot, molten fluid) rose up from subterranean reservoirs and intruded the overlaying sediments of the Galisteo Formation. After cooling, the magma turned into igneous rocks which developed a large number of cracks and fractures. The fractures were then filled with ore-bearing deposits. One group of deposits contains zinc, lead, copper, silver, and (very little) gold, another type of deposit is known for its turquoise.

More than 1000 years ago, Native Americans mined the Cerrillos Hills for turquoise. Mount Chalchihuitl and Turquoise Hill were the main sources for turquoise. Turquoise mining on a small scale continues today. Spanish colonists mined silver and lead in the 17th century. The year 1879 brought new discoveries of lead-zinc-silver ores, igniting a mining boom that lasted for a few years. Thousands of prospectors worked claims that rarely panned out. The last of the metal mines was closed in the 1950s.

In early 2000, Santa Fe County purchased 1116 acres of the Cerrillos Hills and in 2003 opened the Cerrillos Hills Historic Park. The driving force behind the acquisition and development of the park is the Cerrillos Hills Park Coalition, a group of local citizens who want to preserve this special place.

Driving Directions

Take NM14, the Turquoise Trail, which can be reached by taking I-25 south toward Albuquerque and getting off at the NM 14 exit, or by taking Cerrillos Road and driving south until it crosses under I-25 (where it becomes NM 14). Follow NM 14 south past the State Penitentiary for about 11 miles. Note the cone-shaped peaks to the right, which are the Cerrillos Hills. At the sign for "Los Cerrillos Traditional Village," turn right just after the railroad overpass onto CR 57. At the first intersection in town, First Street, turn right, cross the railroad tracks, continue north as the road turns to dirt, and continue on CR 59 (also known as Camino Turquesa) past a side road leading to the Broken Saddle stables. In a few moments you will pass the Catholic cemetery on the right and will see the park's parking area on the left. Park here. The large map board will give you a sense of the geography and the trail system. Help yourself to a park brochure. Before starting the hike, note that just north of the lot, there is a toilet and an unusual structure called an "analemma" or noon sundial, with a large plaque explaining how it works. Note that dogs are permitted only on leash.

Hiking Instructions

From the parking lot, walk across the road and up the 1.2-mile Jane Calvin Sanchéz Trail. After about 10 minutes you will reach the *Christian Lode* mine shaft, fenced-off on your left. Further up the trail (~5 min) you can visit the fenced shaft of the *Amsterdam, Rotterdam & Copenhagen Lodes,* slightly off the trail on the right. After checking it out, return to the trail. There is a bench a short distance further. Soon the trail will turn sharply left, leaving the old road, which enters private property. In a few feet and off the trail to the left, you can visit the *Moonstone / Jewell Lode.* Returning to the trail, it then heads downhill and ends back at the main road by the Yoh Toh Mineral Spring. A large sign explains the origin of this spring (which is the largest in the park) and identifies some of the nearby vegetation. Reddish-brown slime indicates the high iron content of the spring. You have now completed the first leg of the full loop.

You can return to your car by turning left and hiking down this county-maintained road (Camino Turquesa). However, if you want to continue, turn left and follow the road downhill for about 200 ft, then go up on the right on the Escalante Trail. Soon you will find a bench near an inactive electric fence. The trail continues uphill on this old road where a second bench beckons. As the trail veers north, Grand Central Mountain with its many humps appears prominently on the horizon. Soon you will arrive at a three-way intersection marked by a wooden sign at a triangle and another bench. From here, it is only 1 mile back to the Entrada (park entrance) via the Escalante Trail and Camino Turquesa, or 1½ miles back via the Elkins Canyon Trail to the left. Note that the *Wexford Lode* is visible a few feet to the left, down the Elkins Trail.

To hike the full loop, continue north on the Escalante Trail, past a large sign describing the geology of the Cerrillos Hills, and past the intersections of Coyote Trail on the left and the new Cortez Mine Trail that goes off to the right. (The Cortez Mine Trail will return you to Camino Turquesa.) Continuing on Escalante Trail to the ridge top you will come to a left fork named "Escalante View," which dead-ends in about 2 minutes at an overlook. Check it out. Back on Escalante Trail, you will come to a wide 2-track road that is crossed by a fence marking the park boundary, with a pass through. *(Note: to the left of that road, 100 ft beyond the fence, a path takes off that will provide access to a trail yet under construction on BLM land that will take you to the top of Grand Central Mountain.)*

Do not go beyond the fence. Turn sharply left onto the wide dirt road and follow the sign to Mirador. As the road curves toward the south, look for a two-sided sign that says "Park Entrance" on one side and "Mirador" on the other. Take the narrow path to the right that leads up to the Mirador on the top of a small hill—a great viewpoint with a 360° panorama and a sign showing the profiles of all the high points on the horizon and a bench on which to relax and enjoy the view.

After taking in this glorious panorama, go back to the dirt road, and follow it downhill for about 200 ft. Stay on the trail, which at the "Coyote Trail" sign bears left, off of the 2-track. Once across the arroyo in front of you, you will come to a sign about Stephen Elkins, and the steel footbridge over the *Pride of the Camp* mine. From here you can either take the short detour over the top of the shaft, or continue on the main trail. Next, you arrive at the mesh-covered *Rosellia Lode* mine. Immediately afterwards is a T-intersection. You may go left and quickly get back to the Escalante Trail. To continue on the full loop (the more interesting option), however, go straight ahead. This branch of Coyote Trail bears to the right (southwards), proceeding downhill toward a deep arroyo. You can check out the *Canton Lode* shaft (to the right), and downhill to the left you will find the *Josh Lode*, covered by a metal grate. The trail continues downhill, crosses the arroyo, veers east, and follows its narrow streambed to an intersection with the Elkins Trail. Turning left at this intersection would again take you back to the Escalante Trail, but turning right continues the longer loop we have been following.

The Elkins Canyon Trail follows the high ridgeline south. At the highest point, there is a bench along with great views of the rugged Ortiz Mountains. The trail slowly descends along the ridges, then veers left at a small saddle. Here another bench awaits, and, if you are lucky, you might see the eastbound or westbound Amtrak train on the tracks far below. The trail descends around the side of a hill and into the short but impressive rock-faced narrows of Elkins Canyon. Soon the cliffs end and, almost immediately, the trail veers left out of the gully (easy to miss), heading toward the southern boundary of the park. The trail comes out to a dirt road by a wooden fence. Turn left and walk the dirt road (Yerba Buena) for about 5 minutes. You will reach a broad arroyo, just this side of Camino Turquesa (the road you drove in on). A small sign directs you to a path on the left up the arroyo and back to the parking lot.

For more information about the Cerrillos Hills Historic Park, see the Cerrillos Hills Coalition website www.cerrilloshills.org

Note: Jane Calvin Sanchéz Trail, named for the Cerrillos native, New Mexico historian and park activist who died in 2006, may be indicated on older maps by the name "Mountain Lion Trail."

The Many-Humped Grand Central Mountain

20 Apache Canyon / Glorieta Baldy

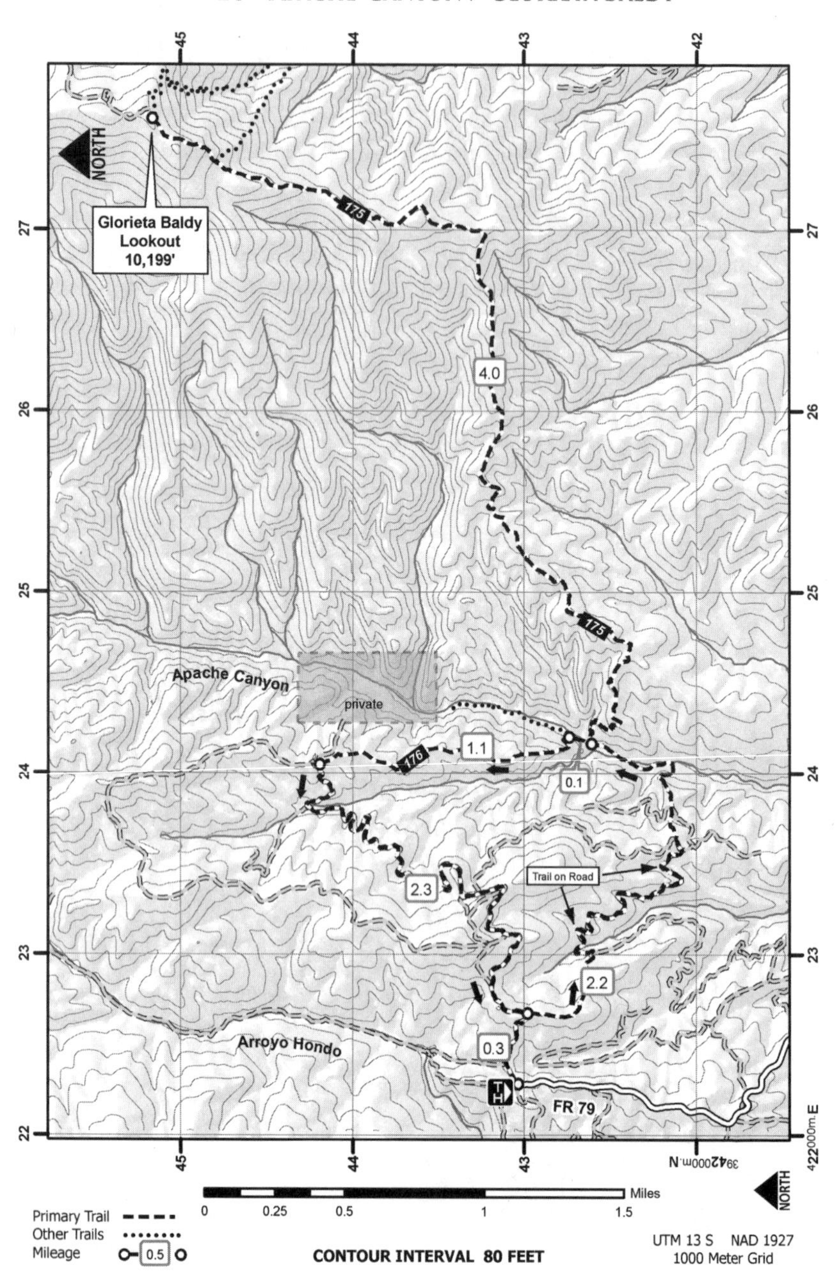

20 - APACHE CANYON / GLORIETA BALDY

by Ned Sudborough

Starting in a ponderosa forest, this hike takes you down to a creek surrounded by towering conifers. From the creek, a steep trail leads you to the top of Glorieta Baldy.

RT Distance: 6.5 miles (Apache Canyon Loop)
13 miles (Apache to Glorieta Baldy)

Time: 4 hrs (Apache Canyon Loop)
8 hrs (Apache to Glorieta Baldy)

Elevation Range: 7760-8400 ft; gain 800 ft (Apache Loop)
7760-10,199 ft; gain 2820 ft (to Baldy)

Rating: Moderate (Apache Canyon Loop)
Strenuous (Apache to Glorieta Baldy)

RT Drive: 27 miles; 1½ hrs

Seasons: The Loop Trail can be hiked in all seasons. Glorieta Baldy is not usually climbed until after snows have melted. The approach on FR 79 may be a problem in wet weather of any season.

Maps: USGS Glorieta and McClure Reservoir - 7.5' series. Drake's *Map of the Mountains of Santa Fe* and Sky Terrain's *Santa Fe, Bandelier & Los Alamos* are recommended.

Trailhead: 422,267 mE 3,943,034 mN elev.8178'

Summary

Apache Canyon and Glorieta Baldy are located in the southern tip of the Sangre de Cristo Range, southeast of Santa Fe. The two hikes described here share the same route into Apache Canyon, starting on a ridge in the ponderosa forest west of the canyon. After reaching the canyon bottom, where tall conifers line the creek, the Apache Canyon loop trail continues on, returning to the trailhead, and the Baldy Trail takes you to the top of Glorieta Baldy. Wildflowers are abundant provided there has been sufficient moisture.

Driving Directions

From downtown Santa Fe, drive south on Old Santa Fe Trail, setting the odometer at Paseo de Peralta, by the New Mexico State Capitol. Continue south on Old Santa Fe Trail and bear left at 0.4 miles, where it separates from Old Pecos Trail. At 8.0 miles, the road tops a ridge. At 8.3 miles, take the left branch at the fork (Cañada Village Road). The road goes downhill and passes through the village of Cañada de Los Alamos (Cottonwood Canyon). At the lower end of the village, the pavement ends. The road then crosses a drainage and climbs up toward a ridge top. Take the left branch at subsequent road forks.

After crossing a cattle guard at mile 10.6, take the left branch, FR 79, and drive an additional 2.9 miles to a four-way intersection with parking spaces on the left. Park here. Trailhead signs (Baldy Trailhead) were missing in early 2006.

Hiking Instructions

The hike starts across from the parking area on the road that goes off to the east. In early 2006, this road was not marked. Follow the road for ¼ mile to a locked gate. At the ridge top beyond the gate, find a sign for Trail 175 on the right. Trail 175 will take you to Glorieta Baldy and is the first part of the Apache Canyon Loop Trail. Follow this trail along a ridge ¼ mile and then down to an old logging road. In 2006, there was a cairn and a bare post where the trail meets the road. Take note of this junction if you plan to return this way. Turn left onto the road and follow it for about a mile (20 minutes) to a spot where a faint trail goes off to the right. There should be a sign (Baldy Trail 175) on the right side of the road. Take this trail to the right. It gets you to the canyon bottom in about 20 minutes.

As you near the canyon bottom, the trees change from ponderosa pine to Douglas fir, white fir, aspen, southwestern white pine and blue spruce. These are species that usually succeed ponderosa pines above 8,200 ft, but here grow below them because of the cooler canyon air. Cottonwood, box elder, willow and Rocky Mountain juniper also grow in the canyon.

At the bottom of Apache Canyon is a stream. This is a good place to eat lunch in the shade, as less than ½ mile of trail is in the canyon. Beyond the grove of Douglas firs the trail crosses the stream. In the flat on the right, the forest is reclaiming a logging campsite. Soon, a trail sign on the right announces Trail 176, which is the Loop Trail. The sign also directs a right turn to the canyon wall for the climb east out of the canyon to reach Glorieta Baldy on Trail 175. *Continued description of the Glorieta Baldy trail begins following the next paragraph.*

Loop Trail - To complete the Loop Trail, continue across the stream to the left side of the canyon. Here, the trail is obstructed by fallen trees. About 100 yards past the stream crossing, Trail 176 climbs out of the canyon. This trail is difficult to find. Look carefully for a cairn and a jumble of logs. The trail climbs 300 ft up the steep canyon wall back to the open ponderosa pine forest. In the next mile, the path rises gently on a ridge above Apache Canyon, with views of Thompson Peak and Glorieta Baldy. Some 30 minutes after leaving the stream, you will come to a road. This is the road you were on at the beginning of the hike. A sign indicates 2½ miles to the trailhead. Turn left onto the road. It climbs over ridges and dips into drainages, taking you back to your car in a little over an hour.

Apache Canyon To Glorieta Baldy - The trail climbs steeply out of Apache Canyon with many switchbacks At about 2 miles out of the canyon, the trail bears right onto the crest of a ridge. The trail is easy to follow as it climbs, passing craggy Shaggy Peak, which is on your right.

In about 3 miles out of Apache Canyon, the trail passes between two posts that once held signs. You still have approximately 1 hour and 800 ft of elevation gain to get to the top. Enter a meadow just beyond the posts, veer left and, following trail markers, cross toward the trees, where the trail will reappear. This is the first of five meadows between here and Glorieta Baldy. You may see purple asters, composites, blue harebells, Indian paintbrush, scarlet bugler, scarlet gilia and white yarrow. After the second meadow are the first views to the east; you will see the lower Pecos Valley, with a glimpse of I-25 and the top of Rowe Mesa. From the third meadow, the Glorieta lookout tower—your destination—can be seen above the trees. Just beyond this meadow, on the left, is a small abandoned mine opening. The tower can be seen again on entering the fifth meadow. The trail breaks from the trees just below the top, passes through a junction with the trail from Glorieta (see GLORIETA BALDY Hike #21), and takes you to the last turn of the tower's service road. You are at the base of the tower and the top of the mountain.

To the southeast, the plains may be visible. To the southwest, across the desert valleys, you can see smooth, round Sandia Mountain (10,678 ft) on the horizon and the pointy, smaller San Pedro and Ortiz Mountains in front of it.

On returning, note the trail junction just down from the top: continue straight ahead to return the way you came. On hiking down Trail 175 in warm weather, you can anticipate the cool, shallow water of Apache Canyon for head, hands and feet.

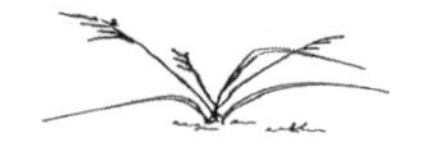

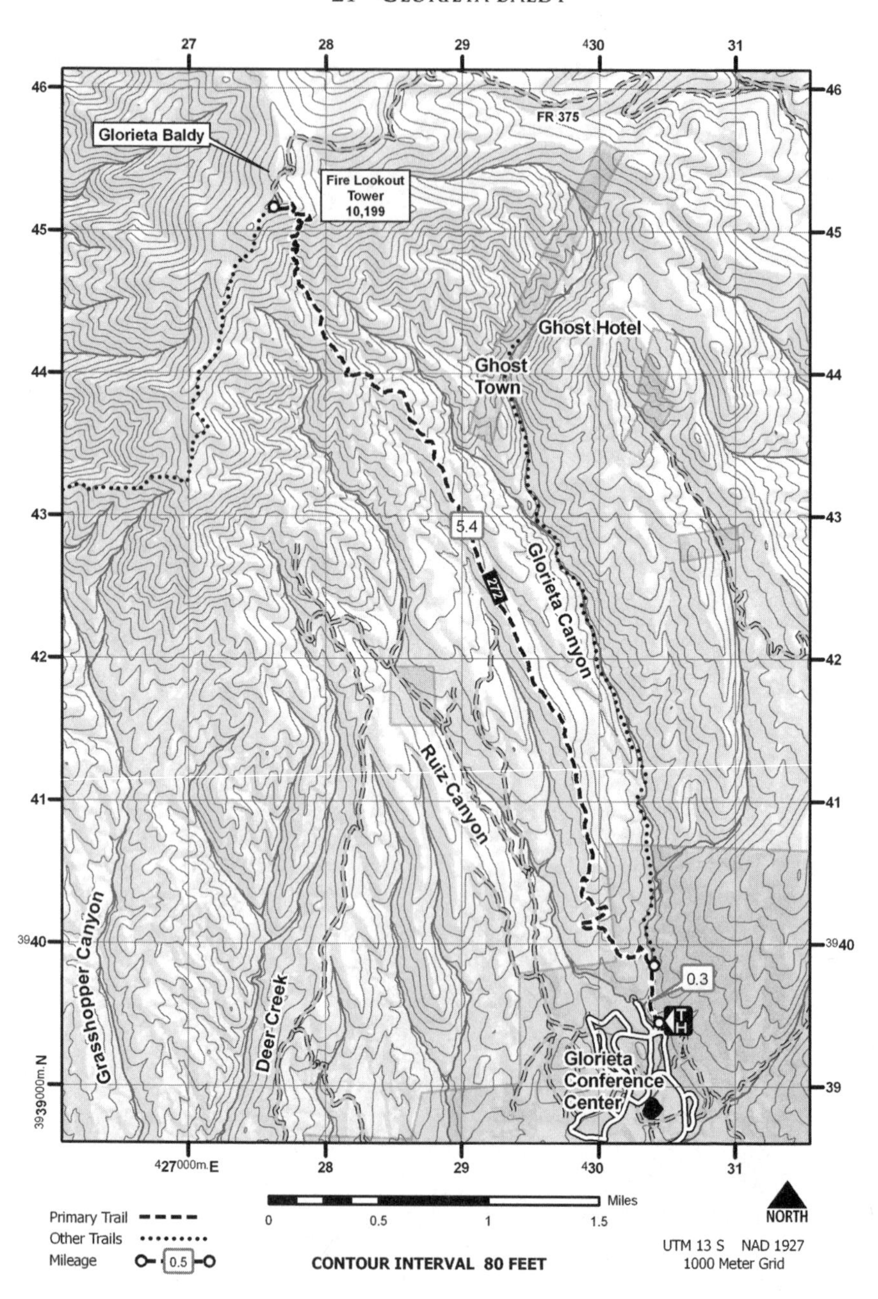
Glorieta Baldy
Fire Lookout Tower 10,199
FR 375
Ghost Hotel
Ghost Town
5.4
272
Glorieta Canyon
Ruiz Canyon
Grasshopper Canyon
Deer Creek
0.3
TH
Glorieta Conference Center
427000m.E
3939000m.N
Primary Trail
Other Trails
Mileage
0.5
Miles
0
0.5
1
1.5
CONTOUR INTERVAL 80 FEET
NORTH
UTM 13 S NAD 1927
1000 Meter Grid

21 - Glorieta Baldy

by Bill Chudd

A steady ascent in the woods to a prominent peak east of Santa Fe.

Distance:	11.5 miles
Time:	6 hrs
Elevation Range:	7475–10,200 ft; total gain 2800 ft
Rating:	Strenuous
RT Drive:	44 miles; ~1 hr
Seasons:	Excellent in spring, summer and fall. Start early to avoid thunderstorms.
Maps:	USGS Glorieta and McClure Reservoir - 7.5' series. Drake's *Map of the Mountains of Santa Fe* and Sky Terrain's *Santa Fe, Bandelier & Los Alamos* are recommended.
Trailhead:	430,427 mE 3,939,410 mN elev.7485'

Summary

Easy approach on paved roads to the trailhead. A steady uphill trail, quite steep in places, to a 10,199-ft peak with an old fire look-out tower with sweeping views. There is no dependable water on the trail, so take enough for the whole trip.

Driving Directions

Take I-25 north toward Las Vegas (NM) to the Glorieta off-ramp (Exit 299). Turn left over the bridge and again left at the T-intersection parallel to I-25, following the signs to the Glorieta Conference Center. Stop at the gatehouse. If the gate is closed, use the intercom located on the gatehouse, follow the printed instructions and inform them you are day hikers and how many cars are with you. On leaving the gatehouse, immediately turn right onto Oak Street. Follow Oak Street through the conference grounds. At 0.6 miles from the gate, Oak Street turns right. Continue on Oak Street to the right (don't go straight on Willow Street). At 0.9 miles you will see an isolated building with two large glass doors (the old firehouse) on your right. Park to the left of this building at the "Hiker's Parking" sign.

Hiking Instructions

Continue a short distance on Oak Street, then turn right at a sign directing you to the RV Park. In a few minutes, you will reach an information board with a map and a trail register where you should sign in. Next, go through the RV Park. Follow the road as it curves left, crosses the creek bed, and goes through a gate in the fence. Turn left as the sign indicates for Glorieta Baldy, following the fence, and in a short distance, there is a sign directing you to Glorieta Baldy on the right.

Follow this trail a short distance uphill through scrub oak and to the left where it levels off among large boulders where you will see an arrow pointing to your right. As you turn right and climb up onto the rock outcropping, look to the left and you will see two arrows pointing in the direction of the trail on the other side of the outcropping. Follow the arrows and shortly you will see and pass through a wooden gate, after which the trail is much clearer.

The trail climbs gradually with nice views toward the west where you can see the top of Shaggy Peak. Continue on the Glorieta Baldy trail (ignoring a branch on the right to Broken Arrow), and shortly you will reach the top of a ridge, a good place to get your bearings. Eastward, to your right, you will be looking down into Glorieta Canyon or across to La Cueva Ridge. Westward, to your left, you are looking into Ruiz Canyon. The broad trail follows the top of the ridge, climbing gently. You will see occasional blazes on trees. Along the trail are bright scarlet gilia as well as other wildflowers.

At about halfway (2½ miles into the hike), the trail widens at an area where there is evidence of previous campfires. Gradually, the trail becomes steeper. After you have been hiking for about 3 miles, the trail becomes sharply steeper and narrower. You should have your first clear view of the fire tower ahead. You descend for a few hundred feet to cross a small, often dry drainage, which eventually runs into Glorieta Canyon. After crossing the ravine, the trail turns left and goes steeply upward on the right side of the drainage.

The ponderosas have given way to fir and, at about 9500 ft, patches of aspen appear. These will announce themselves with shouting golden hues in late September and October. From time to time you will get dramatic views back toward Glorieta and an occasional view of the lookout tower ahead through the tree tops.

In the last mile, the slope becomes increasingly steep and the trail begins to switchback across a runoff channel that is often used as the trail. Stay on the switchbacks. Your trip will be only slightly longer, and you will not contribute to erosion.

Just before reaching the top, this trail meets Trail 175 coming from Apache Canyon (see APACHE CANYON / GLORIETA BALDY Hike #20). Continue on up to the fire tower.

At the top, you can see the Conference Center, I-25, Starvation Peak to the southeast and the Ortiz Mountains in front of Sandia Mountain to the south. The view is obstructed to the north and west.

Return the way you came. Although much of the trail is broad and descends gently, the initial steep decent is precarious with loose rocks on the trail. Enjoy the scent of sunbaked pine needles as you move along. After descending off the ridgeline, and going back through the wooden gate, turn left at the first arrow (which points to the gate you just came through) and look further left for a red arrow pointing across the rock outcropping to the trailhead.

When you get back to the Conference Center, remember to sign out at the trail register. From the parking area, you may choose to drive to the left on Oak Street, which completes a circuit of the Conference Center grounds and returns you to the entrance gate.

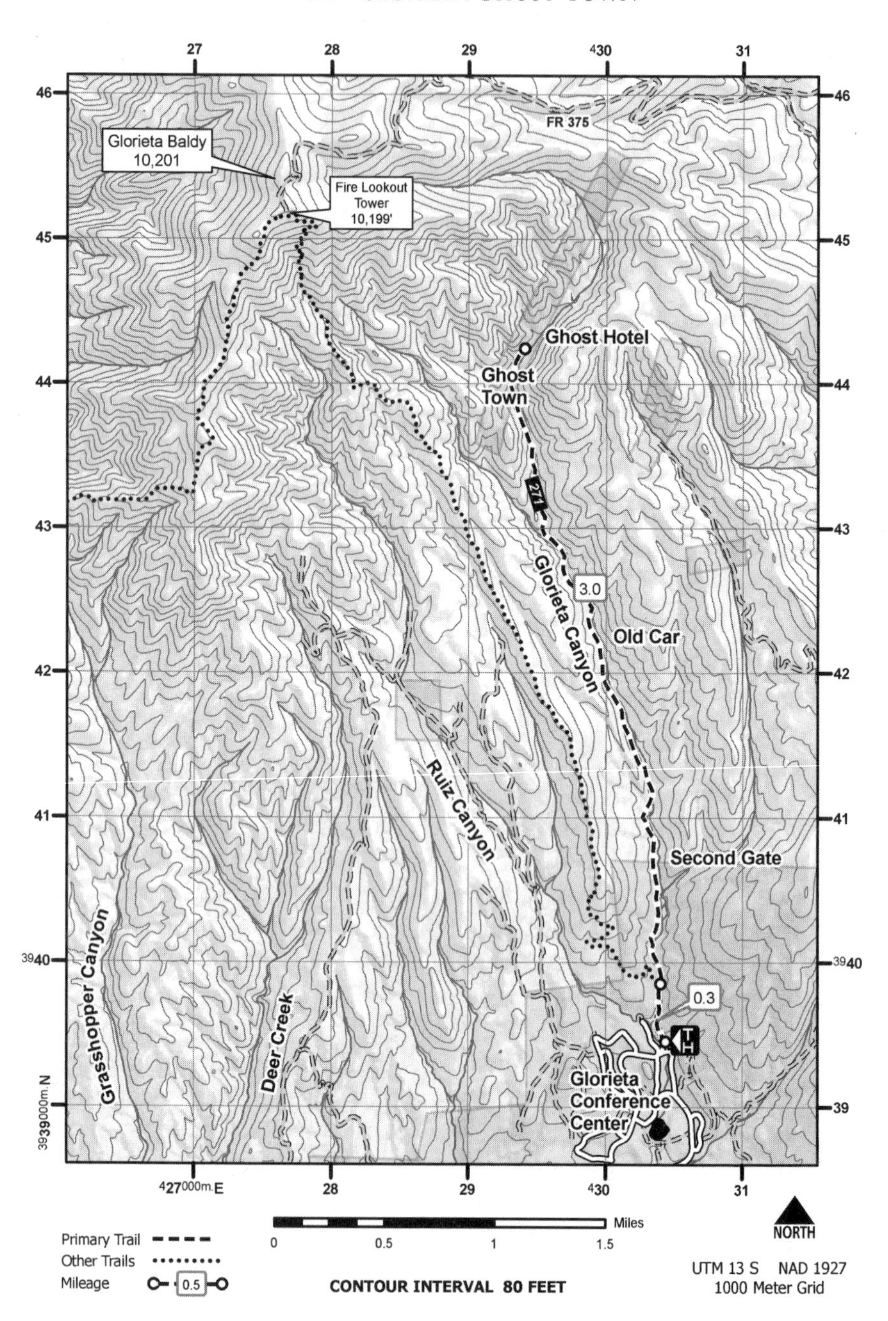

Glorieta Baldy
10,201
Fire Lookout
Tower
10,199'
FR 375
Ghost Hotel
Ghost
Town
271
Glorieta Canyon
3.0
Old Car
Ruiz Canyon
Second Gate
0.3
TH
Glorieta
Conference
Center
Grasshopper Canyon
Deer Creek
27
28
29
430
31
46
45
44
43
42
41
3940
39
427000m.E
3939000m.N
Primary Trail
Other Trails
Mileage
0.5
Miles
0
0.5
1
1.5
NORTH
CONTOUR INTERVAL 80 FEET
UTM 13 S NAD 1927
1000 Meter Grid

22 - GLORIETA GHOST TOWN

by Bill Chudd

A pleasant walk in the woods along Glorieta Creek to the remains of an old settlement.

RT Distance:	7 miles
Time:	3-4 hrs
Elevation Range:	7475-8420 ft; total gain 945 ft
Rating:	Easy to moderate
RT Drive:	40 miles; <1 hr
Seasons:	Delightful spring to fall, winter depends on snow level. Stream crossings generally not a problem. Horses seen frequently on trail during summer.
Maps:	USGS Glorieta and McClure Reservoir - 7.5' series. Drake's *Map of the Mountains of Santa Fe* and Sky Terrain's *Santa Fe, Bandelier & Los Alamos* are recommended.
Trailhead:	430,427 mE 3,939,410 mN elev.7485'

Summary

A shady, easy to hike trail along the intermittent Glorieta Creek. Along the way there are seasonal wildflowers, abandoned mines and the remains of a sawmill. The trail travels through mixed conifers and aspen, opening up several times to lush meadows. Access to the trailhead is on Glorieta Conference Center. The remaining trail is in the Santa Fe National Forest.

History

Located adjacent to the Santa Fe Trail, the area has quite a history. Various Native American tribes traded at the Pecos Pueblo and camped nearby. In 1879-80, the Atchison, Topeka & Santa Fe Railroad came through, and the area became a mining and lumber center.

Driving Directions

Take I-25 north toward Las Vegas (NM) to the Glorieta/Pecos off ramp (Exit 299). Turn left over the bridge and again left at the T-intersection parallel to I-25, following the signs to the Glorieta Conference Center. Stop at the gatehouse. If the gate is closed, use the intercom located on the gatehouse, follow the printed instructions and inform them you are day hikers and how many cars are with you. On leaving the gatehouse, immediately turn right onto Oak Street. Follow Oak Street through the conference grounds. At 0.6 miles from the gate, Oak Street turns right. Continue on Oak Street to the right (don't go straight on Willow Street). At 0.9 miles you will see an isolated building with two large glass doors (the old firehouse) on your right. Park to the left of this building at the "Hiker's Parking" sign.

Hiking Instructions

Continue a short distance on Oak Street, then turn right at a sign directing you to the RV Park. In a few minutes, you will reach an information board with a map and a trail register, where you should sign in. Next, go through the RV Park. Follow the road as it curves left, crosses the creek bed, and goes through a gate in the fence. Ignore a sign pointing to the left where the trailhead for Glorieta Baldy can be reached. Follow the main road to the right. It crosses an area that is used for feeding horses. At the next road fork, take the right branch. A bit further along, ignore a bridge on your left. The road soon turns left and goes over a dam. Five minutes later, the road crosses a fence at a metal gate and comes to an open area. After about 1 mile, a rusted old car will be on your right. It's a good spot for a water break and is a wonderful photo-op location. Sometime after the old car, the trail separates. Take the left fork.

About 3 miles into the hike, you will see the remnants of an old wooden bridge on the left. There is another fossilized car further up on your left. The first of the two ruins, two old wooden buildings, will be on your left further into the meadow. The big pile of wood on your right is the remains of a sawmill. Here the trail narrows to a thin path between the ruin and the stream, then broadens again to the width of a primitive road.

In less than ½ mile you will come to another meadow with towering cliffs to the right. The "ghost hotel" ruins are up and to the left. Whether it was truly a hotel or not, the Bradley family took in roomers who prospected or hunted in the area.

The two-storied wooden structure, built around 1883, collapsed sometime after 1956, but the stone foundation is still intact. One can but wonder how much time it took to hew those huge beams and what effort to lift them. To the west of the ruin are several abandoned mines. There were precious metals found in the area—gold and silver—but not in great profusion. The trail continues a bit further and then disappears. Your return is a reversal of the way up. Be sure to register your return at the trail register. Either road, right or left, from the parking area will get you back to the Conference Center entrance.

Glorieta Ghost Hotel

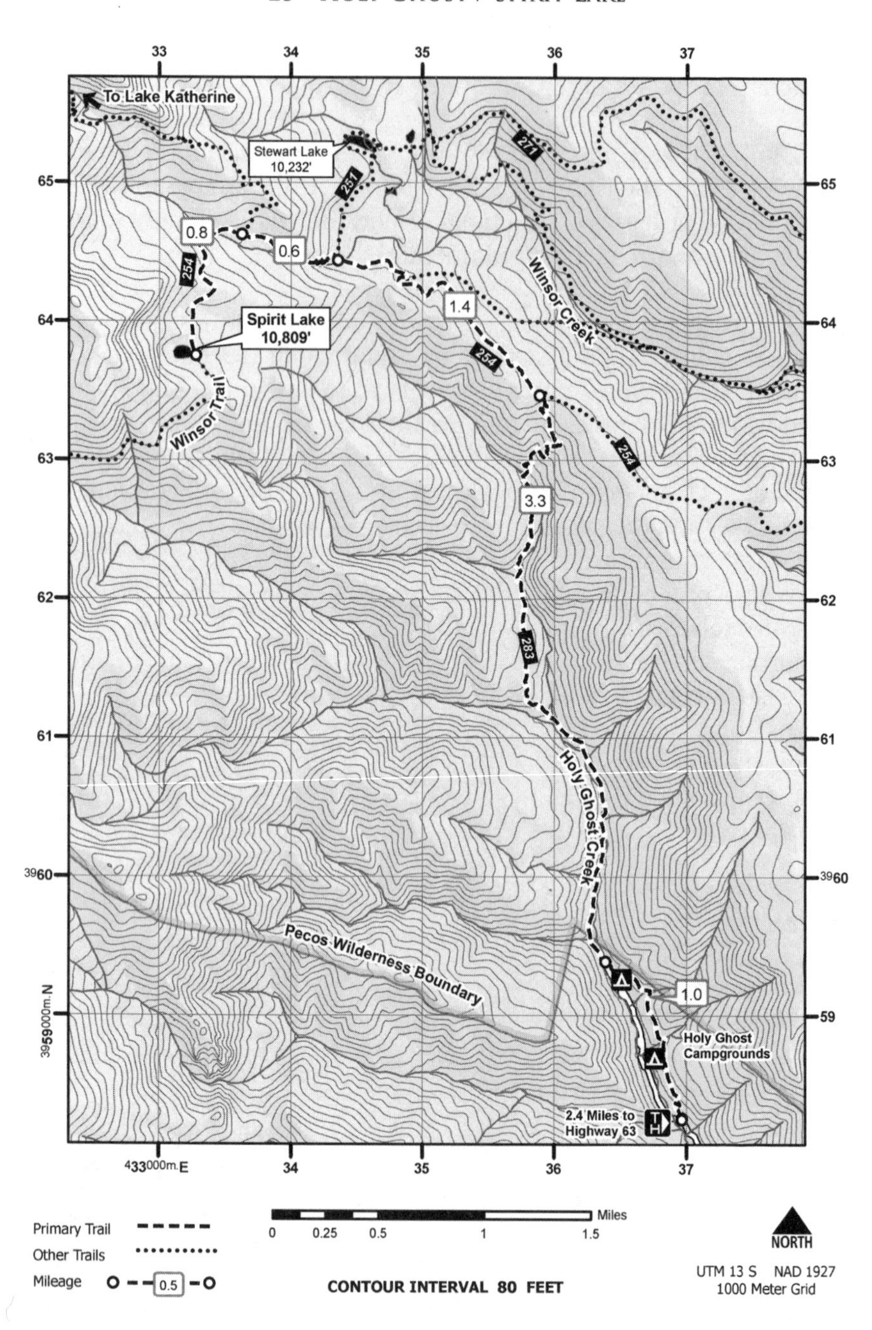
To Lake Katherine
Stewart Lake 10,232'
Spirit Lake 10,809'
Winsor Trail
Winsor Creek
Holy Ghost Creek
Pecos Wilderness Boundary
Holy Ghost Campgrounds
2.4 Miles to Highway 63
254
251
271
283
0.8
0.6
1.4
3.3
1.0
433000m.E
3959000m.N
Primary Trail
Other Trails
Mileage
0.5
Miles
0 0.25 0.5 1 1.5
CONTOUR INTERVAL 80 FEET
NORTH
UTM 13 S NAD 1927
1000 Meter Grid

23 - Holy Ghost / Spirit Lake

by Carl Overhage

A hike in the Pecos Wilderness through flowering meadows, aspen and spruce, along a cascading stream, to a lovely mountain lake.

RT Distance: 14.5 miles
Time: 8+ hrs
Elevation Range: 8150-10,800 ft; total gain 2750 ft
Rating: Strenuous
RT Drive: 81 miles; 2-2½ hrs
Seasons: Summer and fall until the first snow. Early in the season, the stream crossings may be difficult due to snow melt.
Maps: USGS Cowles - 7.5' series. Drake's *Mountains of Santa Fe* is recommended.
Trailhead: 436,964 mE 3,958,257 mN elev.8115'

Summary

This is a hike to a mountain lake, mostly in the trees. The lake is surrounded by large firs, and offers a quiet place where you can enjoy your lunch.

Driving Directions

Take I-25 north toward Las Vegas (NM) for about 15 miles and exit at the Glorieta/Pecos off-ramp (Exit 299). Turn left onto the overpass, then turn right onto NM 50 and drive 6 miles to the town of Pecos. At the stop sign, turn left onto NM 63, which leads north into the Pecos River valley. From the stop sign, drive 13½ miles to the Terrero bridge. Just before the bridge, swing left on FR 122 leading to Holy Ghost Campground. There is a direction sign at this intersection. Follow the paved road 2.4 miles to a parking area located about 100 yards before the campground entrance. Watch for speed bumps along this road. A sign opposite the parking area points to the trailhead. Parking in the area before the campground entrance is free. There is additional parking in the campground, but it is only for campground users and costs $8 per day.

Hiking Instructions

Follow the paved road through the camping sites and past the group campground area. Continue past the camping area on a dirt path. In a few minutes, you will come to the footbridge that crosses the Holy Ghost Creek.

Once you cross the footbridge, follow Holy Ghost Creek upstream. After about 20 minutes and after passing through some large meadows, you will cross Holy Ghost Creek from west to east. Another 20 minutes takes you to the second crossing and back to the west bank. In the meantime, you may see many wildflowers, among them blue flag iris.

Next, you have a short steep climb up on a ridge. You come to some aspen groves with beautiful fern; then you descend to the creek where you cross for the third time. You will cross the creek again very soon. After this fourth crossing, the trail goes steeply up to the left. At this point, you will be back on the west bank. You pass a small meadow, and soon afterwards cross the creek for the fifth time.

After the fifth crossing, turn away from the stream and begin the climb up the ridge between Holy Ghost Creek and Winsor Creek. During the next ½ hour, by a series of switchbacks, you will gain 650 ft in elevation. On the way up, you pass a small promontory, from which there is a fine view down into the Holy Ghost valley. At the top of a ridge, and at the northwest end of a large meadow, the trail intersects with the Winsor Trail 254. Trail 283 ends here, so turn left and follow the Winsor Trail in a northwesterly direction. You are now about 2½ hours away from the starting point.

In about 30 minutes, you will come to the intersection with Trail 261 on your right. Stay on the Winsor Trail (left). Fifteen minutes later, you come to a point where you cross the main branch of Winsor Creek, which descends from Lake Katherine. After crossing the creek to its north bank, the trail splits in two. The Winsor Trail to Spirit Lake bears left (west). The trail to the right goes north to Stewart Lake (see STEWART LAKE Hike #24), less than ½ hour away, and only 100 ft above this junction.

After leaving the Winsor Creek crossing, the trail to Spirit Lake climbs fairly steeply, following Winsor Creek upstream. In several places, you get beautiful views of the stream as it cascades down its steep course. The trail becomes less steep as it passes some lush green meadows a short distance to the left. Twenty minutes after leaving the Winsor Creek crossing, you should begin to look for a trail junction, where the trail to Lake Katherine (Trail 251) takes off to the right. Follow the sign straight ahead to Spirit Lake, continuing on the Winsor Trail.

Five minutes later, the trail crosses Winsor Creek from its north bank to the south bank. As you come closer to the creek, keep looking at the opposite bank for a blaze on a large spruce and for a low cairn. This marks the place where the Winsor Trail crosses to the south bank. Disregard the abandoned former Lake Katherine trail, which continues up the north side of Winsor Creek. Once across the creek, the trail is easy to follow as it climbs up the low ridge separating the Winsor and Holy Ghost drainages. You will reach the lake about ½ hour after the last Winsor Creek crossing and about 4-5 hours from the beginning of the hike.

Return the way you came. At the junctions with other trails, remember to keep right. Shortly after the third crossing of Holy Ghost Creek on the return, as you walk parallel to the stream on its right (west) bank, you will come to a trail fork which you may not have noticed on the way up. Take the right branch, which goes up steeply for a short distance. On the home stretch through the streamside meadows, you may now feel that you have time for a more leisurely look at the many wildflowers.

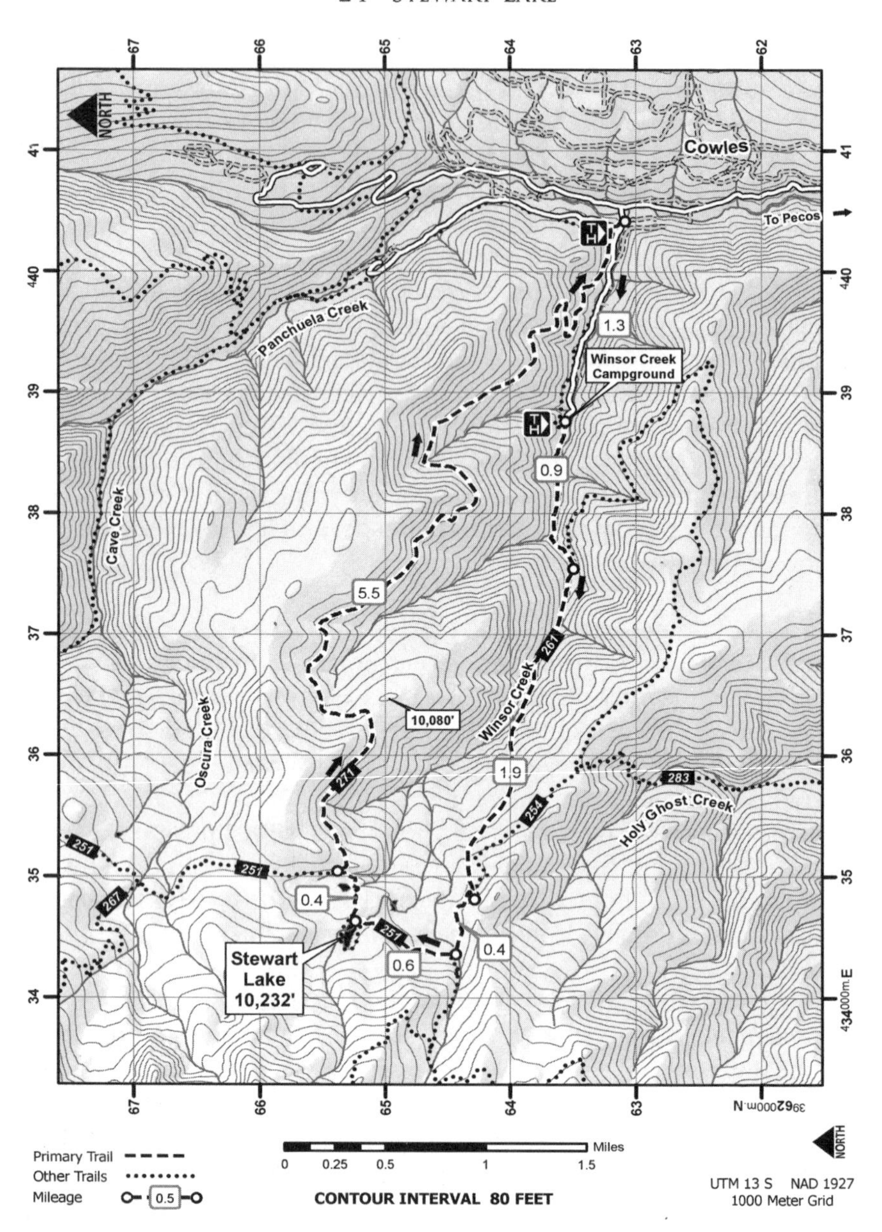
NORTH
Cowles
To Pecos
Panchuela Creek
1.3
Winsor Creek Campground
0.9
Cave Creek
5.5
261
10,080'
Winsor Creek
Oscura Creek
1.9
271
283
Holy Ghost Creek
254
251
267
0.4
0.4
0.6
Stewart Lake 10,232'
4340000m.E
3962000m.N
Primary Trail
Other Trails
Mileage
0.5
Miles
0 0.25 0.5 1 1.5
CONTOUR INTERVAL 80 FEET
UTM 13 S NAD 1927
1000 Meter Grid

24 - STEWART LAKE

by Betsy Fuller and Ann Young

A pleasant loop hike to a lovely mountain lake reached through a deep aspen/conifer forest rife with wildflowers, including a return along a ridge with distant views of the Pecos Wilderness.

RT Distance:	10 miles (loop closed by car) 11 miles (loop closed by walking)
Time:	6½ hrs (+30 min if loop closed by walking)
Elevation Range:	8400-10,332 ft; total gain 2100 ft (+200 ft if loop closed by walking)
Rating:	Strenuous
RT Drive:	90 miles; 2 hrs 20 min
Seasons:	Beautiful in spring as soon as the snow melts; good through fall until the first heavy snow.
Maps:	USGS Cowles - 7.5' series; Drake's *Map of the Mountains of Santa Fe* is recommended. *Pecos Wilderness* put out by the National Forest Service is also helpful.
East TH:	440,408 mE 3,963,060 mN elev.8165'
West TH:	438,824 mE 3,963,510 mN elev.8424'

Summary

A lovely mountain tarn nestled in a deep aspen/conifer forest filled with wildflowers. The return is along a ridge with views of the east side of Santa Fe Baldy and distant views of the Pecos Wilderness.

Driving Directions

Take I-25 north toward Las Vegas (NM) for about 15 miles and exit at the Glorieta off-ramp (Exit 299). Turn left onto the overpass, then turn right onto NM 50 and drive 6 miles to the town of Pecos.

At the stop sign turn left onto NM 63, which leads north into the Pecos River valley. From the stop sign, drive 20 miles to the junction at Cowles. Turn left over the bridge, and immediately turn left again and park at the Cowles Ponds parking area. (The return trail ends across the road from here, at the Forest Service kiosk.)

If you have two or more cars, leave one car here. This will eliminate walking 1.3 miles and climbing 200 ft in elevation. Drive (or walk) 1.3 miles up the road to the Winsor Creek campground parking area. There is a kiosk at the trailhead.

Hiking Instructions

From the parking area, start hiking up Trail 254 (Winsor Trail) that parallels the creek. You will walk through grassy meadows, aspen glades, and wildflower patches. In about 20 minutes, you'll cross the creek to the left bank and continue on the trail still following the creek.

About 100 yards after the creek crossing, you will come to a trail fork. Here, Trail 254 goes off to the left. You continue on the right branch (Trail 261 - Winsor Creek Trail). This trail is not maintained, and because of fallen trees, is not passable for horses, but OK for hiking. It rejoins Trail 254 after about 2 miles.

The aspens give way to deep conifer forests. You may notice a large, low rock sticking out partway into the trail with a USGS marker embedded in it indicating that the elevation is 9,405 ft. This is a good place for a break since you will have been hiking for about 1 hour. Beyond this point, the trail climbs higher above the creek until finally you lose the sound of it below you. After 15 more minutes of climbing beyond the rock, the trail levels out. Another 15 minutes will bring you to a trail joining from the left. You are now back on Trail 254. From here on to Stewart Lake and a little past the lake, your trail traverses granite and gneiss formations, the oldest rocks in this mountain range.

Continue on Trail 254. After 10 minutes of level walking, you will cross the creek over a big log. This is the main fork of the Winsor Creek that you were paralleling down below. At the junction with Trail 251 (Skyline Trail), bear to the right to Stewart Lake (the left branch would take you to Lake Katherine). You will reach Stewart Lake in about 15 minutes.

This little gem of a lake is spring fed, and from its banks you can look up to the west and see the flanks of Santa Fe Baldy. Fishermen have worn a path around the lake. After a snack and a rest you may want to walk around it. It won't take more than 15-20 minutes, including time to admire wildflowers.

To continue, follow the trail in an easterly direction. The trail crosses the outflow from Stewart Lake, goes up a bit and down again to a smaller lake (on your left). After crossing the outflow from the second lake, the trail heads north and in a minute or so reaches the junction with Trail 271 (Winsor Ridge Trail). Here, leave the Skyline Trail and make a sharp right onto Trail 271. You are now hiking on sediments (sandstone, limestone, shale), and the trail is pleasantly smooth for the most part. After 20 minutes or so on Trail 271, you will arrive at a meadow (there may be a sign indicating that this is the Pecos Wilderness), where the trail turns 90° to the left.

As you hike along this gradually descending trail, you will encounter enormous trees (Douglas fir, aspen, ponderosa), meadows, and beautiful views and panoramas of the Winsor Creek Canyon. Looking back to the northwest, you will see the east faces of Santa Fe Baldy and Lake Peak on the horizon.

Trail 271 remains high for the first 90 minutes or so before it descends with a number of switchbacks. You will pass a sign marking the wilderness boundary, and reach a trail junction some 15 minutes later. Continue straight ahead on the trail to Cowles. (The trail that turns sharply right at this point goes down steeply to Cowles Campground.) At the next trail fork, take the right branch toward Cowles, cross the road that goes to Panchuela, and arrive at the kiosk across from the Cowles Ponds parking area.

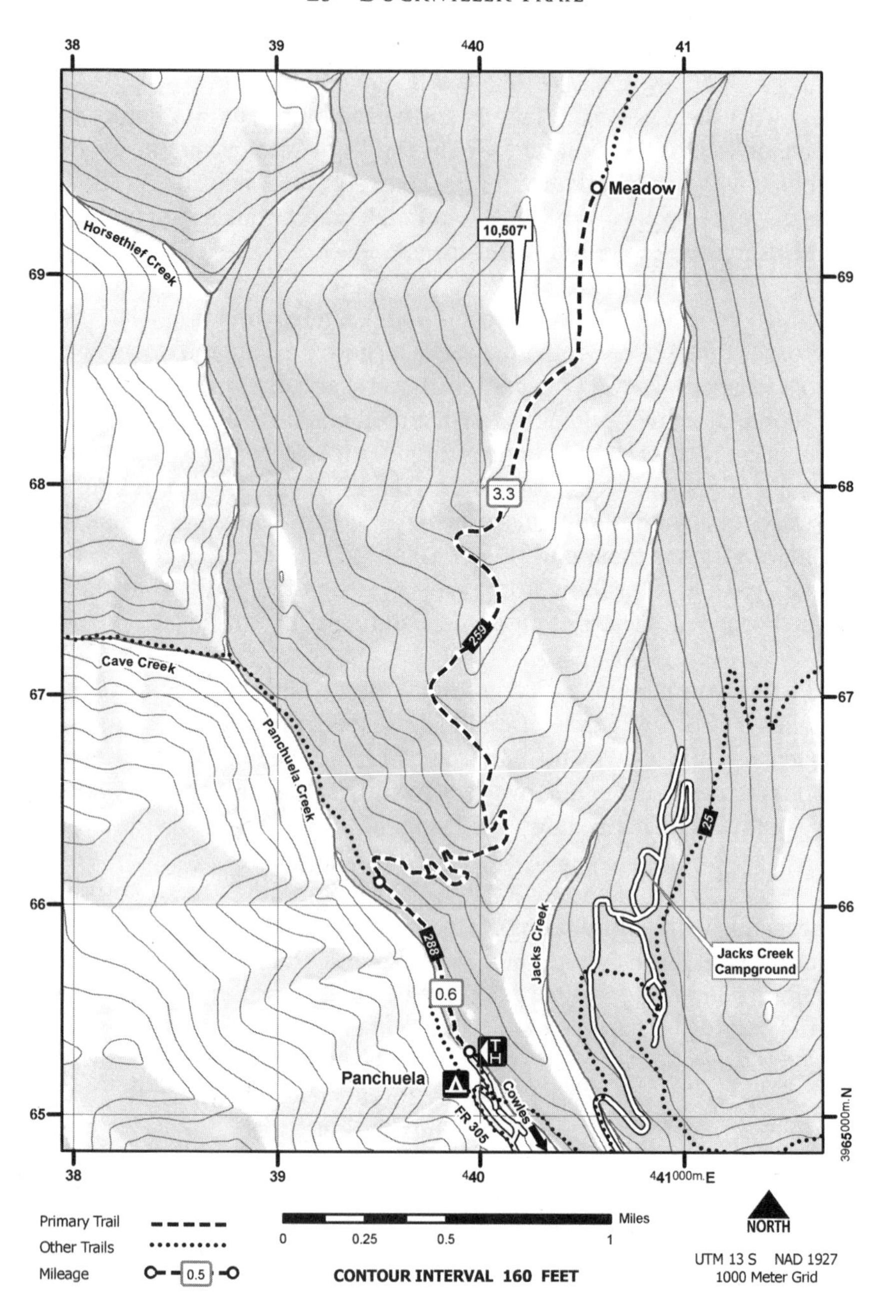

38
39
440
41
69
68
67
66
65
Meadow
10,507'
Horsethief Creek
3.3
259
Cave Creek
Panchuela Creek
25
Jacks Creek
Jacks Creek Campground
288
0.6
Panchuela
Cowles
FR 305
441000m.E
3965000m.N
Primary Trail
Other Trails
Mileage
0.5
Miles
0
0.25
0.5
1
CONTOUR INTERVAL 160 FEET
NORTH
UTM 13 S NAD 1927
1000 Meter Grid

25 - Dockwiller Trail

by Ann Bancroft

A little-used mountain trail in the Pecos with wildflowers, aspens, and high grassy meadows.

RT Distance:	8 miles
Time:	5 hrs
Elevation Range:	8350–10,040 ft; total gain ~1700 ft
Rating:	Moderate
RT Drive:	93 miles; ~3 hrs
Seasons:	Unhikeable in winter. Cool in summer because of dense aspen groves.
Maps:	USGS Cowles - 7.5' series. Also, Drakes's *Mountains of Santa Fe* is recommended.
Fees:	Parking $2/car
Trailhead:	439,941 mE 3,965,303 mN elev.8346'

Summary

This is a little-used trail and, although the views are not expansive, the wildflowers, aspen, and high grassy meadows are beautiful. It is especially wonderful in the fall when the aspen are turning. The opportunity for solitude will invite you to linger.

Driving Directions

Take I-25 north toward Las Vegas (NM) for approximately 15 miles and exit at the Glorieta off-ramp (Exit 299). Turn left onto the overpass, then turn right onto NM 50 and drive 6 miles to the town of Pecos. At the stop sign, turn left onto NM 63, which leads north into the Pecos River valley. From the Pecos stop sign, drive about 13½ miles to the Terrero bridge. Just before the bridge the road forks and you take the right branch. Continue for about 6 miles to Cowles. At a fork in the road, turn left across the bridge onto FR 121 and after just a few hundred yards turn sharply right uphill on

FR 305 toward Los Pinos Ranch and Panchuela Campground. The road dead-ends at Panchuela Campground in about 1½ miles. Park here and pay the parking fee.

Hiking Instructions

Follow the wide trail at the north end of the parking area (just past the fee station). It leads a short distance upstream to a bridge that spans Panchuela Creek. Cross the bridge and continue hiking upstream along a well-defined narrow trail. Twenty or so minutes of walking will bring you to a fork in the trail. Straight ahead is Trail 288 that follows Panchuela Creek (which takes you up to Cave Creek and then on to Horsethief Meadow (see CAVE CREEK / HORSETHIEF / LAKE JOHNSON Hike #26), and to the right is Dockwiller Trail 259. Take the right fork uphill, following Trail 259.

This steeply ascending, switchbacked trail is named after a man who lived in the Cowles area and ran a sawmill. It is also sometimes referred to as the Mystery Ridge Trail. The trail takes you uphill out of the Panchuela Creek drainage, and in about 40 minutes (about half way up the switchbacks), depending on the time of year, you may spot the snow cornice between Santa Fe Baldy and Lake Peak toward the west. These peaks are visible by looking up a canyon at a point where the trail direction changes from west to east.

After more severe switchbacks (at ~9200 ft), you will begin skirting the Jack's Creek drainage on the eastern flank of Mystery Ridge. Continue along the trail through aspen, interrupted by occasional grassy areas. Off and on, aspen art may be spotted: you may find the words "Dios nos libre, Amen" etched around a cross, or names, possibly of sheepherders, dating as far back as 1919, not to mention the numerous carvings of more recent visitors.

After approximately 2½ hours, having taken a leisurely hike with breaks, the turn-around point of this hike comes at a large, sloping, aspen-encircled meadow with a small stream running through it at approximately 10,000 ft. The trail continues on, but for this hike, it's time to turn back, retracing your steps to Panchuela Campground.

This trail leads to many other beautiful areas in the Pecos Wilderness. Someday you may want to go on to Beatty's Cabin or Horsethief Meadow or, if you have someone to do a drive-around, hike to Jack's Creek Campground via the Round Mountain Trail.

Cave Creek 

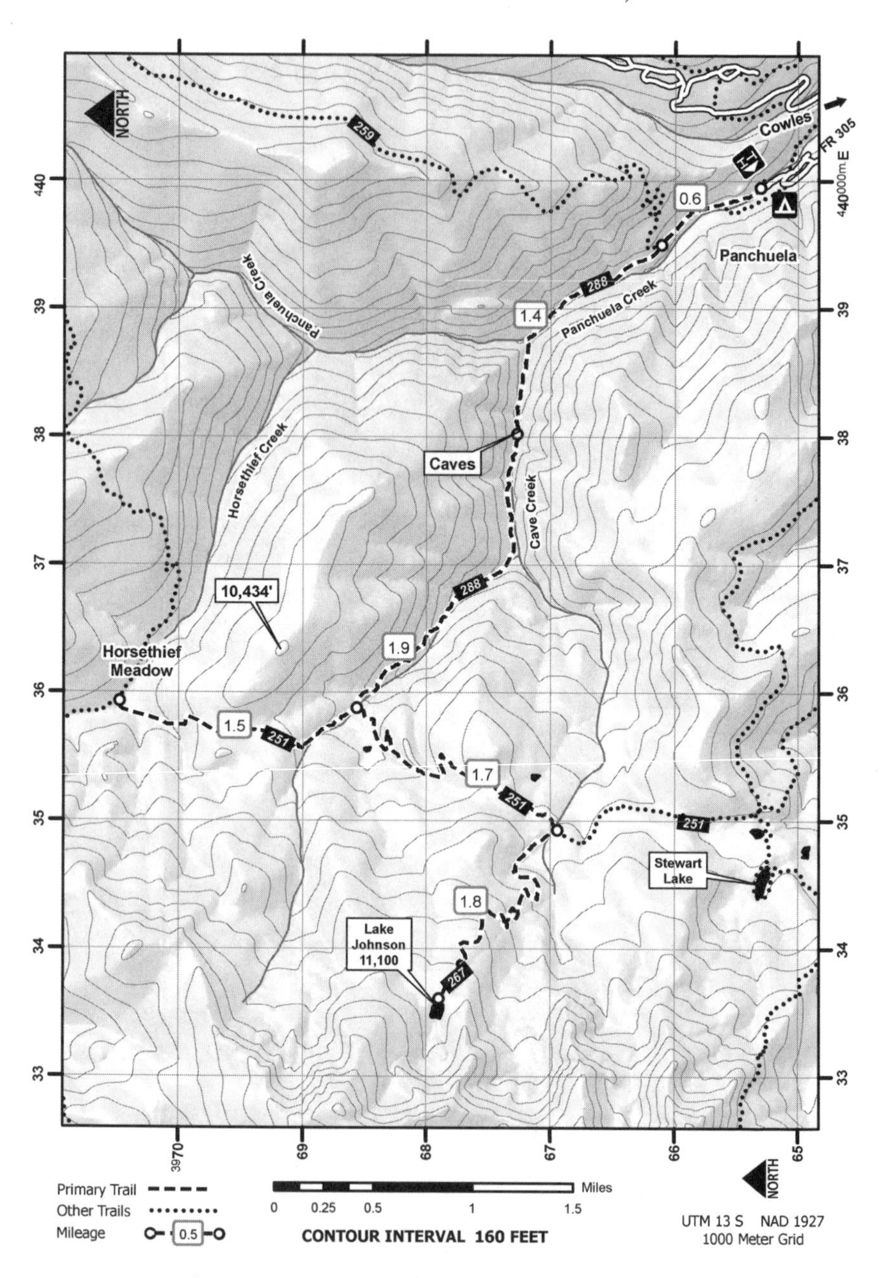
NORTH
259
Cowles
FR 305
440000mE
0.6
Panchuela
Panchuela Creek
288
1.4
Panchuela Creek
Horsethief Creek
Caves
Cave Creek
10,434'
288
1.9
Horsethief Meadow
1.5
251
1.7
251
251
Stewart Lake
1.8
Lake Johnson 11,100
267
440
39
38
37
36
35
34
33
3970
69
68
67
66
65
Primary Trail
Other Trails
Mileage
0.5
Miles
0 0.25 0.5 1 1.5
CONTOUR INTERVAL 160 FEET
NORTH
UTM 13 S NAD 1927
1000 Meter Grid

26 - CAVE CREEK / HORSETHIEF MEADOW / LAKE JOHNSON

by Norbert Sperlich

This hike in the Pecos Wilderness takes you to caves created by a creek. Beyond the caves, you can continue to a large mountain meadow or to a lovely alpine lake.

RT Distance:	4 miles (Caves only) 11 miles (Horsethief Meadow) 15 miles (Lake Johnson)
Time:	2+ hrs (Caves only) 7 hrs (Horsethief Meadow) 8+ hrs (Lake Johnson}
Elevation Range:	8350-8800 ft; gain 500 ft (Caves) 8350-10,150 ft; gain 2200 ft (Horsethief) 8350-11,000 ft; gain 3000 ft (Lake Johnson)
Rating:	Easy (Caves only) Strenuous (Horsethief or Lake Johnson)
RT Drive:	93 miles; 2½ hrs
Seasons:	Mid-June to mid-October, snow conditions permitting
Maps:	USGS Cowles and Truchas Peak - 7.5' series. Drake's *Mountains of Santa Fe* and the FS *Pecos Wilderness* Map are recommended.
Fees:	Parking $2/car
Trailhead:	439,941 mE 3,965,303 mN elev.8346'

Summary

Once a hiding place for horses stolen from ranches in the foothills of the Sangre de Cristos, Horsethief Meadow is the destination of a pleasant mountain hike. You will encounter caves along a mountain stream, wildflowers, and a beautiful, large meadow in the heart of the Pecos Wilderness. For a longer hike, skip Horsethief Meadow and go to the rarely visited Lake Johnson instead.

Driving Directions

Take I-25 north toward Las Vegas (NM) for about 15 miles and exit on the Glorieta off-ramp (Exit 299). Turn left onto the overpass, then turn right onto NM 50 and drive 6 miles to the town of Pecos. At the stop sign, turn left onto NM 63, and drive 20 miles to Cowles where the road forks. Turn left across the bridge onto FR 121, and after 0.1 mile, turn sharply right uphill on FR 305 toward Los Pinos Ranch and Panchuela Campground. The road dead-ends at Panchuela Campground in about 1½ miles. Park here.

Hiking Instructions

Trail 288 (Cave Creek Trail) starts left of the pay station. After a short distance, it crosses Panchuela Creek on a small bridge and continues a gradual climb along the stream. It traverses sediments (shale, limestone, sandstone) from the Pennsylvanian age.

Some 10 minutes into the hike, a trail coming from the left (Horse Trail to Cowles) merges with your trail. Continue on Trail 288. About 20 minutes from the trailhead, you will come to a fork, where Trail 259, the Dockwiller Trail (see DOCKWILLER TRAIL Hike #25) branches off to the right. Continue straight ahead on Trail 288. Some 20 minutes past the intersection with Dockwiller Trail, you will come to a sign "Cave Creek 288" pointing in the direction from which you came, and a white arrow pointing to the left. Here, your trail turns left and crosses Panchuela Creek at a wide, shallow spot over a crude log bridge. The trail now follows Cave Creek in a westerly direction. After you have hiked some 15 minutes along Cave Creek, the stream moves away from the trail, leaving a dry creek bed on your left. Soon, the trail moves close to the creek again. Look for a cairn at a small clearing on your left. Here, a short trail leads to the creek where a cave is visible on the other side. Continue on the main trail for another minute or so to another clearing, with a huge tree trunk on your left, lying at a right angle to the trail. Go left here to the creek, where more caves appear in the cliffs on the other side of the creek. The caves were created by water from the creek entering and enlarging cracks in the soluble limestone. About half of the stream flow is diverted into the caves. Be careful when visiting the caves, as it is dark, damp, and slippery inside (and pleasantly cool on a hot summer day). If all you wanted to do was an easy hike, stop here.

To reach Horsethief Meadow or Lake Johnson, continue on Trail 288. The trail climbs high above the creek for a while. Some 60 minutes past the caves and about 900 vertical feet above them, and close to the creek again, you will come to the junction with Trail 251, the Skyline Trail. Here you have the option of continuing either to Horsethief Meadow or to Lake Johnson.

Horsethief Meadow - To reach Horsethief Meadow, follow the Skyline Trail to the right. The trail moves away from the stream and goes uphill by steep switchbacks. You have crossed a major geological fault that runs in a north-south direction. The fault separates Precambrian granite on the west from Pennsylvanian sediments on the east. Note the gray granite boulders on the way up. After 15 minutes of climbing, the trail tops out on a ridge. The ridge top is fairly level, with small meadows, aspens and alpine flowers.

The trail continues northward, now downhill, and crosses a small creek before reaching the grassy expanse of Horsethief Meadow and Horsethief Meadow Creek. There is a sign on the north side of the creek, pointing to Horsethief Meadow, Panchuela West, Pecos Baldy, and Stewart Lake. To reach a nearby spot with great views, go up on the grassy slope on the other (NE) side of the valley for about 5 minutes. You will see Redondo Peak (aka Capulin Peak) on the horizon, and Horsethief Meadow below you. Enjoy the lovely setting. This is a good place to eat your lunch.

Lake Johnson - From the junction of Trails 288 and 251, take Trail 251 across Cave Creek northwest 45-50 minutes uphill to the junction with Trail 267, then right on Trail 267 another 50 minutes uphill to Lake Johnson. It is rare to see anyone there, and worth the effort. Return the way you came.

27 Pecos Baldy Lake / Pecos Baldy

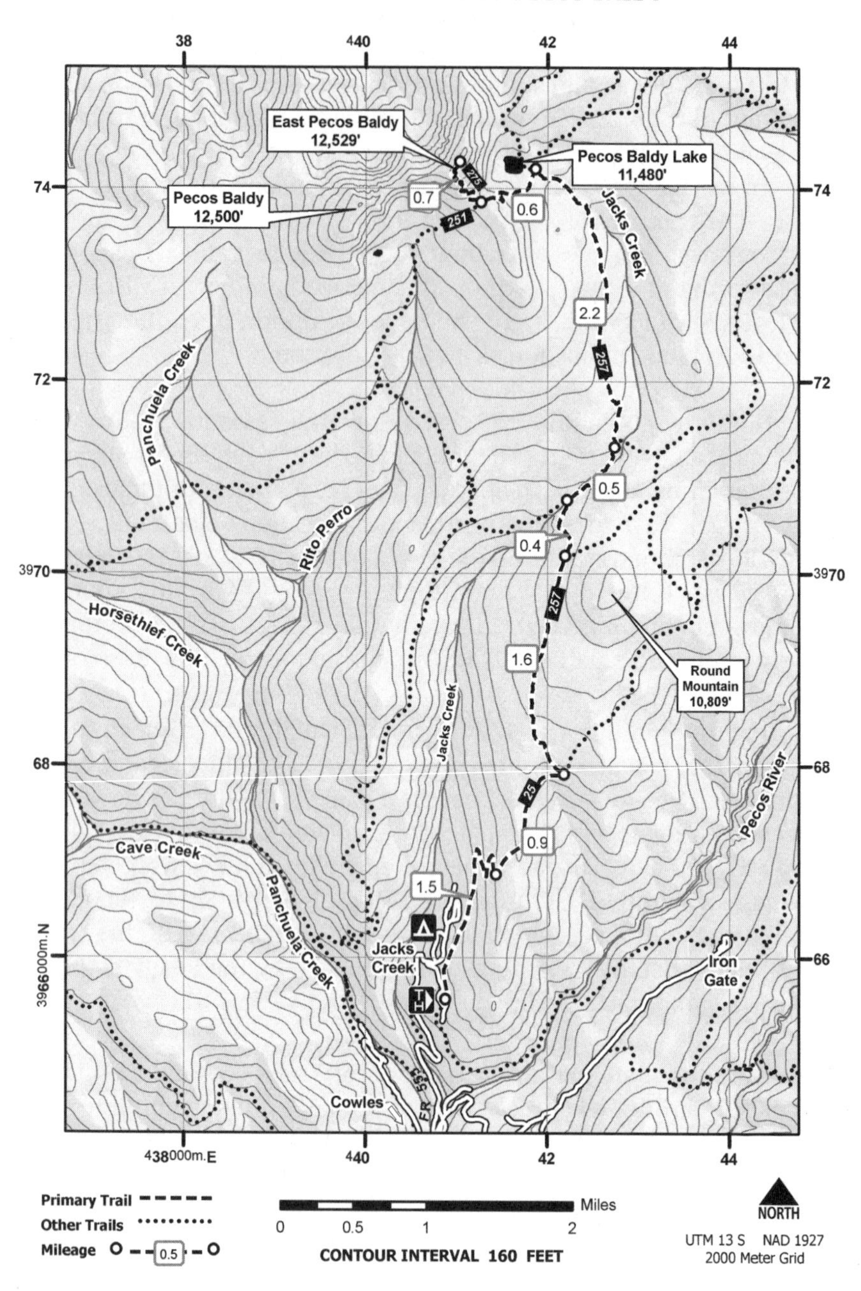

27 - PECOS BALDY LAKE / EAST PECOS BALDY

by Betsy Fuller

High country hike that includes great vistas, high grassy meadows with wildflowers in summer, a beautiful mountain lake and a rugged peak.

RT Distance:	15 miles (Pecos Baldy Lake) 17 miles (East Pecos Baldy Peak)
Time:	7½ hrs (Pecos Baldy Lake) 9 hrs (East Pecos Baldy Peak)
Elevation Range:	8850-11,320 ft; gain ~2600 ft (lake) 8850-12,529 ft; gain ~3800 ft (peak)
Rating:	Strenuous
RT Drive:	102 miles; 3½ hrs
Seasons:	Good in summer and early fall. Likely impassable after first heavy snow. Spring flowers. Higher sections of trail can be muddy and boggy or even snow-packed in spring and early summer.
Maps:	USGS Cowles and Truchas Peak - 7.5' series; Drake's *Map of the Mountains of Santa Fe* is recommended.
Fees:	Parking $2/day; camping $10/night
Trailhead:	440,891 mE 3,965,611 mN elev.8843'

Summary

This high country hike to a beautiful mountain lake has magnificent vistas and the possibility of seeing bighorn sheep. There are high grassy meadows with wildflowers in summer (late June and July), and fall colors in September and early October. Allow at least 11 hours round trip from Santa Fe. It's a long drive and a long hike, so get an early start. If your schedule allows, consider camping at Jack's Creek Campground the night before.

Driving Directions

Take I-25 north toward Las Vegas (NM) for approximately 15 miles and exit on the Glorieta off-ramp (Exit 299). Turn left onto the overpass, then right onto NM 50 and drive 6 miles to the town of Pecos. At the stop sign, turn left onto NM 63, and drive 20 miles to the road fork at Cowles. Do not take the road to the left which crosses the river, but keep straight ahead for another 3 miles following the Forest Service signs to Jack's Creek Campground. Keep to the right at every junction following the road to "Wilderness Parking" until you arrive at a large loop where there are picnic tables, corrals, and parking areas. Pay your fee at the self-service payment box.

Hiking Instructions

The trailhead is north of the parking areas, next to a Forest Service sign. The trail starts with a long climb (~1 mile) through a conifer forest up the side of a hill. During this climb you will enter the Pecos Wilderness. Soon after the initial long climb, the trail becomes a series of steep switchbacks, until finally after about 1 mile, the trail levels off. Then comes another short climb and you will reach an open sloping grassy area. At this point, there is a signpost marking a "Y" trail junction. You will have walked about 2½ miles and climbed about 1050 ft. Elevation here is 10,026 ft.

Take the left (north) fork of the trail and continue through the meadow toward the aspen trees. Watch for beautiful distant views of the Pecos River valley to the east and the mountains to the west. The trail climbs up through an open meadow in a northerly direction. Soon you will get your first view of the bare Pecos Baldy Peaks looming above the forests to the northwest. At the northern end of this meadow, the trail enters a conifer forest and drops down to Jack's Creek, which is shallow most of the year and can easily be crossed on stepping stones. At this point, you will have walked another 2 miles in about 45 minutes to an hour.

Cross Jack's Creek and follow the trail to the right, paralleling the creek. In 5 minutes, the trail swings away from the creek. Fifteen minutes after crossing Jack's Creek, the trail splits. Go straight ahead to Pecos Baldy, not right to Beatty's Cabin. Continue climbing through deep and dark conifer forests. Your elevation here is now over 10,500 ft and the trail is steep in some places, so take it easy as you continue your ascent.

Finally, about 2 miles (and over 1-hour's walking) after you cross Jack's Creek, you will leave the forest behind and see the summit of East Pecos Baldy Peak ahead. One last steep climb brings you to another junction where you will see Pecos Baldy Lake a few hundred feet away. As you approach the lake, note the ridgeline of East Pecos Baldy Peak sloping downward to your left and ending at a high open saddle. This is the open saddle you cross on the way up to the peak.

If you're tired (and you will be!), go down to the lake for a snack and a rest. As you're recovering from the steep walk, search the sides of the mountain for bighorn sheep, which are often found here in the summer months. Sometimes the sheep are overly friendly, nuzzling into your knapsack if it's left unattended. It will make a great picture, though.

You may want to turn back here. If you still have enough energy and time, you might want to consider two options: climb East Pecos Baldy Peak or climb the ridge north of the lake.

East Pecos Baldy Peak – To climb East Pecos Baldy (2 miles RT, 1100 ft up), go back up a couple of hundred feet to the place where you first saw the lake and where there is a marker prohibiting camping in the lake basin. Take the trail to the southwest (to your right as you walk away from the lake) and follow it for about ½ mile through a forested hillside south of the lake until it comes out onto an open saddle. *Note: Be sure to turn around and note where you came out of the woods so you can pick up the trail on the return.* Don't take the trail to the left that goes downhill through the woods, but continue across the open saddle in the same general direction that you were following when you arrived. You will have no trouble finding the rocky path that zigzags up the steep side of the mountain. The climb from the saddle to the top of East Pecos Baldy is another 680 ft and a hard pull at this elevation (12,529 ft when you reach the top), so take your time and enjoy the ever-expanding views as you climb to the top. Don't attempt this part of the hike if it's stormy. There's no protection on top, and lightning and strong winds are not good companions when you're on the top of a bare rocky peak in the high mountains. Frequently, there is a snow cornice along the peak, with a considerable overhang. *Note: Do not walk out on any snow field along the edge of the peak.*

North Ridge of Lake – To go up to the saddle on the ridge north of the lake (1 mile RT, 400 ft up), keep the lake on your left, walk to the north side of the lake and then up to the saddle. There are several trails leading in the same direction. Your reward will be terrific views of the mountains to the north. And yes, those are fossils in the gray shale outcrops. Go back to the lake the same way you came up.

Return the way you came.

Pecos Baldy Lake

Bighorn sheep at Pecos Baldy Lake

28 BEATTY'S CABIN / PECOS FALLS

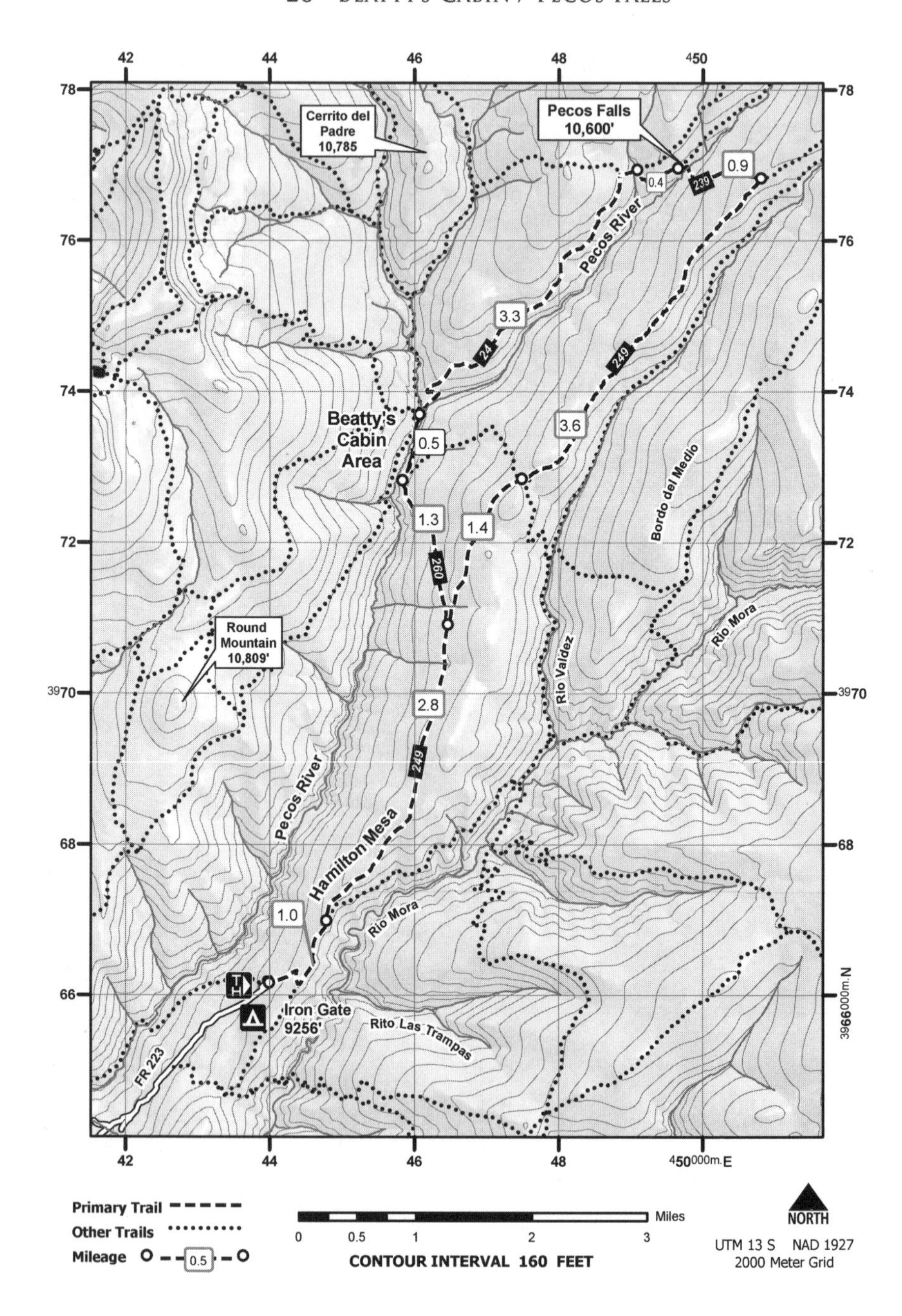

28 - Beatty's Cabin / Pecos Falls

by Philip L. Shultz

This hike takes you through some of the most beautiful high meadows of Hamilton Mesa, with spectacular irises in the early summer and golden aspens in late September.

RT Distance: 11.5 miles (Beatty's Cabin)
19.5 miles (Pecos Falls)

Time: 5+ hrs (Beatty's Cabin)
9+ hrs (Pecos Falls)

Elevation Range: 9400-10,200 ft; total gain ~1640 ft (Cabin)
9400-10,600 ft; total gain ~1300 ft (Falls)

Rating: Strenuous/Very Strenuous

RT Drive: 94 miles; 3½ hours

Seasons: This is not a winter hike. Four-wheel drive is required whenever the road is likely to be muddy. Trail can be muddy during monsoon season (July, August)

Maps: USGS Pecos Falls and Elk mountain - 7.5' series
"Beatty's Cabin" is called "Beatty's" on the Pecos Wilderness map and "Beatty's Flats" on the USFS map. Beatty's Flats is also shown on Drake's *Map of the Mountains of Santa Fe.*

Fees: Parking $2/day; Camping $4/night

Trailhead: 444,031 mE 3,966,246 mN elev.9361'

Summary

This hike goes through some of the most beautiful high meadows of the Pecos Wilderness, with outstanding views of the Truchas Peaks, Pecos Baldy and Lake Peak from the east side. In early summer, the blue flag iris are spectacular.

Driving Directions

Take I-25 north toward Las Vegas (NM) for approximately 15 miles and exit at the Glorieta off-ramp (Exit 299). Turn left onto the overpass, then right onto NM 50 and drive 6 miles to the town of Pecos. At the stop sign, turn left onto NM 63, and drive 18½ miles, passing several camp and picnic grounds and the little settlement of Terrero. At the top of a grade, turn right onto FR 223. A sign here will direct you to Iron Gate Campground. The distance between this junction and the campground is 4 miles; the road is steep, rutted and rough. A high-clearance vehicle is essential. Four-wheel drive is necessary when the road is wet and muddy. (Remember the road may be dry in the morning but wet in the afternoon when you return after a summer shower.) Near the entrance of the campground you will find a parking area for hikers. Pay your fee before starting your hike.

Hiking Instructions

The trail starts at the far end of the campground. Trail 249 gently zigzags northeast from the gate at the Iron Gate Campground. It rises about 300 ft, through spruce, fir and aspen to a usually well-marked junction with Trail 250 (which goes essentially straight and makes up the right fork of the junction). Remain on Trail 249, bearing slightly left and still climbing. This is a popular trail for hikers and equestrians, so the trail marker signs may be torn down or defaced. In ¼ mile or so, the trail comes out of the aspen, still climbing gently through the first meadow. You are now on the beautiful expanse of Hamilton Mesa. In June, the iris are gorgeous. Also, look for mariposa lilies. Kestrels are common as is evidence of elk in these meadows. The trail tops out at about 10,200 ft, a beautiful point for a rest stop, with fine views of the Truchas Peaks to the north. At 3.8 miles from the start, there is a marked trail junction. This is the point where you must decide whether to do the long walk to Pecos Falls or the shorter one to Beatty's cabin.

Beatty's Cabin - If you decide on the shorter trip to Beatty's Cabin, bear left (downhill to the northwest), entering the woods promptly for the winding descent to the Pecos River. Cross the bridge and find a spot on the lovely grassy slope for a rest. The original cabin is long gone. It was upstream near the confluence with the Rio del Padre. However, for those who like to see cabins, there is a new one located southwest of the bridge up on the side of the ridge. Return by the same route for a lovely, not too strenuous hike.

Pecos Falls - If you decide on the longer trip to Pecos Falls, instead of taking the left-hand trail to Beatty's Cabin, bear right on your original Trail 249. The trail generally follows the 10,200-ft contour through meadows and islands of aspen for about 6 miles to the falls, which are quite beautiful during the spring runoff. Return the way you came all the way back to Iron Gate Campground. Alternatively, you may cross the river at the trail junction just before the falls and return by the slightly shorter loop that goes to Beatty's Cabin and meets up with Trail 249. This adds 600 ft of elevation to the hike making it a total of 1900 ft.

This wonderful high country is at its best in early summer when the wildflowers are at their height and in late September when the aspen leaves are golden. Enjoy it!

The View from Hamilton Mesa

29 Hermit Peak

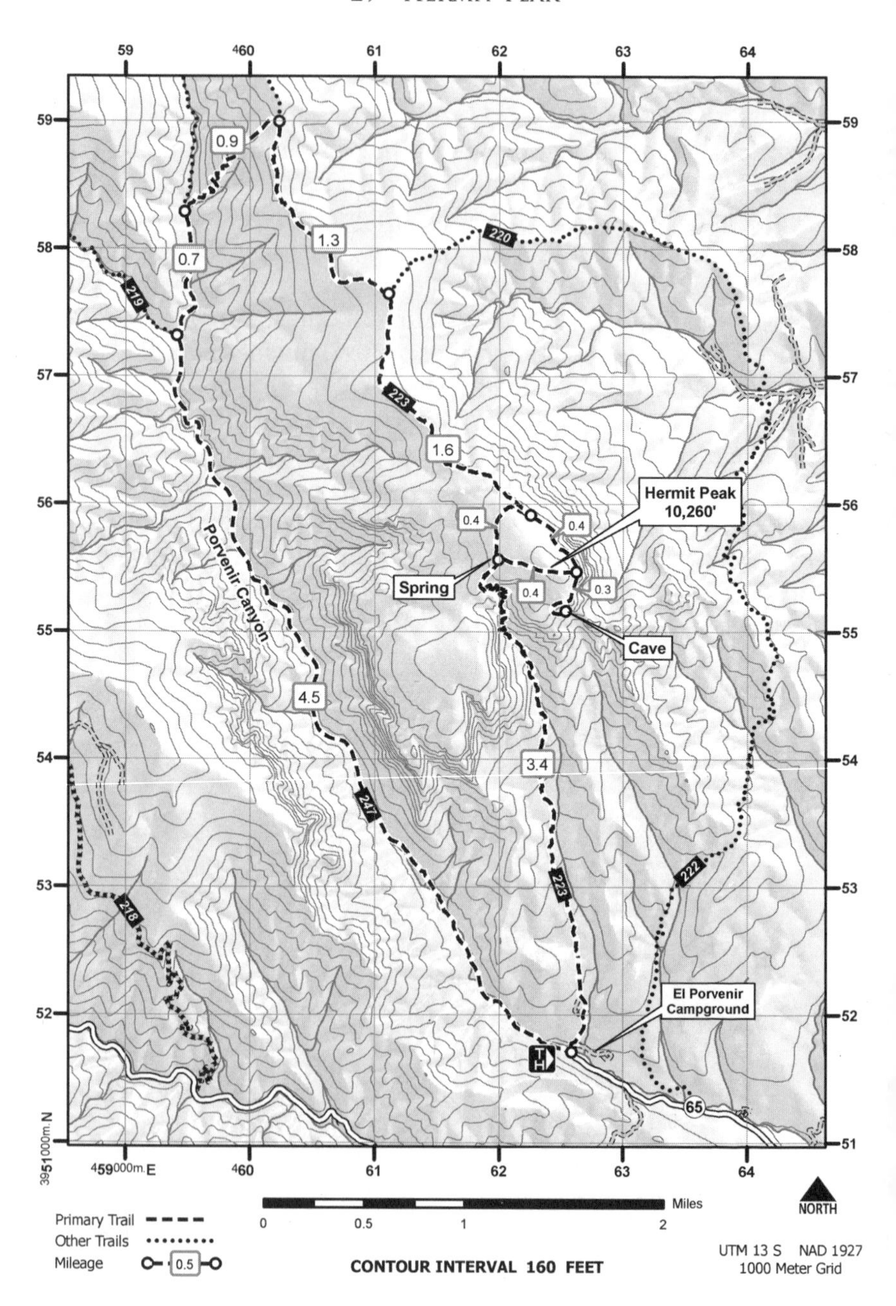

29 - Hermit Peak

by Norbert Sperlich

A hike near Las Vegas (NM) to a towering peak at the edge of the Sangre de Cristos, with great views and an extended return hike through a beautiful canyon.

RT Distance:	8 miles (Hermit Pk only) 14 miles (Hermit Pk & Porvenir Cyn)
Time:	5 hrs (Hermit Pk only) 7+ hrs (Hermit Pk & Porvenir Cyn)
Elevation Range:	7550-10,260 ft; total gain ~2750 ft (Hermit Pk) ~2850 ft (Hermit Pk & Porvenir Cyn)
Rating:	Moderate to Strenuous (Hermit Pk only) Strenuous (Hermit Pk & Porvenir Cyn)
RT Drive:	170 miles; ~3 hrs 30 min
Seasons:	Not a winter hike. For the El Porvenir Canyon portion of the hike, avoid the spring runoff.
Maps:	USGS El Porvenir (Rociada for the extended hike) - 7.5' series. Also, USFS map *Pecos Wilderness.*
Trailhead:	462,588 mE 3,951,722 mN elev.7506'

Summary

Hermit Peak is a rugged granite peak and major landmark in the southeastern corner of the Pecos Wilderness. It is named for a hermit who lived in a cave near the summit in the 1860s. The approach to the trailhead is on paved roads. The trail is quite steep. The summit affords great views toward the eastern plains.

The extension of this hike takes you into beautiful El Porvenir Canyon with its meadows, wildflowers, waterfalls and rugged cliffs. You will be challenged by 27 stream crossings. An extra pair of sneakers and socks, a walking stick and mosquito repellent might be helpful for this adventure. Don't attempt the canyon during spring runoff! It is a long hike and a long drive, so start early. To get an early start, you might want to spend the night at El Porvenir Campground.

Driving Directions

Take I-25 toward Las Vegas (NM) Take the first exit (Exit 343) in Las Vegas, go under the interstate, and turn left onto NM 329 in about ¼ mile. There is a sign, "United World College," at the turnoff. Turn left again at a stop light where NM 329 crosses Hot Spring Road. You are now on NM 65, which will take you to the trailhead. After passing United World College on the right (formerly the Montezuma Castle Harvey Hotel), the road starts to climb and becomes narrow, with many blind curves. When you approach the village of Gallinas, the rocky face of Hermit Peak appears in the background. A few miles past Gallinas you will come to a fork. Take the right branch to El Porvenir. After 2.7 miles, you will reach the parking lot at the entrance to El Porvenir Campground. Park here. A sign, "Hermit Peak Trailhead," points to a wooden bridge.

Hiking Instructions

Cross the wooden bridge next to the parking lot. After a few minutes, you will be back on the road that leads to the campground. Look for a trailhead marked "Hermit Peak, Trail 223" just before the road comes to the campers' self-service pay station and toilet. The trail starts to climb right away. After a few minutes, it goes through a fence. Shortly after, the Dispensas Trail branches off to the right. Go straight ahead, following a sign "Hermit Peak Trail 223." The trail crosses a drainage, then turns left just before crossing a second drainage. Next, a trail joins your trail from the right at an unmarked intersection. Your trail then comes to a T-intersection with a dirt road. Go left on this road for a short distance. Your trail then leaves the road and goes off to the right at a right angle and up a ridge between two drainages. There should be a sign pointing the way.

From now on, the trail is wide and obvious and there are no more forks until you reach the summit plateau. You can forget about the trail for a while and enjoy your surroundings. As you go up, ponderosas give way to Douglas fir and aspen. The slope gets steeper and the trail starts to zigzag up a canyon formed by the cliffs of Hermit Peak. After about 2 hours of hiking, you will come to the top of the cliffs. Enjoy the view.

The trail now moves away from the rim. In a few minutes, you will reach a fork, where the trail has been rerouted. Take the right fork. After a rocky stretch, the trail reaches a clearing. Here is Hermit Spring, enclosed in rock walls and protected with a metal cover. Trail 223 continues to the left of the spring in a northerly direction. It reaches the east rim of Hermit Peak in a roundabout way. Leave Trail 223 here and go right in front of the spring on an unmarked but well-traveled trail that goes east and uphill. This trail is often lined with wooden crosses and traverses the gray limestone that makes up the top of the peak. After about 10 minutes, you will approach the precipitous rim of Hermit Peak. Some 20 yards before reaching the rim, your trail crosses a trail that runs parallel to the rim. There is a fire ring and a huge limber pine with three trunks nearby. Memorize this unmarked intersection. From the rocky edge, you get expansive views of the eastern plains and glimpses of the high peaks (Truchas, Chimayosos, and Santa Barbara Divide) to the northwest.

If you have extra time (30 min or more), you might consider a side trip to visit Hermit's Cave. From the edge, go back to the aforementioned intersection, turn left (south) and follow the trail along the mountain edge. In about 3 minutes, you will reach an overlook with views toward the south. Just before you come to the overlook, and close to a huge anthill, a trail branches off to the right (west). This trail will take you to the cave, some 250 ft below the rim, in less than 10 minutes. The trail soon veers left and starts descending some steep and rocky switchbacks until it ends at the cave. Pilgrims still come to this shrine to pray and to light their candles. Return to the overlook on the east rim the way you came. To return to the car, go back to Hermit Spring and turn left on Trail 223.

If you are planning to take the long way back by way of El Porvenir Canyon, check the time. You have 10 more miles and at least 5 hours of hiking before you. This is for experienced hikers only. The trail is faint in places and may be obstructed by fallen trees. From the overlook at the edge of the peak, go some 20 yards to the trail crossing and turn right onto the trail that follows the edge in a northerly direction. In about 7 minutes, you will reach a trail fork. There may be two signposts without signs marking this spot. The left fork, clearly visible, curves to the left of the second signpost in a westerly direction. It will take you back to the spring in about 10 minutes. The right fork, not very distinct, goes to the right of the second signpost in a northwesterly direction toward Lone Pine Mesa. This is *your* trail. Soon it starts to drop down, staying on a ridge all the time. The trail is faint at times and follows the ridge, with several ups and downs, in a northwesterly direction.

About 2 miles from Hermit Peak, you will come to a trail junction marked by signposts and a cairn. Your trail (Trail 223) goes left toward Lone Pine Mesa. Trail 220 curves to the right. Your trail, little used and faint in places, goes down, then up again, following the ridge which becomes narrow and rocky. About 30 minutes after the last trail fork, you will come to a fence on your right and then to another fork marked by signposts and cairns. Take the trail that goes down to the left, towards Beaver Creek Canyon. On your way down, you will get glimpses of the canyon, and after about 25 minutes of steep downhill hiking, you will reach Beaver Creek and a "T" junction marked by a cairn and a signpost. A marker, "Lone Pine Mesa, Hermit Peak," points in the direction you have come from. This is a great place for a stop. Right across from the trail, Beaver Creek forms a waterfall and a pool.

To continue the hike, take the left branch of the "T" junction, following Beaver Creek downstream. From now on, you will hike along lively streams, first Beaver Creek, then Porvenir Creek. This is the wild and wonderful part of the hike, 5 miles of hiking through meadows and woods, alongside rushing water and towering cliffs. You may see the rare wood lily. If you brought extra sneakers for the stream crossings, now is the time to put them on.

After crossing Beaver Creek four times, you will reach a marked trail junction where the trail you are on (Trail 247) meets Trail 219

(Hollinger Creek Trail), the latter coming in from the right. Continue downstream on Trail 247.

You are now in Porvenir Canyon. Soon the canyon narrows, with the granite cliffs of Hermit Peak on one side and El Cielo Mountain on the other. The trail crosses the creek many times. The last 2 miles of the hike are on private land; stay on the trail to avoid trespassing. When the canyon widens again, you are coming to the end of the hike. You will pass campsites and the remains of a log cabin, and reach a sign directing you to the Parking Area. Go through a gate and soon you will arrive at the parking lot where you left your car. By now, you may be bouncing along in exhilaration, looking for more stream crossings, or you may be staggering on wobbly legs!

30 Diablo Canyon

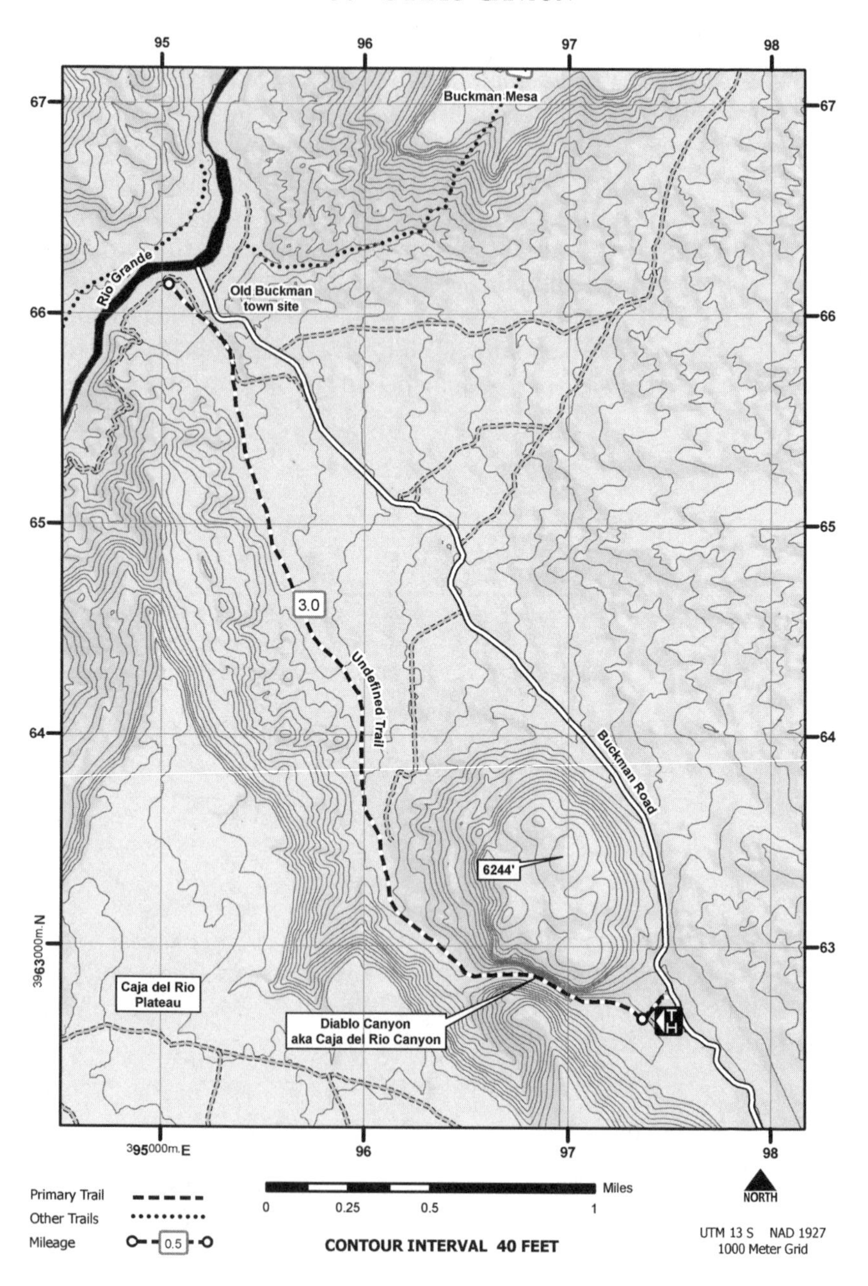

30 - DIABLO CANYON

by Polly Robertson and Norbert Sperlich

A short but spectacular hike, beginning in a canyon with vertical walls of basalt, and continuing along a sandy arroyo to the Rio Grande.

RT Distance: 6 miles
Time: 3 hrs
Elevation Range: 5450-5850 ft; total gain 400 ft
Rating: Easy
RT Drive: 37 miles; 1 hr 20 min (dependent on road conditions)
Seasons: Too hot in summer, unless you go early in the morning. Plan on the temperature in the Canyon being at least 10° warmer than in town. Road may not be passable after heavy rain or snow.
Maps: USGS White Rock - 7.5' series. On the map, Diablo Canyon is called Caja del Rio Canyon.
Trailhead: 397,480 mE 3,962,809 mN elev.5873'

Summary

This is a perfect winter hike, with great views all along the way. The access road is poorly maintained and can be very rough. Four-wheel drive and a high clearance vehicle are advantages when road conditions are less than perfect.

Driving Directions

Take US 84/285 to the first exit north of Santa Fe, NM 599. After 4.3 miles south on NM 599, exit at Camino La Tierra and turn right at the stop sign at the bottom of the exit. Proceed straight ahead through a four-way stop intersection. Farther on, where the road forks, stay on the left branch (La Tierra). Do not take the right branch to Las Campanas. At 0.8 miles past this fork, you will reach a second fork. Take the right branch, which in October 2006 was an unmarked gravel road. Do not take the paved left branch. Soon the road leaves the development and turns into a rough washboard road (Buckman Road). Look for cattle guards, ruts, and deep sand where the road is crossed by drainages. After a little over 3 miles on the dirt road, you pass a green windmill frame and corral on your left. Take a mileage reading here. The Caja del Rio volcanic field is now visible on your left, forming a basalt-capped escarpment. Soon, the vertical cliffs of Diablo Canyon will appear ahead of you to the left. The canyon separates a small mesa from the lava mesa to the west. At 4.1 miles from the windmill, look for a secondary road branching off to the left toward Diablo Canyon. Take this road to an open area close to the mouth of the canyon. Park your car here. Best not to leave valuables in your car.

Hiking Instructions

Head toward the arroyo that goes into the canyon and cross through one of the several breaks in the barbed wire fence. At the entrance of the canyon, vertical cliffs rise up about 300 ft. As you go deeper into the canyon, you will notice that the basalt columns rest on sand and gravel—a very unstable foundation, indeed. About 10 minutes into the hike, you will come to a place where water is seeping out of the ground. To the right of this spot, where basalt columns form an overhang, cliff swallows build their nests. In the summertime, you can see swallows feeding their young. The unique descending-scale song of the canyon wren can often be heard here. Soon, the canyon widens and, on your right and toward the top of the mesa, basalt cliffs give way to layers of ashes and cinders that have been eroded into jagged shapes.

As you walk out of the canyon, the arroyo widens and heads north for a while, toward Buckman Mesa (see BUCKMAN MESA Hike #31). The arroyo then swerves left (northwest) and descends slowly toward the Rio Grande. You may see hawks or ravens circling above. Ahead of you, on the other side of the (still hidden) Rio Grande, you will see dark basalt cliffs topped by orange tuff. The basalt comes from the Caja del Rio volcanoes; the tuff was produced by eruptions of the volcano that created the Jemez caldera. After hiking about 1½ hours, you will come to the river. From this point look upstream toward Buckman Mesa and its small peak. Look for a hound dog or a crocodile in profile. Had you been here around the turn of the 19th century, you would have seen a bridge crossing the river, the Chili Line railroad track, and a settlement built by lumberman Henry Buckman, all of which are now gone. The Buckman area is important for Santa Fe because of the wells that produce part of the water supply.

Return to your car the way you came.

Diablo Canyon

31 Buckman Mesa

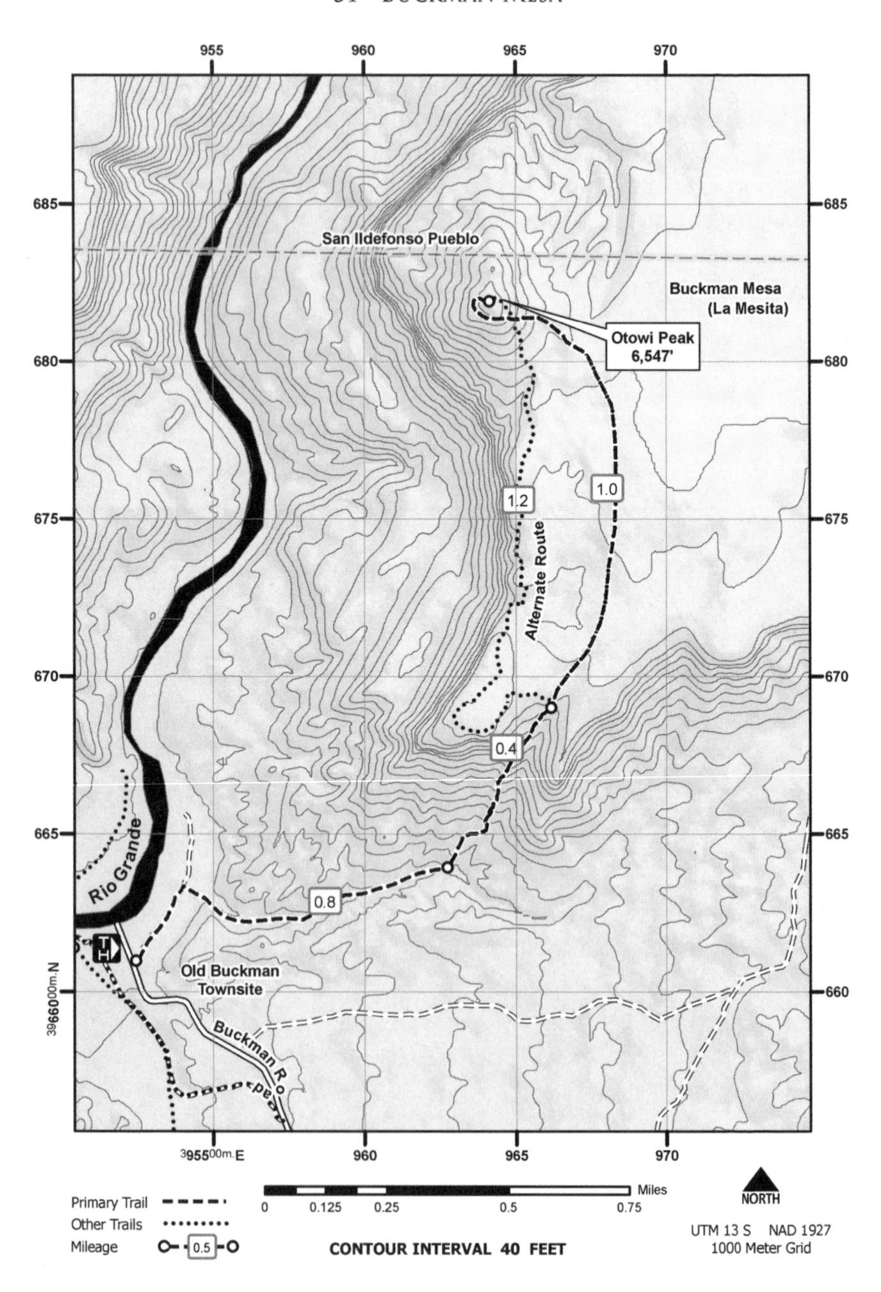

31 - BUCKMAN MESA

by Polly Robertson and Norbert Sperlich

A rugged mesa with an extinct volcano on the Rio Grande, guarding the entrance to White Rock Canyon and offering magnificent views.

RT Distance: 5 miles
Time: 4 hrs
Elevation Range: 5450-6547 ft; total gain 1100 ft
Rating: Moderate
RT Drive: 46 miles; ~2 hrs
Seasons: Very hot in summer. Road may not be passable after heavy rain or snow.
Maps: USGS White Rock - 7.5' series
Trailhead: 395,240 mE 3,966,060 mN elev.5500'

Summary

Buckman Mesa is the prominent mesa south of Otowi Bridge that guards the entrance to White Rock Canyon. Most of the mesa top is flat except for its western corner, where Otowi Peak, the remnant of a volcano, rises 1100 ft above the Rio Grande. The peak offers magnificent views in all directions.

Some of the hike goes over rough terrain. The trail is faint in places on top of the mesa, but often marked with cairns. The access road includes 11 unpaved miles, much of it with a washboard surface, and can be rough or muddy after rain or snow. Four-wheel drive and a high clearance are a great advantage when road conditions are less than perfect. Bring plenty of water because this can be a hot hike (no shade).

Driving Directions

Take US 84/285 to the first exit north of Santa Fe, NM 599. After 4.3 miles south on NM 599, exit at Camino La Tierra and turn right at the stop sign at the bottom of the exit. Proceed straight ahead through a 4-way stop intersection. Further on, where the road forks, stay on the left branch (La Tierra). Do not take the right branch to Las Campanas. At 0.8 miles past this fork, you will reach a second fork. Take the right branch, which in October 2006 was an unmarked gravel road. Do not take the paved left branch. Soon the road leaves the development and turns into a rough washboard road (Buckman Road). Look for cattle guards, ruts, and deep sand where the road is crossed by drainages. After a little over 3 miles on the dirt road, you pass a green windmill frame and a corral on your left. At 4.1 miles from the windmill, the road takes you past the turnoff for Diablo Canyon (see DIABLO CANYON Hike #30). Continue straight ahead. You have 3 more miles to go to the end of Buckman Road. A grove of tamarisks ahead will tell you that the river is near. Shortly after the Rio Grande comes in sight, the road turns left and you will immediately see an open area where you can park your car.

Hiking Instructions

Before starting the hike, you may want to spend a few minutes at the bank of the river. Its muddy waters are always a welcome sight in this dry country. Upstream, to your right, Buckman Mesa rises steeply. No trail going up can be seen from here. This hike will take you to the southern end of the mesa. There, Buckman Mesa ends in two long "fingers," and a rough trail climbs up to the mesa top between the two fingers.

From the river, walk back on the road that you just drove on. While still in the tamarisk grove, look for a secondary through-road that goes off to the left (north). Follow this road for about 5 minutes to a fence (with a gate/cattle guard) and some 30 yards beyond the fence to a wide sandy arroyo. Follow the arroyo upstream. Soon it narrows into a canyon with vertical walls of compacted sand. After hiking in the arroyo for about 8 minutes, you will come to a place where the arroyo turns to the right. On your left is a vertical wall of sand. Some 30 yards further, you will see an eroded trail going up on the left, usually marked by cairns. If you miss the trail, you will see a small drainage coming in from the left at ground level, creating a break in the canyon wall and affording you a glimpse of the southern tip of Buckman Mesa. You have gone too far! Go back about 30 yards and look for the trail.

The first part of the trail is rough. Look for cairns and footprints if you lose sight of the trail. The general direction is up, keeping the drainage on your right. After about ½ hour of climbing, you are close to the top of the mesa. Just before you reach the mesa top, the trail moves into the drainage and then to the right side of it.

Otowi Peak is not yet in sight, but keep going straight ahead on the path. In a minute or so you will see the peak. Go for it!

After hiking for about 20 minutes on the flat mesa top, you come to the cinder-strewn slope of Otowi Peak. Some 20-30 yards south/southeast of the top (and easy to miss) is the blowhole—an opening dating back to the time when the volcano was spewing steam or hot gases. This entrance to the underworld is hidden from view behind rocks until you are very close to it. It is dangerous and drops down steeply after a few yards, so keep out of the hole. Most likely, you will reach the top without having seen the blowhole.

Time to enjoy the views. To the west and southwest, the Rio Grande flows through White Rock Canyon, and the Jemez Mountains appear in the distance. Black Mesa can be seen to the northeast and the Sangre de Cristos stretch across the horizon toward the east and northeast. Closer by, to the south, you will see the Caja del Rio volcanic field with its dark hills. *Note: Otowi Peak is just south of the San Ildefonso Indian Reservation boundary, beyond which a permit is needed. Respect the land and do not wander any further north than the peak itself.*

Return - To return, retrace your route and go back the same way you came.

Alternate Return - Instead of heading straight for the trail, you can follow the western edge of the mesa all the way to the tip of the west "finger" and then continue along the east side of the finger to your trail. This route offers dramatic views into White Rock Canyon.

Leave the peak in a southerly direction and, after bypassing the first gully at the foot of the peak, head for the edge of the mesa on your right. Stay close to the edge, swerving left only to avoid steep drainages. Take time to look back once in a while. Awesome views of Otowi Peak and the canyon below!

Just before you reach the tip of the finger, you will come to a place where the mesa's edge on your right forms an overhang. Watch it! Some 40 minutes after leaving the peak, you should come to the tip of the finger. Turn left now, still following the edge of the mesa. You are heading toward the place where the two fingers join. Stay on top of the mesa, close to the edge. Soon the terrain descends a bit and you will come to a drainage. Cross the drainage and remain on top of the mesa. Two or three minutes later, you will come to a second drainage. This drainage is your landmark. Look for a trail or cairns on the other side of the drainage and start heading down. Go down the way you came up and back to your car.

This grand show is eternal. It is always sunrise somewhere; the dew is never all dried at once; a shower is forever falling; vapor is ever rising. Eternal surnrise, eternal sunset, eternal dawn and gloaming, on sea and continents and islands, each in its turn, as the round earth rolls.

~ John Muir

View of the Rio Grande in White Rock Canyon

Petroglyphs in White Rock Canyon

32 Blue Dot / Red Dot Trails

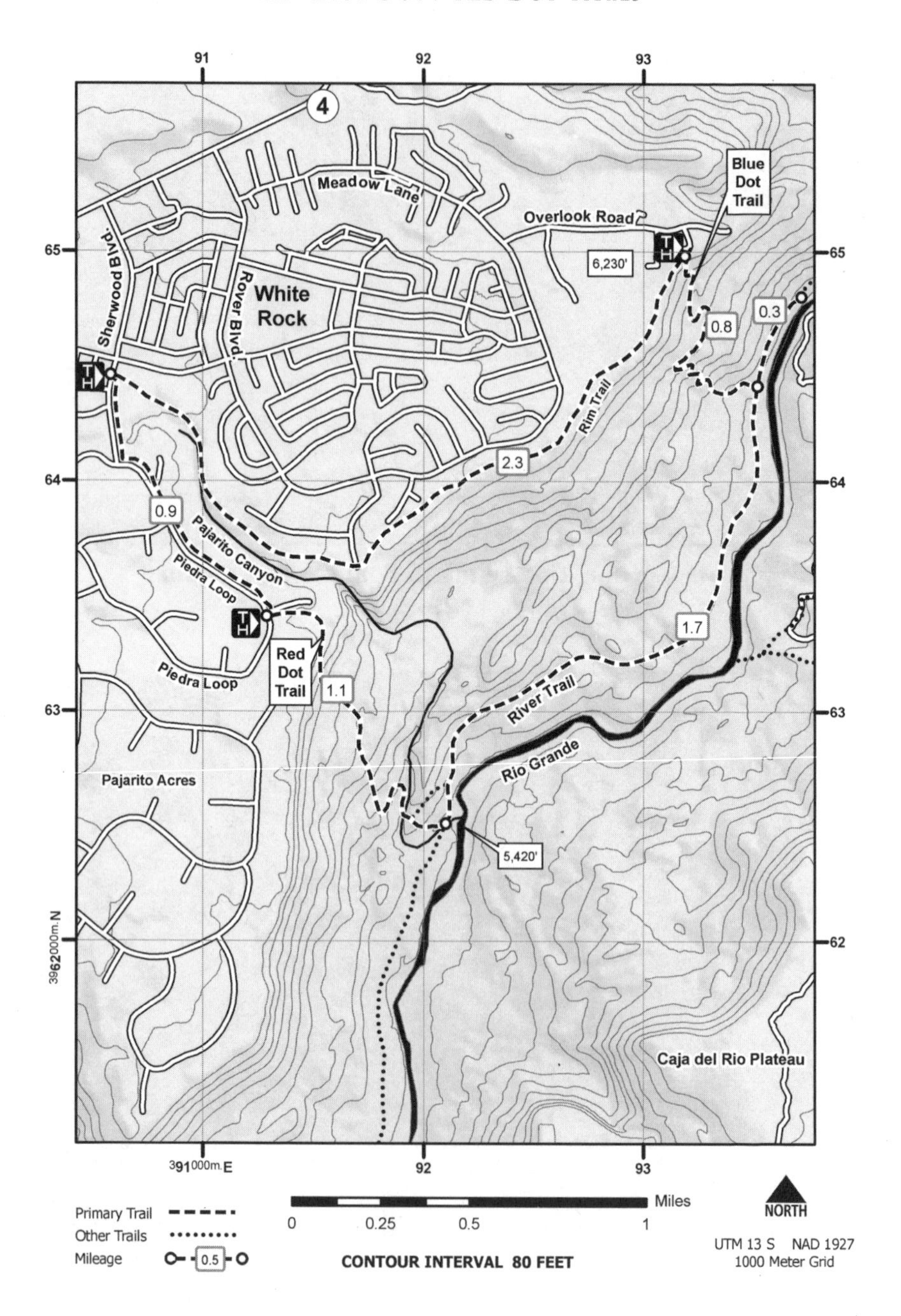

32 - Blue Dot / Red Dot Trails

by Eliza Schmid and Norbert Sperlich

Two rocky trails that lead from the rim to the bottom of White Rock Canyon, connected via a serene trail along the Rio Grande, including petroglyphs, springs, a waterfall, and great views of the river.

RT Distance: 2.5 miles (Blue Dot only)
2.5 miles (Red Dot only)
7.5 miles (Blue Dot/Red Dot Loop)

Time: 3 hrs (Blue Dot only)
3 hrs (Red Dot only)
6+ hrs (Blue Dot/Red Dot Loop)

Elevation Range: 6250-5450 ft; gain 800 ft (Blue Dot only)
6330-5420 ft; gain 850 ft (Red Dot only)
gain 1000 ft (Blue Dot/Red Dot Loop)

Rating: Moderate, short, steep (Red or Blue Dot)
Strenuous (Blue Dot/Red Dot Loop)

RT Drive: ~70 miles; ~1½ hrs

Seasons: Hike can be done year round. Not much shade. Very hot in summer - start early.

Maps: USGS White Rock - 7.5' series.

Blue Dot TH: 393,222 mE 3,964,982 mN elev.6231'
Red Dot TH: 391,300 mE 3,963,417 mN elev.6335'

Summary

From the outskirts of White Rock, two trails, marked by blue or red dots, respectively, take you from the rim to the bottom of White Rock Canyon, offering sweeping views along the way. White Rock Canyon is a rugged gorge, cut by the Rio Grande through lava flows that originated some two to three million years ago. The dominant rock in the canyon is dark, almost black basalt. White rock formations (ash layers from more recent eruptions) are few and far between.

Dropping 800 ft in less than a mile, the Blue and Red Dot Trails are not for hikers used to well-maintained paths. Steep, rocky sections require some scrambling, and loose gravel makes for poor footing. Sturdy hiking boots and hiking poles will help you navigate the difficult sections. Do not drink water from the springs along the way. Bring your own water, and plenty of it. Respect the petroglyphs (please do not touch) and other signs of past human occupation. Ancestors of today's Tewa Indians were cultivating their fields in the canyon until the mid-1500s.

For a short but rugged excursion (~2½ miles RT), take either trail down to the river. If you want to add a few miles, continue along the River Trail. For a longer hike, try the Blue Dot / Red Dot loop. This loop combines Blue and Red Dot Trails with the River Trail and the Rim Trail and includes hiking on pavement for about one mile.

Driving Directions

Take US 84/285 north to Pojoaque (~16 miles). There, take the Los Alamos exit (NM 502) on the right. After a traffic light, the road goes through an underpass and on toward Los Alamos. In about 7 miles, NM 502 crosses the Rio Grande and climbs to a Y-intersection, where you take the right branch towards White Rock and Bandelier. About 1½ miles past the "Y," continue straight ahead through a traffic light (the intersection with the Los Alamos Truck Route) toward White Rock. Continue to the first traffic light in White Rock.

Blue Dot Trail or Blue Dot / Red Dot Loop – At the traffic light, take a left onto Rover Blvd., then take the first left onto Meadow Lane. After 0.8 miles on Meadow Lane, take a left onto Overlook Park Road. Drive for ½ mile, turn right (after a fenced soccer field) at a sign "Blue Dot Trail" and park in the spacious parking area.

Red Dot Trail – At the traffic light, go straight ahead for 0.3 miles, then turn left onto Sherwood Blvd. Stay on Sherwood for 0.9

miles, until it ends at a T-junction with Piedra Loop. Go left on Piedra Loop for 0.6 miles to a trail sign (on the left or east side of the road). Park near the sign, on the side of the road.

Hiking Instructions

Blue Dot Trail only - The trail starts at an information kiosk near the parking area. Some 30 yards from the kiosk, at a trail crossing, continue straight ahead to a T-junction at the canyon rim. Go left to an opening in a fence, marked with a blue dot on a piece of wood. The descent begins here on a steep slope with poor footing. Next comes a level section with sagebrush and river gravel, followed by more switchbacks and loose gravel underfoot. There are great views of Buckman Mesa (see BUCKMAN MESA Hike #31) and the Sangre de Cristo Mountains to the northeast. After another level stretch, the trail descends again. About 30 minutes into the hike, it enters a juniper forest. In another 10 minutes, you will come to a small creek to the right of the trail and to a trail fork, marked by a cairn. The left branch of the trail is the continuation of the Blue Dot Trail; the right branch is the River Trail that goes downstream to meet the Red Dot Trail in about 2 miles. Take the Blue Dot Trail to the left. Soon, it approaches the river and follows it upstream. There are several short spur trails that go down to the water. The main trail is obstructed first by boulders, then by vegetation. About 10 minutes past the cairn, it ends at a small sandy beach. A nearby cottonwood provides shade. This is a great rest stop. Check the sand for animal footprints and enjoy the river. Return the way you came.

Blue Dot / Red Dot Loop - Take the Blue Dot Trail (previous section) to the trail fork with the cairn. There, take the River Trail to the right. It crosses a small stream and enters a forest of tall junipers. After crossing a swampy spot and two more small streams, it reaches a more open area where the junipers are small. Soon, the trail passes badly eroded land on the right and crosses a drainage. The junipers get taller again, and the Rio Grande appears on the left. After crossing another little stream, the trail traverses a steep slope and crosses an arroyo. Next, it moves away from the river, crossing first a sandy, open stretch with lots of prickly pear cactus, then traversing ground that is covered with rounded river rocks.

After about 1 hour of hiking on the river trail, you will reach a high point. Twenty minutes later, the trail enters another juniper woodlands and crosses another little stream. The trail moves closer to the Rio Grande, and in a few minutes reaches a more substantial stream that is fed by the nearby Pajarito Springs. At this point, leave the River Trail (it continues downstream for about a mile or so) and follow the little stream uphill (to the right). After a few minutes, you will come to a delightful spot where a small waterfall drops into a little pool. Take a rest, a dip in the pool, perhaps eat lunch, and watch dragonflies hovering over the water.

Cross the stream and find the Red Dot Trail (look for the red dots). It runs parallel to the stream, going over some rocky areas and then crossing to the right side of the stream. Keep looking for red dots or painted arrows. At the next trail fork, take the right branch that heads towards a steep slope (the left branch goes toward the stream). Look for a red dot up ahead. The trail goes up a ridge and soon returns to the stream. It crosses the stream at a beautiful spot, with large boulders and small pools. This is another good place for a break before the climb that lies ahead. The trail now ascends steeply. For a few minutes, tall junipers shelter you. As the view opens, look up and ahead. See any petroglyphs? After reaching a level area, the trail starts climbing again. Follow the red dots. About 1 hour after the last stream crossing, you will reach the rim of the canyon. In another five minutes you will arrive at the Red Dot trailhead and Piedra Loop Road (paved).

Turn right and follow Piedra Loop for about ½ mile, then turn right onto Sherwood Blvd. After passing intersections with Cañada Way and Barcelona Avenue on your left, look for a gate (two metal poles and a chain) and a trail sign on your right. Go through the gate and look to the right for an information board and the trailhead for the White Rock Canyon Rim Trail. You have about 2½ miles yet to go. The trail is poorly marked, with spur trails going off on both sides, those on the right going to the edge of Pajarito Canyon, and those on the left going to nearby houses. Stay on the main trail. After about 30 minutes of hiking through a landscape that is less than inspiring (dead piñons, eroded soil), you will reach the edge of the mouth of Pajarito Canyon. Breathtaking views! And there is a trail marker. Finally! A few minutes later, you will reach an overlook with dramatic views over White Rock Canyon. From here on, hike close to the rim and stay to the left of it. Step up to the rim once in a while to enjoy the views. After 30 minutes of hiking along the rim, you will see floodlights sticking up above the trees to the left of you. Stay on the trail close to the rim. In about 10 minutes, you will come to the fence and the blue dot marker where the Blue Dot Trail goes through the fence. It is only one more minute to your car.

Red Dot Trail - Follow Driving Directions to Red Dot Trail. A few wooden steps will take you from the road where you parked to the trailhead. In about 5 minutes, you are at the rim of White Rock Canyon. The first part of the steep descent looks a bit intimidating. You have to scramble down over basalt rocks before the trail levels out at the base of the cliffs. There is another steep descent, followed by a more level section, and yet another steep drop. Along the trail, you will see junipers, cholla and prickly pear cacti, and yucca plants. As you get further down and closer to the stream that comes from the nearby Pajarito Springs, vegetation is more abundant. Close to the water, the junipers are tall. The first stream crossing is at a beautiful spot with large basalt boulders near the stream and watercress lining the banks. The trail then briefly climbs above the stream over a ridge and goes down again. As it approaches the second stream crossing, look for red dots painted on rocks. The trail now goes to the left, following the stream. Ignore trails that branch off the main trail and do not have red dots. Some five minutes after the second stream crossing, listen for the sound of a small waterfall (not visible from the trail) on your left. The water drops into a small pool, and dragonflies congregate here in the summer. This makes a very nice rest spot. To reach the Rio Grande, follow the Red Dot Trail for another couple of minutes.

Just before you get to the banks of the Rio Grande, you cross the River Trail. You can extend your hike by following the River Trail in either direction. This unmarked trail goes upstream for about 2 miles to connect with the Blue Dot Trail, and downstream for about 1 mile or so. If the trail you are on fizzles out soon, you are on a spur trail branching off from the River Trail. Try again!

To return to your car, retrace your steps. By following the red dots, you will again cross the stream twice, and then the steep uphill climb begins. Once you leave the thicket of tall junipers, look up ahead and to the left. You might see some petroglyphs, among them the depiction of three snakes in an almost abstract, contemporary style. Make sure you stay on the trail. Let the red dots guide you back to the rim.

Petroglyphs near the Red Dot Trail

White Rock Canyon

33 Ancho Rapids

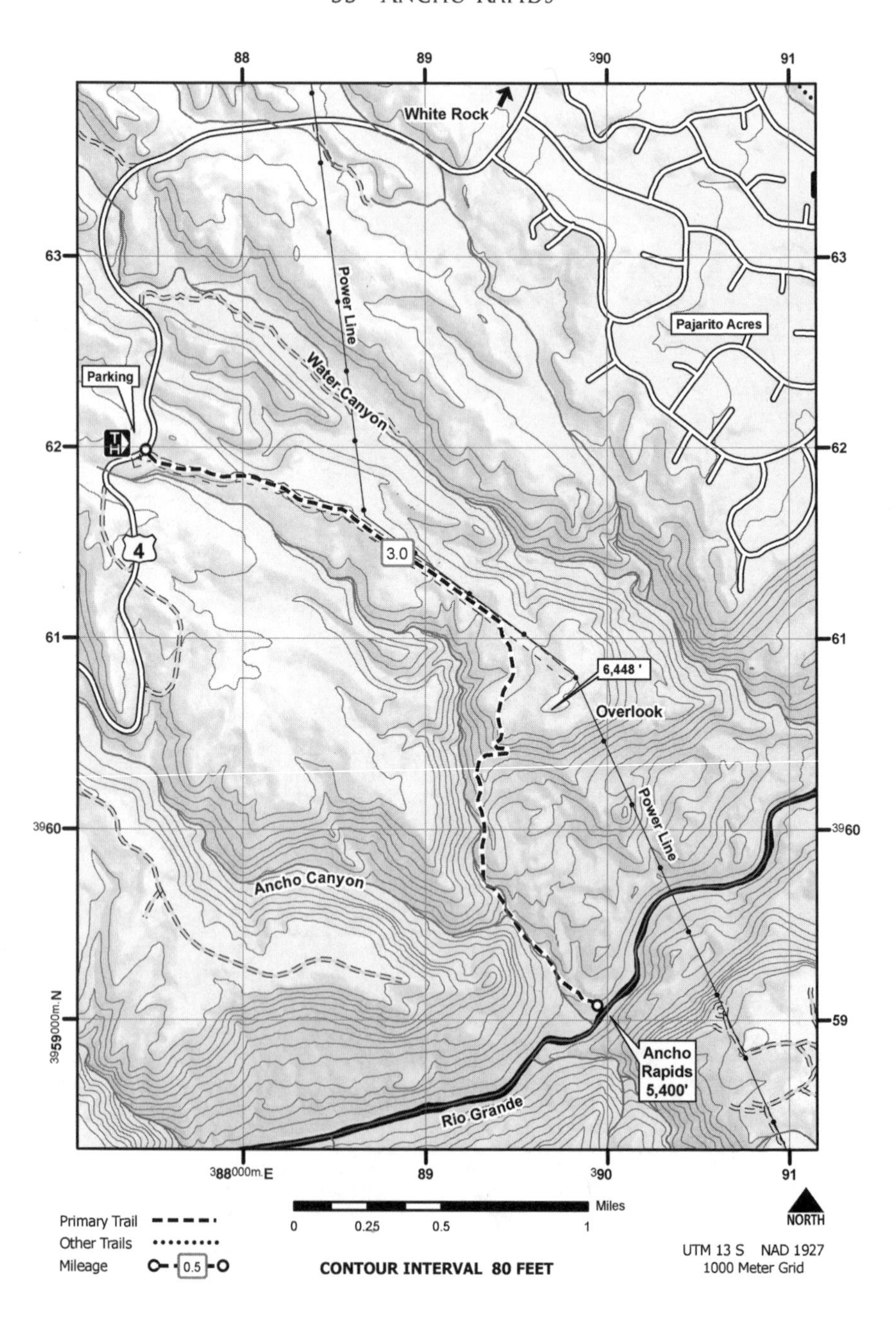

33 - Ancho Rapids

by Bill and Linda Zwick

A rugged steep hike to the Rio Grande at the bottom of White Rock Canyon.

RT Distance:	6 miles (7 miles if side trip included)
Time:	3 hrs (+30 min for side trip)
Elevation Range:	5460-6500 ft; total gain 1040 ft
Rating:	Moderate
RT Drive:	74 miles; 1½ hrs
Seasons:	Potentially very hot in summer and may be slippery when wet or after snowfall, but generally a year-round hike.
Maps:	USGS White Rock - 7.5' series.
Trailhead:	387,405 mE 3,961,956 mN elev.6530'

Summary

This hike starts along a service road and then descends steeply into scenic Ancho Canyon (ancho means "wide" in Spanish). There you will follow a little stream down to the Rio Grande. Sturdy shoes are recommended. Cacti abound, so people and dogs should be careful not to get spines in their feet.

Driving Directions

Take US 84/285 north to Pojoaque (~16 miles). There, take the Los Alamos exit (NM 502) on the right. After a traffic light, the road goes through an underpass and on toward Los Alamos. In about 7 miles, NM 502 crosses the Rio Grande and climbs to a Y-intersection, where you take the right branch towards White Rock. About 1½ miles past the "Y," continue straight ahead through a traffic light (the intersection with the Los Alamos Truck Route) toward White Rock and Bandelier. After driving through the first traffic light in White Rock, you arrive at the second traffic signal (the intersection with Pajarito Road). Check your odometer reading here and continue straight, still heading south, in the direction of Bandelier for 3.2 miles.

As you approach a yellow diamond-shaped sign indicating that the road will turn left (the fifth such sign after White Rock), look for gate No. 4 on the left side of the road. There is a graveled parking area and a metal "Notice" sign in front of this gate. Pedestrian access is through an entrance to the right of the large gate.

Hiking Instructions

Proceed through the angled pedestrian access. The hike follows a road built for the installation of power lines. This portion of the hike toward the Rio Grande provides spectacular vistas of the Sangre de Cristo Mountains (especially nice in the fall when the aspen are golden) and the return provides nice views of the Jemez Mountains and Bandelier. You will cross under a power line that heads north and south, and about 1 mile into the hike, the road will converge with another power line that heads east. Note the radio telescope dish to your right (south). This Los Alamos facility is part of an array of radio telescopes stretching to the South Pacific. Continue walking east on the road. Looking down, you might notice large ant hills shimmering in the sunlight, a result of the ants mining quartz grains to make their homes.

About 1¾ miles from the start of the hike, the road will descend and then begin to rise toward the canyon rim. Shortly after you begin ascending, a road branches off to the right (southeast). Here you have a choice of going directly down into White Rock Canyon (on the right branch of the road fork) or to continue on the road straight ahead that follows the power line to an overlook with spectacular views of the canyon. The side trip to the overlook will add about 1 mile to the hike. The road that goes off to the right ends in about ½ mile. At this point, you are at the rim of Ancho Canyon. Note the broken-down fence and gate that once prevented cattle from descending into the canyon to graze. Bear to your right (toward the sandstone cliff) and you will find a trail winding through rockfall, which will then begin a steep traverse to the bottom of the canyon. The trail shows little sign of use, is eroded and rocky in places, but is easy to follow.

At the bottom of the canyon, the trail is mostly obvious, but cairns aid your travel here. When the canyon bottom levels out, you will find a spring-fed stream to your right. It's a nice place to rest after your climb down or before beginning your climb back up. The authors shared this rest spot with a large, but shy, black bear! The river is not far from here and the trail and cairns will take you to the water's edge. If you see the skeleton of a fallen cottonwood on the way to the river, take a closer look. Teeth marks at the bottom end of the trunk will tell you that beavers cut the tree down.

You can explore the bank of the river for varying distances, depending on the water level. Note the dead tamarisk and oak high on the river banks—a result of the high water level of Cochiti Reservoir some years ago. Rocks and debris washed from Ancho Canyon in flash floods have formed Ancho Rapids, the most difficult rapid in White Rock Canyon for river runners.

Return the way you came.

Watching the circling seasons, listening to the songs of the waters and winds and birds, would be endless pleasure. And what glorious cloud-lands I would see, storms and calms, a new heaven and a new earth every day.

~ John Muir

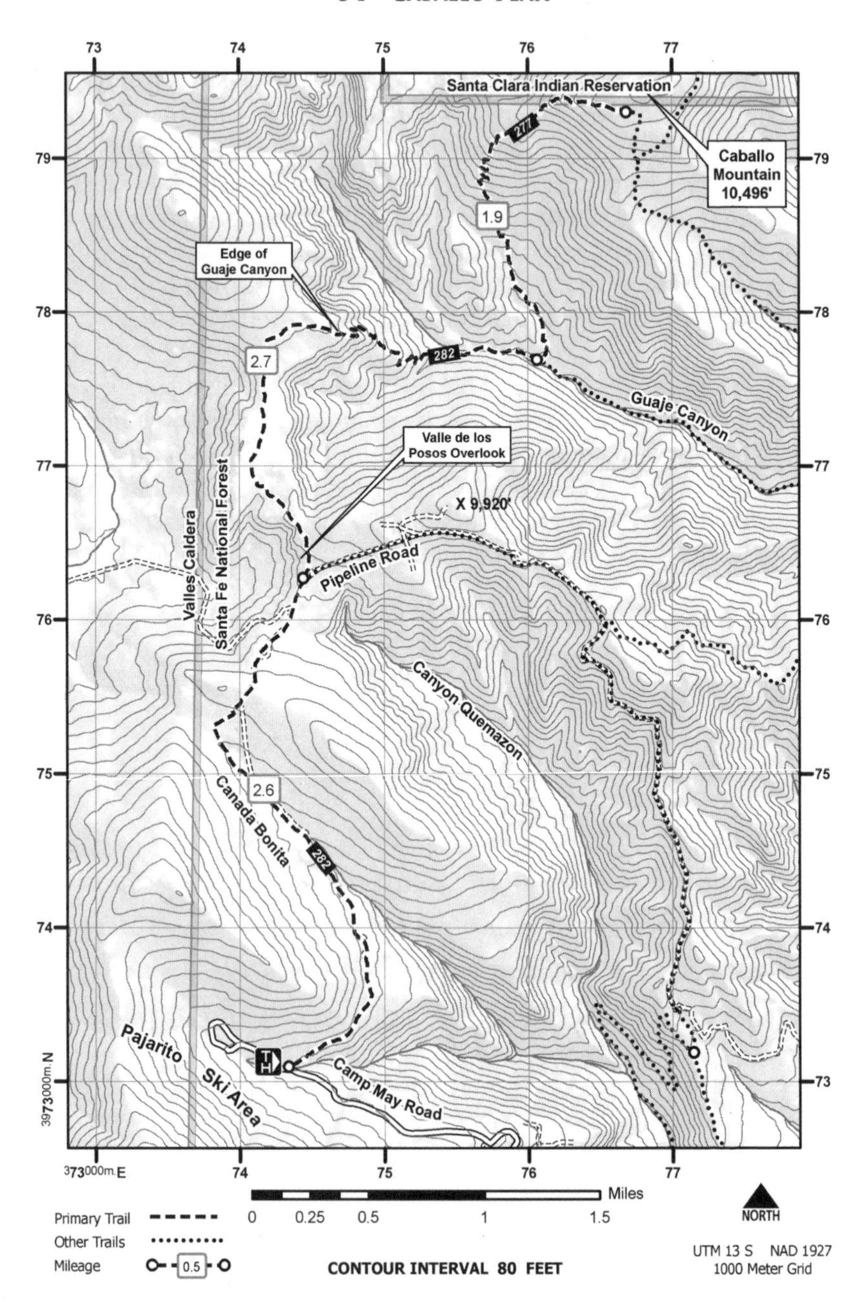
Santa Clara Indian Reservation
Caballo Mountain 10,496'
277
1.9
Edge of Guaje Canyon
2.7
282
Guaje Canyon
Valle de los Posos Overlook
X 9,920'
Pipeline Road
Valles Caldera
Santa Fe National Forest
Canyon Quemazon
2.6
Canada Bonita
282
Pajarito Ski Area
Camp May Road
373000m.E
3973000m.N
Miles
0 0.25 0.5 1 1.5
NORTH
Primary Trail
Other Trails
Mileage
0.5
CONTOUR INTERVAL 80 FEET
UTM 13 S NAD 1927
1000 Meter Grid

34 - CABALLO PEAK

by Norbert Sperlich

A high country hike near Los Alamos, offering a pleasant serene meadow on the first (easy) portion, and a sweeping panorama at the top of Caballo Mountain on the final portion.

RT Distance: 3.5 miles (Cañada Bonita)
6 miles (Valle de los Posos Overlook)
8.5 miles (Edge of Guaje Canyon)
15 miles (Caballo Mountain)

Time: 2 hrs (Cañada Bonita)
3 hrs (Valle de los Posos Overlook)
4 hrs (Edge of Guaje Canyon)
8 hrs (Caballo Mountain)

Elevation Range: 9220-9650 ft; gain 650 ft (Posos Overlook)
9220-9650 ft; gain 1000 ft (Guaje Cyn)
8600-10,450 ft; gain 3800 ft (Caballo Mtn)

Rating: Easy/Moderate/Strenuous, depending on the distance hiked.

RT Drive: ~86 miles; 2+ hrs

Seasons: Not a winter hike. Trails might be clear of snow from May to October. Cañada Bonita is especially beautiful in the fall, when the aspens are golden, and in the early summer when wild irises bloom.

Maps: USGS Valle Toledo, Guaje Mountain (for the top of Caballo Mountain) - 7.5' series. On the Valle Toledo map, look in the lower right corner for a road called "Camp May Road." Just past the ski area (toward Camp May), a trail goes off in a northerly direction. This is your trailhead. Sky Terrain's *Santa Fe, Bandelier & Los Alamos* is also recommended.

Trailhead: 374,350 mE 3,973,077 mN elev.9235'

Summary

A hike to the high country near Los Alamos. The first part is an easy walk and takes you to a high meadow (Cañada Bonita) and to the rim of the Valles Caldera (Valle de los Posos Overlook). For a moderate hike, continue to the edge of Guaje Canyon. For a strenuous hike, cross Guaje Canyon and climb to the top of Caballo Mountain. Great views across the Rio Grande Valley! Leave early with plenty of water if you plan to do the whole hike.

Driving Directions

Take US 84/285 north to Pojoaque (~16 miles from Santa Fe). There, take the Los Alamos exit (NM 502) on the right. After a traffic light, the road goes through an underpass and on toward Los Alamos. In about 7 miles, NM 502 crosses the Rio Grande and climbs to a Y-intersection, where you take the right branch toward White Rock and Bandelier. About 1½ miles from the "Y," turn right at a traffic light. You are now on East Jemez Road (the Los Alamos Truck Route). After about 5½ miles, East Jemez Road approaches an intersection and traffic light. A left turn takes you through the Los Alamos National Laboratory (LANL) guard gates (where you should be able to pass through showing some form of identification—e.g., a driver's license), allowing you to continue onto West Jemez Road. (If you go straight through the traffic light, it will take you over the Omega bridge in the direction of the Los Alamos townsite.) If, because of a heightened security level, you are not allowed to pass through the Laboratory gates, you may be re-directed—e.g., to West Road on the north side of the bridge (a left turn), which will connect via a bypass to the Los Alamos Ski Area road and, to the left, West Jemez Road; or the longer way via NM 4 past the entrance to Bandelier.

For this hike, you want to reach the Pajarito Ski Area. If you passed through the LANL guard gates, continue up West Jemez Road about 1½ miles to the Ski Area road on your right. Turn right here and drive 4.4 miles on a narrow, winding road. Drive through the parking area, then down a short hill. At the bottom of the hill, park in a small parking area on your left.

Hiking Instructions

Across from where you parked, on the other side of the road, a dirt road goes off the main road. The dirt road crosses and then follows a seasonal stream off to your right. This is your trail. Some 40 yards along this road there is an information board for Santa Fe National Forest on your left and a worn sign "Guaje Canyon Trail 282, Cañada Bonita 1, Pipeline Road 3" to your right. Shortly after, the road reaches a gate and then heads uphill. At the crest, choose one of two routes of equal length to Cañada Bonita; one goes left and along a foot-worn cross-country ski path, and the other is the road you are on. By either way, you will hike in the shadow of enormous aspens and Douglas fir. In about 30 minutes, you will reach Cañada Bonita, a meadow that has not been grazed since Los Alamos was established in 1943. For approximately ½ mile, you hike on a footpath and gently uphill along the western edge of the meadow. Soon the trail turns right, crosses the meadow and goes up a slope toward and through a stand of aspens. The trail then crosses a ridge and heads down among Douglas fir. You will next reach and cross a gate, after which the trail widens to a road that heads north and gently uphill. A short distance from the gate, the road forks. The right fork is Pipeline Road. Take the left and less-traveled fork, which, in another 50 yards, will take you to the first overlook of the Valle de los Posos. The "Valley of the Holes"—the holes are prairie dog burrows—is part of the huge Valles Caldera, a 13-mile-diameter, crater-like depression that originated about a million years ago after the eruption and collapse of an enormous magma chamber. From the overlook, rejoin the trail, go left at a Y intersection, and look left for a signpost indicating "Guaje Canyon, Trail 282, Guaje Canyon 2." Bear left at this sign to follow the Guaje Canyon Trail. You are now hiking on the narrow rim of the Valles Caldera. The trail heads uphill and north. After the trail crests and gently descends, look left and walk toward a rocky outcropping and prominent cliff above the Caldera. From here, you have another and grander view into the Valle de los Posos. It's also a good place to rest. If you came for an easy hike, turn around here.

The Guaje Canyon trail meanders in a northerly direction until it turns east and begins a gradual descent toward the edge of Guaje Canyon. The descent then becomes straight and steep. Just when it seems the trail would end at the edge of a cliff, look for the trail's hairpin turn to the left and down into Guaje Canyon. The turn should be marked by cairns. Before continuing on, step to the edge for a view. To the northeast and across Guaje Canyon is Caballo Mountain. Santa Fe Baldy and Lake Peak are in the distance to the east. For a moderate hike, this is a good place to turn around.

Those with time and energy to spare will now head down the steep trail into Guaje Canyon. After a descent of 700 ft in about ½ mile, the trail levels, nears the canyon bottom, and crosses a permanent stream. The trail then goes east, with the stream at your right. Follow the trail downstream for about 10 minutes to reach the intersection with the Caballo Trail. The junction, marked with cairns, is the lowest point of the hike. The highest point is only 2 miles away but 1900 ft up. A campsite and small fire ring along the Guaje Canyon Trail just opposite the Caballo trailhead might help you spot the turn.

Turn left onto the Caballo Trail. After a brief climb, the trail drops into a drainage before turning right to ascend the east side of the drainage. In about ½ mile, the trail levels off slightly, and comes alongside a trickle fed by a nearby spring. The trail jogs left across a runnel and then bears left (west) and up just before reaching the source of the spring. Time to catch your breath. You have about 1½ miles and an hour or so to go.

Within a few minutes, you begin a series of switchbacks that alternate east and west. Afterwards, the trail levels off and meanders northeast through thick stands of Douglas fir. Near the top, the trail comes to a small clearing in the trees. Go straight across the clearing (heading east) and find the trail on the other side.

You are now minutes from your destination—Caballo's wide, south-facing meadow near the peak. A sign at the edge of the meadow tells you to stay on the trail and not to disturb sacred objects. The sign also refers to the Agua Piedra Trail, which, in days past, crossed the top of Caballo Mountain and entered Santa Clara Pueblo land. Hikers are no longer welcome on Santa Clara land. Therefore, stay on the south side of the summit and don't go into the trees at the very top.

Enjoy the sweeping panorama south to east along the Rio Grande Valley, with the Sangre de Cristos in the background toward the east, the Sandias and Ortiz toward the south, and, closer by, Pajarito Mountain and St. Peter's Dome. For views toward the north, go past the sign and walk east with the edge of the trees to your left. In a few minutes, you will reach a place where the forest forms a corner. Turn left at the corner, still keeping the trees to your left. Ahead in the distance, the Truchas come into view.

Return the same way you came.

Upper Crossing

☞

Frijoles Canyon

35 Upper Crossing Loop

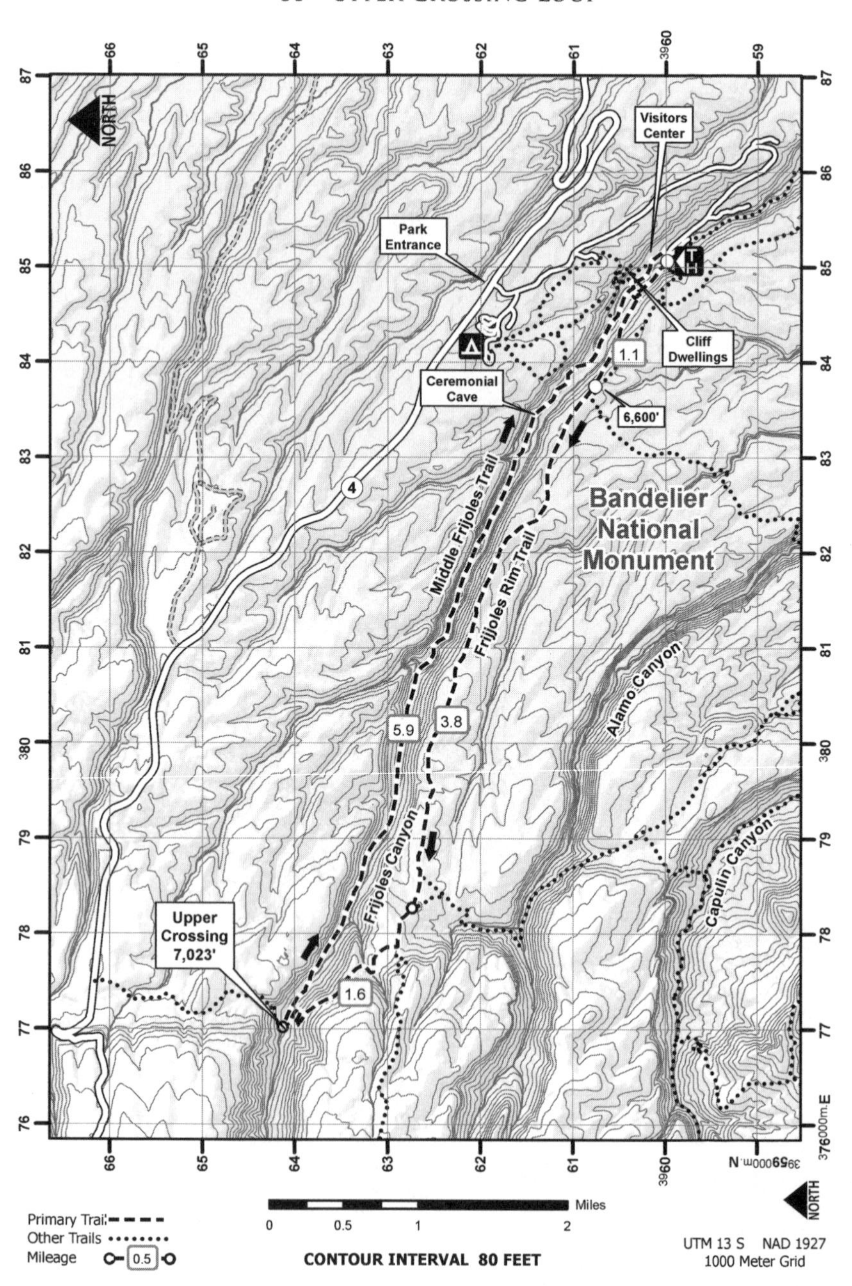

35 - UPPER CROSSING LOOP

by Joe Whelan

This scenic hike follows the southern rim of Frijoles Canyon and returns along Frijoles Creek at the bottom of the canyon.

RT Distance: 13 miles
Time: 7 hrs
Elevation Range: 6066–7400 ft; total gain ~1600 ft
Rating: Strenuous
RT Drive: 92 miles; ~2 hrs 30 min
Seasons: Can be uncomfortably hot in midsummer. In winter, the mesa top is usually lightly snow-covered or muddy, and the stream crossings are icy. Most beautiful during late fall.
Maps: USGS Frijoles - 7.5' series. *Bandelier National Monument, Trails Illustrated* shows all the trails (available at Bandelier Headquarters). Sky Terrain's *Santa Fe, Bandelier & Los Alamos* is also recommended.
Fees: Entrance $12/car
Trailhead: 385,113 mE 3,959,960 mN elev.6064'

Summary

The first part of this well-marked loop hike takes you up to the high mesa that rims Frijoles Canyon. You will enjoy views of nearby Indian ruins and distant mountain ranges. On the return, you will hike at the bottom of the narrow canyon, with its sparkling stream, mixed forests and orange tuff cliffs. If you hike quietly, you may see deer along the trail. In the fall, large herds of elk enter this part of the monument to escape hunters in the adjacent Santa Fe National Forest. On the mesa top, the trail passes through two burn eas: the 1977 La Mesa Fire and the Lummis Canyon Burn of 1997. The return trail features 25 stream crossings on flattened logs or flat rocks. In winter, these crossings are usually icy and very slippery, making this part of the loop especially challenging. No dogs are allowed in Bandelier.

Driving Directions

Drive north on US 84/285 (~16 miles) to Pojoaque. Take the Los Alamos exit from the right lane, then turn left under the overpass and proceed west towards Los Alamos on NM 502. In about 7 miles, NM 502 crosses the Rio Grande and climbs to a well-marked "Y" intersection. Take the right leg, NM 4, toward Bandelier and White Rock. About 1½ miles from the "Y" is a stoplight. You drive straight ahead toward White Rock and Bandelier. The entrance to Bandelier is beyond White Rock, about 12½ miles from the "Y." There is an entrance fee. Drive to the Visitor Center and across the bridge over Rio Frijoles, turn left, and park in the area designated for back country hikers.

Hiking Instructions

From the back country hikers' parking area across the bridge from the Visitor Center, walk back up the paved road past the bridge about 50 yards to a posted map and information board. Your trail starts here on the right of the map. It leads uphill to a sign listing Frijolito, Yapashi and Painted Cave. Take the trail behind the sign about 100 ft to a junction and second sign. Follow the sign for the Yapashi Pueblo Trail to the right (northwest) for ¼ mile to another junction and sign, where you will turn left onto the uphill switchback to Yapashi Pueblo Trail and follow it to the top of the south rim. On this portion of the trail, there are good views of the ruins in and on the north side of Frijoles Canyon. From the top of the rim you can see the Ceremonial Cave and the long ladders leading up to it, directly across the canyon.

Once on the rim, there will be five trail junctions before you return to the bottom of Frijoles Canyon. At all five of these junctions, take the trail to your right. At the first four junctions, the signs will point toward the Upper Crossing; at the fifth junction, follow the sign toward Ponderosa Campground. The trail descends in this last mile to the bottom of the canyon. Here again, you will go to your right toward the Visitor Center.

Before you start hiking downstream, you might enjoy having lunch at a clearing a few feet further along the Ponderosa Campground trail. Go about 50 ft along the trail and cross the creek on a log bridge to the small clearing where the trail begins to climb out of the canyon. This area is usually sunny even in winter. There are several large rocks on which to rest.

After this detour to the clearing, cross back over the creek to the Upper Crossing signpost. Return to the Visitor Center by following the sign at Upper Crossing to the Park Headquarters (6 miles) downstream. This return trail through the narrow canyon bottom and along the stream is bordered by steep, colorful tuff formations and is heavily wooded. There are no junctions along the 6 miles of return trail, but there are 25 stream crossings, most of them with primitive bridges. At the Ceremonial Cave ruins, (1 mile from Visitor Center), the trail widens to a nature trail and finally reaches the paved picnic grounds road and back country hikers' parking area.

Stone Lions ☞

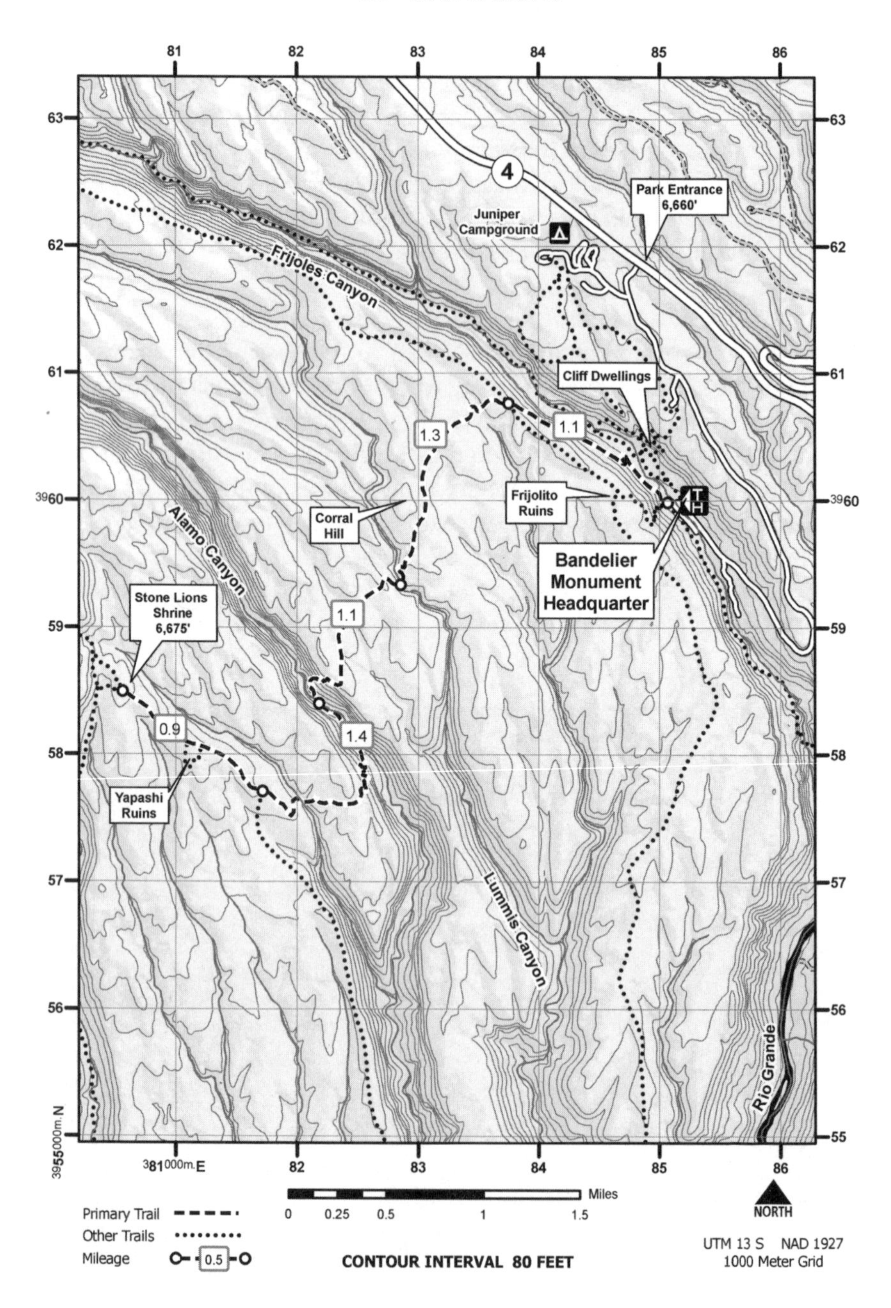

Park Entrance 6,660'
Juniper Campground
Frijoles Canyon
Cliff Dwellings
Frijolito Ruins
Corral Hill
Bandelier Monument Headquarter
Alamo Canyon
Stone Lions Shrine 6,675'
Yapashi Ruins
Lummis Canyon
Rio Grande
1.3
1.1
1.1
1.4
0.9
Miles
0 0.25 0.5 1 1.5
Primary Trail
Other Trails
Mileage 0.5
CONTOUR INTERVAL 80 FEET
NORTH
UTM 13 S NAD 1927
1000 Meter Grid

36 - Stone Lions

by Mickey Bogert

A challenging hike in the Bandelier backcountry.

RT Distance: 13 miles
Time: 8 hrs
Elevation Range: 6066-6660; total gain ~2700 ft
Rating: Strenuous
RT Drive: 92 miles; 2½ hrs
Seasons: Can be uncomfortably hot in summer. Snow may linger in winter.
Maps: USGS Frijoles - 7.5' series. More convenient is the Bandelier National Monument Map 209 made by Trails Illustrated showing hiking trails (available at the Visitor's Center). Sky Terrain's *Santa Fe, Bandelier & Los Alamos* is also recommended.
Fees: Entrance $12/car
Trailhead: 385,113 mE 3,959,960 mN elev.6064'

Summary

This is a challenging walk to an ancient shrine still used by Indians from the nearby pueblos. It is a strenuous hike because of the climbs in and out of several beautiful canyons, especially Alamo.

The walks across the mesa tops are easy, on good trails, with views of the Sangre de Cristo and Jemez Mountains. Vegetation has suffered greatly from drought and bark beetles. In the fall of 2004, most piñons and many ponderosa pines were dead but still standing. Will scrub oak take the place of the piñons? Just before the Stone Lions Shrine is Yapashi Pueblo, a large, unexcavated pueblo ruin. *Note: It is unlawful to remove anything from the National Monu-*

ment, especially Indian artifacts. No dogs are allowed in the National Monument. Carry plenty of water.

Driving Directions

Take US 84/285 north to Pojoaque (~16 miles). There, take the Los Alamos exit (NM 502) on the right. After a traffic light, the road goes through an underpass and on toward Los Alamos. In about 7 miles, NM 502 crosses the Rio Grande and climbs to a "Y" intersection, where you take the right branch toward White Rock and Bandelier. About 1½ miles from the "Y" is a stoplight (intersection with the Los Alamos Truck Route). You drive straight ahead through this light toward White Rock and Bandelier. The entrance to Bandelier is beyond White Rock, about 12½ miles from the "Y." There is an entrance fee. Drive to the Visitors Center and across the bridge over Rio Frijoles, turn left, and park in the area designated for back country hikers.

Hiking Instructions

From the parking area, walk back up the paved road, past the bridge about 50 yards where you will see an information board with a map on your left. This is your trailhead. Take the trail to the right of the board. It heads uphill to a sign listing Frijolito, Yapashi and Painted Cave. Thirty yards further up, the trail splits into three branches. Take the right branch to Yapashi Ruins. After ¼ mile, you will reach another fork. Take the left branch to Yapashi Ruins. The trail now climbs away from the canyon bottom. This is a fairly gradual climb and affords good views of the ruins in Frijoles Canyon. When you reach the top of the mesa you can see the Ceremonial Cave, with the long ladders leading up to it, directly across the canyon. A few yards further is a junction (1 mile from the Visitors Center), where you turn right toward Stone Lions. At the nearby next junction take the left branch to the Stone Lions via Yapashi, 5 miles. Continue on the Stone Lions Trail, crossing Lummis Canyon (identified by a sign) and the two tributary canyons on each side of it, and then on to the rim of Alamo Canyon.

For most of this distance, the vegetation is varied: juniper, scrub oak and some ponderosa, as well as yucca and cactus. Most of the once numerous piñons died in the drought years of 2002-2003. The previous canyon crossings are semi-shaded and fairly easy, so Alamo Canyon comes as a shock, as well as a spectacular surprise. There are beautiful views, but no shade, and there is a very steep switchback trail down a precipitous cliff.

The canyon bottom does have trees, and a stream during certain times of the year. Do not drink the water without treating it. The trail goes downstream for several hundred yards before crossing and starting steeply upwards on the south side of the canyon. The south rim of the canyon is a good place for a snack break, to enjoy the view, and to gather strength for the next 2 miles. One-half mile further, the trail crosses a shallow canyon with some nice shady spots. Next there is a trail junction with Lower Alamo Trail going left. Continue straight ahead to Yapashi. The vegetation south of Alamo is quite different: more arid in appearance, no more ponderosa. The junipers are shorter and the piñons are dead. Cactus is much more abundant. (From here on, when covered with snow, the trail may be difficult to follow. Look for cairns.)

One mile beyond the little canyon, in a westerly direction, is Yapashi Pueblo, now a mound of rubble. From here you will have magnificent views of many mountains—to the west, the San Miguel Mountains; south, the Sandias; southeast, the Ortiz and San Pedro Mountains; northwest, the Jemez; and to the northeast, the Sangre de Cristo Mountains. One-half mile beyond the Yapashi ruins, on your left and near a trail junction, you will see a small enclosure made of piled-up stones. In the middle is what's left of the stone lion carvings. Time and the elements have obliterated the heads but the backs and haunches remain. Most of us who come here sense a special atmosphere about this place. Remember, it is a sacred area, so please respect and enjoy it accordingly.

You may enter the circle with respect, but are requested not to sit, stand or climb on the stones, leave anything, or disturb the site in any way.

Return to your car over the same trails.

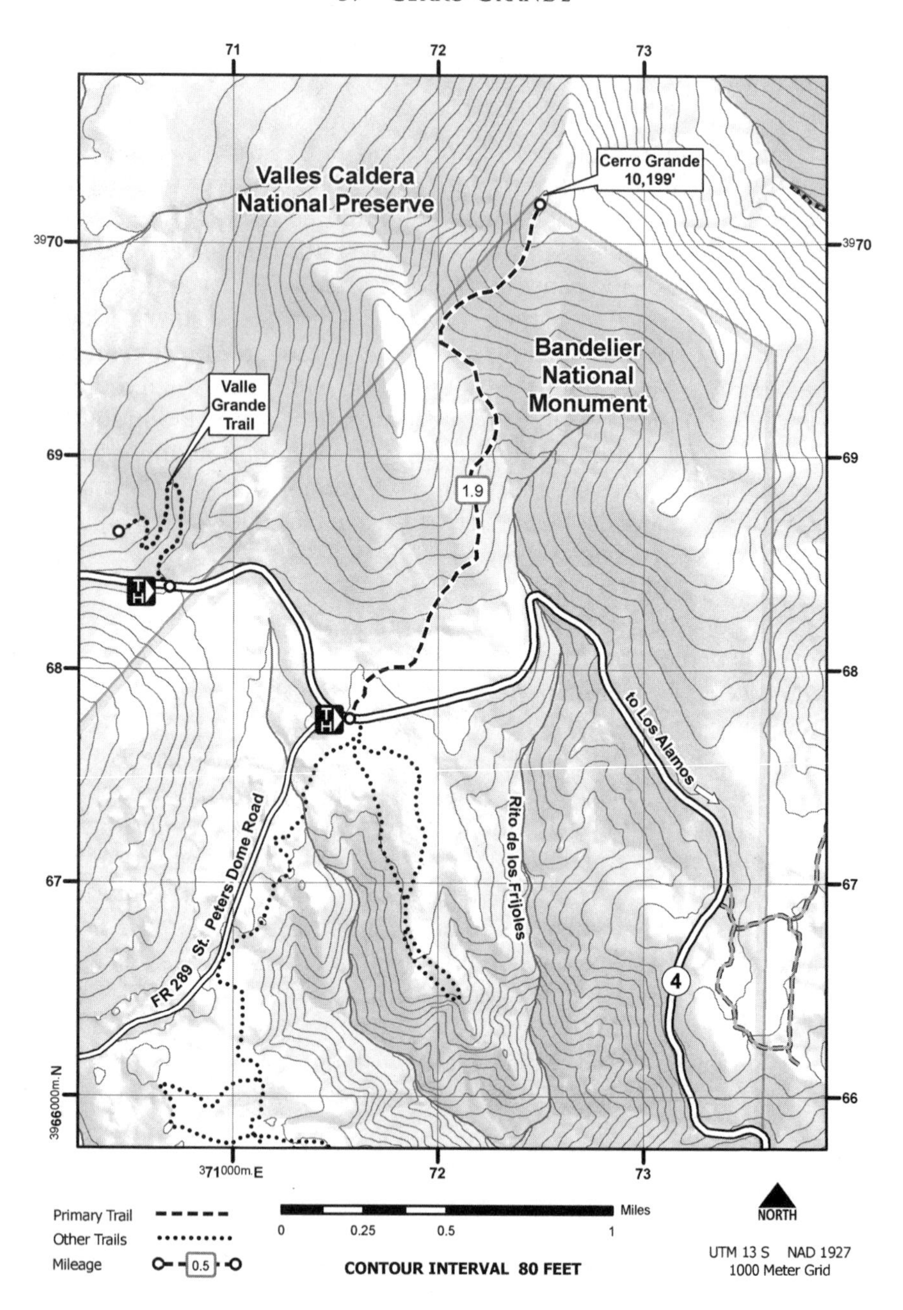
71
72
73
Cerro Grande
10,199'
Valles Caldera
National Preserve
3970
Bandelier
National
Monument
Valle
Grande
Trail
69
1.9
68
to Los Alamos
Rito de los Frijoles
St. Peters Dome Road
FR 289
67
4
3966000m.N
371000m.E
66
Primary Trail
Other Trails
Mileage
0.5
Miles
0
0.25
0.5
1
CONTOUR INTERVAL 80 FEET
NORTH
UTM 13 S NAD 1927
1000 Meter Grid

37 - CERRO GRANDE

by Norbert Sperlich

This hike leads through an open forest of ponderosa, aspen and conifers to the top of Cerro Grande (highest point in Bandelier) on the rim of the Valles Caldera with sweeping views into the Valle Grande and beyond.

RT Distance:	4 miles
Time:	3+ hrs
Elevation Range:	8,960–10,199 ft; total gain 1,300 ft
Rating:	Moderate; short but steep
RT Drive:	~90 miles; ~2½ hrs
Seasons:	Best from late spring to fall. Great for snowshoe hikes in winter.
Maps:	USGS Bland - 7.5' series. Bandelier National Monument, Map 209, by Trails Illustrated, and Sky Terrain's *Santa Fe, Bandelier & Los Alamos* are recommended.
Trailhead:	371,548 mE 3,967,751 mN elev.8955'

Summary

Located on the rim of the Valles Caldera, this is the highest part of Bandelier National Monument. Opened in September 2005, a primitive hiking route (unmaintained trail) leads through an open forest of ponderosa, aspen and conifers to the top of Cerro Grande, with sweeping views into the Valle Grande and beyond. Good chance of seeing game. Area closes at dusk. Dogs are not permitted in Bandelier (neither are off-road vehicles, cows, nor hunters). A hiker's paradise!

Driving Directions

Take US 84/285 north to Pojoaque (~16 miles from Santa Fe). There, take the Los Alamos exit (NM 502) on the right. After a traffic light, the road goes through an underpass and on toward Los Alamos. In about 7 miles, NM 502 crosses the Rio Grande and climbs to a Y-intersection, where you take the right branch toward White Rock and Bandelier. About 1½ miles from the "Y," turn right at a traffic light. You are now on East Jemez Road (the Los Alamos Truck Route). After about 5½ miles, East Jemez Road approaches an intersection and traffic light. A left turn takes you through the Los Alamos National Laboratory (LANL) guard gates (where you should be able to pass through showing some form of identification—e.g., a driver's license), allowing you to continue onto West Jemez Road. (If you go straight through the traffic light, it will take you over the Omega bridge in the direction of the Los Alamos townsite.) If, because of a heightened security level, you are not allowed to pass through the Laboratory gates, you may be re-directed—e.g., to West Road on the north side of the bridge (a left turn), which will connect via a bypass to the Los Alamos Ski Area road and, to the left, West Jemez Road; or the longer way via NM 4 past the entrance to Bandelier.

For this hike, you want to reach the end of West Jemez Road, which is approximately 5 miles after bypassing the Laboratory. At the end of West Jemez Road, you come to a "T" intersection with NM 4. Turn right here and check your odometer. NM 4 winds upward and twists sharply (blind curves). At 4½ miles you will see a sign that notes it is 1½ miles to the Cerro Grande Trail. Just past a sign "Congested Area," you will see a paved parking area on your right. Park here. This is 0.1 mile before the intersection with FR 289.

Hiking Instructions

Read the Bandelier Backcountry display board and take a flyer with area map from the box. Go through the opening in the fence and look for the next yellow diamond on a tree. Hikers and elk have created a well-worn path. Stay on the trail. At first, you are surrounded by ponderosa pines and aspens. Here and there, trees burned in the Cerro Grande fire have fallen across the trail. Some of the stumps have weathered enough to display a sculpted look. After passing a fenced area (elk exclosure) on your right, the trail begins to climb, then briefly drops down twice before going up again.

The drainages that you cross go down into Frijoles Canyon. As you go higher, ponderosa pines are replaced by Douglas fir and spruce.

After about an hour of hiking, the trail approaches a saddle and a large meadow. Here, the trail turns right and heads up the grassy slope that leads to the summit. Markers will guide you along the way. As you climb higher, the views to the south and west unfold. The nearby Valle Grande and Redondo Peak, the high plateau of the San Pedro Parks to the right of Redondo, the nearby brown-toned San Miguel Mountains, Boundary Peak and Sandias further to the south and the southern tip of the Sangre de Cristos to the east are all part of the panorama. Resting on top of Cerro Grande one sunny day in late September, we could hear elk bugling below us in the valley, as hawks and ravens circled above.

Return the way you came, using the trail markers as guide.

Note: In May of 2000, the Cerro Grande fire was started as a controlled burn on the lower portion of this mountain, but alas, high winds escalated it to a massive wildfire that burned over 200 homes in Los Alamos before it was contained.

The top of Cerro Grande

38 Valle Grande / Coyote Call Trails

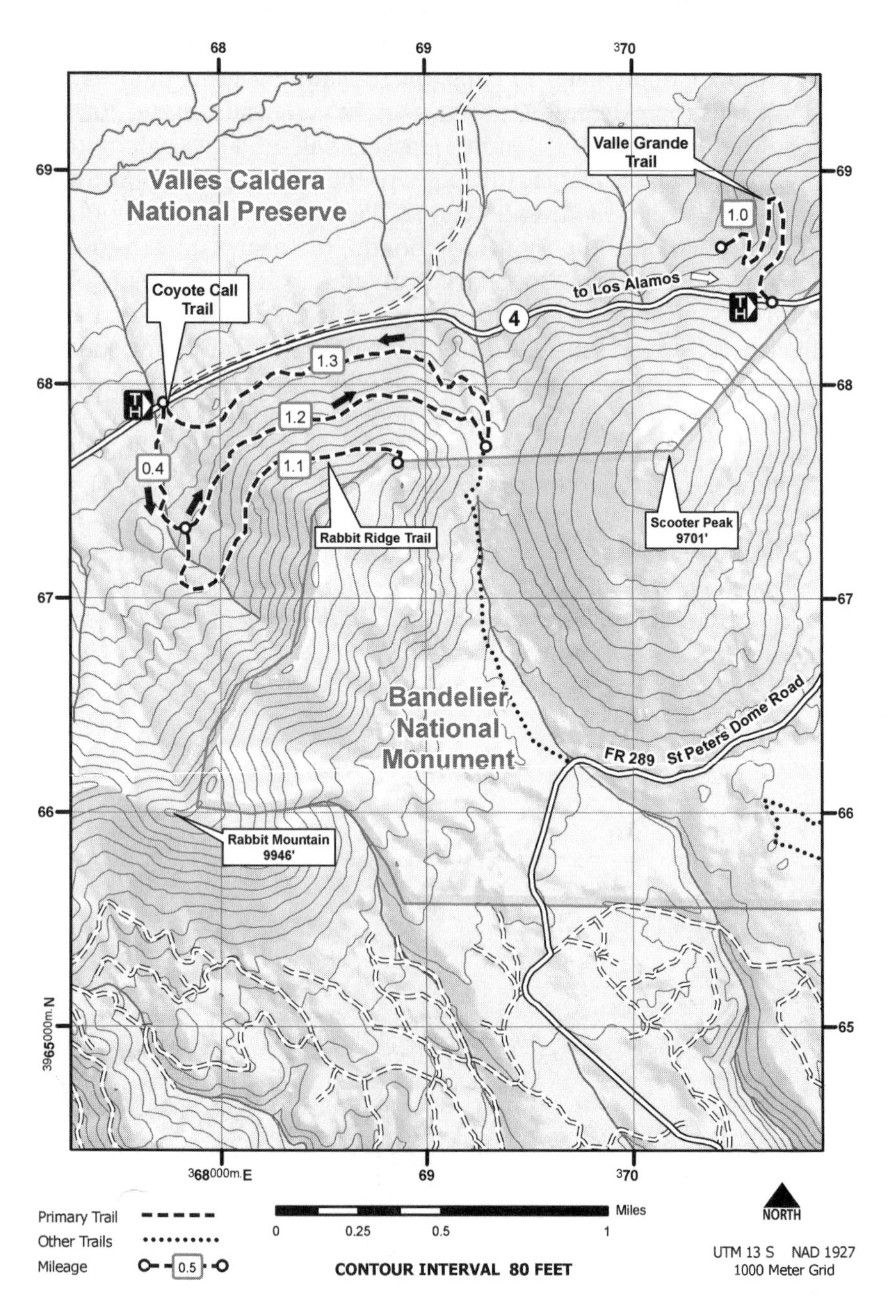

38 - VALLE GRANDE / COYOTE CALL TRAILS

by Norbert Sperlich

Two easy Jemez Mountain hikes with lovely views of the Valle Grande.

RT Distance:	2 miles for Valle Grande Trail 3 miles for Coyote Call Trail loop
Time:	1+ hr for Valle Grande Trail 2 hrs for Coyote Call Trail
Elevation Range:	8600-9050 ft; gain 450 ft (Valle Grande) 8720-9160 ft; gain 370 ft (Coyote Call Tr)
Rating:	Easy
RT Drive:	~96 miles (Valle Grande Trail); ~100 miles (Coyote Call Trail); ~2½+ hrs
Seasons:	May through October, snow conditions permitting.
Maps:	USGS Bland - 7.5' series. Trail maps can be downloaded at www.vallescaldera.gov. Sky Terrain's *Santa Fe, Bandelier & Los Alamos* is recommended.
Valle Grande TH:	370,726 mE 3,968,420 mN elev.9058'
Coyote Call TH:	367,713 mE 3,967,898 mN elev.8720'

Summary

The Valles Caldera National Preserve, created by Congress in 2000, is located in a huge collapsed crater in the Jemez Mountains. Before 2000, this area was a private ranch. The preserve is open to the public, but access is limited. As of May 2006, there were only two very short hikes available that are free of charge. These hikes, accessed from NM 4, are described in the following hiking instructions. Trails are open from dawn to sunset. No pets are allowed.

Note: To find out about other backcountry hikes that require reservations and a fee, visit www.vallescaldera.gov.

Driving Directions

Take US 84/285 north to Pojoaque (~16 miles from Santa Fe). There, take the Los Alamos exit (NM 502) on the right. After a traffic light, the road goes through an underpass and on toward Los Alamos. In about 7 miles, NM 502 crosses the Rio Grande and climbs to a Y-intersection, where you take the right branch toward White Rock and Bandelier. About 1½ miles from the "Y," turn right at a traffic light. You are now on East Jemez Road (the Los Alamos Truck Route). After about 5½ miles, East Jemez Road approaches an intersection and traffic light. A left turn takes you through the Los Alamos National Laboratory (LANL) guard gates (where you should be able to pass through showing some form of identification—e.g., a driver's license), allowing you to continue onto West Jemez Road. (If you go straight through the traffic light, it will take you over the Omega bridge in the direction of the Los Alamos townsite.) If, because of a heightened security level, you are not allowed to pass through the Laboratory gates, you may be re-directed—e.g., to West Road on the north side of the bridge (a left turn), which will connect via a bypass to the Los Alamos Ski Area road and, to the left, West Jemez Road; or the longer way via NM 4 past the entrance to Bandelier.

For this hike, you want to reach the end of West Jemez Road, which is approximately 5 miles after bypassing the Laboratory. At the end of West Jemez Road, you come to a "T" intersection with NM 4. Turn right here and check your odometer. The road winds and twists sharply (blind curves). At 6.2 miles, you will pass a parking area for the Cerro Grande Trail on your right. About 0.1 mile further, you will pass the turnoff to FR 289 on your left. Less than a mile past this turnoff, look for a sign "Entering Valles Caldera" on your right. Some 70 yards past this sign, just before the road starts to descend, there is a parking area on your left. Park here for the Valle Grande Trail.

For Coyote Call Trail, drive two more miles down into the Valle Grande, past two paved pullouts on your right, to a gate and trail sign on your left. Park near the gate or at the nearest pullout.

Hiking Instructions

Valle Grande Trail - This trail takes you from the crater rim to the bottom of the Valle Grande. From the parking area, cross the road and look for the Valle Grande trail sign. The trail first follows, then crosses, a fence and starts to descend on switchbacks through a forest of huge ponderosas, aspen, spruce and Douglas fir. Even at this high elevation, there is some evidence of tree die-off. The trail ends at a scenic spot at the edge of the Valle Grande, a vast, open grassland valley. Return the way you came. For more hiking, drive a mile east to the Cerro Grande trailhead (see CERRO GRANDE Hike #37) or drive 2 miles west to the Coyote Call trailhead.

Coyote Call Trail - Go through the gate on the south side of the highway and up an old logging road. After 40 yards, the trail forks. Take the right branch that goes uphill. (You will return on the other branch.) Note blue diamonds on trees and brown plastic stakes that serve as trail markers. Some ten minutes into the hike, the trail turns left and levels out. You will come to a fork with a trail sign. The Coyote Call Trail continues on to the left, while the Rabbit Ridge Trail goes right, climbing up the ridge. If three miles of hiking is enough for you, continue on Coyote Call Trail. Rabbit Ridge Trail is a spur trail that comes to a dead end after about 1½ miles. It takes you to a ridgetop almost 800 ft above the Coyote Call Trail, with nice views into the Valle Grande. This detour will add 1 hour or more to the hiking time.

From the junction with the Rabbit Ridge Trail, the Coyote Call Trail runs fairly level and parallel to the ridge on your right. As you enter a grassy, open ridgetop area about 30 minutes past the intersection with Rabbit Ridge Trail, the Coyote Call Trail suddenly turns left, goes down steeply, then swings west and runs parallel to the highway below. Watch for the blue diamonds. The trail goes in and out of the trees, offering wonderful views of the Valle Grande along the way, and takes you back to the trail fork close to the start of the hike.

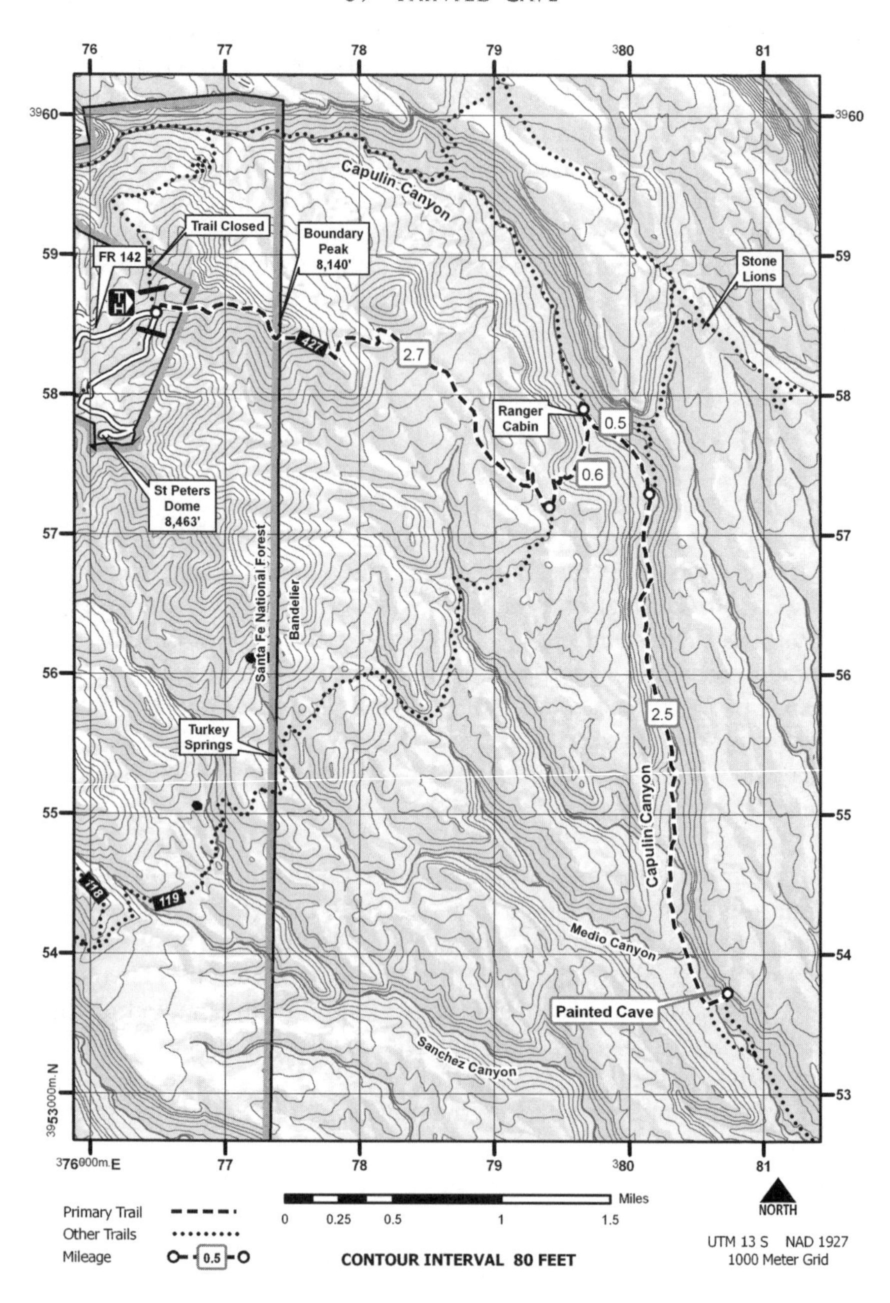
Capulin Canyon
Trail Closed
Boundary Peak 8,140'
FR 142
Stone Lions
427
2.7
Ranger Cabin
0.5
0.6
St Peters Dome 8,463'
Santa Fe National Forest
Bandelier
2.5
Turkey Springs
Capulin Canyon
118
119
Medio Canyon
Painted Cave
Sanchez Canyon
Primary Trail
Other Trails
Mileage
0.5
Miles
0 0.25 0.5 1 1.5
CONTOUR INTERVAL 80 FEET
NORTH
UTM 13 S NAD 1927
1000 Meter Grid

39 - PAINTED CAVE

by John Masters

This is a very beautiful hike in the Bandelier backcountry, with great views over canyons and the Rio Grande, as well as Indian pictographs at the Painted Cave.

RT Distance:	13 miles
Time:	8 hrs
Elevation Range:	5713-8108 ft; total gain 2400 ft
Rating:	Strenuous
RT Drive:	112 miles; 4 hrs
Seasons:	Best in spring and fall. FR 289 is usually closed in winter and early spring. Call the Jemez Ranger (505-829-3535) for information about road closings and driving conditions.
Maps:	USGS Bland, Frijoles and Cochiti Dam - 7.5' series. It is more convenient to use Bandelier Map 209 by Trails Illustrated. Sky Terrain's *Santa Fe, Bandelier & Los Alamos* is also recommended.
Trailhead:	376,486 mE 3,958,577 mN elev.8099'

Summary

The first half of this hike is all downhill, and the return all uphill. This is a very beautiful hike, especially in fall from the colors, and in spring from the rush of water in Capulin Creek. There are distant views of Chicoma Peak and Caballo Mountain, and the Truchas Peaks across the valley. You will see great cliff formations of tuff as you drop into Capulin Canyon.

In April 1996, the Dome Fire roared through this area, decimating the forest. The piñon trees that survived the fire were killed by e drought in 2002-2003. Many burned trees have toppled, sometimes obstructing the trail. It is best to call Bandelier Headquarters for an update on conditions. With all the devastation of the fire and the drought, this is still a very beautiful hike. *Note: you may need a vehicle with high clearance to navigate the last 3½ miles to the trailhead. Also, dogs are not permitted in Bandelier.*

Driving Directions

Take US 84/285 north to Pojoaque (~16 miles from Santa Fe). There, take the Los Alamos exit (NM 502) on the right. After a traffic light, the road goes through an underpass and on toward Los Alamos. In about 7 miles, NM 502 crosses the Rio Grande and climbs to a Y-intersection, where you take the right branch toward White Rock and Bandelier. About 1½ miles from the "Y," turn right at a traffic light. You are now on East Jemez Road (the Los Alamos Truck Route). After about 5½ miles, East Jemez Road approaches an intersection and traffic light. A left turn takes you through the Los Alamos National Laboratory (LANL) guard gates (where you should be able to pass through showing some form of identification—e.g., a driver's license), allowing you to continue onto West Jemez Road. (If you go straight through the traffic light, it will take you over the Omega bridge in the direction of the Los Alamos townsite.) If, because of a heightened security level, you are not allowed to pass through the Laboratory gates, you may be re-directed—e.g., to West Road on the north side of the bridge (a left turn), which will connect via a bypass to the Los Alamos Ski Area road and, to the left, West Jemez Road; or the longer way via NM 4 past the entrance to Bandelier.

For this hike, you want to reach the end of West Jemez Road, which is approximately 5 miles after bypassing the Laboratory. At the end of West Jemez Road, you come to a "T" intersection with NM 4. Turn right here and check your odometer.

NM 4 winds uphill and twists sharply and the scenery is beautiful, so drive carefully (large trucks use this road). After driving about 6 miles on NM 4, you will come to FR 289.

Turn left here onto FR 289. You have 11 more miles to go to reach the trailhead. After 2 miles on FR 289 you will cross a cattleguard. Shortly after, several roads branch off FR 289. Stay on FR 289, following signs that say "Dome Wilderness." After 7½ miles on the well-maintained gravel road, you will come to a "T" junction. "Dome Lookout" and "Dome Wilderness" signs direct you to the left onto a narrow, rocky and rutted road, FR 142. This road is 3½ miles long, requires a vehicle with high clearance, and is hazardous when wet.

While driving on FR 142, ignore secondary roads going off to the left and right. Park as the road turns sharply right and comes out on a steep edge overlooking the Rio Grande Valley. This is the trailhead and access to St. Peter's Dome Lookout. There are two signs at the trailhead. One sign informs you that the Capulin Trail is temporarily closed. The other sign indicates that Bandelier is 0.8 miles ahead. This is your trail, Boundary Peak Trail 427, which goes to the right of this sign. You will return on the same trail.

Hiking Instructions

From the parking area, take Trail 427 heading northeast, and for a short distance, uphill. Next, the trail turns east and wends down the side of Boundary Peak. After about 1 hour, the trail approaches a drainage on the right and seems to disappear. Cross the drainage, turn sharply right on the other side, and look for the continuation of the trail. In a few minutes you will come to a junction with the Turkey Springs Trail (there may be a sign). Take the left fork (north), which goes down into Capulin Canyon. After about 15 minutes, cross Rio Capulin at a large log cabin (a ranger station). Continue on the trail downstream to a marked trail junction. You continue straight ahead toward Painted Cave. The trail on the left goes to Ponderosa Campground and the Visitor's Center.

As you hike, you will see all three types of juniper (one seed, Rocky Mountain and alligator), as well as magnificent stands of ponderosa pine. You may see hoof/paw marks and scats of black bear, deer, and elk.

Proceed downstream with several stream crossings for about another 45 minutes, where you will see the big scooped-out overhang of the Painted Cave to your left. Follow the side trail that takes off toward the cave, crossing the stream. Do not attempt to climb up to the cave itself. Get out your binoculars instead and have a closer look at the pictographs. You will see horned serpents, stars, kachinas, stepped-cloud designs, strange animals, a man on horseback, etc. Many of the paintings were made between 1300-1600. More were added after the arrival of the Spaniards. The Painted Cave has been an important shrine for many centuries and is still a sacred site revered by the Indians from the nearby Pueblos.

When you're ready to return, go back the same way you came. Follow the signs that point you to the Dome trailhead. After passing the log cabin, make sure you take the trail that branches off to the left.

Alligator Juniper

Painted Cave

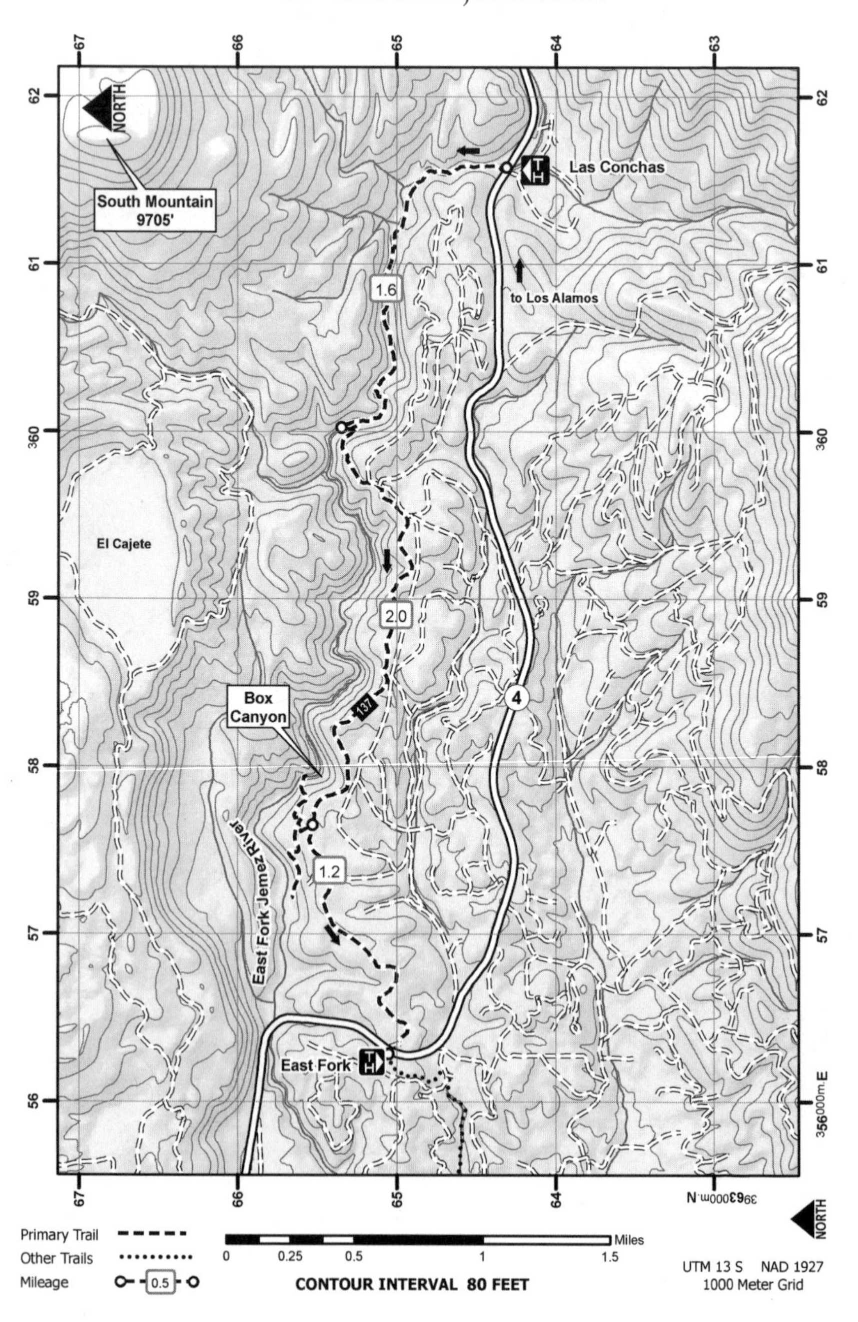
NORTH
South Mountain
9705'
Las Conchas
to Los Alamos
1.6
El Cajete
2.0
137
4
Box
Canyon
East Fork Jemez River
1.2
East Fork
67
66
65
64
63
62
61
360
59
58
57
56
3963000m.N
356000m.E
Primary Trail
Other Trails
Mileage
0.5
Miles
0
0.25
0.5
1
1.5
CONTOUR INTERVAL 80 FEET
UTM 13 S NAD 1927
1000 Meter Grid

40 - East Fork Jemez River

by Tom Ribe

A lovely hike along and above the Jemez River with striking cliffs, abundant wildflowers, and many river crossings.

RT Distance:	10 miles (full main trail) 8 miles (East Fork Box only) 5 miles (main trail with car shuttle)
Time:	6 hrs (full main trail) 4-5 hrs (East Fork Box only) 3 hrs (one way with car shuttle)
Elevation Range:	8080-8560 ft; gain 640 ft (main trail) 8000-8560 ft; gain 720 ft (East Fork box)
Rating:	Easy to moderate (depending on distance hiked)
RT Drive:	110 miles; 3+ hrs
Seasons:	Spring through fall, depending on snow conditions.
Maps:	USGS Redondo Peak - 7.5' series. *Note: the trail is not outlined on this map.* The Santa Fe National Forest map is recommended.
East Fork TH:	356,302 mE 3,965,052 mN elev.8084'
Las Conchas TH:	361,558 mE 3,964,329 mN elev.8396'

Summary

A lovely hike in the Santa Fe National Forest that begins along the Jemez River. The trail passes through a canyon of blue spruce, fir and pine growing among volcanic cliffs, and is lined with wildflowers. The trail is well marked, with log and rail bridges (some in disrepair) over river crossings. After leaving the river, the trail winds through a pleasant forest of mixed conifer and aspen.

Note that this trail, Trail 137 (called the "East Fork Trail"), has two trailheads located off of NM 4. The starting trailhead for this hike is called the "Las Conchas Trailhead," and the turnaround point for the full main-trail hike is at the "East Fork Trailhead." If your group has more than one car, you could arrange a car shuttle between the two highway trailheads, (3.7 miles apart on NM 4), cutting the hiking distance in half.

History

The Jemez Mountains are the remains of a field of volcanoes that erupted over many thousands of years. Two miles to the northwest of the trailhead, a large volcanic vent called El Cajete spewed light, chalky pumice into great drifts across the landscape about 60,000 years ago. This pumice, visible in road cuts but otherwise hidden beneath the mantle of forest soil, was targeted by miners. The Jemez National Recreation Area was created by Congress in 1993, thanks to the efforts of the East Fork Preservation Coalition and the Sierra Club, to protect this area from pumice strip mining.

Driving Directions

Take US 84/285 north to Pojoaque (~16 miles from Santa Fe). There, take the Los Alamos exit (NM 502) on the right. After a traffic light, the road goes through an underpass and on toward Los Alamos. In about 7 miles, NM 502 crosses the Rio Grande and climbs to a Y-intersection, where you take the right branch toward White Rock and Bandelier. About 1½ miles from the "Y," turn right at a traffic light. You are now on East Jemez Road (the Los Alamos Truck Route). After about 5½ miles, East Jemez Road approaches an intersection and traffic light. A left turn takes you through the Los Alamos National Laboratory (LANL) guard gates (where you should be able to pass through showing some form of identification—e.g., a driver's license), allowing you to continue onto West Jemez Road. (If you go straight through the traffic light it will take you over the Omega bridge in the direction of the Los Alamos townsite.) If, because of a heightened security level, you are not allowed to pass through the Laboratory gates, you may be re-directed—e.g., to West Road on the north side of the bridge (a left turn), which will connect via a bypass to the Los Alamos Ski Area road and, to the left, West Jemez Road; or the longer way via NM 4 past the entrance to Bandelier.

For this hike, you want to reach the end of West Jemez Road, which is approximately 5 miles after bypassing the Laboratory. At the end of West Jemez Road, you come to a "T" intersection with NM 4. Turn right here and check your odometer. NM 4 winds uphill and twists sharply and the scenery is beautiful, so drive carefully. The trailhead is 13.7 miles from the right turn.

Once in the Jemez Mountains, the road winds along the Frijoles Canyon watershed until you drop down into the Valle Grande, a huge caldera and grassland surrounded by the Jemez peaks. The road then leaves the Valle Grande and crosses the Jemez River at Las Conchas Campground. A half-mile further, the road again crosses the river in an open area where a few houses stand on the left side of the road. Park in the gravel parking area on the right side of the road at the river crossing, directly across the road from a private driveway. There is a Forest Service sign that indicates "Las Conchas."

Hiking Instructions

Look for the gate north of the parking lot that marks the Las Conchas Trailhead of the East Fork Trail. The trail descends steeply to the river, then follows the river and crosses it at several log and rail bridges. The river meanders between steep canyon walls covered with an amazing variety of orange, chartreuse, pale green and black lichens. Alert hikers may see dippers (water ouzels) along the stream, in addition to Steller's jays, western tanagers, and Rocky Mountain chickadees.

About 2 miles from the trailhead, the river leaves the meadow and forest bottom land and enters a box canyon. The trail leaves the river a few yards before a cattle fence and gate where the river turns left. Continue on the main trail, which bears uphill and to the left. There are signs noting that the trailhead (where you began) is 2 miles back and the East Fork Trailhead is 3 miles ahead. The trail switchbacks up the north-facing slope to a ridgetop, passing through a wooden gate about one-third the way up. At the top, you can see Redondo Peak directly to the north, with its forested ramparts and montane grasslands gleaming among aspen groves.

On the ridgetop, the forest tells the story of logging and fire suppression, which has changed it from open park lands of big ponderosa before 1900 to the thickets of small locust and aspen that grow here today. After hiking 20 minutes on the ridgetop, the trail is crossed by a logging road. Shortly thereafter, it merges with a ski trail that comes in from the left and is marked by blue diamonds nailed to the trees. On occasion, the trail runs closely parallel to the logging road, but stay on the narrow trail.

Soon you will come to a trail junction marked by a sign. Trail 137 continues straight ahead to reach the East Fork Trailhead in a mile, and another trail goes off to the right, reaching the river in about ½ mile. This right-hand trail soon branches into Trails 137A and 137B. The right branch goes to the East Fork Box where the river leaves the box canyon. If you are planning to hike to the East Fork Box, this is your trail. The trail makes a very steep descent to reach the river and cross a bridge. You can then head upstream after crossing the bridge to where the river comes out of a wild, rocky canyon. This spot makes an excellent lunch area and turn-around point for the hike. If you wish, follow the river upstream into the canyon (you will get your legs wet!) for 5 more minutes to a popular picnic area.

You can return the way you came, or, at the junction of the main trail (Trail 137), you can turn right and continue one additional mile to the East Fork Trailhead. Here is where your hike ends if you arranged for a car shuttle.

If you are returning the way you came (no car shuttle), note that after hiking about 20 minutes on the main trail past the junction to the river, the blue-diamond ski trail separates from Trail 137 by veering off to the right (there is a lot of downed timber at this fork). Make sure you stay left on the better-defined main hiking trail to return to the Las Conchas Trailhead and your car.

East Fork Box

41 Los Griegos Ridge

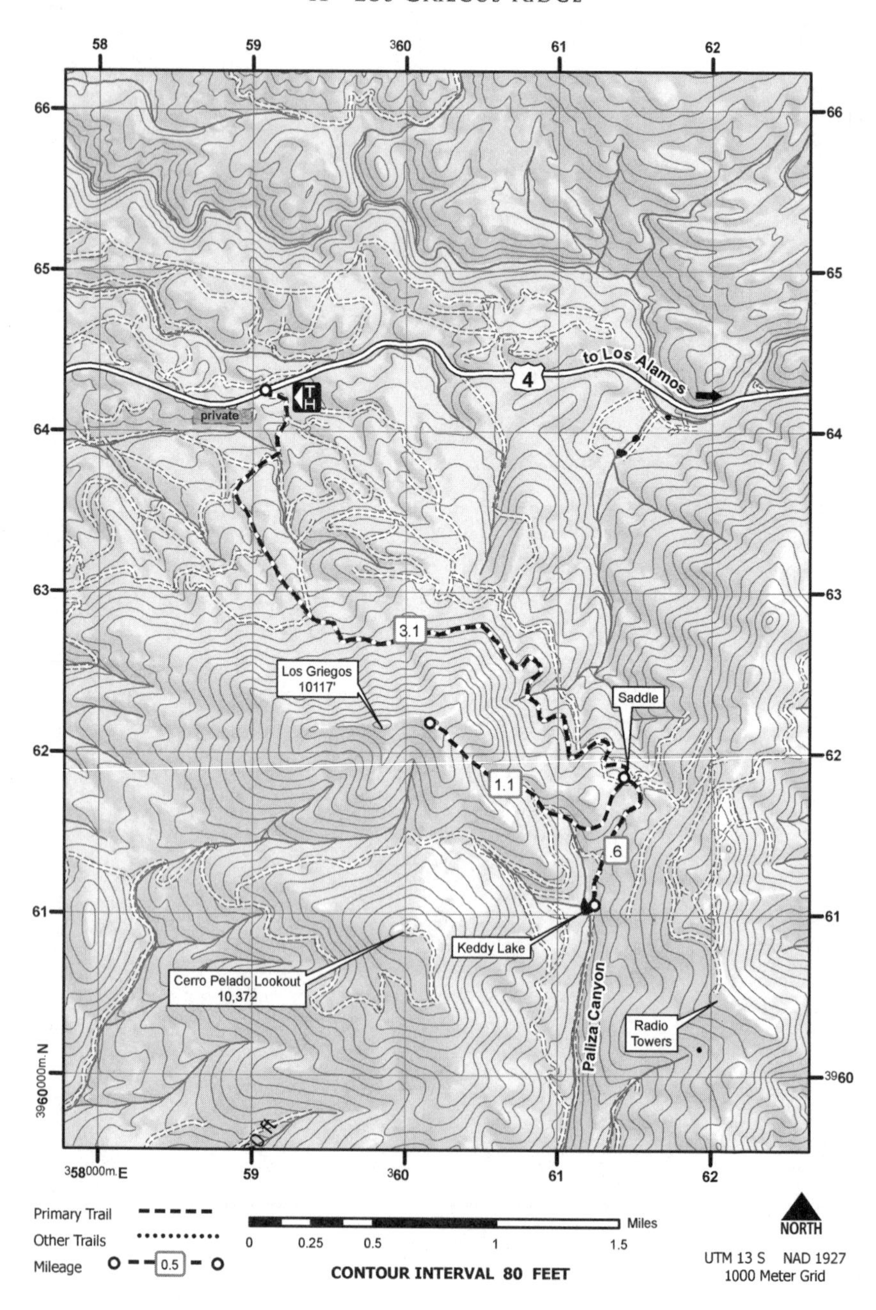

41 - Los Griegos Ridge

by Norbert Sperlich

A beautiful Jemez woodlands hike to a ridge overlooking the Valles Caldera, mostly along an old forest road with sweeping views from the top.

RT Distance:	6.5 miles to saddle 8.5 miles to east peak
Time:	~4 hrs to saddle ~6 hrs to east peak
Elevation Range:	8400-10,100 ft; total gain 1300 ft to saddle, 2000 ft to east peak
Rating:	Moderate hike to saddle overlooking Paliza Canyon; strenuous to east peak of Los Griegos
RT Drive:	114 miles; ~3 hrs
Seasons:	Most enjoyable from mid-May (aspens leafing out) to early October (aspens turning color). Can be warm in summer.
Maps:	USGS Redondo Peak - 7.5' series. Your destination is the eastern-most part of Los Griegos ridge.
Trailhead:	359,075 mE 3,964,270 mN elev.8403'

Summary

This hike takes you to the south rim of the Valles Caldera—a basin formed by a volcanic eruption 1.2 million years ago. Most of the hike follows a forest road that gradually climbs the north side of the ridge. The last section of the hike is off-trail and steep and requires some route-finding skills (bring topo map and compass). You will encounter a forest of conifers and aspens, and depending on the time of the year, wildflowers, berries, butterflies, and birds. There are sweeping views from the top. You may meet cattle and/ or noisy off-road vehicles. Flowers are abundant in late spring and summer, after the rains have come and before cows get to them.

Driving Directions

Take US 84/285 north to Pojoaque (~16 miles from Santa Fe). There, take the Los Alamos exit (NM 502) on the right. After a traffic light, the road goes through an underpass and on toward Los Alamos. In about 7 miles, NM 502 crosses the Rio Grande and climbs to a Y-intersection, where you take the right branch toward White Rock and Bandelier. About 1½ miles from the "Y," turn right at a traffic light. You are now on East Jemez Road (the Los Alamos Truck Route). After about 5½ miles, East Jemez Road approaches an intersection and traffic light. A left turn takes you through the Los Alamos National Laboratory (LANL) guard gates (where you should be able to pass through showing some form of identification—e.g., a driver's license), allowing you to continue onto West Jemez Road. (If you go straight through the traffic light, it will take you over the Omega bridge in the direction of the Los Alamos townsite.) If, because of a heightened security level, you are not allowed to pass through the Laboratory gates, you may be re-directed—e.g., to West Road on the north side of the bridge (a left turn), which will connect via a bypass to the Los Alamos Ski Area road and, to the left, West Jemez Road; or the longer way via NM 4 past the entrance to Bandelier.

For this hike, you want to reach the end of West Jemez Road, which is approximately 5 miles after bypassing the Laboratory. At the end of West Jemez Road, you come to a "T" intersection with NM 4. Turn right here and check your odometer. NM 4 winds uphill and twists sharply and the scenery is beautiful, so drive carefully. The trailhead is 15.4 miles from the right turn.

Once in the Jemez Mountains, the road winds up along the Frijoles Canyon watershed until you drop down into the Valle Grande, a huge caldera and grassland surrounded by the Jemez peaks. The road then drops out of the Valle Grande and crosses the Jemez River at Las Conchas Campground. A half-mile further, the road recrosses the river where a few houses stand on the left side of the road. On the right is the parking area for the Las Conchas trailhead. From here, keep on driving for another 1.7 miles. As you approach a yellow sign indicating that the road will veer right, look for a hard-to-see road coming in on the left, about 60 yards before the yellow sign and turn left here. (Don't take the more prominent road opposite the sign.) Go through a gate and a cattleguard, and note a large corral to the right. Do not park here, as the corral is used by ranchers, and a small sign says "No camping within ¼ mile." Instead, proceed left up the dirt road about 60 yards to where it forks, and take the right fork. Shortly you will see a pull-off area on the right where you can park.

Hiking Instructions

Start hiking up the road. You are walking among tall aspens, ponderosas, scrub oak, and locust trees. About 15 minutes into the hike, the road forks. Take the left fork that goes uphill and towards Los Griegos Ridge. At further forks in the road, stay on the obvious main road. The road traverses an area of pumice deposits. Note the small grayish pebbles on the road. If you pick one up, you can feel how light pumice is. Pumice holds water, hence the large size of the trees. Ponderosas soon give way to Douglas fir and spruce.

Some 40 minutes into the hike, the road turns east. On your left, you will have glimpses of Redondo Peak, a "resurgent dome" that was pushed up inside the caldera after the initial eruption. Further along, and before the road turns sharply right and downhill, step onto a pull-off on the left which affords a great view of the Valle Grande and the rounded hump of Chicoma Peak beyond it. The road now goes into a southeasterly direction, and after several ups and downs, approaches a saddle, a good 2 hours into the hike. Look for a fence on your right and go through it over a small cattleguard. On the far side of the fence is a good spot for a break, or the endpoint of a moderate hike. You get good views to the south into Paliza Canyon, a green valley surrounded by Douglas firs and aspen. (If you hike down Paliza Canyon for 15 minutes, you will come to Keddy Lake, a large stock pond.)

The east peak of Los Griegos is about 1 mile away and 700 ft up. To continue your hike, still at the southside of the fence and looking at the fence, turn left (west) and take the narrow trail, a short distance away, heading uphill. This trail follows the fence in a westerly direction, first uphill, then down again. After about 10 minutes, the trail turns left, away from the fence, and drops down to a drainage. There is a small wooden bridge across the drainage. Just before you get to the bridge, leave the trail you were on and follow an old logging road that goes up to the right parallel to the drainage. In a few minutes, you will have to step around aspens that have fallen across the road. Continue on the road to a small meadow where the road disappears, but is replaced by a cattle trail. Staying on the right edge of the meadow, continue on this small cattle trail. This trail briefly gets lost in a second meadow, but looking straight ahead, you will see it re-emerge in the distance. Don't take the faint trail to the left of the drainage. The cattle trail continues along the right side of the drainage until you reach a grassy slope where the trail disappears. Follow the small drainage (now on your right) up a broad grassy slope. This is the steepest part of the hike, with an abundance of flowers if there has been rain.

Close to the ridge top, the grass is tall. Step across an old fence and proceed to a large rock outcrop/cairn at the high point. This makes a good lunch spot. There is a small rock shelter on the far side, should the wind be blowing. The view to the north (ahead of you) is partially obstructed by limber pines. Go past these trees for a view of Redondo, of the cliffs overlooking the canyon of the Jemez, and—smack in the middle of all this beauty—the El Cajete Pumice Mine. Way in the distance, to the left of Redondo, the high plateau of San Pedro Parks is visible. Looking into the opposite direction (south), you will see nearby radio towers on Peralta Ridge, and further back, the Sandia, San Pedro, and Ortiz Mountains. For more views (Mount Taylor, a glimpse of Cabezon, and the nearby Cerro Pelado), explore the ridge to the west.

Return to your lunch spot. Follow the drainage down (heading in the direction of the radio towers). Soon you will be back at the trail intersection with the little wooden bridge. If you have ½ hour to spare, follow the drainage down to the stock pond. From there, a road brings you back up to the saddle and the fence. The other option is to turn left at the little bridge and follow the trail you came in on back to the saddle. Go through the fence, take the road to the left and follow it back to your car.

View into Paliza Canyon from saddle on the Los Griegos Hike

When one comes out of the woods everything is novel... even our fellow beings are regarded with something of the same keenness and freshness of perception that is brought to a new species of wild animal.

~ John Muir

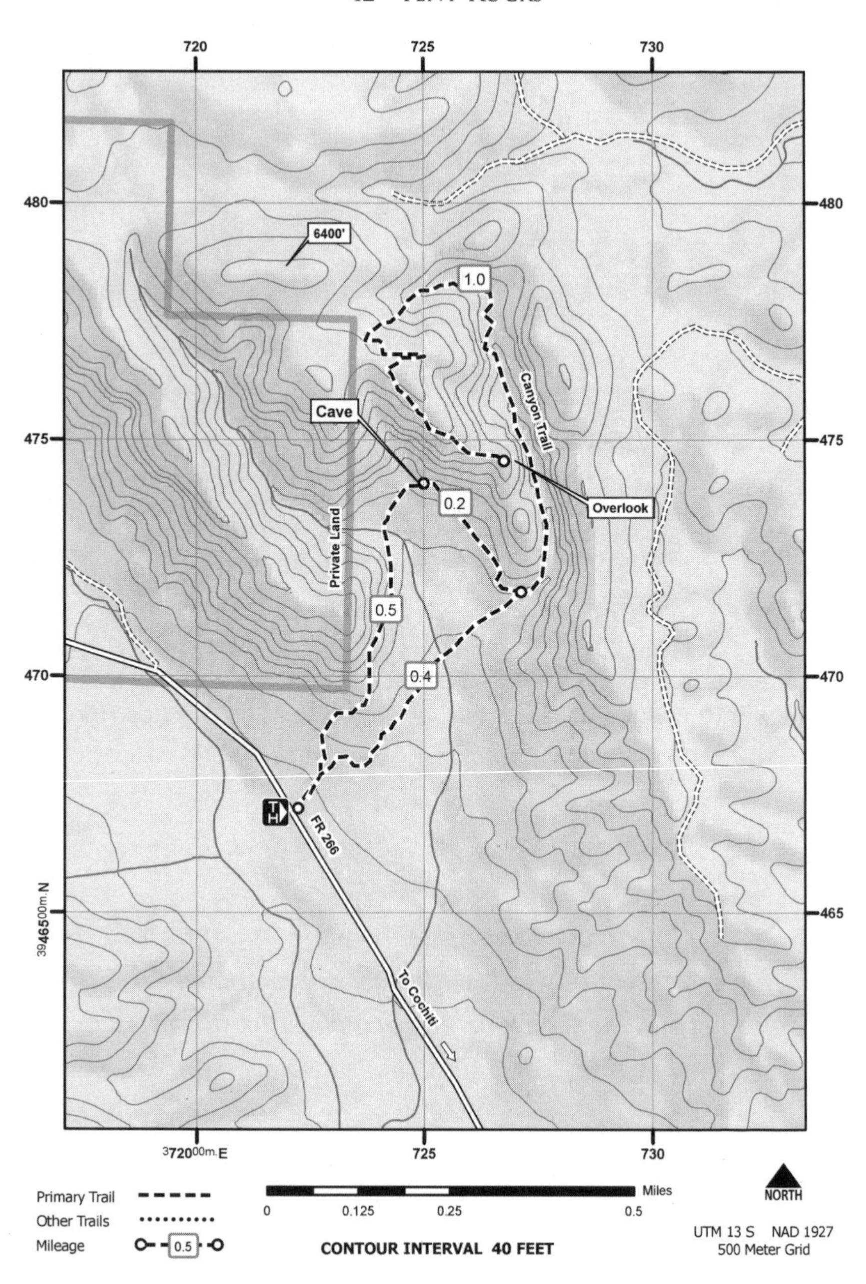
720
725
730
480
475
470
465
6400'
1.0
Cave
Canyon Trail
0.2
Overlook
Private Land
0.5
0.4
TH
FR 266
To Cochiti
3946500m.N
372000m.E
Primary Trail
Other Trails
Mileage
0.5
Miles
0
0.125
0.25
0.5
CONTOUR INTERVAL 40 FEET
NORTH
UTM 13 S NAD 1927
500 Meter Grid

42 - Tent Rocks

by Alan and Jenny Karp

A geological wonderland 40 miles southwest of Santa Fe, featuring cone-shaped tent rocks, narrow canyons and sweeping views from the ridge tops.

RT Distance:	1.5 miles (Cave Loop only) 3.5 miles (Cave Loop and Canyon Trail)
Time:	~1 hr (Cave Loop only) 2-3 hrs (Cave Loop and Canyon Trails)
Elevation Range:	5750-5975 ft; gain 225 ft (Cave Loop only) 5750-6375 ft; gain 675 ft (to ridge top)
Rating:	Easy
RT Drive:	80 miles; ~2 hrs
Seasons:	Spring, fall or early summer morning hours make this an idyllic, short, comfortable hike. Not a winter hike if there has been heavy snowfall.
Maps:	USGS Cañada - 7.5' series
Fees:	$5/car
Trailhead:	372,235 mE 3,946,730 mN elev.5730'

History

Formerly known as "Tent Rocks," this place is now Kasha-Katuwe Tent Rocks National Monument. Kasha-Katuwe means "white cliffs" in the Keres language of the nearby Cochiti Pueblo. The white cliffs came into being millions of years ago, after volcanic eruptions in the Jemez Mountains created large deposits of pumice, tuff and ashes. Wind and water sculpted this material into tent rocks, canyons, mesas and arroyos. In 2001, Tent Rocks was designated a National Monument.

Summary

Add to the sculpted landscape piñon, juniper, ponderosa pines, desert plants and flowers, and a variety of birds and animals, and you have the special place known as Tent Rocks. Since it was designated a National Monument, the number of visitors has increased dramatically. To beat the crowds, visit early in the day and/or on weekdays. There is only so much traffic this small area can bear. Keep your dog leashed, don't litter, don't go off the trail and don't come in large groups. The area is administered by the BLM. There is a $5 fee per vehicle, but no fee for holders of Golden Eagle or Golden Age cards. Visitation hours are 8 am to 5 pm from November through March, 7 am to 6 pm from April through October. Access is controlled by a gate and pay station booth about 5 miles before you reach Tent Rocks. Access may be closed occasionally by order of the Cochiti Tribal governor. Call Cochiti Pueblo (505-465-2244 or 505-465-0121) to verify if the road is open.

Driving Directions

Take I-25 south toward Albuquerque and get off at Exit 264 to Cochiti. Take the right turn (west) off the exit ramp onto NM 16. In about 8 miles, you will come to a "T" intersection. Turn right here onto NM 22 and follow this road for about 2½ miles. Look for an intersection where you will take a sharp turn left (still NM 22) toward Cochiti Pueblo. Stay on this road for 1.8 miles. To the right of the road you will see a water tower painted like an Indian drum and then a similar but narrower tower. After passing a sign "Cochiti Pueblo" you will come to an intersection where a paved road comes in from the right. This road is marked "266, Tent Rocks." Turn right onto this road.

Soon it becomes a gravel road that takes you to the aforementioned gate and pay station booth. After 4.8 miles (part of which will be through Cochiti Pueblo land), you will come to the well-marked entrance to the Tent Rocks area on your right.

Hiking Instructions

Look for a wide trail that will take you to an information board protected by a roof. On the board you will find a map, descriptions and pictures of the area. The map shows two trails. One is a loop trail (also referred to as Cave Loop on signposts) that starts and ends at the information board. It is well maintained and marked with wooden posts with arrows. You can do this loop in 1 hour or less. The other trail is the Canyon Trail, which branches off the Cave Loop and takes you through a slot canyon and up on a ridge top with dramatic views. Both trails are described in the paragraphs that follow.

The Cave Loop Trail goes past the information board and, after some 50 yards, branches to the left. You will be hiking amidst tent rocks that have lost their "caps." The trail climbs up a slope, with cliffs on your left, then drops into a bowl that is surrounded by sculpted cliffs on three sides. The trail starts to climb again and goes up to the right, past a cave in the cliff wall. From here you have beautiful views to the south. The trail follows the cliffs, then descends steeply through manzanita bushes down to a drainage where it meets the Canyon Trail. Here, you can either continue on Cave Loop to the parking lot, or go left onto Canyon Trail to the ridge top. If you choose to take Canyon Trail, it will take you into an enchanted world.

Mother Nature's imagination went wild in this stone wonderland. Over the ages, wind and water have sensuously carved out this inspiring miniature canyon that envelopes and entices you with its cap rocks and volcanic tuff, ponderosa-lined trail and cheerful wildflowers. It gives you a very special spiritual feeling. The arroyo funnels into this inner sanctuary. As you wind your way up the canyon, the soft curving walls provide you with meditative niches. The sky appears a deeper blue than imaginable and provides a dramatic backdrop for the still-forming tent rocks. After 5 minutes of hiking on the Canyon Trail, a ponderosa pine and a lone tent rock appear at the base of the left wall of the canyon. The wall bears "petroglyphs" depicting serpents, and handprints of unknown origin.

The canyon narrows into a stone hallway where at several places you must scramble over rock steps. At one point you will need to duck under a huge boulder. Some hikers may require a helping hand or a boost on this section of the trail. The trail continues to wind, alternating between open and narrow sections.

Next to a large fallen tree to the right, the trail will leave the slot canyon, and continue out and up to the top of the ridge. It is well traveled and well marked by signs with arrows. The trail starts to climb out of the canyon, ascending along a small, steep ridge. There is one spot where hikers will need to scramble up a small rocky area. For a short while, the trail follows the edge of the canyon, then turns away from the canyon and up. Just before you reach the top you will come to a fork. Follow the main trail to the right, which will bring you to the ridge top (a branch trail goes off to the left). Once you are at the top, you can enjoy your lunch while taking in the 360° views. You will see the Tent Rocks area nearby as well as the slot canyon below. To the east is the familiar shape of Tetilla Peak above Cochiti Lake, to the north are the Sangre de Cristo Mountains, and to the south, Sandia Peak. To extend the hike, continue on the trail that follows the ridge top in a southeasterly direction. In a few minutes, you will come to an overlook with great views and a precipitous drop off.

Return to where you left Cave Loop trail and follow the signs to the parking area.

Tent Rocks

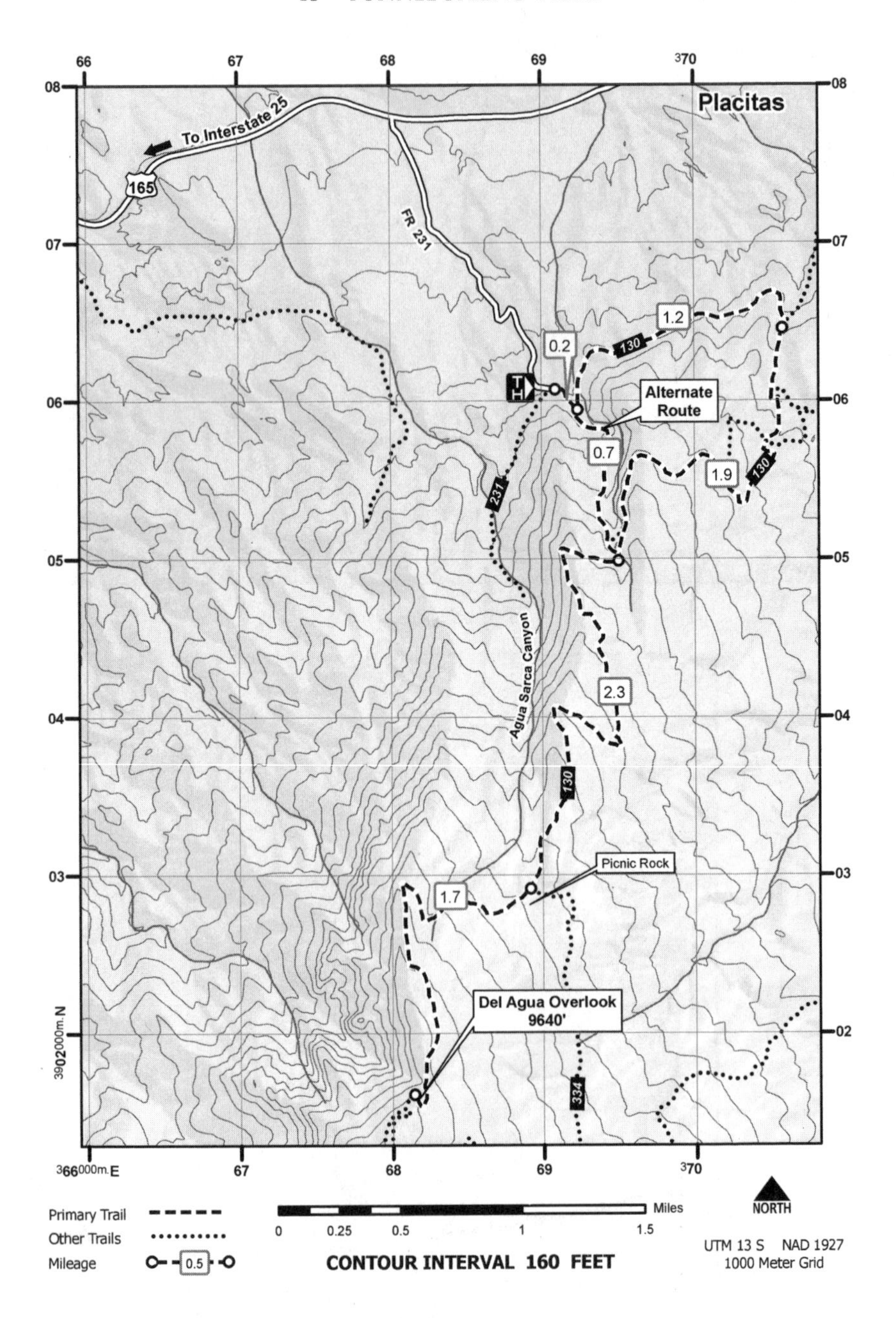

Placitas
To Interstate 25
165
FR 231
231
130
334
0.2
1.2
0.7
1.9
2.3
1.7
Alternate Route
Agua Sarca Canyon
Picnic Rock
Del Agua Overlook 9640'
Primary Trail
Other Trails
Mileage
0.5
Miles
0
0.25
0.5
1
1.5
CONTOUR INTERVAL 160 FEET
NORTH
UTM 13 S NAD 1927
1000 Meter Grid

43 - Tunnel Spring Trail

by Polly Robertson

This hike is on the northern side of Sandia Crest and offers sweeping views and lovely wildflowers.

RT Distance:	15 miles - can be cut to any length as an "out and back" hike (if you take the alternate route up or down Del Orno Canyon, subtract 2 miles; if taken both ways, subtract 4 miles).
Time:	7-10 hrs
Elevation Range:	6400-9640 ft; total gain ~3240 ft
Rating:	Moderate to strenuous
RT Drive:	108 miles; ~2 hrs
Seasons:	Best in spring or fall. Snow may linger in the upper reaches in early spring. Summer is hot.
Maps:	USGS Placitas - 7.5' series. However, we recommend you use the *Sandia Mountain Wilderness* map, published by the USFS.
Fees:	Parking $3/car
Trailhead:	369,161 mE 3,906,055 mN elev.6435'

Summary

This hike gradually ascends the northernmost section of the Sandia Crest Trail and offers sweeping views and lovely wildflowers. There is no water along the trail.

Driving Directions

Take I-25 south toward Albuquerque. About 47 miles from Santa Fe, take Exit 242 (Placitas). Make note of your odometer reading at the highway and go 5.2 miles east toward Placitas. After passing a street sign, "Puesta del Sol," on your right, look for the next dirt road on your right, marked "Tunnel Springs Road," with a group of mail and newspaper boxes. There is a small sign (FR 231) a few yards up this bumpy dirt road. Turn right here and drive 1½ miles past several houses, bearing left if in doubt. You will pass a spring on your right gushing through a pipe behind a stone wall. This is Tunnel Spring, and the water is non-potable. The large parking area with toilet facilities is immediately beyond. Park here and pay the parking fee.

Hiking Instructions

Trail 130 (North Crest Trail) starts next to an information board with a map. Crest Trail signs give the distance to Agua Sarca Overlook as 5 miles, Del Agua Overlook 8 miles and Sandia Crest 11 miles. The trail starts at an elevation of 6400 ft. Agua Sarca Lookout is at 7800 ft and Del Agua Lookout at 9640 ft. The time given on the sign to reach these spots is probably exaggerated for most experienced hikers. Trail 130 ultimately reaches Sandia Crest after 11 miles and continues to the southern end of the Sandias. Any part of this distance is a lovely walk.

Close to the trailhead, your trail crosses a drainage. Here, there is a wooden sign, "Sandia Mountain Wilderness." An unmarked trail goes to the right and steeply up into Del Orno Canyon. (This is a shortcut that rejoins the official trail after a steep ascent over rough terrain. It offers more shade than the official trail and saves you about 2 miles. If you take the shortcut by turning right, you will reach the main trail in about 50 minutes.)

For the main trail, continue straight ahead on Trail 130. To your left, in the distance, you can see Cabezon Peak, a volcanic neck, and closer by, the Jemez Canyon reservoir and the fingerlike mesas of the San Felipe volcanic field.

The trail is a long, gentle traverse going northeasterly (toward Placitas) for about 1 mile, then it bears due south (right) and up Arroyo Colorado. You are hiking on gray limestone, deposited in an ocean 300 million years ago. Look for fossils!

About 1 hour into the hike, old cart tracks cross the trail at right angles. Five minutes later, another track approaches the trail from the left, runs parallel to the trail, then veers left again. Stay on the narrow trail to the right of this track. To the east, the Ortiz and San Pedro Mountains are coming into view. Soon the trail turns west and takes you to the rim of Del Orno Canyon. Looking down the canyon, you can see your car. In the distance to the west is Mount Taylor; to the north are the Jemez Mountains with Redondo Peak prominent.

For a while you will hike below the vertical cliffs that form the east rim of Del Orno Canyon. About 3½ miles from the start of the hike, just before you come to the head of the canyon (where your trail crosses a drainage and turns sharply right), you will notice an unmarked trail that drops down to the right into the canyon. This is the shortcut mentioned earlier. Note this junction since you may want to return on it and it may be difficult to find on the way down.

About 10 minutes after passing this trail junction, you will reach the east rim of Agua Sarca Canyon. There is a low stone wall on the right, overlooking a steep escarpment with expansive views to the west. It takes a little under 2 hours to reach this point (1 hour if you take the shortcut). This overlook makes an excellent place to stop for a break.

The trail now moves away from the edge, then returns briefly to the rim of Agua Sarca Canyon about ½ hour farther on. This overlook also offers great views. Soon the vegetation changes as piñon and juniper give way to dense scrub oak. Near some rock outcrops, you will come to a trail fork, with the Peñasco Blanco Trail heading off to the left. Stay on the main trail. A short distance past a trail sign, a short narrow path to the left leads to a large flat rock which offers a great spot for lunch and a good turnaround point if you don't want to hike the entire distance. This "picnic rock" offers striking views to the east and is generally protected from the winds that often sweep across the Sandias.

Continue straight ahead and up through the oak thicket. In late May, you should see lots of flowers along this section of the hike; the scrub oak will have leafed out and the gorgeous Fendler's cliffrose should be in bloom. About ½ hour past the trail junction, the trail returns briefly to the rim again, then turns left at a stone wall and keeps climbing in a southerly direction. The air is getting thinner and the scrub oak smaller, and you will have magnificent views to the north. In another ½ hour, the trail approaches the rim once more, and leaving the oak behind, goes into the fir trees. The trail makes a hairpin turn to the right and soon runs alongside the rocky rim, with great views to the west. There is no sign marking the Del Agua overlook; however, a stone bench close to the trail marks the place. Strong hikers can reach this point in 4 hours or less, if they take the shortcut.

You may return to your car by the same route or take the shorter route previously mentioned. The shortcut saves you about 2 miles. The trail descending through Del Orno Canyon is steep, a bit of a scramble, and rough in spots with a lot of loose rock, making for poor footing. Caution should be exercised while descending. Don't use this trail during or after heavy rains. Should you return via the standard trail, be forewarned that you will encounter a gentle uphill section before reaching your car.

Del Agua Overlook, Sandias

Let children walk with Nature, let them see the beautiful blendings and communions of death and life, their joyous inseparable unity, as taught in woods and meadow, plains and mountains and streams of our blessed star, and they will learn that death is stingless indeed, and as beautiful as life... All is divine harmony.

~ John Muir

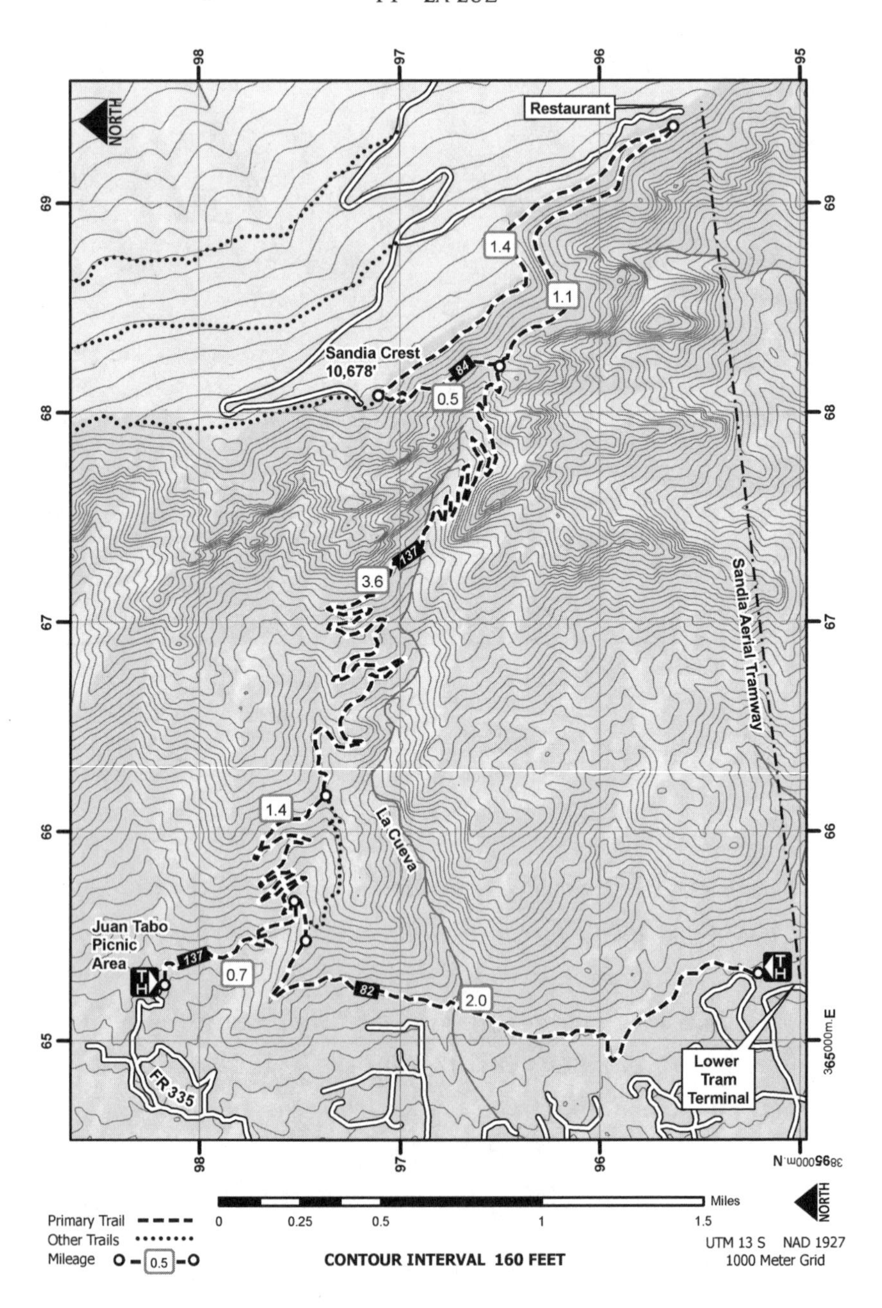
Restaurant
NORTH
Sandia Crest
10,678'
1.4
1.1
0.5
84
137
3.6
1.4
La Cueva
Sandia Aerial Tramway
Juan Tabo
Picnic
Area
T
H
0.7
82
2.0
FR 335
Lower
Tram
Terminal
98
97
96
95
69
68
67
66
65
365000m.E
3895000m.N
Miles
0
0.25
0.5
1
1.5
Primary Trail
Other Trails
Mileage
CONTOUR INTERVAL 160 FEET
UTM 13 S NAD 1927
1000 Meter Grid

44 - LA LUZ

by Lionel Soracco

This is a hike up a magnificent granite escarpment to the top of the Sandias, with spectacular cliffs and spires and bird's-eye views of Albuquerque below.

RT Distance:	14 miles (La Luz TH to Sandia Crest) 15 miles (La Luz TH to upper tram terminal) 8.5 miles (one way lower to upper tram terminals)
Time:	8-10 hrs (La Luz TH) 5+ hrs (one way from lower tram terminal)
Elevation Range:	7036-10,678 ft; gain 3800 ft (La Luz TH to Sandia Crest) 6659-10,378 ft; gain 4200 ft (lower tram to upper tram terminals)
Rating:	Strenuous
RT Drive:	112 miles; 2½ hrs
Seasons:	May - October, conditions permitting. The lower regions are very hot in summer. Snow and ice on the upper sections are hazards during winter and early spring. We recommend you call the Sandia Ranger Station (505-281-3304) for trail conditions. Start early.
Maps:	USGS Sandia Crest - 7.5' series or the US Forest Service Map of the Sandia Mountain Wilderness in the Cibola National Forest.
Fees:	Parking $3/car (La Luz TH) Parking $1/car (lower tram)
Juan Tabo TH:	365,229 mE 3,898,208 mN elev.7041'
Tram TH:	365,322 mE 3,895,116 mN elev.6523'

Summary

This is a hike up a magnificent granite escarpment, capped on top by bands of white fossiliferous limestone. This escarpment rises one mile above the Rio Grande valley. From the trailhead to the top, the La Luz Trail (Trail 137) climbs slightly less than 4,000 ft, passing through four of our six life zones. As you climb, you'll see the vegetation change, greening as you enter the higher elevations. The trail rises near granite cliffs and spires hundreds of feet high, finally reaching the high altitude spruce and fir at the top.

There are two trailheads. The La Luz trailhead is in Juan Tabo recreation area, just above the picnic grounds. The other trailhead is at the lower tram terminal. If you plan to hike up and take the tram down, park at the lower tram terminal and take Trail 82. It reaches the La Luz Trail in about 2 miles. The entire La Luz trail is on Sandia Pueblo land, although it is still administered by the US Forest Service. Please respect their land. The Albuquerque Trail Runners maintain the trail.

We recommend taking 2-3 quarts of liquid. There are drinking fountains at the top.

History

Sandia Mountain is the result of Rio Grande rifting, a widening crack in the plate beneath our feet starting up in Colorado and ending in Mexico. This crack caused Sandia Mountain to rise while the valley sank. Because the pink granites glow a rich watermelon color at sunset, the mountain may have been named "Sandia," which means watermelon in Spanish.

Driving Directions

Take I-25 south to Tramway Blvd (Exit 234) in north Albuquerque, and then set your odometer. Turn east and drive uphill on Sandia land, past Sandia Casino on the left and Bien Mur Indian Market on the right. For the La Luz trailhead in Juan Tabo, turn left onto FR 333, which is 4 miles from I-25. Drive uphill in a northeasterly direction 2 miles and turn right onto FR 333A (through stone pillars) and go into the parking lot at the end. Pay the fee (free with Golden Age Pass). Alternatively, for Trail 82 at the base of the tram, stay on Tramway Blvd as it turns south, and turn left (east) at a 3-way stop sign to go to the upper parking lot at the tram terminal.

Hiking Instructions

La Luz Trail 137 begins on the uphill side of the parking lot, where you enter the Sandia Mountain Wilderness. Juniper, cactus, Apache plume, mountain mahogany, cholla, live oak, piñon, cottonwoods in the draws, thistles with magenta blossoms, prickly pear cactus and more greet the eye. After about 30 minutes you'll pass a large arroyo. The trail forks with signs indicating straight ahead for the La Luz Trail and right (Trail 82) for the tramway station. Stay on the La Luz Trail. The first Gambel oak appears. The TV towers atop Sandia Crest are regularly in view.

As you climb, take a look back towards Albuquerque, noting how the vegetation density increases as you rise from the barren plane. You'll reach a shaded cove, with a stream, about 1¼ hours from the start. This is a good spot for a break. Soon you'll pass over a ridge separating two major canyons, Chimney Canyon on your left and La Cueva Canyon on your right. The trail hugs the northeast side of La Cueva high above the bottom. You may hear water running below.

Another hour or so brings you to a lookout point, with massive granite walls and spires to your left and across the canyon. The trail then descends into La Cueva canyon. Here you'll find a lovely, sheltered rest stop with cliffs on either side. You're less than 3 miles from the top. A sign warns that ice and snow may make the higher trail impassable (a problem from late fall to early spring). Continuing, you pass to the opposite side of the canyon and cross a number of rock slides. High above you, just below the Sandia Crest, you'll see limestone strata and, beneath your feet, you'll start to see grey limestone rocks along the trail. You just crossed the great unconformity, the granite-limestone junction, separating 1.1 billion years of geologic record.

Shortly after crossing the last of the rock slides, you'll move into forest and rise in a series of short, steep switchbacks through aspen to a saddle, where the trail forks. The right fork is the La Luz Trail, which leads you to the tramway terminal and a restaurant (High Finance, 505-243-9742) in about 45 minutes of fairly level walking. The view to your right is dramatic, as the canyon is very deep. You may spot a tramcar or two crossing this canyon, suspended thousands of feet above ground. The left fork involves a bit more climbing (400 ft higher). It brings you to Sandia Crest after ½ mile, and concludes with a concrete stairway. At the crest is a curio shop, restrooms and snacks (but no restaurant). The way back is the same as the way up, with more time to enjoy the views.

The Thumb, on La Luz Trail

Petroglyph National Monument, Piedras Marcadas ☞

45 Petroglyph National Monument

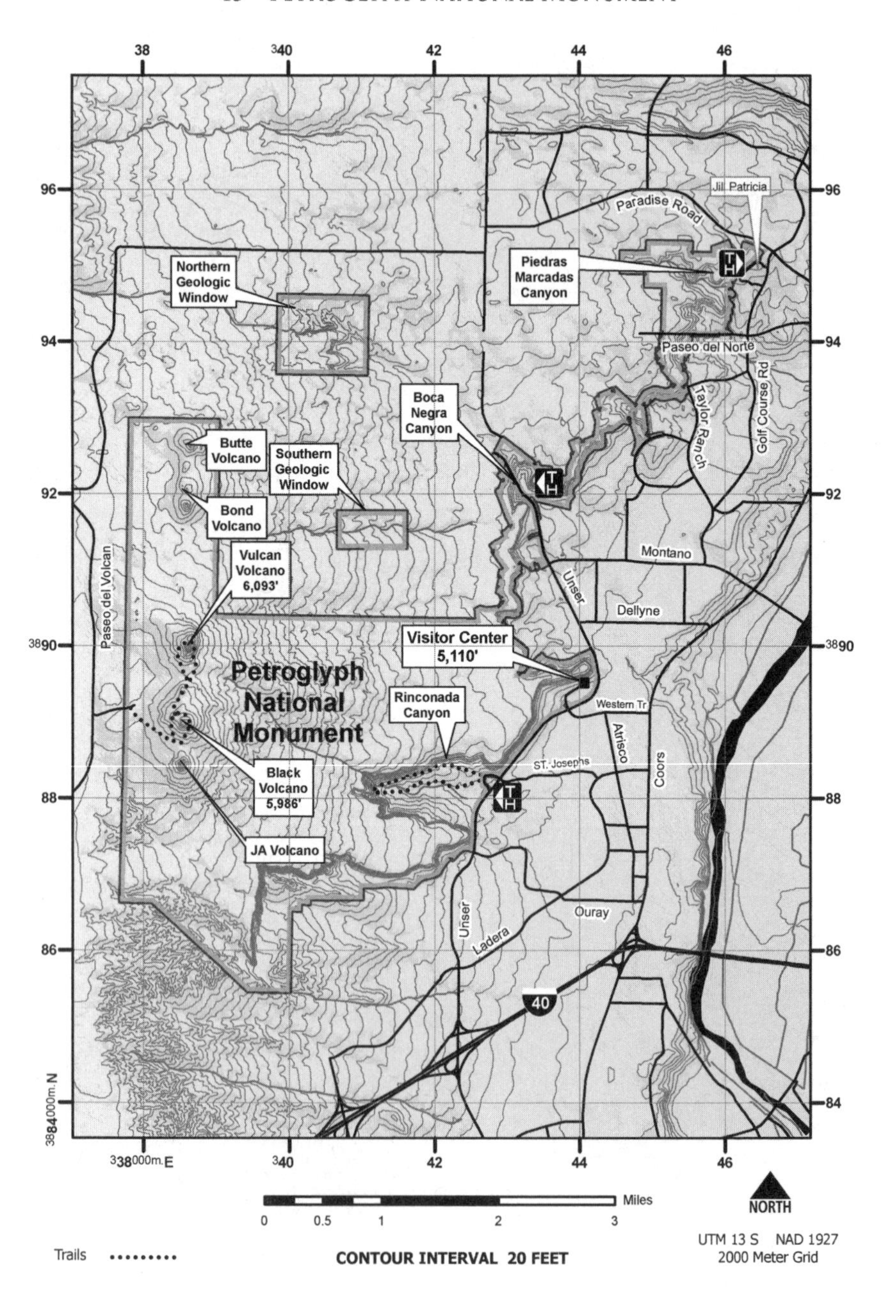

45 - PETROGLYPH NATIONAL MONUMENT

by Norbert Sperlich and Eleanor Eisenmenger

The monument at the edge of Albuquerque is a sacred place for today's Pueblo people as it was for their ancestors. It features images, created hundreds of years ago, that depict elements of the Pueblo spiritual world.

RT Distance:	1 mile (Boca Negra Canyon) 2 miles (Piedras Marcadas) 2.5 miles (Rinconada Canyon)
Time:	1 hr (Boca Negra Canyon) 2+ hrs (Piedras Marcadas) 2+ hrs (Rinconada Canyon) *(Note: Distances are short but with much to see, so you don't want to rush)*
Elevation Range:	5200-5300 ft; total gain 100 ft
Rating:	Easy
RT Drive:	~140 miles; ~2½ hrs
Seasons:	The monument is open year round, with many visitors coming during October's Balloon Fiesta. Late fall and winter are great times to visit because the light is perfect for viewing the petroglyphs, and there are fewer visitors.
Maps:	Topo maps are not needed. Brochures with maps available at Visitor Center.
Fees:	Parking at Boca Negra $1 on weekdays; $2 on weekends.
Piedras M. TH:	346,422 mE 3,895,072 mN elev.5236'
Boca Negra TH:	343,613 mE 3,892,105 mN elev.5203'
Rinconada TH:	342,674 mE 3,888,288 mN elev.5181'

Summary

Petroglyph National Monument, established by Congress in 1990, contains the greatest concentration of petroglyphs along the Rio Grande. Included in the monument are 17 miles of lava escarpment west of Albuquerque and five extinct volcanos that are lined up on top of the mesa. Most of the petroglyphs were made between 1300 and 1600 AD, but some are much older. Three trails are described, viz., Boca Negra Canyon, Piedras Marcadas, and Rinconada Canyon, with both driving and hiking instructions. Hiking boots recommended. During warmer months, bring water, wear a hat and look out for rattlesnakes. Mornings are quieter, with chances for seeing wildlife.

Background

For Pueblo people, the monument is an important spiritual center and shrine, a place of reverence and prayer, a pathway to the spirit world and a link to their ancestors who created the petroglyphs. For lovers of the outdoors, the monument is an oasis at the edge of the city. For those who benefit from urban sprawl, the petroglyphs are an annoying obstacle to Albuquerque's westward expansion.

The Friends of the Albuquerque Petroglyphs and other groups, including the Sierra Club, were involved in the effort to create the monument. Controversy erupted when the City of Albuquerque asked Congress to withdraw land from the monument to allow the extension of Paseo del Norte, a major thoroughfare. Despite considerable protest, the extension was completed in 2005.

Beleaguered and threatened as it is, with housing developments coming right up to its eastern and northern boundaries, the monument is still a wonderful place to visit, not just once, but many times. Ranger-guided tours are available on summer weekends. Call the Visitor Center (505-899-0205, ext 335) for more information. Bring binoculars to watch wildlife and to look at petroglyphs that are far from the trails. Dogs are not allowed in Boca Negra Canyon.

Driving Directions

Take I-25 south to Albuquerque, and take Exit 228, Montgomery-Montaño. Turn right at the traffic light onto Montaño Road. Go straight on Montaño Road, across the Rio Grande, past the intersections with North Coors and Taylor Ranch Road, to the intersection with Unser Boulevard (6 miles west of I-25). Turn left onto Unser. Go south on Unser past the Dellyne intersection, around a bend, and on to the intersection with Western Trail Road, where you take a right to the Visitor Center. Hours are 8 am to 5 pm daily except Thanksgiving, Christmas, and New Year's Day. Summer hours are 8 am to 6 pm. The Visitor Center has restrooms, maps, pamphlets and books with information about the area.

To get to the hiking trails requires more driving. Further driving instructions are included in the hiking instructions.

Hiking Instructions

Boca Negra Canyon – This site gives quick access to short, self-guiding trails. Trailside signs explain petroglyphs and other features. Water, restrooms and picnic tables are available. Start early to avoid the crowds.

From the Visitor Center, drive north on Unser, past the Dellyne and Montaño intersections. Turn right into Boca Negra Canyon (2 miles north of the Visitor Center) and drive to the pay station and the first parking lot. From there the Mesa Point Trail, quite steep in places but paved most of the way, will take you to the mesa top in about 20 minutes, past many petroglyphs. The view from up there is striking: you are right at the edge of housing developments. Worlds in collision - urban sprawl held in check by the magic of the petroglyphs!

Two shorter trails start at the next parking area. These are the Macaw and the Cliff Base Trails. Among the highlights of these trails are the petroglyphs of a parrot and a mysterious star being.

Rinconada Canyon - This easy hike takes you away from the road and the suburbs into a secluded area where you can truly appreciate the petroglyphs in their natural setting. A pamphlet with a map of Rinconada is available at the Visitor Center. The parking lot at the entrance to the canyon is open from 8 am to 5 pm.

From the Visitor Center, drive south on Unser for 0.8 miles, then turn right at a traffic light (intersection with St. Joseph's Road). Park in the designated area. Don't leave valuables in your vehicle. Thieves know about this place! As you start walking the sandy trail that follows the escarpment, you will notice countless boulders riddled by bullets. Was this once a war zone? No, just a place for target practice.

Further away from the road, there are fewer shot-up rocks and more petroglyphs. Don't touch them or climb on them, they are fragile. Stay on the trail, and don't trample the rattlesnakes. If you get tired of the petroglyphs, look out for the rabbits, squirrels, quail and other wildlife. The vegetation of the high desert, mostly shrubs and grasses, is quite different from what we have in Santa Fe. There are no shade trees.

As you approach the head of the canyon, you will encounter the last large group of petroglyphs. By now, your mind has calmed down, your eyes have learned to recognize subtle designs on the rocks, and the urge to rush from one roadside attraction to the next has vanished. Enjoy the feeling! This is what you came here for.

Retrace your steps, or continue along the southern escarpment toward Unser. If you continue, look back once in a while and you will catch glimpses of the volcanos on the mesa top. Before you reach Unser, turn left (north) and go back to your car.

Piedras Marcadas Canyon – The northernmost part of the monument, with suburbs on two sides, holds a treasure trove of petroglyphs in a setting somewhat like Rinconada Canyon. The extension of Paseo del Norte cuts this area off from the rest of the monument.

From the Visitor Center, drive north on Unser and turn right at Montaño Road. Proceed east on Montaño to Taylor Ranch Road. Turn left onto Taylor Ranch Road and set your odometer. After ½ mile, continue straight onto Golf Course Road as Taylor Ranch Road bears left. At 2½ miles, turn left onto Jill Patricia, one block before the major intersection of Golf Course with Paradise Road. Piedras

Marcadas parking is on the right on Jill Patricia, behind the oil change station.

When you pass from the closely spaced houses of the suburb into the open canyon, you know that you have entered a parallel universe. Be extra careful not to disturb this special place. Follow the sandy trail that runs along the escarpment of the lava mesa. Many petroglyphs are to be found in little side canyons, on south-facing boulders. You will see depictions of masked beings, birds, animals, stars, hands and many other things. You might also notice grinding slicks (stones with a smooth surface where grains or herbs were ground). Here and there, you will startle a rabbit or quail that was hiding between the rocks. Notice the many bird and animal tracks that crisscross the sand. Before long, you will forget how close you are to the city. Return the way you came.

You can return to I-25 via Paseo del Norte.

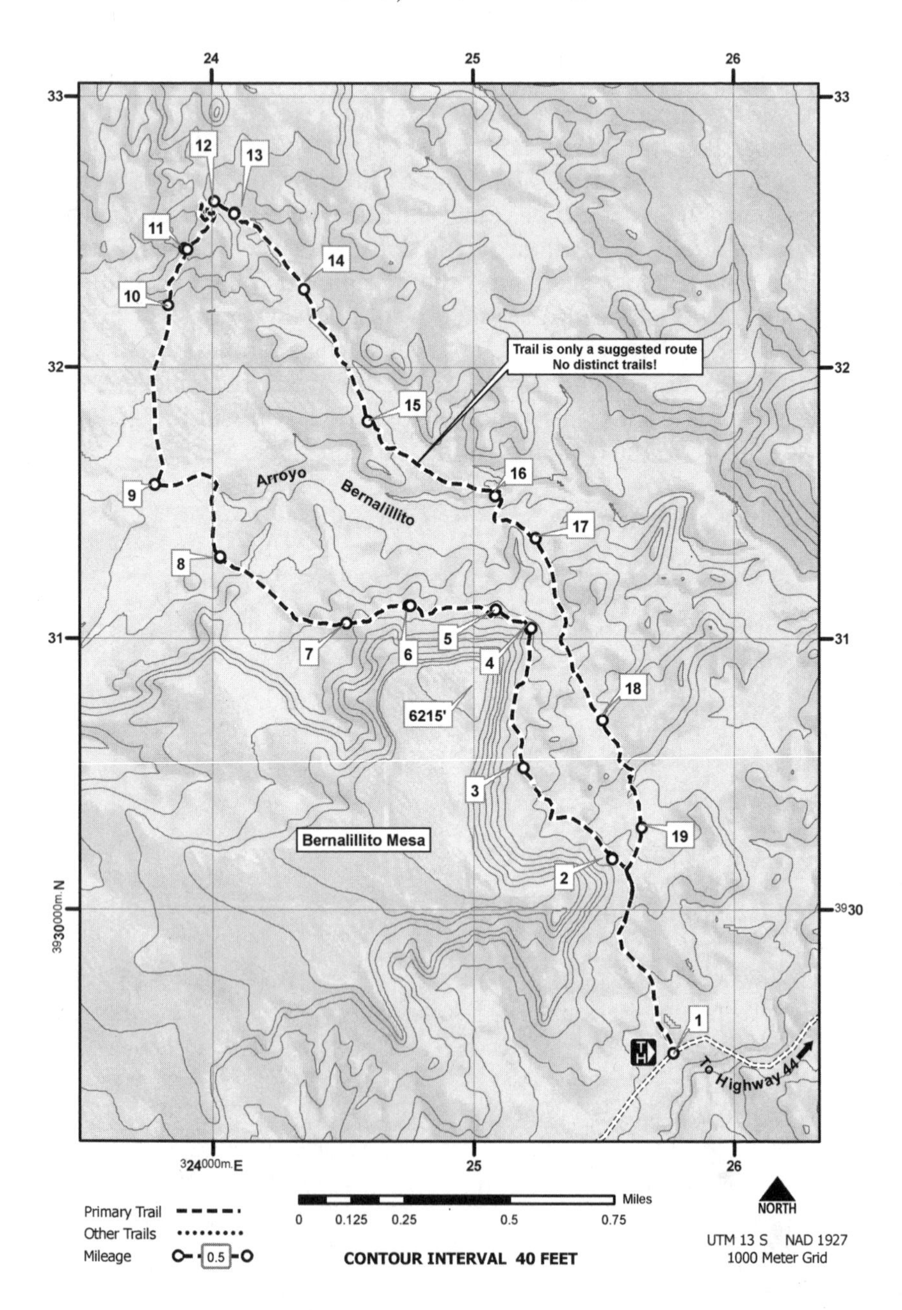
24
25
26
33
32
31
3930000m.N
3930
324000m.E
Trail is only a suggested route
No distinct trails!
Arroyo
Bernalillito
Bernalillito Mesa
6215'
To Highway 44
1
2
3
4
5
6
7
8
9
10
11
12
13
14
15
16
17
18
19
Primary Trail
Other Trails
Mileage
0.5
Miles
0
0.125
0.25
0.5
0.75
CONTOUR INTERVAL 40 FEET
NORTH
UTM 13 S NAD 1927
1000 Meter Grid

46 - Ojito Wilderness

by Stephen Markowitz

An off-trail hike west of San Ysidro in picturesque badlands, requiring a good sense of direction and a GPS receiver.

RT Distance: 6 miles

Time: 5 hrs

Elevation Range: 5750-6000 ft; total gain 600 ft

Rating: Moderate

RT Drive: 150 miles; 3 hrs

Seasons: Late fall, winter and early spring. This hike is not appropriate for hot weather. Beware of rattlesnakes during warmer weather.

Maps: USGS Ojito Spring Quadrangle - 7.5' series. The trailhead is located in USGS Sky Village NW - 7.5' series.

GPS Required: A GPS receiver with spare batteries or a fresh recharge is required.

Trailhead: 325,769 mE 3,929,467 mN elev.5791'

Summary

The Ojito Wilderness is a favorite cool-weather hiking area, a dry and much eroded place of high desert scenery with stark distant vistas of the Cabezon volcanic plug and the Red Mesa cliffs. The hikes there take you on top of mesas and into arroyos and past the remains of old homesteads and corrals, and 19th century Indian and ancestral Puebloan ruins. The Ojito Wilderness Act, passed and signed into law in October 2005, permanently protects the wilderness from exploitation. There are few trails; hiking there consists of following old jeep roads, cattle and game trails or just dead reckoning off-trail, on sandstone ledges, or trekking through arroyos and brush on uneven, rocky, and potentially very muddy soils.

This hike is moderate in length and elevation gain but over rough and uneven terrain, and requires careful route finding.

Please don't remove any artifacts or fossils, as these are protected under law. This area should be avoided during wet conditions, as the roads can become very muddy and impassable, even for 4-wheel drive.

Note: The hike description below is for experienced off-trail hikers with a good sense of direction and a thorough knowledge of how to use maps, a compass and a GPS. Do not hike this suggested route alone, and leave plenty of daylight before starting out.

Driving Directions

Drive southwest on I-25 to Exit 242 at Bernalillo. Turn right onto US 550 (old State Hwy 44) and set your odometer. Drive northwest and in about 18 miles you will pass Zia Pueblo. There are wonderful views of White Mesa at 12 o'clock, the Nacimiento mountains at 1 o'clock, the Jemez fault uplift at 2 o'clock, and the Jemez volcanic mountains at 3 o'clock. Just past the 21-mile road marker, turn left onto Cabezon Road. After turning, stop and reset your odometer. Bear left immediately at a fork to continue on Cabezon Road. At about 4 miles, you will cross from Zia Pueblo land onto Ojito BLM land. You will pass Gasco Road at 4.8 miles. The road turns sharply to the right at 5.9 miles. At about 10 miles, you will pass a parking area on the left, which is parking for a short hike to the Seismosaurus State Dinosaur site. At about 11 miles, you will cross an arroyo and you will see an old road on the right. This is waypoint (WP) 1. Park on the right just beyond the sign saying "area closed to motor traffic." The hike starts here.

Hiking Instructions

The hike requires good route-finding skills. The first part follows an old jeep road. Later, it coincides in places with game and cattle trails, and occasional hiker footprints. A part is across open country.

Upload the following waypoints prior to hike. (GPS Data Format: UTM NAD 27 ZONE 13S ElevFeet):

#	WP	mE	mN	Elev. (ft)
1	TH	325,769	3,929,467	5791
2	Cone	325,530	3,930,188	5866
3	Hoodoo	325,190	3,930,520	5914
4	Point	325,215	3,931,034	5887
5	Fence	325,085	3,931,105	5882
6	6	324,751	3,931,117	5904
7	7	324,517	3,931,053	5916
8	Survey	324,030	3,931,295	5823
9	Homes	323,703	3,931,731	5839
10	Rocks	323,831	3,932,226	5877
11	Enter	323,896	3,932,435	5964
12	Down	323,962	3,932,602	5956
13	13	324,089	3,932,567	5906
14	14	324,354	3,932,288	5852
15	15	324,597	3,931,800	5822
16	Arroyo	325,081	3,931,524	5754
17	17	325,237	3,931,370	5776
18	18	325,493	3,930,697	5845
19	Gate	325,644	3,930,302	5822
1	TH	325,769	3,929,467	5791

Start at WP 1 and head toward WP 2 by hiking north on the old jeep road. Leave the road shortly before reaching WP 2 and cross the barbed wire fence at the sandstone stepping stone, west of a cone. Head for WP 3, following as best you can on the tracks of earlier trekkers. You might find a game trail heading in that direction or footprints in the sand. WP 3 is on a rise with an interesting combination of desert hoodoos and ponderosa, a good spot for your first break.

Continue to WP 4, below the point of Bernallilito Mesa on your left. There are good views of the Red Mesa cliffs to the northeast. Red Mesa is the southernmost area of the Nacimiento Mountain range. Round the point on a game trail and go toward WP 5, while viewing Cabezon straight ahead. Go over a downed fence and work your way west toward WP 6. Go around a drainage and follow the game trail. Proceed to WP 7. Then head west-northwest cross-country to WP 8, keeping the windmill far to your left and the pond straight ahead. Go north on the dam and cross low ground going left, and then west on higher ground to WP 9 crossing downed barbed wire on the way. There are two homestead ruins at WP 9. This is another good spot for a break.

Hike north to WP 10, deviating slightly west to cross a downed fence, to a line of broken boulder debris, and then hike up the sandy ridge on a game trail. Hike northeast on the ridge to the base of the cliff and then work your way left to WP 11 and ascend the sandstone mesa top. This is a good place for a lunch stop or a break. The hike is half over, but the return is harder, so save your energy if you can. If you have time, explore the interesting geologic formations, north, toward the cone-shaped mesa.

Next, head for WP 12, by not falling off the cliff. The way down is west and north of where you think it is. Pass a small Navajo ruin and then another as you hike toward WP 13. Go southeast to WPs 14 and 15, being careful at a stone dam, and cross an arroyo at 16. Be very careful at arroyo edges, as the walls are steep and unstable. Find a way out of the arroyo center on the game trail that goes up the side drainage. Climb to level ground and then around the drainage. From here, head to WP 17 where there is an abandoned water trough. Head south-southeast through the maze to WP 18, and then find a way to WP 19 where there is a gate through a fence. Follow the path and then return on the old jeep road from whence you came (end of hike).

In the Ojito Wilderness

47 Brazos Cabin

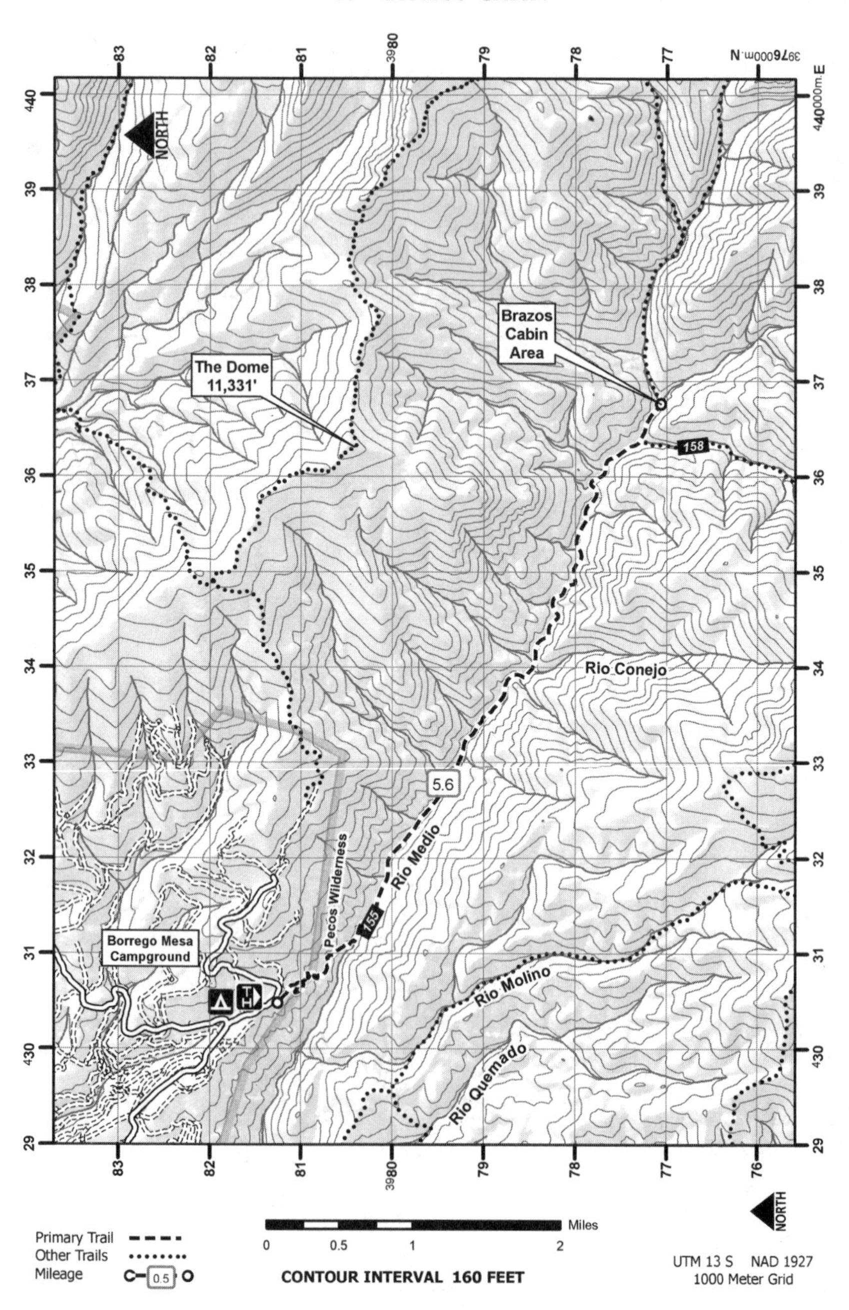

47 - Brazos Cabin

by John O. Baxter

The destination of this hike is a high meadow with views of Pecos Baldy.

RT Distance: 11 miles
Time: 8 hrs
Elevation Range: 8250-9200 ft; total gain 2500 ft
Rating: Strenuous
RT Drive: 78 miles; ~2½ hrs
Seasons: May be snowed-in in winter.
Maps: USGS Sierra Mosca and Truchas Peak - 7.5' series. The trail shown on these maps is different from the current trail described here. Drake's *Map of the Mountains of Santa Fe* shows most of the hike except for the trailhead.
Trailhead: 430,508 mE 3,981,289 mN elev.8805'

Summary

This trail into the Pecos Wilderness is used far less than trails starting at the Santa Fe Ski Basin. A beautiful mountain country hike, mostly in the trees, with good bird and flower sightings likely. The destination of this hike is a high meadow with views of Pecos Baldy. There is a sharp drop (8850 to 8250 ft) in the first ½ mile, then a gradual climb to Brazos Cabin at 9200 ft.

After prolonged rains or snow, we recommend you check with the Forest Service on the condition of FR 306, which takes you to the trailhead. We also recommend you carry a trash bag to collect items that mar the landscape.

Driving Directions

Take US 84/285 north to Pojoaque (~16 miles from Santa Fe). Continue across the bridge in the Española lane and turn right onto NM 503 at the Nambé turnoff (traffic signal). Note the mileage at the turnoff. At the Cundiyo-Chimayo junction (about 7½ miles), go straight ahead toward Cundiyo. Drive carefully through Cundiyo (~10 miles on a narrow road with free-roaming dogs). About 2 miles past Cundiyo, you will pass a turnoff to Santa Cruz Lake on your left, CR 98A. About 100 yards past this turnoff (13½ miles from the Nambé turnoff), look for FR 306, a dirt road that goes off to the right (there is a very small sign displaying "306"); turn right here. If you drive past the top of the ridge you've gone too far.

When you turn right onto FR 306, reset your odometer to zero. You will enter the burn area of the 12,700-acre 2002 Borrego Mesa fire. At about 7½ miles, you will pass a turnoff on your right marked "Trail 150, Borrego Trail." This is **not** your trail. At 9 miles, close to the Borrego Mesa Campground, the road forks. Take the right fork (FR 435), which takes you to the entrance of the campground. Take the road in front of the entrance that goes off to the right. The trailhead (Trail 155) is about 300 yards further. The last part of this road can be very rutted. You might want to park closer to the entrance of the campground, especially if rain is expected, and just walk the extra 300 yards.

Hiking Instructions

At the trailhead to the right of the road, you will find an information board. A wooden sign directs you to Rio Medio Trail 155, which reaches the junction with the Rio Capulin Trail after 5 miles and Trail Riders Wall after 10 miles. Follow this trail to Brazos Cabin for about 5½ miles. The trail sets off in an easterly direction, rising slightly for 100 yards before plunging sharply down into Rio Medio Canyon. Much of this trail was re-routed in 1992. If you find yourself on a washed-out, rutted trail, you have probably strayed from the new, narrow trail onto the old one, which forks off to the right. Retrace your steps and get back on the new trail. Or, trudge on; the new and old trails rejoin a short way further down.

On the southern horizon, the green silhouette of Sierra Mosca looms over the valley to the south. Winding through towering ponderosas and patches of oak, the trail makes a descent of 600 ft in the first ½ mile, leading to the clear waters of the Rio Medio (not to be confused with Rio en Medio). This part of the trail has many false paths and shortcuts, but the main course is clear. It takes about ½ hour to reach Rio Medio.

Continuing eastward, the trail follows the north bank of the river upstream. Birders should find several mountain species in this area such as Steller's jays, hairy woodpeckers and western wood peewees. Broadtailed hummingbirds are often seen feeding at the scarlet penstemon blossoms that border the trail. Unfortunately, the canyon is also the home of some of New Mexico's most belligerent insects, including clouds of voracious gnats in June and equally hungry deer flies later on. That's why they call it Sierra Mosca (Fly Mountain)!

After staying close to the Rio Medio for about 1 mile, the trail leaves the bottom of the canyon, turning abruptly left. The trail climbs up on the north bank for the next 2½ miles or so, making several swings away from the river to cross a series of arroyos and occasional streams which come down from the north. If a snack now seems in order, reward yourself with the tiny raspberries that grow in profusion nearby as the trail returns to the Medio.

After making an easy stream crossing on a huge fallen ponderosa, followed by a few minutes through fallen trees, the trail passes through a log fence into a horse corral and comes to a marked fork. Here, Trail 158 goes off to the right toward Horsethief Meadow. Stay on the left fork, Trail 155, the Rio Medio Trail. It takes you out of the corral, through a most picturesque section of the canyon. In a few minutes, you cross a small stream and find yourself in a beautiful meadow where the Brazos Cabin once stood, and where only a few of its foundation stones remain. In this part of the valley, which opens rather suddenly, there are many pleasant locations to enjoy your lunch and the beauty of the Sangre de Cristos before retracing your footsteps to the trailhead.

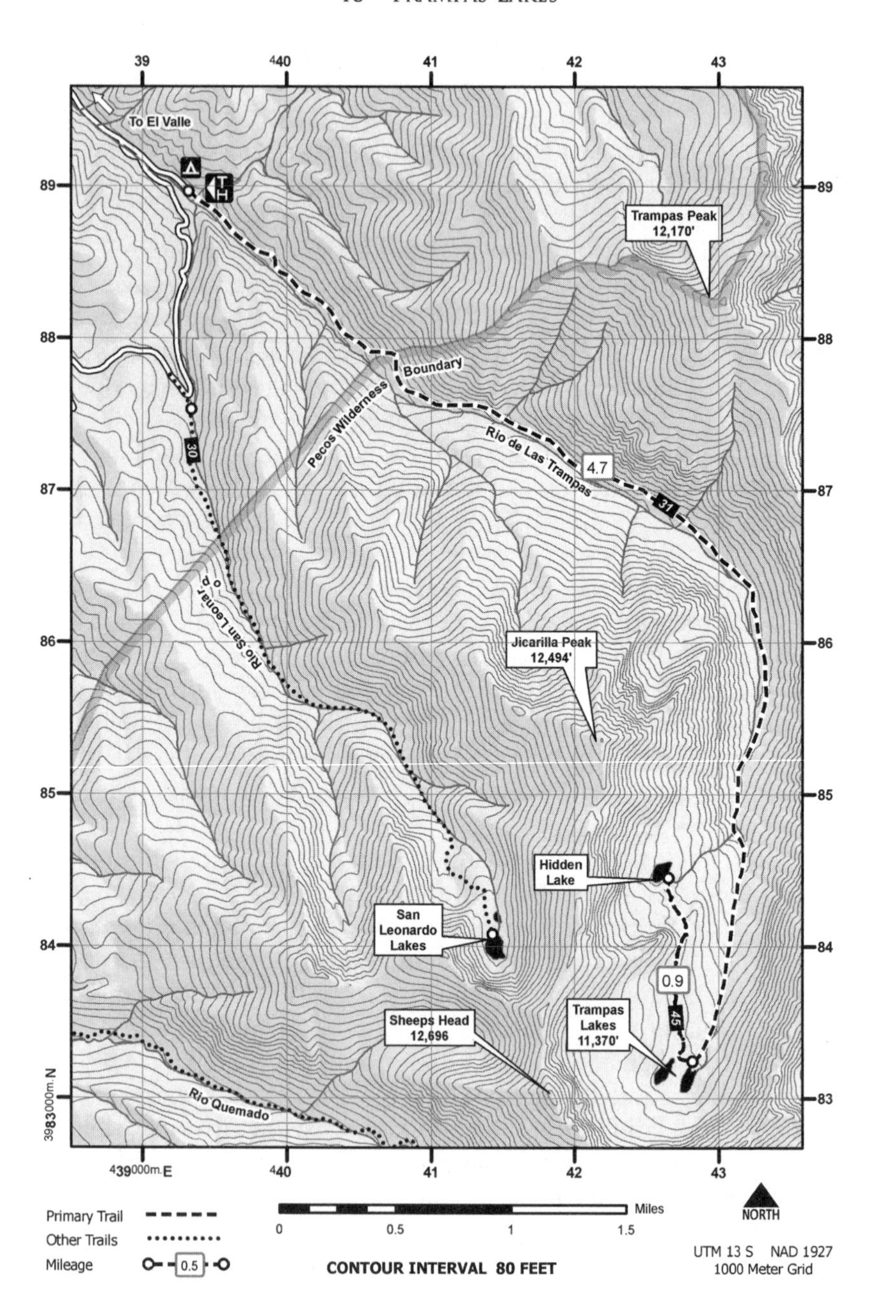
To El Valle
Trampas Peak
12,170'
Boundary
Pecos Wilderness
Rio de Las Trampas
4.7
31
30
Rio San Leonardo
Jicarilla Peak
12,494'
Hidden
Lake
San
Leonardo
Lakes
0.9
45
Sheeps Head
12,696
Trampas
Lakes
11,370'
Rio Quemado
439000m.E
3983000m.N
Primary Trail
Other Trails
Mileage
0.5
Miles
0
0.5
1
1.5
NORTH
CONTOUR INTERVAL 80 FEET
UTM 13 S NAD 1927
1000 Meter Grid

48 - Trampas Lakes

by Betsy Fuller

Lovely hidden lakes in the northern part of the Pecos Wilderness surrounded by towering peaks with a trail through deep coniferous forests.

RT Distance:	11.5 miles (Trampas Lakes only) 13.5 miles (with extension to Hidden Lake)
Time:	6+ hrs (Trampas Lakes only) 7+ hrs (with extension to Hidden Lake)
Elevation Range:	9000–11,410 ft; gain 2450 ft (Trampas Lakes only); gain 2700 ft (with extension to Hidden Lake)
Rating:	Strenuous
RT Drive:	108 miles; 3 hrs
Seasons:	A late spring, summer and early fall hike.
Maps:	USGS El Valle and Truchas Peak - 7.5' series. FS *Pecos Wilderness* Map is also recommended.
Trailhead:	439,311 mE 3,988,982 mN elev.8939'

Summary

A good, gradual uphill trail through thick shady forests, much of the time near a clear fast-running stream. The trail takes you to two picturesque alpine lakes nestled in a bowl formed by glaciers. There are abundant wildflowers along the stream.

Driving Directions

Take US 84/285 north to Pojoaque (~16 miles from Santa Fe). Continue over the bridge as you leave Pojoaque (in the Española lane) and turn right onto NM 503, the Nambé turnoff at the traffic signal. About 7½ miles from the turn-off onto NM 503, take a left turn (north) onto CR 98 to Chimayo. Go through the village of

Chimayo until you come to the junction with NM 76. Turn right (east) on NM 76 toward Truchas. About 8 miles from this junction and just as you get into the village of Truchas, NM 76 takes a sharp turn to the left (north). The turn here is between two buildings and hardly looks like a main thoroughfare, but there is a sign showing that the road goes to Peñasco and Taos.

Continue on NM 76 through the villages of Ojo Sarco and Las Trampas. Soon after you pass through the village of Las Trampas, be sure to notice the old log flume on the right, still carrying water from the higher elevations over the ravine to the irrigation ditches of the village below. About 1 mile beyond Trampas, take the road to El Valle going off to the right. From El Valle, continue on FS 207 for about 8 miles to the end of the road. Park at the primitive campground.

Hiking Instructions

Now you can get a close look at the Rio de las Trampas whose course you have been following in the car. It comes rushing out of a deep little canyon, probably the reason the road comes to an end here.

Look for a sign reading "Trampas Lake Trail 31" near an outhouse sited on a bank to the left of the road. Start walking up the trail, a steady upward path. You have about 2400 ft to climb to the lakes, and over 5 miles. You will soon pass through a gate (be sure to close it behind you). Close to 1 hour in, the trail will cross to the south side of the stream and then again to the north side. This is where an avalanche came down the side of the mountain years ago, taking all the trees with it. The area is now regenerating into an aspen forest usually filled with a profusion of wildflowers. Shortly after this open spot, rimmed on the north with striking cliffs, you will encounter a large blowdown which extends the better part of a mile or more. Fortunately, the Forest Service sawed off a sufficient number of the trees that were blocking the trail, providing an easy passage through the devastation.

Until you get very near the lakes, you will be walking along the left side of the river, most of the time quite far above it, but within earshot of it and with occasional glimpses of it rushing below you.

Occasionally, the trail traverses rock slides and talus slopes formed by Precambrian quartzite, the predominant rock of this area. In spite of avalanches, rock slides and blowdowns, the trail is usually well maintained.

There are many long switchbacks that help ease your way up. There is a river crossing which, except during the spring snow melt, should be no problem. Fallen tree trunks and stepping stones can be useful in crossing.

At the right time of year, usually early to mid-July, you find unbelievably beautiful gardens of marsh marigolds, brook cress, false hellebore, wild candytuft, thimbleberry, monkshood, cranesbill, osha, cow parsnip, Parry's primrose and many other flowers. Look back down the valley once in a while and you may catch a glimpse of the flat land around Española far below you in the Rio Grande Valley.

Finally, you will reach a level marshy area and a junction with a sign indicating Trampas Lakes ahead to the left and Hidden Lake straight ahead. To go to the Trampas Lakes, veer left and you will see a faint path along the shallow streamlet. Although you cannot see the lakes from here, in a few minutes you will see a sign identifying Lower and Upper Trampas Lakes. A walk of a few hundred yards further ahead will bring you to Upper Trampas to the right and Lower Trampas to the left. They are separated from each other by a low ridge and both provide majestic sites for lunch and photographs. Visit both lakes to enjoy their different colors and the striking views of the cliffs towering above.

From these lakes you can either return directly to your car down the trail over which you have just come, or you can take the trail to Hidden Lake at the junction you passed.

Extension Note - Given that returning from Hidden Lake requires an uphill walk, some may prefer to visit it first, then the Trampas Lakes. This extension will add about 1¼ hours and about 2 miles to the total distance. You will be walking along a good trail that is almost parallel with the trail you came on, but above it. Gradually the trail to Hidden Lake will bear off to the left, and, after a couple of mild switchbacks, you will descend to the lake itself. You will have dropped about 280 ft from the Trampas Lakes to Hidden Lake, and you will now have to climb back up to start the return trip home.

The return trip to your car is over the same trail on which you walked to get to the lakes.

(Note: Winter cross-country skiers who may be tempted to ski in the Rio de las Trampas Canyon from the campground to Las Trampas Lakes should be fully aware of the avalanche danger. This danger becomes greater toward spring and on warm winter days with widely-changing temperatures. Traveling the Rio de las Trampas Canyon trail during such conditions is to be avoided.)

Trampas Lake

Near Trampas Lake

49 SANTA BARBARA WEST FORK

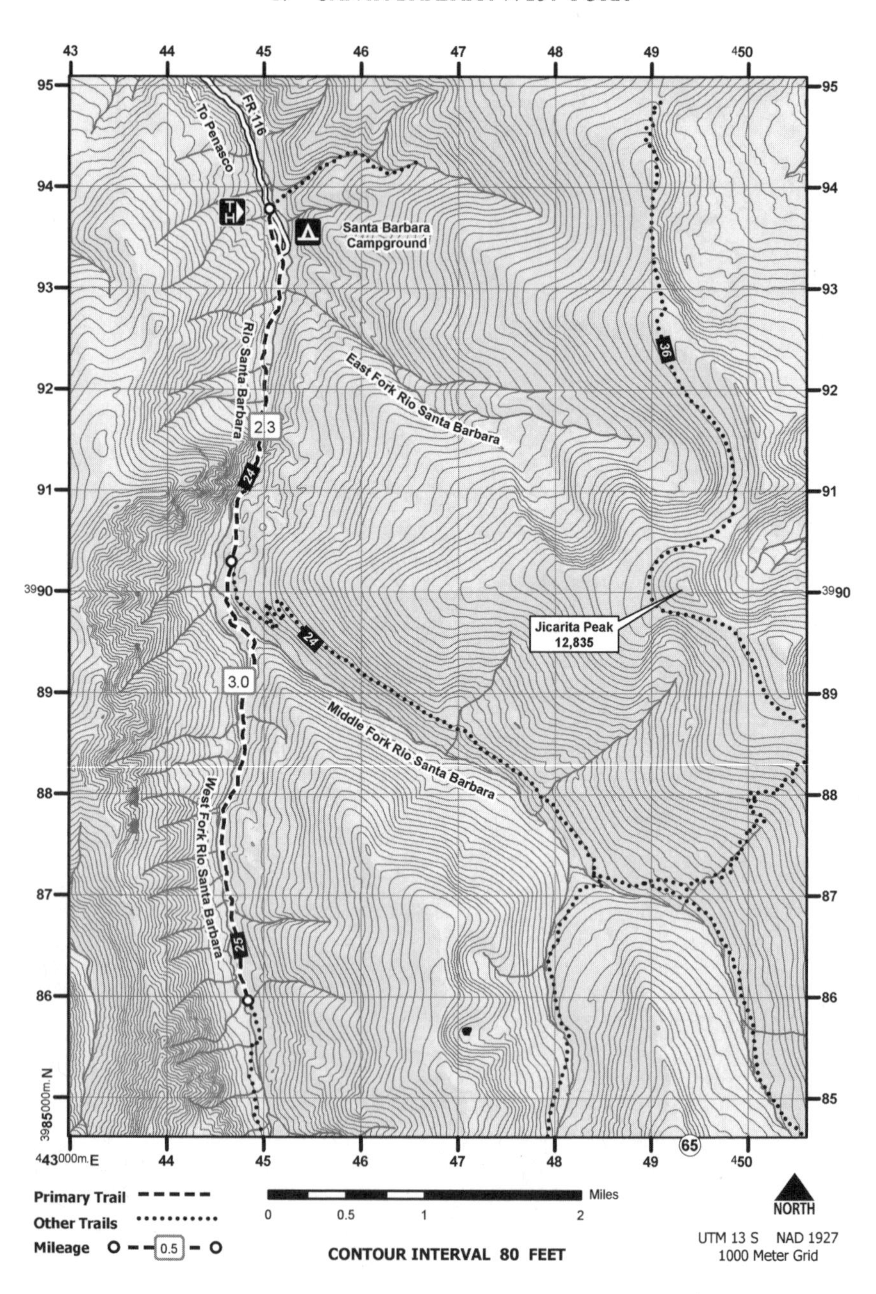

49 - SANTA BARBARA WEST FORK

by Linda and John Buchser

A beautiful hike with stunning views at the north end of the Pecos Wilderness, following the West Fork of Rio Santa Barbara.

RT Distance:	12 miles
Time:	7 hrs
Elevation Range:	8868-9880 ft; total gain ~1100 ft
Rating:	Strenuous
RT Drive:	143 miles; 3-3½ hrs
Seasons:	Late spring through fall. Road closed several miles before Santa Barbara campground during snow season.
Maps:	USGS Jicarita Peak - 7.5' series.
Trailhead:	445,051 mE 3,993,801 mN elev.8371'

Summary

This trip takes you to the north end of the Pecos Wilderness. Following the West Fork of Rio Santa Barbara, you will hike through lush meadows and aspen forest bordered by towering cliffs.

Driving Directions

Take US 84/285 north to Española, continuing straight through Española on NM 68 headed toward Taos. Go through Velarde and along the Rio Grande just past Embudo, where you turn right (east) onto NM 75. Continue through Dixon and Peñasco. When you come toward the end of Peñasco, NM 75 turns sharply left (toward Vadito). Don't take this left turn. Keep going straight ahead toward Rodarte, on what is now NM 73. After about 1½ miles, turn left onto FR 116. There is a brown Forest Service sign directing you to Santa Barbara campground. Follow this road (initially paved) for 6 miles to the Santa Barbara campground. About 100 yards before reaching the Fee Area, the road forks at a trail sign and there is a small parking area at your left. Parking here is free. Day parking in the Fee Area is $2.

Hiking Instructions

Walk the lower road through the campground. At the top end of the campground, a gate allows access to the trail that starts to the right of the parking area entrance (Trail 24). At about ½ mile, the trail is rerouted past a washed-out area and ascends through an aspen stand. Later, the trail continues along the main flow of Rio Santa Barbara.

The entire trail offers great views, wonderful stream sounds, and has an excellent shady canopy that is quite beautiful in the fall. In a wet year, there is a continuous show of wildflowers from April through September. The variety of wildflowers is considerable, since the changes in elevation provide a wide range of growing conditions. At about 1½ miles, there is a wooden bridge crossing Rio Santa Barbara. This first section of trail is an easy day hike. As the trail increases its rate of ascent, towering cliffs come into view. At 2¼ miles, you will reach a fork in the trail marked by a sign. Go straight ahead on West Fork Trail 25. The left fork, which you do not take, is Middle Fork Trail 24.

In another ¼ mile, there is a stream crossing that often has fallen logs you can use as a makeshift bridge. Your safest option is to use hiking poles to navigate the stream. If you are backpacking, unfasten your waistbelt before crossing. In the spring, it is common for folks to turn around at this point. There are some fine views about ¼ mile up Trail 24, if you backtrack to the junction of Trails 24 and 25.

The stream you have just crossed is a combination of the East and Middle Forks, and you are now between them and the West Fork, which is out of sight at this point. The trail moves higher up the mountainside, and though the West Fork is now often visible far below, access to it is inconveniently steep and hazardous.

At about 4¾ miles, you come out of the trees and pass through open areas. These intermittent meadows continue to the end of the valley. There are several large beaver dams on the stream below. Cattle-grazing is permitted here only in the fall of every third year, so meadow wildflowers can be magnificent when there has been sufficient rain. Chimayosos Mountain comes into view spectacularly to the south.

At about 5½ miles, on your right are two large rock cairns. Several more cairns appear, marking the beginning of the Dominguez trail. This trail, re-constructed by the Sierra Club in the 80s, follows an old sheep-herding route. The trail goes to the top of the ridge, offering some of the finest aspen viewing on the west side of the Pecos Wilderness. Bristle-cone pines are common on the top of this ridge. The trail continues, steeply dropping to the Rio Trampas, with considerable blowdown obstructing it.

But back to our trail! At about 6 miles, you enter a mile-long meadow. It is worth going at least halfway up this meadow, as it offers magnificent views in all directions.

Return by the same route.

Glory be to God for dappled things...
All things counter, original, spare, strange;
Whatever is fickle, freckled (who knows how?)
With swift, slow; sweet, sour; adazzle, dim;
He fathers-forth whose beauty is past change;
Praise him.
~ Gerard Manley Hopkins

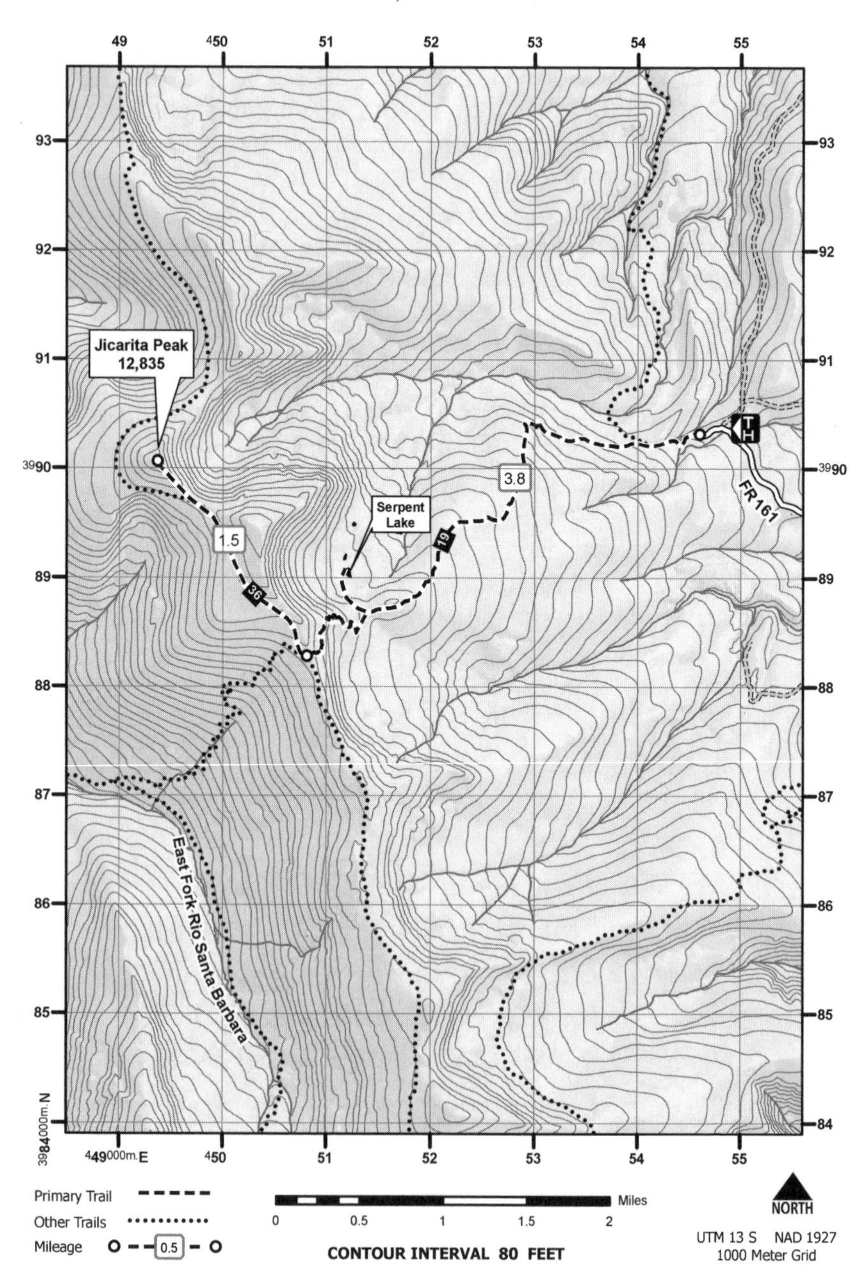

Jicarita Peak
12,835
Serpent Lake
1.5
36
19
3.8
FR 161
T H
East Fork Rio Santa Barbara
49
450
51
52
53
54
55
93
92
91
3990
89
88
87
86
85
84
449000m.E
3984000m.N
Primary Trail
Other Trails
Mileage
0.5
0
0.5
1
1.5
2
Miles
CONTOUR INTERVAL 80 FEET
NORTH
UTM 13 S NAD 1927
1000 Meter Grid

50 - Jicarita Peak

by Norma McCallan

A hike to a high peak at the north end of the Pecos Wilderness, with marvelous vistas, incredible displays of alpine wildflowers, and a sense of being on top of the world.

RT Distance:	11 miles
Time:	8 hrs
Elevation Range:	10,383-12,835 ft; total gain 2452 ft
Rating:	Strenuous
RT Drive:	150 miles; 4 hrs
Seasons:	June to October is best; otherwise you may run into snow. The dirt road to the trailhead is not plowed in winter.
Maps:	USGS Jicarita Peak - 7.5' series. USFS *Pecos Wilderness* map is recommended *(note that it shows this trail as Serpent Lake Trail 19).*
Trailhead:	454,594 mE 3,990,315 mN elev.10404'

Summary

This hike takes you to one of the highest peaks in New Mexico. The peak itself is easily climbed and can be done as a day hike. Because the peak and its approach are well above timberline, caution is urged in the event of approaching storms. Frequent thunderstorms occur around the Santa Barbara Divide in the summer, and exposed terrain is not the place to be when lightning strikes.

Driving Directions

Take US 84/285 north to Pojoaque (~16 miles from Santa Fe). Continue over the bridge as you leave Pojoaque (in the Española lane) and turn right onto NM 503, the Nambé turnoff at the traffic signal. About 7½ miles from the turnoff onto NM 503, take a left turn (north) onto NM 520 to Chimayo (you'll see a blue sign indicating Restaurante de Chimayo). Go through Chimayo until you come to the junction with NM 76. Turn right (east) onto NM 76 toward Truchas. About 7½ miles from the turn into the village of Truchas, NM 76 takes a sharp turn to the left (north). The turn here is between two buildings and hardly looks like a main thoroughfare, but there is a sign showing that the road goes to Peñasco. Continue on NM 76 through the villages of Ojo Sarco, Las Trampas and Chamisal. Turn right onto NM 75 and continue through Peñasco. At the end of Peñasco, turn left, still on NM 75, through Vadito. Ten minutes from Peñasco you come to a "T" intersection. Reset your odometer and turn right onto NM 518. You will go 13½ miles on this road, past a number of Forest Service campgrounds, and through the small village of Tres Ritos. After the private Angostura Camp and at about 1 mile past the sign for Mora County, turn right onto FR 161. It is marked with a large brown sign on the highway. Stay on this rough but passable road until it dead-ends in about 4½ miles at a roadblock (dirt piled up) and park.

Hiking Instructions

At the roadblock, there is a small sign "Head Trail" pointing toward the extension of the road you have been driving on. Proceed on the road for about 5 minutes until the road ends. There is a sign indicating that the trail to the right is Angostura Trail 493. The trail to the left goes to Serpent Lake and Santa Barbara Campground. Follow the left trail, and in about 10 minutes, you will see a trail coming in from the right, which you should ignore. Very shortly you will cross a ditch with fast-flowing water; there should be enough stones and logs to make a relatively easy crossing.

The trail continues through the forest, going upward at a comfortable incline. About 1½ miles in, you will pass a series of meadows. These make good spots for rest stops since this part of the trail is mostly heavy forest. In 2½-3 miles, you will come to a boundary sign for the Pecos Wilderness. Soon thereafter, the trail makes a sharp turn, and you will see the stark outline of the Santa Barbara Divide through the trees. Shortly, you will come to the intersection of the spur trail to Serpent Lake, heading off to the right, while the main trail has a sign showing that it is 11 miles further to Santa Barbara Campground and 10 miles back to Agua Piedra Campground. You have now traveled 3½ miles from the trailhead.

Note: Serpent Lake is only about ¼ mile down the spur trail. The origin of the name is not known, but the several grassy hummocks in the lake look rather like a small serpent swimming along, when viewed from the top.

Continue up the main trail. It soon leaves the forest and starts to switchback up through the scree and isolated clumps of stunted spruce and bristlecone pine. As you go higher, these pygmy forests give way to dense patches of willow, and magnificent bouquets of alpine flowers dot the scree. By the end of summer, the willows are turning gold and so are the aspen in the surrounding forests.

Just before you get to the top of the Santa Barbara Divide, you will pass a small spring, which takes the form of a shallow pond, on the right. On the top, you will find a barely legible sign that points the way back to Serpent Lake and Agua Piedra Campground. About 50 ft further, there stands a post where you should turn right off the main trail, following a series of cairns as a faint trail contours along the ridge near the top of the divide. This route detours around the south side of a large unnamed 12,828-ft peak. In some stretches, alternate trails and cairns exist—likely ending up in the same place.

Not until you are well around this unnamed peak will Jicarita Peak be visible. Its flat top and trapezoidal shape will suddenly dominate the horizon in front of you. Stay on this small trail until you reach the closest corner of Jicarita. The trail contours around the south and west sides of Jicarita and meets the trail coming up from Indian Creek at the northwest corner of Jicarita. Get off the trail and walk up the southeast corner of Jicarita. If you watch closely, you will find intermittent paths going up through the scree and grass of the slope. Soon you will be on the flat, wide top, with vistas in all directions and several rock shelters where you can eat your lunch out of the wind. The southern horizon is particularly awesome, with the jagged Truchas Peaks and the gentler slopes of Trampas and Chimayosos Peaks dominating the skyline. Always observe caution when up on the divide and watch for storm clouds; summer thunderstorms can roll in fast and you do not want to be above timberline when lightning strikes.

To return, carefully retrace your steps, veering slightly to the right and downhill, instead of staying at contour, or you will end up in a large pile of scree. When you come to the post, turn left (northeast) and follow the trail back.

Note: If you want to make this into a backpack trip, Serpent Lake is an ideal campsite part way up the trail. It is situated in a lovely grassy meadow, just below the steep cliffs of the Santa Barbara Divide. You can set your tent up in the grove of large trees near the faint path just north of the lake, or by the more open dwarf trees just beyond. Depending on the time and weather, you can then proceed back to the main trail and on up to the Peak, or wait till the next morning, when there is less likelihood of storms. Camping here also gives you the option of returning to the divide and turning left, in the opposite direction from Jicarita Peak to enjoy another hike. There are faint paths to follow southeast along the divide as far as your time, energy, and the weather permits. Drink in the magnificent 360° views and the sense of being on top of the world!

Walking is man's best medicine.
~ Hippocrates

Jicarita Summit

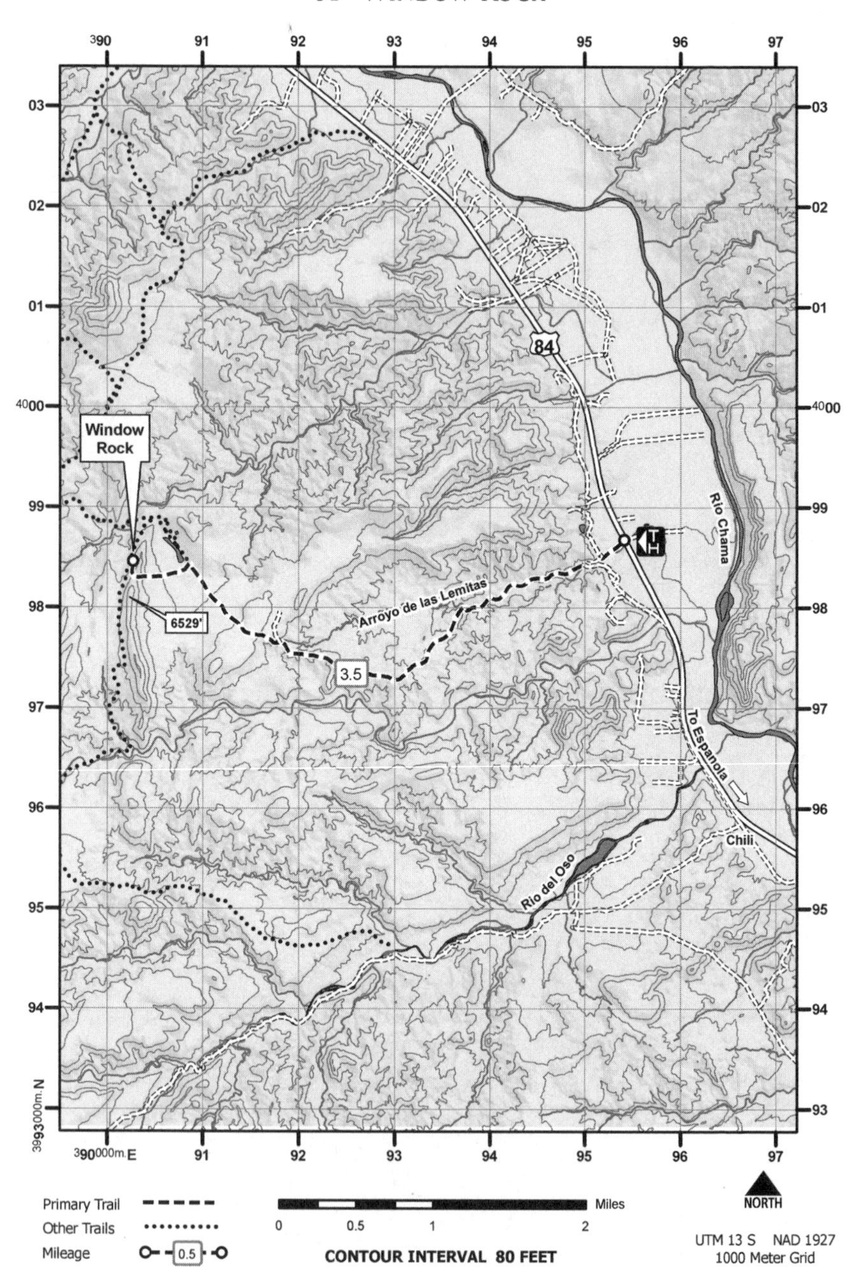

Window Rock
6529'
3.5
Arroyo de las Lemitas
84
Rio Chama
To Espanola
Chili
Rio del Oso
390
91
92
93
94
95
96
97
03
02
01
4000
99
98
97
96
95
94
93
3993000m.N
390000m.E
Primary Trail
Other Trails
Mileage
0.5
0
0.5
1
2
Miles
CONTOUR INTERVAL 80 FEET
NORTH
UTM 13 S NAD 1927
1000 Meter Grid

51 - Window Rock

by Norbert Sperlich

A hike up through badlands and a sandy arroyo to a "window" in a rock wall with great views along the way as well as from Window Rock.

Distance:	7.5 miles
Time:	5 hrs
Elevation Range:	5800-6463 ft; total gain 1000 ft
Rating:	Moderate
RT Drive:	70 miles; 1½+ hr
Seasons:	All seasons, but not recommended in hot weather. If you go in summer, take extra water.
Maps:	USGS Chili and Medanales - 7.5' series.
Trailhead:	395,440 mE 3,998,625 mN elev.5790'

Summary

Since the jeep trail you will hike on is not marked or maintained, this is a hike for experienced hikers only. Much of the terrain is sandy (look for animal tracks), but there are some rough and rocky spots as well. You will hike in a sandy arroyo, go up on a ridge through badlands, and come to a "window" or hole that has been weathered out of a dike (a rock wall formed by igneous rocks). You are in the piñon-juniper belt (or what is left of it after drought and bark beetles decimated the piñons), and you will also encounter cottonwoods, tamarisk, mountain mahogany and a stand of ponderosa.

Driving Directions

Drive north on US 84/285 to Española (~20 miles), follow the signs for US 84/285, cross the Rio Grande and head toward Chama.

Continue north on US 84/285 out of Española where, at about 6 miles, US 84 and US 285 separate. Keep going straight on US 84. Look for the green mileposts on the right side of the road. Slow down when you pass milepost 200. At 0.1 miles after this post, look for a gray, barn-like building made from corrugated sheet metal on your right. Some 40 yards past this building, a powerline crosses the highway, and a paved private driveway goes off to the right. Go just past this driveway and park your car on the side of the highway.

Hiking Instructions

Cross the highway. On the west side of the highway is a fence marked "Property Boundary, National Forest." Climb over the fence and go down into a sandy arroyo that comes in from the west. Follow the car tracks that run parallel to the arroyo along its right (north) side. If the tracks are gone, follow the arroyo, staying on its right side. Disregard a jeep trail that goes off to the right. Some 7 minutes or so into the hike, you should see a freestanding, orange-brown rock ahead of you on the right side of the arroyo. In another 5 minutes or so, you will be close to this rock. In front of the rock is a rectangular, green water tank and a well. The car tracks (your "trail") pass the tank on the left and go in and out of the arroyo. There are cottonwoods, elm trees and tamarisks along your way, and sandy hills with piñon and juniper along the sides of the arroyo. Here and there, you will encounter light gray rocks, formed by sand particles that have been cemented together. Often, the surface of these rocks is covered with balls or nodules consisting of cemented sand in different sizes—from peppercorns to tennis balls.

A little over 1 mile into the hike (it seems longer because of the sandy terrain), the arroyo narrows. Just where it makes a turn to the right, look for a jeep trail that goes out of the arroyo and uphill on your left. This is your trail to Window Rock.

The trail climbs to the top of a ridge and follows the ridgeline. Here and there, the trail is blocked by mounds of dirt. You are surrounded by badlands dotted with juniper and mountain mahogany. There are more of the gray sandstone formations sculpted by the elements. About 20 minutes after leaving the arroyo, you come to a high point on the ridge, with splendid views in all directions. Ahead of you are the Jemez Mountains; to the east you will see the Sangre de Cristo Range, with the flat-topped Black Mesa in the foreground. As you continue your hike, the ridge widens and levels out. Soon, it narrows again and the trail goes steeply uphill. Here, the ground is covered with loose rocks and the going is rough until you reach level ground again. You have now hiked about 1½ hours.

At this point, the jeep trail branches. Stay on the left branch. After a few minutes of hiking, look ahead and to the left. You will see a ridge that is crested by a dark rock wall, sticking out like a spine. Look for a hole in the rocks. That's Window Rock about 1 mile away. For about ¾ mile, the jeep trail goes gently downhill, taking you to a flat, treeless area. This is an area where water collects after heavy rains. Window Rock is to your left. Here you leave the jeep trail and go toward Window Rock. Just below the ridge, there is a sandy bank with tall ponderosa. This is a great spot for a break before ascending the ridge.

Look for a drainage coming down to the left of Window Rock. Climb up on the trail to the left of this drainage. As you near the top of the ridge, the trail bears to the right and goes to the other side of the dike and to the window. Caution should be taken if you climb up on the dike. It is only 6 ft wide. Do not attempt to cross over the top of the window. Enjoy the views and the solitude, then return the way you came.

Window Rock

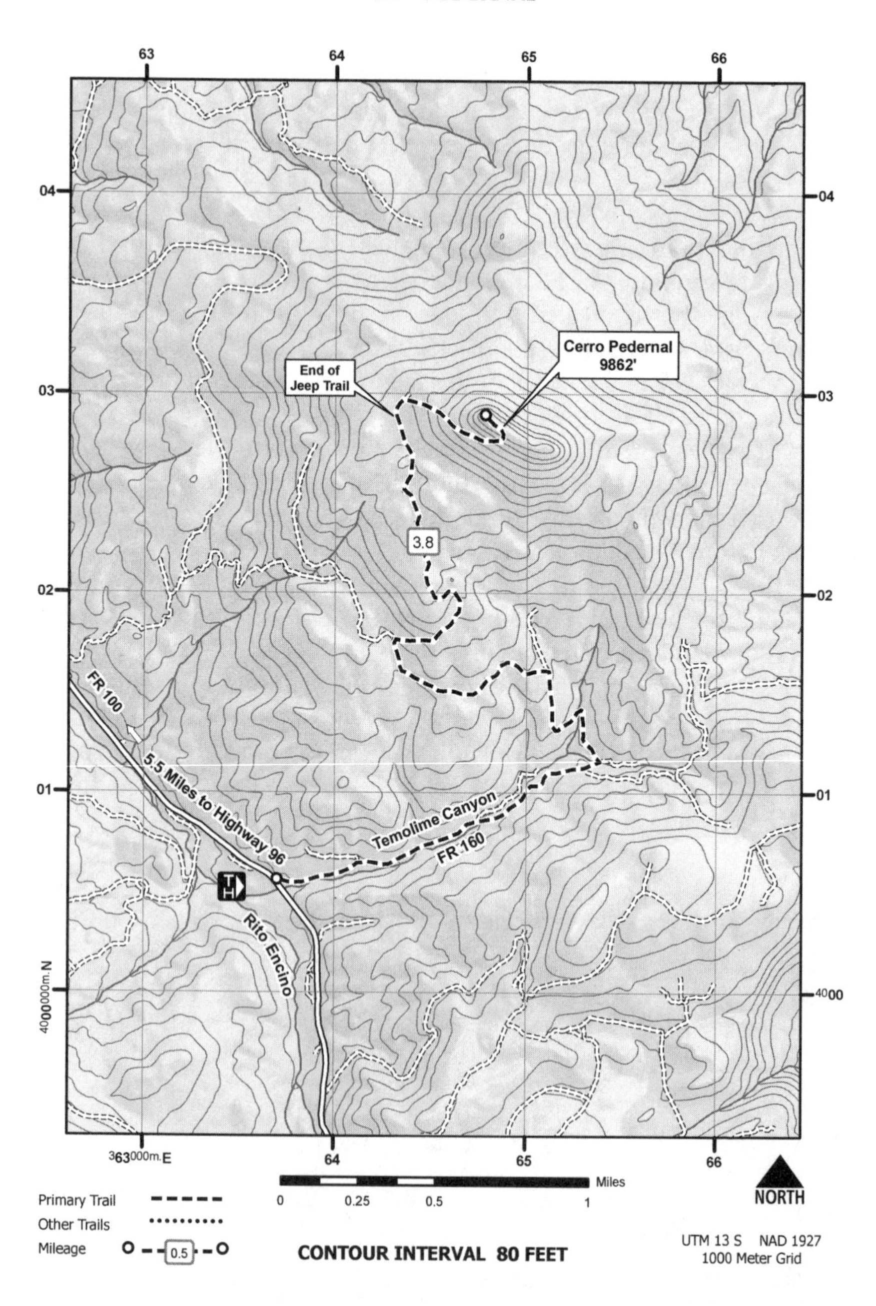
63
64
65
66
04
03
02
01
4000000m.N
4000
Cerro Pedernal
9862'
End of
Jeep Trail
3.8
FR 100
5.5 Miles to Highway 96
Temolime Canyon
FR 160
Rito Encino
363000m.E
Primary Trail
Other Trails
Mileage
0.5
Miles
0
0.25
0.5
1
CONTOUR INTERVAL 80 FEET
NORTH
UTM 13 S NAD 1927
1000 Meter Grid

52 - PEDERNAL

by John Muchmore and Norbert Sperlich

Cerro Pedernal's distinctive profile can be seen throughout north-central New Mexico. The summit provides sweeping views in all directions.

RT Distance:	8 miles
Time:	6-7 hrs (including time for stops)
Elevation Range:	8000-9862 ft; total gain 1862 ft
Rating:	Moderate in miles, but strenuous due to steep climbs.
RT Drive:	146 miles; ~3½ hrs
Seasons:	Not safe when snow hides the jeep roads and makes the rocks slippery. Best time to visit is in spring, fall and early winter. A favorite area for elk and deer hunters.
Maps:	USGS Youngsville and Cañones - 7.5' series.
Trailhead:	363,785 mE 4,000,579 mN elev.8019'

Summary

Cerro Pedernal (commonly referred to as simply "Pedernal") is a landmark well known throughout north-central New Mexico. Its truncated pyramid shape is visible from Taos to Cuba and from Chama to Española. The mountain has appeared in works by famous American artists, including Georgia O'Keeffe. From its summit, you will enjoy sweeping views in all directions.

Much of the hike is on unmarked jeep roads; the last part is very steep with only a faint trail. This hike is not suitable for inexperienced hikers and **not** recommended for solo hiking. The last part of the hike is steep and rocky, and can be dangerous unless you are confident of your ability to climb up and down a vertical 15-ft rock face (dogs will not be able to negotiate this rock face). Sturdy boots with good traction are required. This is dry country, so carry sufficient water and be prepared for wind, cold and rain.

History

Cerro Pedernal is Spanish for "Flint Hill." Flint (a variety of quartz) can be found on the lower slopes of the mountain at about 8,500 ft. For more than 10,000 years, Indians have used the flint from Cerro Pedernal to make arrowheads and tools.

Driving Directions

Drive north on US 84/285 to Española (~20 miles). Follow the signs for US 84/285, cross the Rio Grande and head toward Chama. Continue north on US 84/285 out of Española where, at about 6 miles, US 84 and US 285 separate. Continue straight (north) on US 84 past Abiquiu to the Abiquiu Dam turnoff (NM 96) where you turn left. Take your mileage at this intersection, and continue for about 11 miles to the outskirts of Youngsville. As you approach Youngsville, look for a gravel road on your left. This is FR 100 (Rito Encino Road). Turn left onto FR 100 and follow it for about 5½ miles, until you see a dirt road branch off to the left. Turn left onto this road and park your car in the meadow immediately after the turnoff. You are now on FR 160, the Temolime Canyon jeep road. The road is not marked at the turnoff. However, a sign "160" appears some 100 yards along the road.

Hiking Instructions

Follow FR 160 up Temolime Canyon for about 1 mile (~20 min) to a fork in the road. FR 160 effectively ends as further passage is blocked by dirt berms. Follow the main road that goes to the left (north). Ignore an abandoned logging road that branches right. In a few minutes, you will cross a drainage where the road turns to the left and starts climbing. Soon the road turns to the right (north) again and it appears to head toward the eastern end of the Pedernal summit ridge. Some 5 minutes after crossing the drainage, you will reach an area that is covered with pieces of flint. Flint comes in many colors: white, pearly gray, blue-gray, red and more.

In a few more minutes, you will encounter a fork in the road. The road that goes straight ahead (toward the summit) is blocked with a pile of dirt. Continue on the unobstructed road that goes off to the left, in a westerly direction. About 15 minutes after taking the left fork, as you are going uphill, you will notice a drainage on your left, where Gambel oaks are growing. Just before the road is about to cross the drainage and make a turn to the left, a road comes in sharply behind you on the right. There should be a cairn marking this intersection.

Take the rocky road that comes in from the right. At first, the road climbs steeply in an easterly direction. Then the road turns north, toward the summit ridge. It crosses a drainage and starts climbing again, turning to the left, away from the summit. This is obviously not the shortest way to get to the top, but it is the easiest! After briefly heading south, the road turns right to almost level ground. In a few minutes, you will come to the first of a series of meadows. From the last intersection you have now hiked some 25 minutes or more.

For a while, the road heads toward the center of the summit ridge, then turns left and runs parallel to the ridge. In the meadows, the jeep tracks are less distinct but still visible. Follow the jeep tracks past the western end of the summit ridge to a level spot between two pine trees with a nice sitting rock. You have now hiked about 40 minutes since the last intersection. Ahead of you, the terrain starts to descend, opening up splendid vistas over valleys, mesas and mountain ranges. Take a break and enjoy the views.

It will take another hour or so of strenuous hiking to reach the summit. Look to your right. A talus slope, studded with scrub oak and piñon, rises up to the lower end of the basalt ridge that forms the summit. Walk several hundred feet up to the end of the jeep tracks. Turn right and head up toward the narrow end of the ridge, veering a little to its left. You should shortly see cairns marking a faint path which becomes more discernible as you get higher. This zigzag trail ends at a layer of boulders which you must cross with care. When you reach the vertical basalt cliffs, note where you crossed the boulder field for your return trip. Go to the right and follow a faint trail that runs along the base of the cliffs. After about 10-15 minutes of hiking, the trail passes between the cliff wall on the left and a large juniper tree on the right. (If you come to a cave in the rocks on your left, you have gone too far. Go back and look for the juniper tree.) Follow the trail 10 yards past the juniper tree. Stop and look. The cliff on your left is somewhat broken up, providing hand and footholds. This is the place to climb up, or to call it a day if it looks too scary to you. The first 15 ft are nearly vertical, but then you will come to a rough trail that goes up to your right, leading to the top of the ridge. Watch for loose rocks! When you come to the flat top, look for cairns. They will tell you where to start your descent on the way back. Any other way down is dangerous. Continue left on the ridge to its western end. This is the highest point of Pedernal.

After you have enjoyed the spectacular views, you might want to go to the other end of the ridge, where the views are toward the east. Then find the cairn that marks the descent and start your way down to the base of the cliffs. Proceed very slowly down the steep, gravelly slopes: loose rocks abound. It helps to have one of the more able members of the party go down the final 15 vertical feet first so he/she can help direct the rest in finding footholds. Once at the base, you will be tempted to head straight down to the jeep trail in the meadow below. However, to stay out of harm's way, avoid loose rocks on a very steep slope and cause less erosion, return to the meadow the same way you came up, along the zigzag trail to the jeep road, and retrace your route back to your car.

Pedernal – the place to climb up

53 Kitchen Mesa

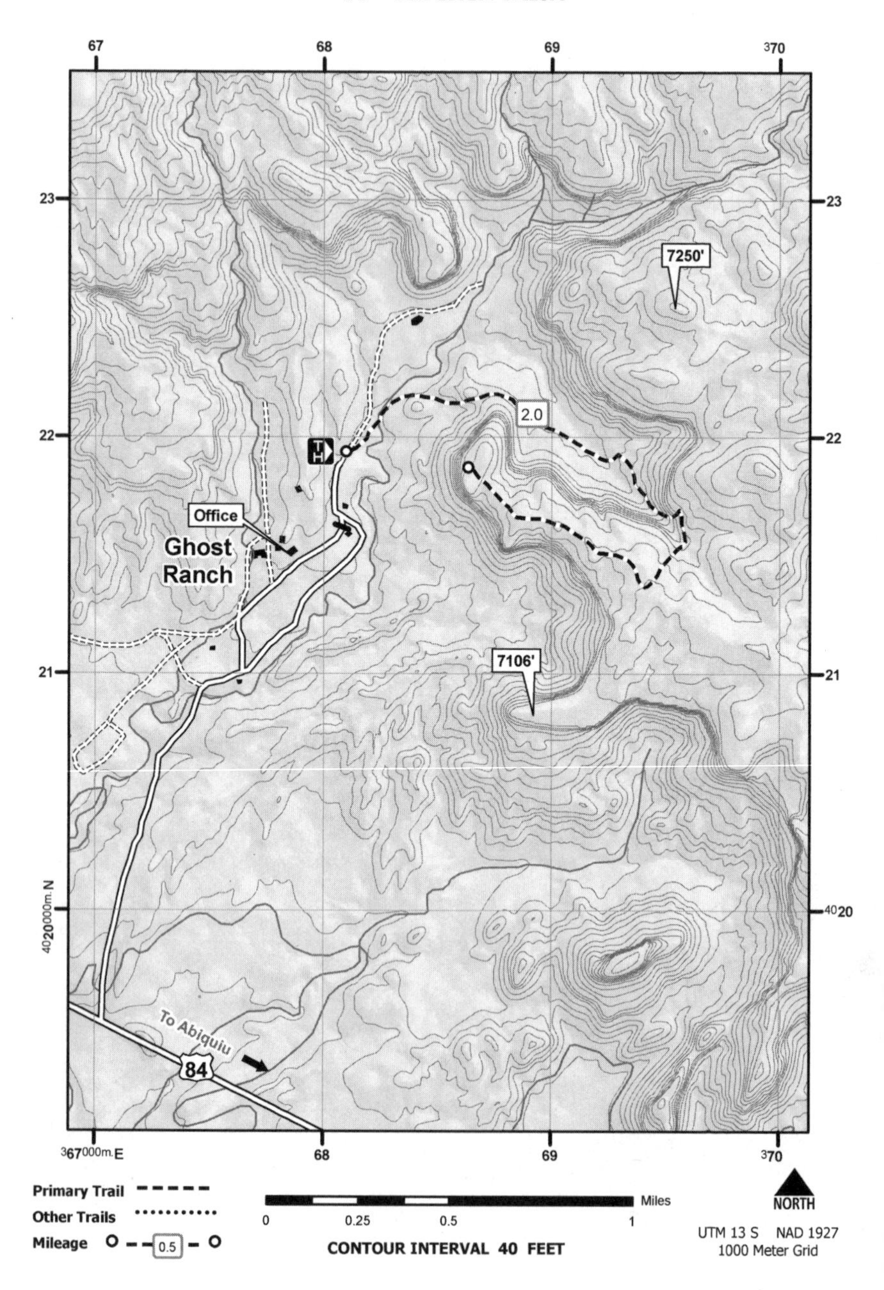

53 - Kitchen Mesa

by Norma McCallan

Striking vistas, interesting geological features, and the best display of red rock in northern New Mexico with expansive views of the country north of Abiquiu.

RT Distance:	4.5 miles
Time:	3+ hrs
Elevation Range:	6500-7077 ft; total gain 600 ft
Rating:	Moderate
RT Drive:	122 miles; 2¾ hrs
Seasons:	Spring and fall are the most pleasant. Winter might be OK if there has not been a recent heavy snowfall or rainstorm in the area. Summer will be hot; try to get an early start in the cool of the morning. *Note: trail is very slick when wet!*
Maps:	USGS Ghost Ranch - 7.5' series (trail does not show on topo map).
Trailhead:	368,146 mE 4,021,950 mN elev.6539'

Summary

This hike starts at Ghost Ranch and takes you through Georgia O'Keeffe country. The cliffs are sediments from the Triassic, Jurassic and Cretaceous ages. Fossils of early dinosaurs were discovered nearby. The origin of the name Kitchen Mesa is unknown. The director of Ghost Ranch suggested it might be due to the fact that it overlooks the dining/kitchen area of the ranch. Owned by the Presbyterian Church, Ghost Ranch is used by many organizations and groups for conferences and retreats. Staff is friendly and knowledgeable about the area.

Driving Directions

Drive north on US 84/285 to Española (~20 miles) and follow the signs for US 84/285, cross the Rio Grande, and head toward Chama. Continue north on US 84/285 out of Española where, at about 6 miles, US 84 and US 285 separate. Continue straight (north) on US 84 past Abiquiu and the Abiquiu Dam turnoff (NM 96). You will begin to see the striking red sandstone cliffs ahead—the setting of the hike. Continue north on US 84 for about 6 miles where you will see, on the right, a wooden sign for Ghost Ranch. Turn here and drive up the dirt road. Note the historic-looking log cabin on the right; it was used as a set in the movie, "City Slickers." At 1.1 miles the road forks. The left fork takes you to the Ghost Ranch office, which is ½ mile away. There you can register your hike and check out the nearby museum and library. To go directly to the trailhead, take the right fork, marked "Dining Hall." In about ½ mile you will pass the dining hall on your left and then drive past a post with many signs, one of them for Kitchen Mesa. Drive ¼ mile to a parking area where the road is closed. This is near the "Long House." Park here.

Hiking Instructions

Follow the dirt road a few yards down a short hill and you will see a sign pointing right for Kitchen Mesa. Follow the trail across a shallow stream and up the far bank. You will start to see coffee cans painted green with a white stripe, nailed upside down on small posts; these markers continue intermittently the whole length of the trail. The trail follows the riverbank a short distance, then joins an old dirt road going up the hill to the right, through the deep red Chinle formation soils of the valley floor. After 5-10 minutes of walking, the trail takes you up to the top of a low, but steep, ridge and down on the other side. You can now see, to your right, the small box canyon stretching southeast, which the trail follows, ascending by degrees to the mesa top at the far end.

After meandering along the base of some wonderfully sculpted Entrada sandstone cliffs, the trail crosses an arroyo and starts going up the rocky talus slope of the canyon wall. The trail is steep from here to the top, so proceed slowly and watch your footing. The loose clay soils can be quite difficult to cross when muddy.

About halfway up, you will begin having to traverse around or over large boulders. There are several dead-end paths branching off to the right of the main trail in this section, so look for the green coffee cans and a few arrows painted on the rocks, which denote the actual trail.

Just before you reach the top, you will find yourself directly in front of a sheer cliff. Look to the left and you will see a slot in the rocks. You will need to scramble up this narrow passage. The first part is the most difficult. There are adequate foot and hand holds if you look around for them; however, you will need to hoist a small child or your dog up the steepest section, and some adults may want help from their hiking companions.

When you reach the top, note carefully where the passage is, since the slot is not easy to see from the top.

The trail now veers right and then left, briefly following an arroyo which is to the right of the trail. Next, the trail crosses the arroyo. Look for a half hidden coffee can on the other side of the arroyo. It is easy to lose the trail here by staying in the arroyo instead of crossing it. The trail now climbs up on a steep, rocky slope in a southwesterly direction. Look for cairns, green arrows, and a few coffee cans to guide you. Once up, you can easily see the trail heading north, to your right, along a flat peninsula to the chalky white, lunar landscape at its end. This porous, hollow-sounding substance is called the Todilto formation and is gypsum deposited by a lake that evaporated during the Jurassic age, more than 100 million years ago. Roam around this point and enjoy the magnificent views, but don't get too close to the edge since the gypsum is crumbly and the cliffs below it are sheer.

Walk back a few hundred yards to the beginning of the vegetation, find a comfortable rock outcropping under a wind-sculpted juniper, take out your picnic lunch and feast your senses. All is silence, sky and magnificent rock formations. Ghost Ranch, surrounded by green fields, sits right under the cliffs. The ridge immediately to the north of it is Mesa Montosa and the further ridge to the northwest is Mesa de los Viejos (see RIM VISTA / SALAZAR TRAILS Hike #54). Abiquiu Reservoir spreads out to the west and

Cerro Pedernal (see PEDERNAL Hike #52) is the prominent flat-topped peak on the southwest horizon. The multi-colored bluffs all around you expose geologic history, from the reddish purple Chinle formation muds at the base to the tree-topped Dakota sandstone at the highest points. At your feet may be brownish patches of cryptobiotic soil or biological soil crusts composed of lichens, mosses, algae, fungi and bacteria, which take many years to form and are easily destroyed. Try not to step on them. The destruction of these crusts is the most significant factor in the erosion of desert soils. You may see the gray-green leaves and small white trumpet-shaped flowers of Bigelow's sand abronia, or tufted sand verbena, a rare plant that grows only on Todilto gypsum soils.

If you have time and want to immerse yourself longer in the red rock, turn south and wander along the relatively flat mesa top, following the undulating edge of the cliffs for 1 mile or so to the southern terminus of this remarkable plateau. Just be careful not to get too close to the edge since the rocks could be crumbly!

Return the way you came. Take time to enjoy the rich hues of the twisted juniper stumps as you return along the ridge, and, when descending the trail back down the canyon, look for a few stately Douglas firs nestled in the coolest, shadiest nooks of the rocky walls. If you signed in, don't forget to sign out at the Ghost Ranch Office.

Note: If you want to spend more time hiking in the area, you can take the short well-marked trail to Box Canyon, which starts at the same trailhead. Follow the signs along the streambed to a picturesque box canyon with steep walls and lush vegetation, whose subdued lighting reminds one of a mysterious grotto. Ghost Ranch also provides a written description (available at the office) of the short Chimney Rock Trail, just north of the Ranch, with much useful geological information.

Climbing the slot at Kitchen Mesa

54 Rim Vista / Salazar Trails

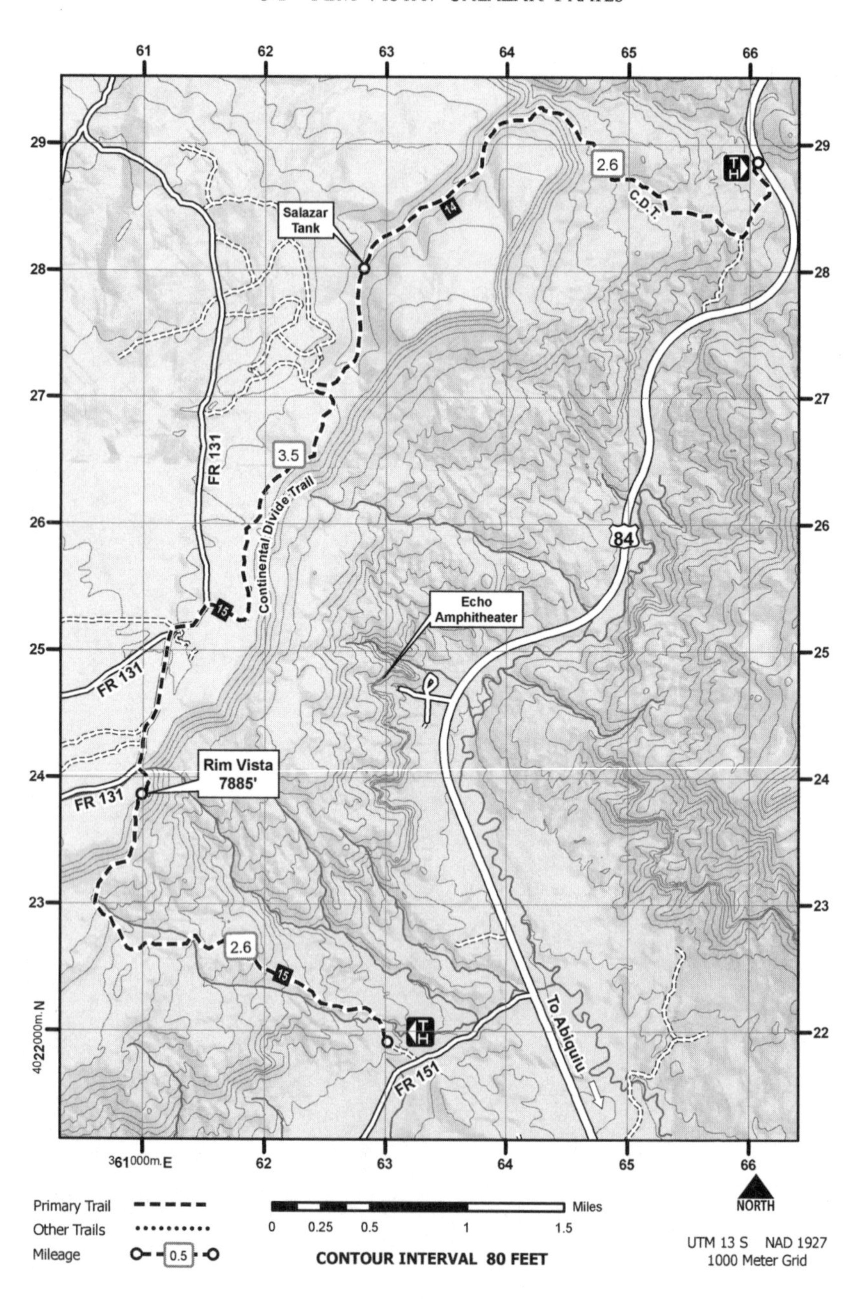

54 - Rim Vista / Salazar Trails

by Norma McCallan

Two short little-used trails connected by mesa-top forest roads with expansive views of the red rock country near Abiquiú.

RT Distance:	9 miles (trailhead to trailhead) 5.5 miles (Rim Vista only) 5 miles (Salazar only)
Time:	5-6 hrs 2½ hrs (Rim Vista only) 3 hours (Salazar only)
Elevation Range:	6200-7900 ft; total gain 1700 ft
Rating:	Easy to moderate
RT Drive:	130 miles (Rim Vista trailhead) 140 miles (Salazar trailhead); 3-3½ hrs
Seasons:	Spring or fall. Summer can be very hot. Winter may entail snow.
Maps:	USGS Alire, Canjilon, Echo Amphitheatre - 7.5' series (trails not shown on topo maps). Carson National Forest map shows both trails and most connecting roads.
North TH:	365,950 mE 4,028,850 mN elev.6984'
South TH:	363,075 mE 4,021,860 mN elev.6647'

Summary

This hike is on two trails connected by sections of Forest Service roads. The southern segment (Rim Vista Trail) offers great views of red rock cliffs and the Ghost Ranch valley. The mesa-top connecting segment of the hike has expansive mountain views. The northern segment (Salazar Trail) takes you through a lovely forested canyon. Can be hiked one-way (TH to TH) with a short car shuttle, or either trail can be hiked up to the Forest Service road with a return on the same route. The hike description proceeds from south to north, Rim Vista Trail to mesa top to Salazar Trail. The Salazar and forest road sections have been designated as a part of the Continental Divide Trail (CDT).

Driving Directions

Drive north on US 84/285 to Española (~20 miles) and cross the Rio Grande, following signs for US 84/285. About 6 miles north of Española, US 84 and US 285 separate. Continue straight (north) on US 84 past Abiquiu and the Abiquiu Dam turnoff (NM 96). You will begin to see the striking red sandstone cliffs ahead—the setting of the hike. After a few more miles, you pass the dirt road to Ghost Ranch, and 1-2 miles further, the Ghost Ranch Piedra Lumbre Education and Visitor Center. In about 1 more mile, you will see a small BLM sign on the right pointing out FR 151 to Rio Chama on the left. This road goes to the Christ-in-the-Desert Monastery and, closer by, to the Rim Vista trailhead. If you want to go up on the Rim Vista trail and come back the same way, turn left onto FR 151, skip the next paragraph, and then read on.

If you will be hiking south to north on the entire hike (as in the hiking instructions below) and want to do a car shuttle, note FR 151, but continue driving north on US 84 past the Echo Amphitheatre Picnic Area. At 5.3 miles beyond the FR 151 turnoff just past mile marker 227, and after a very long guardrail on the left, turn left, although no road is visible. As you are turning, you will see a small shrine and some white crosses on a small knoll ahead of you. Immediately after you turn left at the end of the guardrail, you will be on a section of old highway (now a dirt track). Follow this track to the left, downhill, noting a small black sign "Salazar Trail" on the right, and a CDT sign on the left. A few hundred yards later, you will see a large cairn on the right, with a post on the left and an arrow noting "Trail 14 CDT" to the right. Park here. This is the Salazar trailhead. If you reach an old bridge, you have gone too far. Leave one car here and return in a second car on US 84 to the earlier turnoff to FR 151.

Turn onto FR 151 and go 0.7 miles. Here at the crest of a saddle you will see a narrow dirt road going right, signed "Trail 15." Follow this road and, where it forks, stay right. In ¼ mile you will reach the end of the road and the trailhead for the Rim Vista Trail 15. You will see a sign: "Trail 15 - Rim Vista 2.3 miles." Park here. *Note: In wet weather, these dirt roads may be impassable*

Hiking Instructions

Proceed up the well-defined trail, which slowly wends its way uphill toward the cliff face to the north, passing through piñons and junipers with lots of Indian paintbrush, Perky Sue and blue penstemon. In about 15 minutes, you will start to see old blue diamond trail signs. These blue diamond markers continue the entire length of the hike. Shortly before you reach the cliffs, at a partial clearing in the heavy piñons and junipers, the trail makes a sharp right. The trail is less clear here, but the blue diamond markers will confirm that you are on the right trail. Just before the trail makes a sharp left to go up the cliffs, you will pass a large rock. This is a nice shady spot for a rest before ascending in the full sun.

The trail is now a bit steeper but well graded. Almost immediately you will be rewarded by great views of Abiquiu Lake and the whole Ghost Ranch valley. Near the top, the trail makes a sharp left and then angles gently up to the top.

Once on the top, veer right for a few steps and you will reach a dirt road with a large brown sign facing away from you, which says "Carson National Forest Rim Vista Overlooking Ghost Ranch and Abiquiu Dam - 2.3 miles to FS Rd 151" (which of course is where you have come from). Find a comfortable seat on the rocks at the edge of the cliffs and feast your eyes on the magnificent vista: Pedernal and Chicoma Peaks are prominent to the southwest, US 84 snakes south, the red rock cliffs surrounding Ghost Ranch are to the southeast, with the prominent outline of Sierra Negra immediately behind, and beyond them in the far distance are the peaks of the Sangre de Cristos. Peace and solitude reign, broken only by the caws of the ravens cruising in the thermals and, far below, an occasional car on the highway. If your destination is Rim Vista, you have reached it and you can simply return the way you came.

If you are hiking the entire one-way trip, you now head north, around the turnabout on the dirt road. Soon you will come to a "T" intersection. The Forest Service signs facing away from you on the right say "131 - South Rim 3" ahead and "Rim Vista, 131A" to the left, from which you have just come. Turn right here. From now on you will see new CDT signs and remnants of the blue diamonds the rest of the way, with a few markers that simply say "Trail." Now you are hiking on a high, open, sagebrush-covered plateau called Mesa de Los Viejos (Old Ones' Mesa). In the distance are the Canjilon Peaks and, further still, the high peaks at the southern end of the San Juans. The dirt road heads roughly north; after rain or snow it can be muddy. Soon you will see a white barn slightly to the left of your route that stays prominent for a long time. You will pass a small Forest Service sign (again facing away) indicating you are on Route 131. Stay straight here where a dirt track comes in from the left, which is also signed "Route 131." The map shows that 131 is actually a loop, and you are at the connecting point of the beginning and end of it. In a few yards, the trail starts curving to the right and is joined by a lane on the left. Stay on the main trail. Soon you will cross a cattle guard and briefly find yourself back in the piñons and junipers.

Fairly soon after the cattle guard, where the main road starts to veer left, and there is a very small pond on the left side, the trail turns right. There will be a sign on this less-used road noting "Trail 14" with an arrow pointing ahead. The back of the sign notes "Trail 15" ahead, from which you have just come. Turn right here and follow this track east. The CDT signs and occasional blue diamonds continue to mark your way. Along this section, the trail stays just to the left of a narrow band of woodlands that follows along the edge of the cliffs. You can walk out to the edge at almost any point to take a break while you enjoy the views and watch the ravens play.

After a mile or so, you will come to another "T" intersection with another sign indicating "Trail 14" to the right (again with "Trail 15" on the reverse side) and a CDT sign a bit further on. Go right on this dirt road, which circles northeast, and in ¼ mile you will reach a brown sign noting "Trail Ahead." Ignore the ruts to the right. You will soon come upon a cow pond, which in recent years has become a small puddle (and which may be dry). This is "Salazar Tank" on the map. Here at this pond is where you reach the Salazar Trail. It would be your turn-around point if you had arrived from the north and were doing the Salazar Trail only.

Keep to the left around the pond. You will see a trail sign after the pond and a series of large cairns marking the trail as it moves down the floor of an emerging canyon. In less than ½ mile, the trail leaves the canyon floor and proceeds along a bench on the south side of the canyon. The vegetation is quite different here from that on the mesa top or the Rim Vista Trail; you are walking amidst stately ponderosa pines and scrub oaks and the temperature is 5-10° cooler.

In another ½ mile or so, you will pass through a cattle gate. Then, a little further on, the trail widens and becomes an old, unused, very rocky dirt road, and the side canyon you have been following comes out into the main canyon. The road makes a sharp right to follow the main canyon south. In ¼ mile or less from the right turn, you will see some cairns just where the road is becoming less steep and rocky and more grassy. Here, the trail leaves the road and turns left into the woods, with CDT signs to mark the way. *(Note that the Forest Service map shows only the trail, and not this old road.)* You will see cairns and CDT signs as you follow the faint but discernible trail which heads slowly down toward the canyon floor, then more steeply into an arroyo at the bottom. After crossing the arroyo and going up its steep bank, the trail veers right across a smaller arroyo. It then heads south through an open, sagebrush-covered meadow and in no time at all arrives at the old highway where you parked your first car.

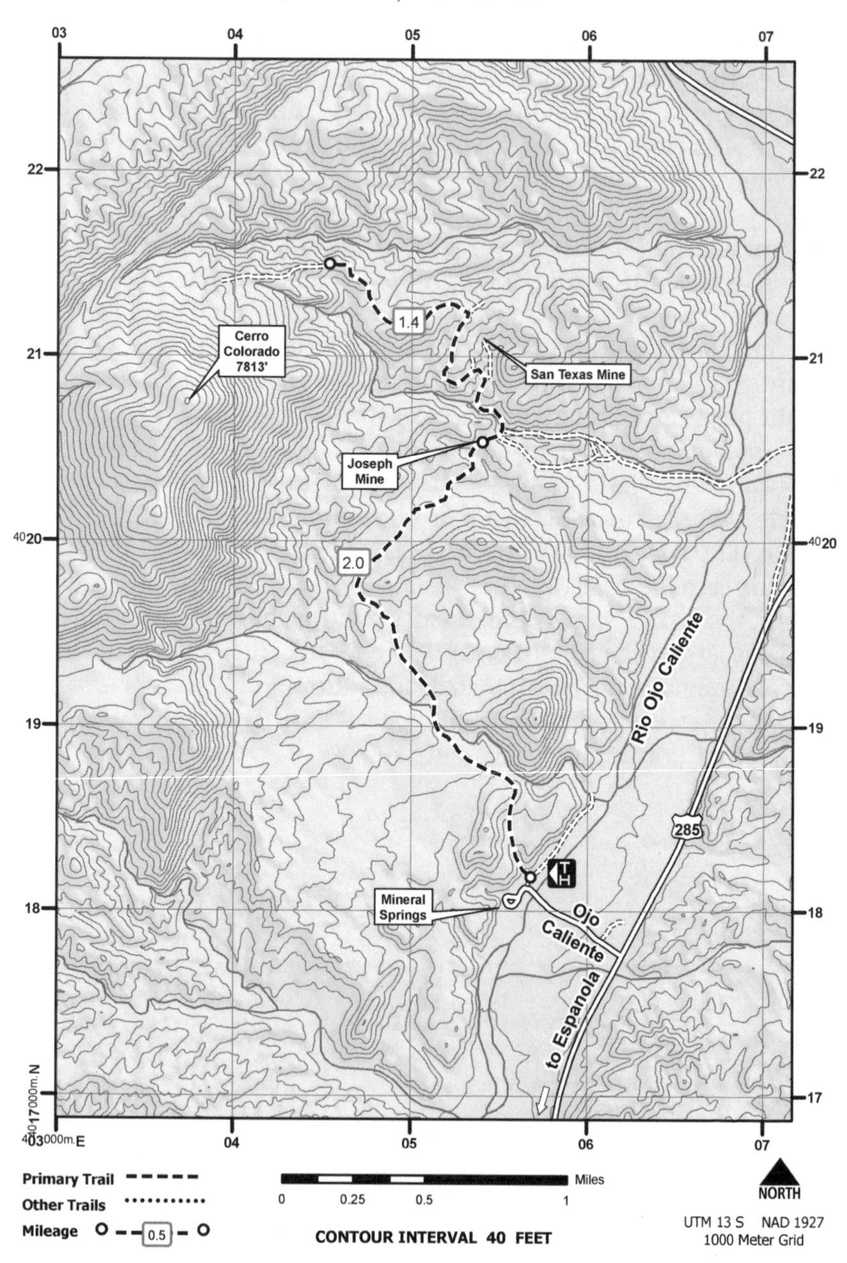
03
04
05
06
07
22
21
4020
19
18
4017000m.N
403000m.E
1.4
2.0
Cerro Colorado 7813'
San Texas Mine
Joseph Mine
Rio Ojo Caliente
285
T H
Mineral Springs
Ojo Caliente
to Espanola
Primary Trail
Other Trails
Mileage
0.5
Miles
0
0.25
0.5
1
CONTOUR INTERVAL 40 FEET
NORTH
UTM 13 S NAD 1927
1000 Meter Grid

55 - OJO CALIENTE

by Norrine Sanders

In the backcountry north of Ojo Caliente, you can explore abandoned mica mines and enjoy sweeping vistas.

RT Distance: 4 miles (to Joseph Mine)
6-7 miles (to overlook rocks)
Time: 2 hrs (to Joseph Mine)
4 hrs (to overlook rocks)
Elevation Range: 6200-6900 ft; total gain 700 ft
Rating: Easy to moderate
RT Drive: 100 miles; 2 hrs
Seasons: All seasons, but not recommended in very hot weather. It can be very muddy after rain or during snowmelt.
Maps: USGS Ojo Caliente - 7.5' series.
Trailhead: 405,654 mE 4,018,212 mN elev.6228'

Summary

This hike follows old dirt roads, through a piñon and juniper landscape. You will be able to explore abandoned mines and enjoy good views. The town of Ojo Caliente is a National and State Historic Site, with an historic adobe church and a round adobe barn. The Ojo Caliente Mineral Springs also make the area worth a visit. You can enjoy a good soak after your hike!

Driving Directions

Drive north on US 84/285 to Española (~20 miles) and follow the signs for US 84/285, cross the Rio Grande and head toward Chama. Continue north on US 84/285 out of Española where, at about 6 miles, US 84 and US 285 separate. Take a right turn here and continue north on US 285 about 17 miles to the village of Ojo Caliente. The Ojo Caliente Post Office is on your left; just past it is the left turn to the mineral springs. Drive toward the springs, turn right just after you cross the river, and park in the large parking area under the cottonwood trees. The road leads to a campground.

Hiking Instructions

From your car, go back a few yards on the road you drove in on and look for a dirt road that goes uphill to the right between two hills. This is your trail. To the right of this road is a brown "TRAIL" sign. For a short distance, this trail, recently established by the BLM, coincides with the dirt road you will be hiking on. Later on, it goes its separate way, then crosses the road again. Ignore the trail signs and stay on the road.

Take the road uphill. In a few minutes, a road comes in from the left (from the water tower above the spa). Ignore it. Some 5 minutes later, the terrain levels out and then the road starts to descend. You will come to an intersection where the BLM trail goes off to the left and a faint jeep trail goes off to the right. The jeep trail takes you to a nearby picturesque canyon with a steep drop to the Ojo Caliente valley. This is a short (~15 min) side trip.

To get to the Joseph Mine, stay on the main road, which goes straight ahead toward the rounded shape of Cerro Colorado. In about 15 minutes, the road approaches and passes a ridge on your right and then turns to the right and northeast. Cerro Colorado is now on your left. Stay on the road, which for a short distance has two tracks that run parallel to each other and then merge. When the road crosses a drainage, it briefly divides into two tracks again. Next, the road starts to climb and the tailing piles of the Joseph Mine come in view on your left. The ground is strewn with glittering mica. The road levels out as you reach the mine pit on your left. There are three mine shafts in the rock wall of the pit. Mica mines were operated commercially until the 1960s.

Continuing on the road, you will soon come to a fork. Ignore the trail marker pointing to the right fork of the road that goes down into the valley. Take the left fork, which goes up and skirts the mine pit on the left. Look for a way to get to the three shafts. On a hot summer day, the shafts offer a cool place for a break. You could make this the end of the hike and spend some time exploring the vicinity.

For a longer hike, continue up on the road. Soon it tops out and goes down into a canyon (Cañada Pueblo). At the bottom of the canyon, on your left, you will notice another mineshaft. This one is propped up with wooden beams and is not safe to enter. Some 30 yards past this shaft, the road curves left and climbs out of the canyon. In a few minutes, you will come to a fork. The right branch, which goes straight ahead and down into a side canyon, would take you to the San Texas mine with more remnants of mining activity. A side trip to this mine adds another 15 minutes or more to the hike.

Overlook Rocks – If you want to enjoy sweeping views of distant mountain ranges (Sangre de Cristos, Picuris, Jemez), take the left fork of the road. In about 2 minutes, you will come to another fork and again take the left branch. In about 10 more minutes, you will reach an outcropping of stone on the left, which makes a good spot for lunch and a turnaround point of the hike. You have now hiked about 2½ miles.

You may want to extend the hike by another mile by following the road up to an even more spectacular outcrop about ½ mile from the first. There is a steep pitch up to these rocks, but the views of the high mountains to the north and east are excellent. On your return, at the bottom of the steep pitch, the main road turns right. It is an easy mistake to go straight ahead on a faint road here.

Return by the same route. A mineral bath makes a nice finish to this hike.

Note: You can also explore the signed BLM trail you saw at the beginning, which heads west then north to a high point below Cerro Colorado before turning east to rejoin the main road. It is about 2 miles long.

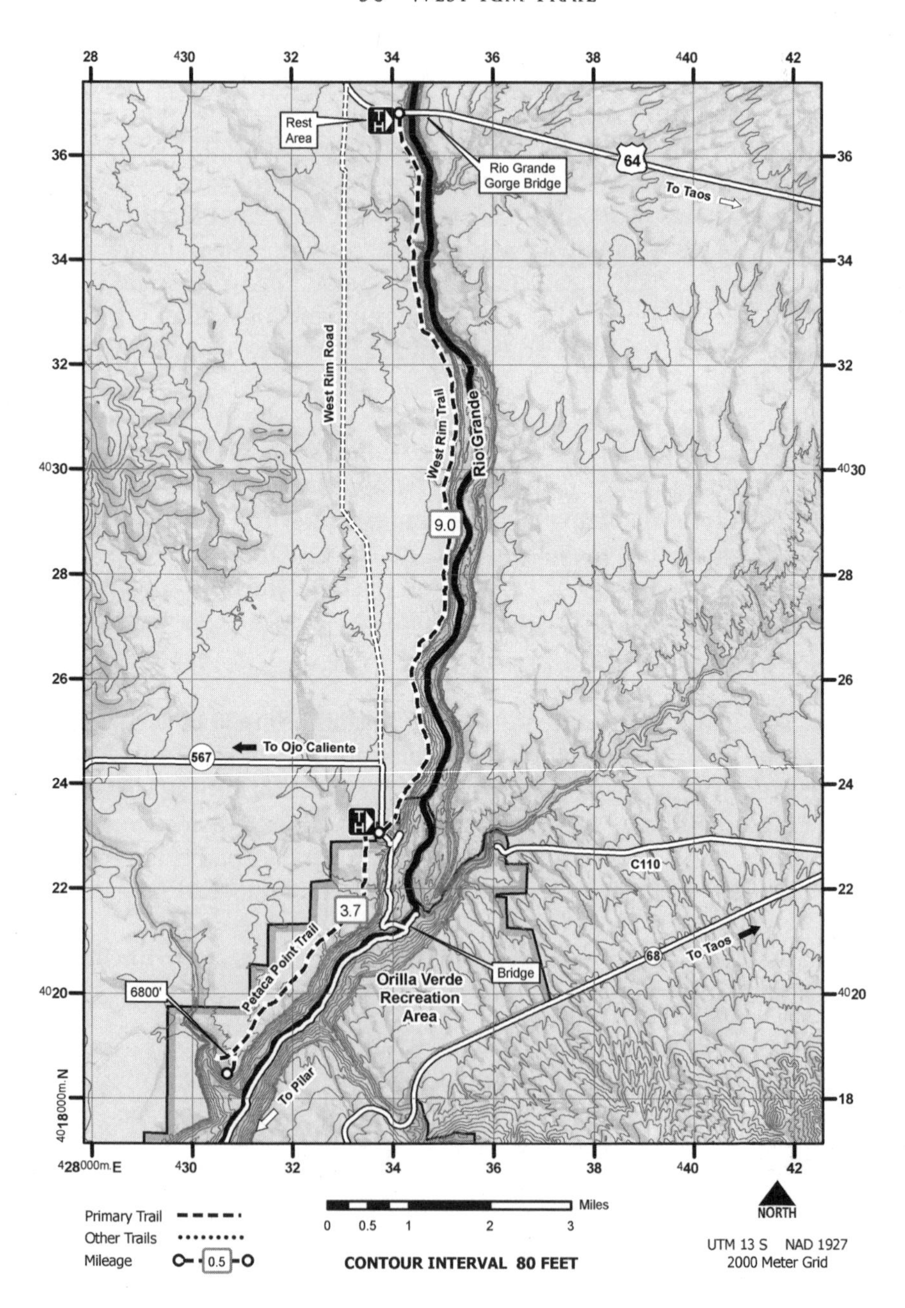
Rest Area
Rio Grande Gorge Bridge
64
To Taos
West Rim Road
West Rim Trail
Rio Grande
9.0
567
To Ojo Caliente
C110
3.7
Petaca Point Trail
Bridge
68
To Taos
Orilla Verde Recreation Area
6800'
To Pilar
Primary Trail
Other Trails
Mileage
0.5
Miles
0 0.5 1 2 3
CONTOUR INTERVAL 80 FEET
NORTH
UTM 13 S NAD 1927
2000 Meter Grid

56 - West Rim Trail

by Norma McCallan

Three connecting hikes along the rim of the Rio Grande Gorge on a broad sagebrush mesa, with fantastic views and a wonderful sense of solitude.

RT Distance:	9 miles (Northern) 9 miles (Southern) 7.5 miles (Petaca Point)
Time:	5-6 hrs (Northern and Southern) 4-5 hrs (Petaca Point)
Elevation Range:	6500-6700 ft; gain 200 ft
Rating:	Moderate
RT Drive:	122 miles; 3 hrs
Seasons:	All year. Summer likely to be very hot (there is no shade). Winter could be cold and windy.
Maps:	USGS Carson, Los Cordovas, and Taos SW - 7.5' series. Also Taos, NM 30'x60' Quad.
North TH:	434,074 mE 4,036,768 mN elev.6979'
South TH:	433,769 mE 4,023,064 mN elev.6751'

Summary

The BLM's 13-mile long West Rim Trail was formed in the mid-1990s from segments of old roads and trails. It can be nicely done as three separate out-and-back hikes: Southern Trailhead up to mid-point of the main trail, Northern Trailhead (Gorge Bridge) down to midpoint, and the Petaca segment. If you have two cars, it is relatively easy to do a car shuttle, and hike the complete 9-mile main trail. Walking just a short distance from any of the trailheads is rewarding and provides great vistas of the surrounding countryside as well as the rugged basalt-walled gorge of the Rio Grande and the river far below.

Driving Directions

Take US 84/285 north to Española, continuing straight through Española on NM 68 toward Taos. About 23 miles from Española you will see a left turn sign for NM 570, Carson, Pilar and the Orilla Verde Recreation Area. The recreation area is named for the lush green banks of the Rio Grande. Before turning left you may want to visit the Rio Grande Gorge Visitor Center, across the highway on the right. It has exhibits of the local area, maps, and a helpful staff. Cross the highway and take NM 570 through the hamlet of Pilar and the BLM Orilla Verde Recreation Area, passing a number of campgrounds and boat launching sites next to the Rio Grande. Right after the Taos Junction Bridge the road turns to dirt and proceeds steeply up through the cliffs for 2½ miles to the rim. The dirt road then becomes paved and is NM 567.

Petaca Point Segment - Almost immediately to the left is a sign for the "West Rim Trail Petaca Point Segment 4 miles" and a parking area. Park here. If this is not your destination, keep reading and driving.

Southern Trailhead - A minute or so later you will see a sign on the right for the "West Rim Trail 0.5 miles," with an arrow pointing to a narrow road on the right. Drive in here, and you will soon come to a parking area. Park here if the Southern access to the main West Rim Trail is your destination. If not, read on.

Northern Trailhead - Continue on the paved road (NM 567) a few minutes more until it turns sharply to the left. Turn right here onto a wide, unmarked dirt road (West Rim Road on the BLM handouts). Though the road is somewhat rutted, and can be muddy after rain or snow, it is usually passable. If in doubt, check with the Visitor Center (505-751-4899). This road ends 8 miles later at NM 64. Turn right here, and in a few moments you will see a sign "Rest Area one half mile." Turn into the rest area, next to the Rio Grande Gorge Bridge, and park. You can also access this Northern Trailhead via NM 64, either west from Taos or east from Tres Piedras on US 285.

Hiking Instructions

Petaca Point Segment - Sign in at the register and follow the trail as it heads down and up through a deep gully. From then on, the trail will stay relatively flat. It is less used than the main West Rim Trail, and stays a bit further from the rim. Enjoy the great solitude, the vistas of the far away Jemez to the west, and the vast expanse of sagebrush flats to the north, rimmed by domes, cones and mesas. You will see Picuris Peak to the south, and the massive peaks in the Wheeler Peak Wilderness prominent to the east. In addition to sagebrush, you will see side-oats gramma, yellow snakeweed, winter fat, and occasional Indian paintbrush. As you walk you will notice intersections which are marked by signs. At the two which are unmarked (the last two), stay left. As you near the end of the trail (a little over 3 miles), you will see a gigantic cleft in the cliffs. When you reach the end of the trail you will be looking into a long side canyon, called Petaca Arroyo which extends 30 or 40 miles. This is your turnaround point. Return the way you came.

It makes an interesting side trip to walk north along the rim of this canyon. You can also walk back to the last unmarked intersection you came to, turn left, and follow this old road as it heads toward the canyon rim and parallels it. Gradually the road fades away. As the side canyon narrows, you begin to see more varieties of vegetation, and you find yourself amidst stands of old, gnarled juniper and new piñons. Take a break or enjoy your lunch beside the huge broken blocks of black basalt at the edge of the rugged cliffs. Return the way you came.

A second side trip is possible about a mile from the trailhead. Watch for a glimpse of a U-shaped break in cliffs at the edge of the rim, and hike toward it as soon as you get to a large depression with a cow pond in the center. After going up and over the berm behind the pond, head down into a short arroyo rimmed by cliffs, with little pools in the rocks at the bottom. If you look closely you will see a few petroglyphs and other signs of ancient habitation! Please do not disturb anything! Return to the main trail and proceed back to the trailhead.

Southern Trailhead - Head for the trailhead sign reading "West Rim Trail, Tres Orejas Segment, Highbridge 9 miles." Follow the trail as it goes in and out of a small gully, then around a small rocky knob. Soon it heads towards the rim, and there it stays. All intersections are marked with arrows. Sometimes you are so close to the rim you can peer down into the canyon from the trail; at other times the trail is a bit farther away, but always within an easy distance to take a look or shoot a picture. There are numerous viewpoints, some marked with cairns. There are vistas of Taos Mountain, the Wheeler Peak massif, and the Latirs beyond to the northeast. The three-eared silhouette of Tres Orejas is prominent to the northwest and the Jemez far to the west. Amongst the sage you will see the dense yellow flowers of snakeweed, prickly pear cactus, Apache plume and fourwing saltbush. In about 1¾ miles and then again in about 2½ miles you will pass under power lines strung across the river. Somewhat farther you will pass a rock inscribed with the enigmatic phrase "Dead Car Rapid - Frank Fernandez 11/24/39." As you get close to a lone juniper or two, you are probably nearing the halfway point. Go back the way you came, and enjoy the ravens and hawks gliding along the thermals. To see the other half of the trail, drive to the Northern trailhead.

For both the Southern trail and the Petaca Point segment, you may want to drive back by a route slightly longer in miles, but shorter in time by continuing out NM 567 past Carson to US 285, where you turn left, go by Ojo Caliente, and turn left where US 285 joins US 84 and takes you into Española and back to Santa Fe.

Northern Trailhead - At the rest area, look for the large trailhead sign "West Rim Trail" with a map, and head through a gate. The huge span of the Rio Grande Gorge Bridge dominates the landscape here, and can be seen when looking back for some time. The trail will stay close to the rim the whole way along the slightly undulating terrain. The first mile or so will probably have a number of tourists, stretching their legs while parked at the rest area, while you will likely see bicyclists your entire way. There are any number of good spots to go peer over the rim. On this segment, more than on the other two, you will see a longer stretch of the cliffs and the river far below. In late fall or early spring, you may see sandhill cranes and geese migrating along the Rio Grande flyway. When you feel like going back, return the way you came. You will see the Gorge Bridge appear from several miles away, then disappear for a time as the river veers slightly to the left. Just before you get back to the rest area you will come to a bench next to the rim. Enjoy a welcome rest and savor the great view of the gorge and the tapestry of earth tones, chocolate, rust brown, orange, tan, on the cliffs, interspersed with gray green patches of sage and other small plants that have taken root wherever enough soil has collected.

Drive back the way you came, or at the far end of the dirt West Rim Road, choose the alternate driving route mentioned above.

Rio Grande Gorge

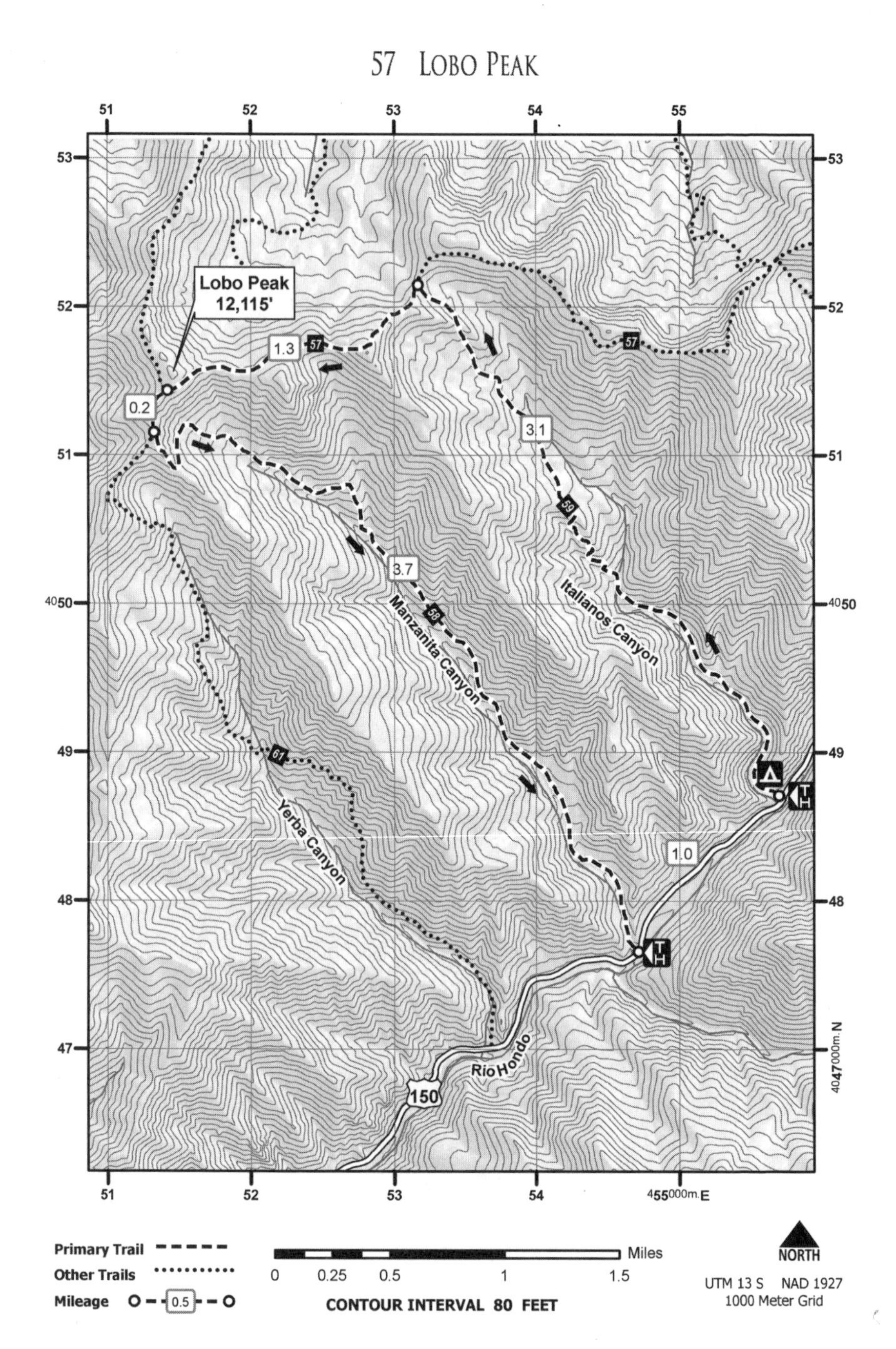

Lobo Peak
12,115'
0.2
1.3
57
3.1
59
3.7
58
Manzanita Canyon
Italianos Canyon
61
Yerba Canyon
1.0
Rio Hondo
150
T
H
51
52
53
54
55
4050
49
48
47
4047000m.N
455000m.E
Primary Trail
Other Trails
Mileage
0.5
Miles
0
0.25
0.5
1
1.5
CONTOUR INTERVAL 80 FEET
NORTH
UTM 13 S NAD 1927
1000 Meter Grid

57 - LOBO PEAK

by David Brown

A steep loop hike to a high peak near Taos with lovely canyons, flowers, rock outcrops, cascading streams, and old growth forest, offering great views in all directions.

RT Distance: 9 miles (if car is used to close the loop);
10 miles (if closing loop by walking or returning on same route)

Time: 6½-7 hrs (+30 min to close loop by walking)

Elevation Range: 8,350-12,115 ft (Manzanita trailhead)
8,650-12,115 ft (Italianos trailhead)
Total gain ~3740 ft (if walking the loop)
Total gain ~3465 ft (if using a car shuttle)

Rating: Strenuous

RT Drive: 178 miles; ~4 hrs

Seasons: June-October, snow conditions permitting.

Maps: USGS Arroyo Seco and Wheeler Peak - 7.5' series. FS Map of Latir Peak and Wheeler Peak Wilderness also recommended.

Manzanita TH: 454,683 mE 4,047,652 mN elev.8376'
Italianos TH: 455,712 mE 4,048,698 mN elev.8647'

Summary

A steep climb to the highest peak of the mountain range located between Rio Hondo and Red River, with lovely canyons, flowers, rock outcrops, cascading streams, and old growth forest. Lobo Peak is above tree line and offers sweeping views in all directions. From the Taos Ski Valley Road (NM 150), there are three trails that lead to Lobo Peak. The trails are named after the drainages that they follow: Yerba, Manzanita, and Italianos Canyon. The loop hike described below goes up Italianos Canyon and follows a ridge to Lobo Peak. The descent is down Manzanita Canyon. The loop is closed by driving or walking one mile on NM 150. Get an early start to avoid thunderstorms above treeline.

Driving Directions

Take US 84/285 north to Española, continuing straight through Española on NM 68 to Taos. After going through the center of Taos, the road forks. Take the left branch toward Questa. Some 3½ miles later, you come to a junction with NM 150. Set your odometer, turn right, and take NM 150 toward the Taos Ski Area. After driving for 11 miles on NM 150, look for highway mile marker "11." The Manzanita Canyon trailhead is nearby on the left side of the road. This is where the hike will end. If you have two or more cars, leave a car here. This will eliminate walking an extra mile (and 300 ft elevation gain) on the road to complete the loop. Continue driving up NM 150 to mile marker "12" and park. On the left side of the road is the Italianos Canyon trailhead where the hike starts.

Hiking Instructions

The trail starts as a dirt road, passes an outhouse, and turns into a hiking trail. For the next 45 minutes or so, it will cross the stream about 15 times. Not all the crossings have stepping stones, but the water is not very deep. Between the second and third crossings, you pass a nice rock outcrop on the right. After about 25 minutes and eight stream crossings, you come to the largest cascade on your left. Stop for a moment and enjoy the sound of the water. Some 20 minutes later, the trail starts to move away from the stream. After another 30 minutes, you come out of the woods into the first meadow. The trail continues straight ahead on the far side of the meadow. There might be a few small cairns to guide you. A second meadow appears about 2 hours into the hike. Go straight ahead into the meadow, looking to the right. The trail leaves the meadow on the right side, before the end of the meadow. Five minutes later, it turns right and crosses two small streams. When you come to the top of the third and largest meadow, look back and enjoy the view of the peaks to the southeast. The trail continues through some open sections, with cairns as markers. About 20 minutes after leaving the third meadow, the trail turns right and starts to climb steeply through the trees. After a few switchbacks, it tops out on a saddle.

You are now on the ridge that connects Gold Hill with Lobo Peak. Here, your trail meets Lobo Peak Trail 57 at a T-junction. A sign indicates Gold Hill to the right and Lobo Peak to the left. From here, it takes about 1½ hours to the summit. The trail is mostly in the trees, either on or below the ridge. The last 10 minutes to the summit are above tree line. Make sure the weather is good before taking the trail (left) to Lobo Peak. After about 30 minutes from the trail junction, you reach a high point at 11,800 ft. The trail then drops down a bit on the north side of the ridge and crosses a steep north-facing slope. If the trail is hidden by snow drifts, look for blazes on the trees. Soon, the trail returns to the south side of the ridge and passes a large rock outcrop on the right. As you approach the rock outcrop, Lobo Peak comes into view. It is less than an hour away.

The trail now goes up again, staying on the ridge or on the north side of the ridge. About 40 minutes after the rock outcrop, the trail crosses the ridge and traverses on a south-facing slope with great views. Shortly, the trail comes to a signed trail junction. Down to the left is the trail that goes to Manzanita Canyon, your descent route. Up to the right is the way to Lobo Peak (~10 more minutes to go!) Take the trail to the right (north) and start up the ridge. When the trail reaches the rocks, it disappears. Stay left on the grass, still heading north. After a minute or two, go diagonally up through the rocks. Soon, you will see the summit sign. Enjoy your lunch on the top, with great views in all directions. To the southeast is the Wheeler Peak area, with some of New Mexico's highest mountains, to the west the Taos Plateau and Rio Grande Gorge, to the north the Latir Mountains, and far in the distance, the 14,345-ft Blanca Peak, and to the east, the nearby Gold Hill (see GOLD HILL Hike #59).

To descend, return to the nearby signed trail junction and continue going straight ahead (south) on the Manzanita Canyon Trail. About 5 minutes down from the signed trail junction, after passing a steep, rocky section, the trail levels out and you will see a trail marked by cairns dropping down off the ridge to the right. Do not take this unsigned trail (the Yerba Canyon Trail). Your trail continues straight ahead on the ridge for a few minutes, then briefly drops below the ridge to the left and regains the ridge again. Some 15 minutes past the signed trail junction, look for a cairn where the trail goes left and away from the ridge, forming a switchback. You are now dropping into the Manzanita drainage. The next ½ mile of trail might be obscured by snowdrifts from late fall into early summer. Look for tree blazes before you lose the trail! The trail descends through a beautiful old-growth forest (with nice duff to walk on) on a series of switchbacks. About 1½ hours after leaving the peak, the trail crosses the main drainage of the canyon, and continues to follows the stream, crossing it several times. It then goes left, leaving the stream on your right. For the last stretch, the trail widens to a road that takes you to the car you left at the Manzanita trailhead, or to a last mile of uphill hiking along NM 150, to get back to Italianos Canyon trailhead.

Lobo Peak Trail

Manzanita Canyon, on the way down from Lobo Peak

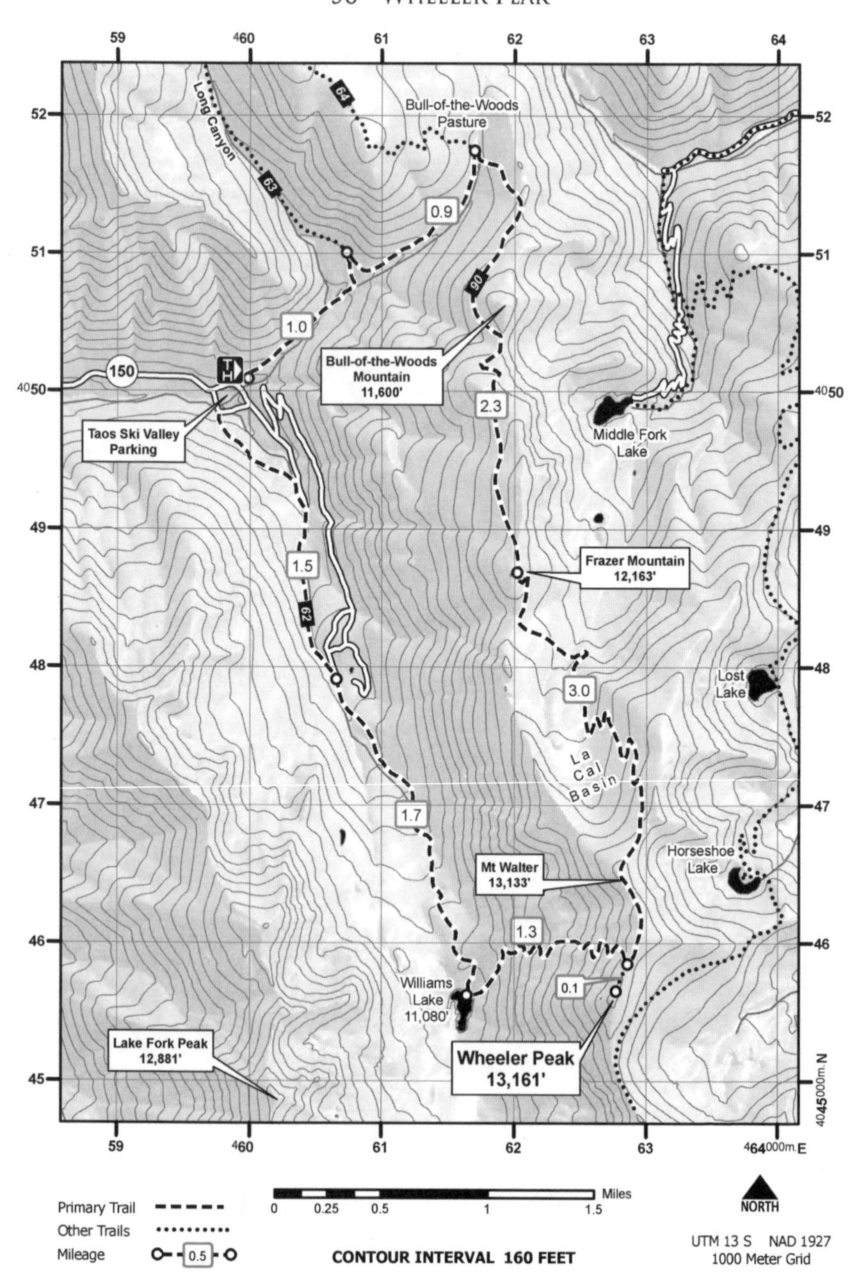
Bull-of-the-Woods Pasture
Long Canyon
64
63
0.9
90
1.0
150
Bull-of-the-Woods Mountain 11,600'
2.3
Taos Ski Valley Parking
Middle Fork Lake
1.5
62
Frazer Mountain 12,163'
3.0
Lost Lake
La Cal Basin
1.7
Horseshoe Lake
Mt Walter 13,133'
1.3
0.1
Williams Lake 11,080'
Lake Fork Peak 12,881'
Wheeler Peak 13,161'
Primary Trail
Other Trails
Mileage
0.5
Miles
0 0.25 0.5 1 1.5
CONTOUR INTERVAL 160 FEET
NORTH
UTM 13 S NAD 1927
1000 Meter Grid

58 - Wheeler Peak

by Matt Gervase

A long, hard (but rewarding) hike to the highest peak in New Mexico.

RT Distance:	15 miles
Time:	8-10 hrs (stops not included) 7 hrs (return via Williams Lake)
Elevation Range:	9,430-13,161 ft; total gain ~4310 ft
Rating:	Strenuous
RT Drive:	184 miles; ~4 hours
Seasons:	June-October, snow conditions permitting. Watch the sky for signs of inbound weather. The main consideration is the likelihood of lightning above tree line.
Maps:	USGS Wheeler Peak - 7.5' series. FS Map of Latir Peak and Wheeler Peak Wilderness also recommended.
Trailhead:	459,855 mE 4,050,055 mN elev.9477'

Summary

One of the finest alpine walks in northern New Mexico. Panoramic views and magnificent displays of wildflowers. Occasional reminders of past mining activity and its prominence in New Mexican history add to the hike's character. Of course, standing on the high point of the state has its own special appeal.

NOTE: Camping or staying in a Taos Valley motel is highly recommended, as it allows you a 7 am start (and some motels have hot tubs, which is great after a long day!).

Driving Directions

Take US 84/285 north to Española, continuing straight through Española on NM 68 to Taos. After going through the center of Taos, the road forks. Take the left branch toward Questa. Some 3½ miles later, you come to the junction with NM 150, marked by a traffic light and sign indicating Taos Ski Area. Turn right onto NM 150 and follow it to the highest parking lot adjacent to the main entrance at the Taos Ski Area.

Hiking Instructions

From the upper parking lot of the Taos Ski Area, at about 9,430 ft, walk to the wooden registration sign declaring Wheeler Peak Wilderness. Look for the trail sign indicating Bull-of-the-Woods 1.8 miles and Wheeler Peak trail. Take this trail. After 15 minutes of ascent from the parking lot, you cross a small stream, then proceed toward the right (northeast) alongside a small feeder stream coming in from the right.

In several minutes you reach a trail intersection. Do not go to Long Canyon. Follow Bull-of-the-Woods trail. In roughly 1 hour of hiking, the trail climbs out of the canyon, with remnants of mines dotting the area. A wooden sign indicating Wheeler Peak Trail 90, La Cal, marks the Bull-of-the-Woods pasture. Take the right fork at the sign, passing a small 20-ft pond on your left.

The trail ascends in a southwesterly direction, with the first views of Kachina Peak and the Taos Ski Area ahead. In 30 minutes from the Bull-of-the-Woods junction, a wood barricade crosses the trail. Here, take a look back and you will see Fishers Peak outside of Trinidad, Colorado, the Latir Mountains to the north and the area comprising Philmont Scout Ranch to the east.

The trail breaks out above treeline and continues south. The trail contours around Frazer Mountain on a low shoulder, then descends eastward into La Cal basin, by now an obvious low point in the trees. In a little over 2 hours of continuous hiking, you reach La Cal Basin at 11,800 ft. Note the protected campsites alongside the stream and plan for a return visit. Shortly after crossing the stream, the trail makes an obvious right turn to the south and continues to climb out of the protection of the densely forested basin. Once the tree line is again reached, the trail is clearly etched into the hillside, ascending toward the ridge.

From La Cal Basin, another hour of hiking brings you to the low saddle (13,080 ft) between 13,133-ft Mount Walter and 13,161-ft Wheeler Peak. If you look carefully down the scree slope to the west, you should see the intermittent outline of a return trail leading to Williams Lake and ultimately the Taos Ski Area parking lot where you began (you may want to return via this route). Continue along the ridge for another 15 minutes and attain the highest point in New Mexico. Thus far you have climbed about 4,030 ft from the parking lot in about 4 hours.

The return presents two options; reverse the hike or return down the scree slope from the saddle between Wheeler Peak and Mount Walter. If you consider the descent to Williams Lake, take note of the 1,800 ft of steep descent. Ski poles can help take the load from the knees on the descent. The climb up from Williams Lake takes about 1 hour 40 minutes. On the other hand, you can expect to reach the lake in about half that time descending. The steep scree route follows the path of least resistance down to a defined trail returning to Williams Lake. The return to trees marks the approach to the lake. You will be walking through as dense a profusion of alpine wildflowers as can be found anywhere in New Mexico.

At Williams Lake (11,080 ft), the trail takes an obvious right turn near a wooden outhouse in the trees to your right. From here, the trail is well worn and hard to lose, descending in 1.9 miles to the Taos Ski Area (Phoenix Lodge). Along the way, you can appreciate the steep avalanche chutes coming down from the high ridge to the east that you just hiked across. The avalanche debris is a vivid reminder of winter. Once at the Phoenix Lodge, look for a trail sign that indicates 1.6 miles back to the Taos Ski Valley base. Thirty minutes of fast hiking along Rubezahl, a beginners trail, takes you back to the parking lot at Taos Ski Valley base.

59 GOLD HILL

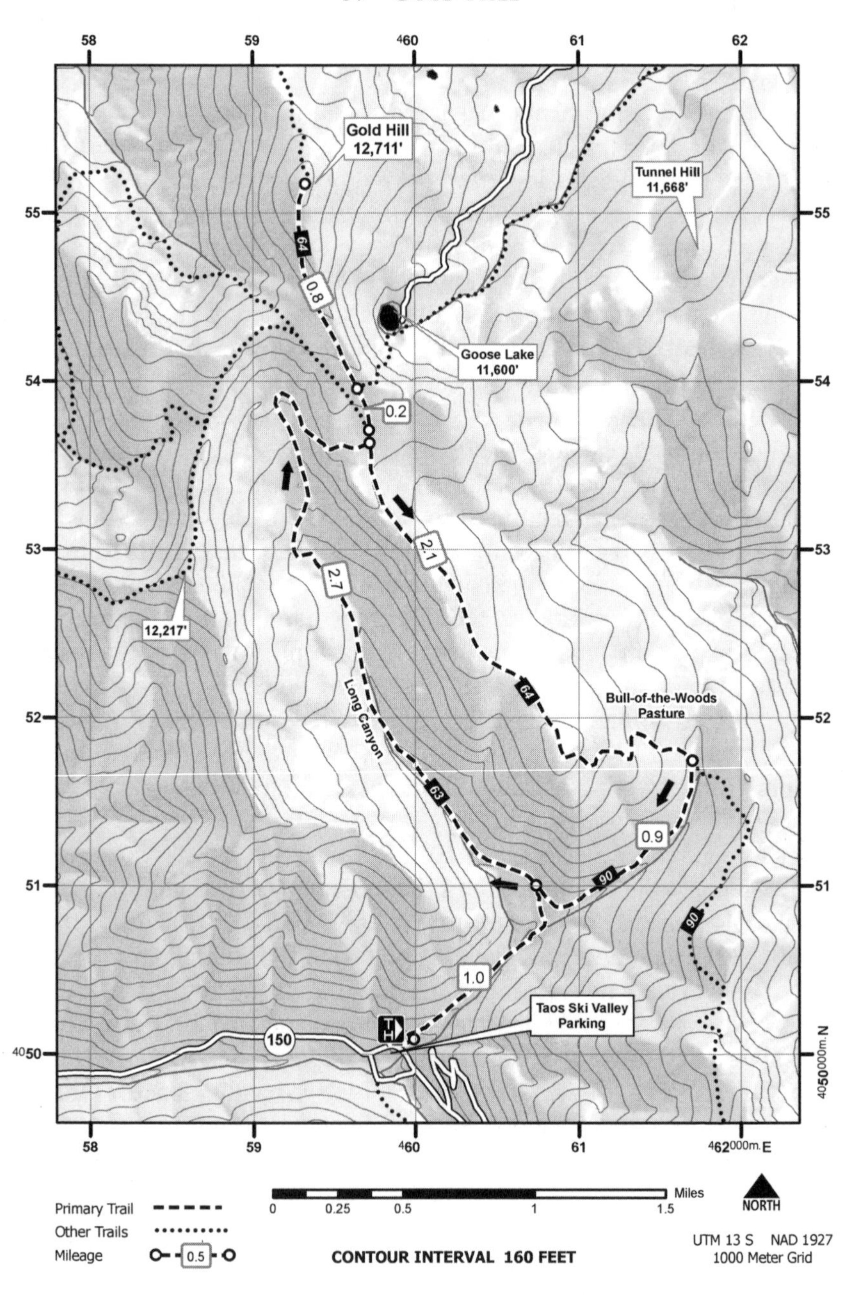

Gold Hill
12,711'
Tunnel Hill
11,668'
Goose Lake
11,600'
12,217'
Long Canyon
Bull-of-the-Woods
Pasture
Taos Ski Valley
Parking
150
0.8
0.2
2.1
2.7
0.9
1.0
64
63
90
58
59
460
61
62
55
54
53
52
51
4050
4050000m.N
462000m.E
Primary Trail
Other Trails
Mileage
0.5
Miles
0
0.25
0.5
1
1.5
NORTH
CONTOUR INTERVAL 160 FEET
UTM 13 S NAD 1927
1000 Meter Grid

59 - GOLD HILL

by John Jasper

An exhilarating hike to a high peak near the Taos Ski Valley.

RT Distance:	10 miles
Time:	7 hrs
Elevation Range:	9,300-12,711 ft; total gain 3411 ft
Rating:	Strenuous
RT Drive:	184 miles; ~4 hrs
Seasons:	Not a winter hike. Parts of the trail may be snow-covered through June, and snowfall comes early in the autumn this far north and this high. Be prepared for high winds and cool temperatures.
Maps:	USGS Wheeler Peak and Red River - 7.5' series. Also, USFS Map of Latir Peak and Wheeler Peak Wilderness is recommended.
Trailhead:	459,855 mE 4,050,055 mN elev.9477'

Summary

A strenuous but enjoyable hike to a high peak north of the Taos Ski Valley. Spectacular views in all directions, remnants of mining activity, alpine flowers in summer, golden aspens in fall. The middle portion of this hike includes a loop. Watch for bighorn sheep. Get an early start, and do not stay above timberline during an afternoon thunderstorm. Bring extra warm clothing and rain gear.

Driving Instructions

Take US 84/285 north to Española, continuing straight through Española on NM 68 to Taos. After going through the center of Taos, the road forks. Take the left branch toward Questa. Some 3½ miles later, you come to the junction with NM 150, marked by a traffic light and sign indicating Taos Ski Area. Turn right onto NM 150 and follow it to the highest parking lot adjacent to the main entrance at the Taos Ski Area.

Hiking Instructions

From the upper parking lot at the Taos Ski Area, look for the Wheeler Peak Wilderness sign and registration board. The trailhead has a carved wooden map that details most of the major hikes in the area. Follow the Bull-of-the-Woods Trail across a road, uphill and eastward. In several minutes the trail forks. Take the left fork, which continues to climb steeply alongside the creek (ignore the horse trail that crosses the hiking trail several times). See if you can pick out the brambleberries, aster, yarrow, harebells and blue gentian growing along the trail.

After about 20 minutes of climbing through the forest, you reach an arrow pointing left into the deep woods. Follow the arrow to a stream crossing, and 5 minutes later, to a trail fork with Long Canyon Trail 63 to the left. Turn left onto Trail 63. The trail climbs consistently through spruce and fir, with dense streamside vegetation.

After about 45 minutes on Long Canyon Trail 63, you will reach a small meadow. Some 30 minutes later, there is another meadow and the trail now turns sharply to the right and climbs out of Long Canyon through a stand of bristlecone. There is a cairn where the trail reaches the high open ridgetop. Here the trail can be faint in the grass. Follow it for a few minutes to a signpost. You are now at the intersection of Long Canyon Trail and Gold Hill Trail. Follow the sign arrow toward Gold Hill by turning left and heading north up towards an open grassy alpine meadow.

The trail follows a well-furrowed course with several rock cairns. Your trail intersects the trail to Goose Lake. Stay on the trail going north. Check the sky for any indications of lightning. This exposed ridge is not friendly in poor weather.

The trail heads up to the edge of the ridge and for the first time you can see off to the east and northeast. Goose Lake is far below.

The hill you've been looking at as you have climbed, probably thinking it is Gold Hill, is a 12,000-ft false peak to the south of Gold Hill. The trail contours around the southwest side of this false peak and continues its steady climb to the real Gold Hill. If the climb has not taken away your breath, the views will. To the north are the Latir Peaks and closer-by slopes scarred by the Molycorp Mine. Farther north are the mountains of Colorado. To the south is Wheeler Peak.

Return on the trail the same way you came. In about 30 minutes you should reach the intersection with Long Canyon Trail. Here Long Canyon Trail goes to the right, which returns you on the trail you came up; however, we recommend you continue on the Gold Hill Trail. This trail might be hard to see if the grass is high. Look east and notice the remnants of an old mining cabin. There is a faint trail marked by cairns going toward the cabin. Take this trail. Explore the cabin site, then continue on the well worn trail that goes to the right (south) in front of the cabin.

At the right time of year, from the point where the return trail enters the woods all the way down to Bull-of-the-Woods Pasture, this is an excellent mushrooming area. Through the end of June, you may encounter big snowdrifts in the trees. The trail is blazed but you must be very observant if the trail is snow-covered. The trail winds in and out of the trees, and there are some spectacular views.

About 3 miles (1½ hrs) from Gold Hill, you intersect Bull-of-the-Woods Road in Bull-of-the-Woods Pasture. There is a nice pond that makes a good break spot. Head downhill on the road. (Uphill, the road goes to Bull-of-the-Woods Mountain and the Wheeler Peak Ridge Trail.) The road has been closed for some years and is reverting to a trail since it has had no vehicular traffic. A little stream runs down the valley to your left. You'll note across the valley signs of mining activity: tailing piles and some stripped timber. After almost a mile, the road turns sharply left. Here is a small trail marker, a post with a very small sign "Twining" with an arrow pointing down a trail. Leave the road and follow the trail, which is well-defined with a small canyon to the left.

Soon you will find yourself at the intersection of the Long Canyon Trail and the trail you came up on from the ski valley, which makes a sharp right turn, downhill, with a small sign "Twining." Proceed down the trail you came up on, back to the parking lot.

View from Gold Hill

La Junta / Wild Rivers ☞

60 Wild Rivers

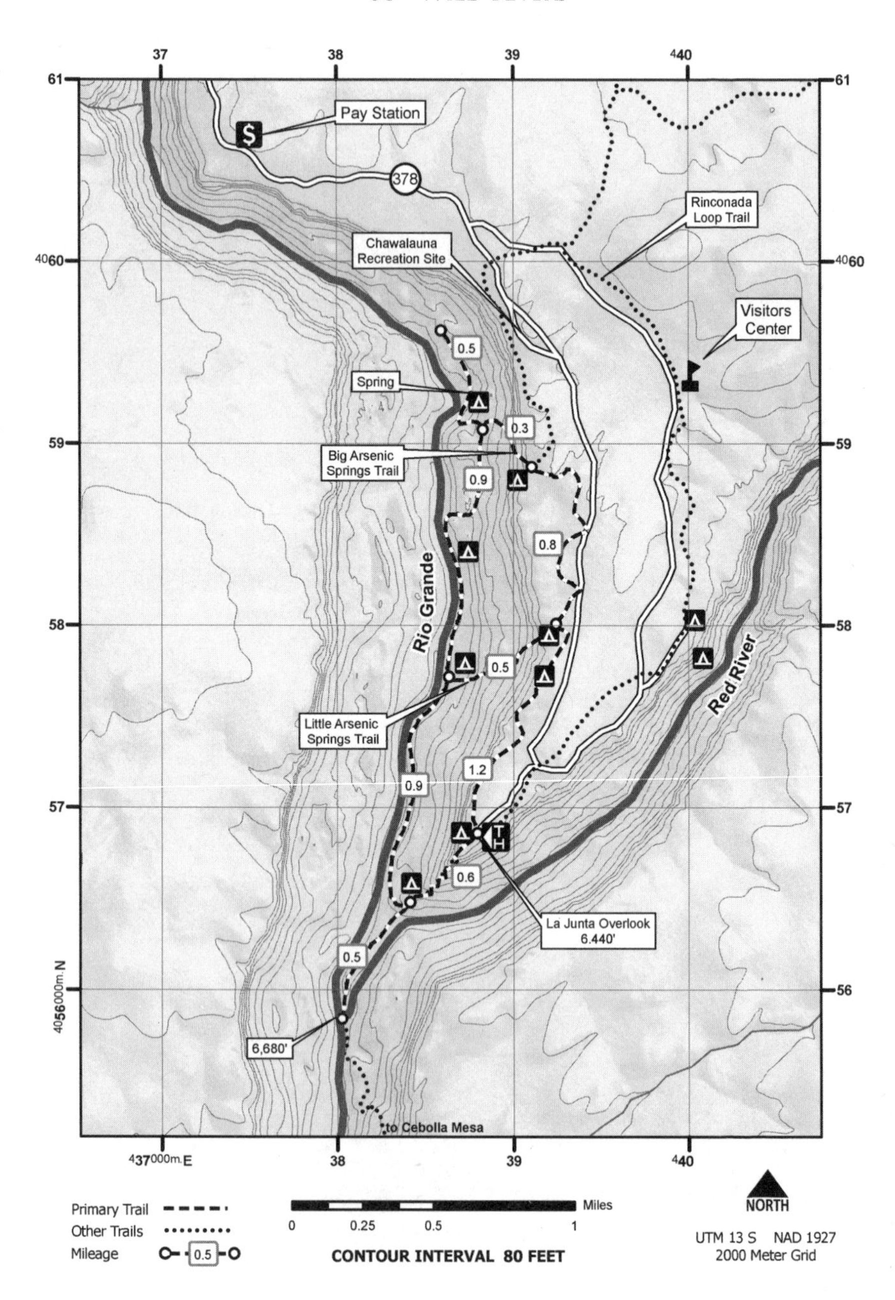

60 - WILD RIVERS

by Norbert Sperlich

From the sagebrush-covered Taos plateau, these hikes take you to the bottom of the Rio Grande gorge where you will encounter lush vegetation, towering ponderosa, and the confluence of two lively rivers.

RT Distance: 4.5 miles (Little Arsenic)
6 miles (Big Arsenic)
8 miles (River Trail)

Time: 3 hrs (Little Arsenic)
4 hrs (Big Arsenic)
6 hrs (River Trail)

Elevation Range: 6600-7400 ft; gain 800 ft (Little Arsenic), 1000 ft (Big Arsenic), 1500 ft (River Trail)

Rating: Moderate

RT Drive: 220 miles; 5 hrs

Seasons: The area is open year round, but access may be difficult in winter. Snow is possible from November to March. Thunderstorms are common in July and August. Summer afternoons in the canyon can be very hot.

Maps: USGS Guadalupe Mountain - 7.5' series. See also trail map on Wild Rivers brochure, available at the Visitor Center.

Fees: Parking $3/day; camping $7/night

Trailhead: 438,715 mE 4,056,806 mN elev.7453'

Summary

The Wild Rivers Recreation Area is north of Taos and west of Questa, where the Red River joins the Rio Grande, and both rivers have cut deep canyons into the Taos Plateau. Sagebrush, juniper and piñon give the plateau its austere character. In the distance, long extinct volcanoes rise above the plain. To the east the towering ridges of the Sangre de Cristo Mountains form a dramatic backdrop, marred only by the highly visible waste piles of the Molycorp Mine! Descending to the bottom of the Rio Grande canyon, one encounters lush riparian vegetation and towering ponderosa.

The area is managed by the BLM and features a Visitor Center staffed from Memorial Day through Labor Day, several campgrounds and picnic areas, and many hiking trails. Fees are charged for parking and camping. Pets must be kept on a leash and are not allowed on Big Arsenic Trail or in fresh-water springs. Wild Rivers telephone number is 505-770-1600.

While a day hike to the river will give you a good introduction to the area, spending a night or two at one of the campsites will make your stay more memorable. Wear hiking boots and carry plenty of water when the weather is warm. Watch out for poison ivy (very common near the springs) and rattlesnakes (hard to find).

Although all three hikes are along the river, the longest hike described (the river trail) follows more of the river and includes La Junta Overlook, La Junta, Big Arsenic Springs and a return by the same path, giving you the most time at the bottom of the gorge. For shorter hikes, you may return by way of Little Arsenic or Big Arsenic Springs Trail and Rinconada Loop Trail, as indicated in the hike instructions. To only go down to the river and back is about 2 miles on steep trails.

Driving Directions

Take US 84/285 north to Española, continuing straight through Española on NM 68 to Taos. After going through the center of Taos, the road forks. Take the left branch toward Questa. North of Taos this highway is called NM 522. Some 3½ miles later, you come to the junction with NM 150, marked by a traffic light and sign indicating Taos Ski Area. Continue straight ahead on NM 522 toward Questa. At the intersection in Questa continue straight ahead. Some 2½ miles past the stoplight in Questa, look for a sign "Wild Rivers" and turn left onto NM 378. This road takes you through the community of Cerro and to the entrance of the recreation area. At 1¾ miles past the entrance, you will pass the turnoff (on your left) to the Guadalupe Mountain trail. Approximately 4 miles further, the road forks, with the left branch going to the Visitor Center. Stay on the right branch, unless you're going to the Visitor Center. In about ½ mile, you will approach a turnout on the right that takes you to Chawalauna ("Hole in the Rock"), an overlook that offers a first glimpse into the canyon of the Rio Grande. We recommend you stop briefly to look below, where you can see the campsites of Big Arsenic Springs. Return to your car and continue south for about 2 miles, past the turnoffs to Big Arsenic Springs, Little Arsenic Springs and Montoso campsites, to the turnoff to La Junta on your right. A short dirt road takes you to a parking area with a pay station and restrooms. Park your car and pay the fee.

Hiking Instructions

All Hikes - Follow the sign to the overlook on a paved trail, along a rock wall and down a few steps to the trailhead. There are awesome views of La Junta (where the two rivers meet 800 ft below). A sign indicates La Junta 1.2 miles, Little Arsenic Springs 1.7 miles. The first part of the descent is the steepest, involving metal stairs at one point and many switchbacks further down. The trail is rough when it crosses boulder fields or loose gravel. After hiking for about 25 minutes, you will come to a trail intersection. Continue straight ahead for another 10 minutes to La Junta. This is a great place to hang out for a while. Several shelters offer shade and a trail takes you right down to the water where the two rivers come together. Large boulders, carved and polished by the water, will remind you of modern sculptures, and there is always a cool breeze blowing at this place. A trail leads to the Red River, across a bridge and up to the Cebolla Mesa campground. You might want to explore that trail.

For now, retrace your steps back ½ mile to the trail intersection and take the trail to the left to both Little and Big Arsenic Springs. The trail goes down to the river, then climbs up above a boulder field. Soon it reaches the Little Arsenic Springs campsites in the shade of huge ponderosa. Next, it climbs away from the trees and intersects a trail that goes up to the rim of the canyon. Here you have two options to continue your hike. You can return to the rim via the Little Arsenic Springs Trail, or continue on the River Trail to Big Arsenic Springs and beyond.

Little Arsenic Trail – If you need to keep your hike short, go up to the rim at this point and you'll be back at your car in less than 1 hour. Once you reach the rim, look for the Rinconada Loop Trail, which will take you back to La Junta overlook, if you follow it in a southerly direction. The trail is marked with brown plastic stakes and coincides (at times) with dirt roads. If you can't find a trail sign right away, follow the nearest dirt road until you come to a trail marker. If in doubt, follow the dirt road to the paved road and go south on the paved road to the La Junta turnoff and your car.

Big Arsenic Trail – Ignore the trail that goes up to the rim and continue on toward Little and Big Arsenic Springs. Your trail soon descends toward the river again and crosses a creek that comes from Little Arsenic Springs. ("Arsenic" is a misnomer, by the way. There is no arsenic in any of the springs that you will encounter.) Next, a branch of the trail goes down to the left to a shelter at the river's edge. Stay on the main trail. Up to this point, the river was running its course fairly quietly, but from here on upstream, its path is blocked by many boulders. If you happen to be here during spring runoff (May/June), you might experience the river at the peak of its power.

The trail climbs up above another boulder field to a level area with sagebrush, where it meets the Big Arsenic Springs Trail, which comes down from the canyon rim on your right. Here again you have two options. You can return to the rim via the Big Arsenic Springs Trail, and follow the Rinconada Loop Trail south (described above) back to your car, or you can continue on the River Trail as described below.

River Trail – This option takes you down to the beautiful Big Arsenic Springs, which are less than ½ mile away. At the intersection with Big Arsenic Springs Trail, take the left fork. The trail heads towards the river, descends steeply, and crosses the creek that comes from the first spring. Huge ponderosa and lush vegetation (lots of poison ivy, too) make you feel that you have arrived at an oasis. Take a little side trail that follows the creek right down to the river. What a lovely spot to eat your lunch. The river makes a bend at this point and the views are grand.

You have hiked about 2½ hours to reach this place, short stops included. If you feel inspired to explore more and have another hour to spare, go up to the main trail and continue on past an outhouse and up some switchbacks. Once you reach level ground again, walk some 60 yards on the trail to where a smaller trail goes off to the left. It leads to a group of boulders with petroglyphs. Petroglyphs are fragile. We trust you will not touch them or climb on them.

Back to the main trail. It goes past another spring and down to a shelter, then crosses the creek from the spring on a wooden bridge. Soon you reach the last shelter, overlooking a wild stretch of the river. Some day you have to come back here and spend the night!

River Trail Return Options - This is as far as the trail goes. Time to go back. The longest and most beautiful way to return would be to retrace your steps. For a shorter return trip, take either the Big or the Little Arsenic Springs Trail up to the rim and then go south on the Rinconada Loop Trail, as described earlier.

Pamphlets available at the Visitor Center will inform you about other trails, including a hike to the top of Guadalupe Mountain, a nearby volcano.

We must be refreshed by the sight
of inexhaustible vigor ...
The wilderness with its living and its decaying trees,
The thundercloud and the rain ...
Some life pasturing freely where we never wander.
~ Thoreau

SAFETY TIPS FOR HIKERS

by Herb Kincey, St. John's College Search and Rescue Team

Certain safety procedures should be followed by anyone going into wild country. Failure to observe these rules can lead to accidents or even death. Chances of becoming a statistic in the records of a search and rescue team will be greatly reduced by following these safety rules.

Do not go alone – Unless you are experienced and prefer solitude, a party of at least four persons is recommended so that if one person is injured, one can remain with the victim while the other two go for help. Try never to leave an injured hiker alone.

Instead of going solo, find an experienced hiker to accompany you or join one of the Sierra Club weekend outings, lead by experienced hikers who are willing to share their knowledge with you. An outing schedule is available in a box outside our office at 802 Early Street or online at http://riogrande.sierraclub.org/santafe/outings.asp.

Plan your route carefully – Know the escape routes. Plan a route ahead of time using U.S. Geological Survey and U.S. Forest Service maps (hikes in this book list many applicable maps). When traveling on foot allow about one hour for each two miles covered plus an additional hour for each 1000 ft of altitude gained. At all times know where you are on the map and the best way out to civilization. A compass (or better yet, GPS with full batteries) can be invaluable for avoiding getting lost. *Note: GPS batteries weaken in cold weather.*

Get weather reports and be prepared for emergencies – Fast-moving frontal systems can bring sudden and violent changes in New Mexico weather. Try to obtain an extended weather forecast before setting out. The highest peaks in New Mexico are above timberline and remote. On hikes above timberline the safe policy is to start for the summit at dawn and turn back about noon, the time when storms begin to form. Storms at high elevations provide two life-threats: hypothermia (from wind and rain) and electrocution (from lightning).

Check with authorities – Most of the New Mexico high country lies within National Forests. Forest rangers know their districts and can offer valuable advice on trails, campsites and potential problems. Many desert lands are administered by the Bureau of Land Management (BLM), whose officials will be glad to help. The New Mexico Department of Game and Fish will make recommendations about where to hike during hunting seasons. Booklets from this department describe the areas open to hunters along with season dates. These are useful publications for hikers wishing to avoid hunting areas. Bright clothing is appropriate for safety during big game hunting season.

Go properly equipped – As a rule the most serious dangers in the wilderness are WIND, COLD and WETNESS. Even during July it can snow on the higher peaks, and hard summer rains occur almost daily in the mountain ranges. It is quite possible to die from "exposure" (hypothermia: a disastrous drop in body temperature) at any time of the year, especially above timberline (about 11,800 ft). Having warm clothing, even during the summer, is vital. A shirt, sweater, socks, mittens and cap (all of wool or polypropylene) should always be carried. Even when wet, wool is warm against the skin. For protection against wind and wetness carry a weatherproof parka or poncho. One of the first signs of hypothermia is shivering. This may be followed by difficulty walking and speaking, confusion, drowsiness and coma. Steps should be taken to restore and maintain body temperature as soon as signs of hypothermia appear. These steps may include locating shelter from the elements, use of warm clothing or blankets, replacing cold wet clothing, providing warm, non-alcoholic drinks and body-to-body transfer of heat. If symptoms intensify, medical help should be obtained as soon as possible.

Always carry these items with you when going into the back country: map, compass, flashlight or headlamp, sunglasses, candle, waterproof matches, whistle, pocket knife, protective clothing, minimum first aid, extra food and water. Water is very scarce in some areas; carry plenty, at least a quart per person. Water purification is recommended for water from streams or lakes. Giardia is now a common problem in wilderness areas.

Allow time for acclimatization – Persons going into high mountains from low altitudes should beware of trying to climb any of the major peaks until they have had a few days to acclimatize. Many people who go too high too fast suffer "mountain sickness." The symptoms are vomiting, diarrhea, and feeling very ill. Pulmonary edema, a major medical emergency, also can occur above the 8,000-ft level. The symptoms include extreme fatigue or collapse, shortness of breath, a racking cough, bubbling noises in the chest, and bloody sputum. Unless transported to a much lower altitude immediately the victim may die within a matter of hours. If available, administer oxygen until reaching a hospital. Several other procedures may help prevent the "mountain miseries:" arrive in good physical condition, get plenty of rest and sleep and avoid alcohol and smoking.

Leave information with relatives or friends – An itinerary of your trip, along with the names and addresses of each member, description and license numbers of vehicles used, and expected time fo return should be left with a reliable person. Once under way, stick to your planned route and schedule. Any time a group is seriously overdue or an accident has occurred, the New Mexico State Police should be called in order to obtain assistance (505-827-9000).

Learn the limitation of each member – Assess the strengths and weaknesses of each member of the party. Do not try anything beyond the ability of the weakest hiker. Set the pace to that of the slowest hiker. Be willing to turn back when conditions warrant doing so.

Keep the party together – Individual members of a group should not be allowed to fall behind the main party or to get ahead of it. Many wilderness fatalities have resulted from disregarding this rule. If the group is large, select one person to set the pace, another to bring up the rear. If hiking in the dark for some reason, assign each hiker a number and count off periodically.

Watch for flash floods – Most New Mexico streams are shallow and present few fording problems. However, flash floods occur in the steep arid canyons and arroyos around the perimeter of the mountains and in desert areas. Be especially careful in these hazardous areas and do not camp or leave vehicles parked there.

Beware of loose rock - In some places loose rock can be a serious hazard. Keep your group bunched together when going up or down this type of terrain. Never roll rocks down a mountainside. Another party may be below you.

Get off exposed ridges during storms - Summer storms move in fast and will bring rain or hail, high winds, low visibility and lightning. Try not to allow your group to be caught on a peak or exposed ridge. If you are unable to get down in a lightning storm, have the group spread out with about 30 feet between each person. Stay away from lone trees or rocks. Avoid shallow caves or depressions, for ground currents may jump from the edge to your body. Insulate yourself from the ground (with pack, rope, clothing) and squat down, allowing only your feet to touch the ground or the improvised insulation.

Emergency calls and signals - Cell phones may be useful, but reception is limited in many canyons and remote hiking areas and batteries weaken in cold weather. Available widely, FMRS and especially GMRS two-way, walkie-talkie type radios may be useful for keeping groups in touch over a few miles depending on terrain. If such modern electronic methods fail, the following signals are considered standard by many search and rescue groups:

Distress - 3 evenly-spaced signals given within 30 seconds. Repeat as required.

Acknowledgement - 2 signals given in quick succession.

Return to camp - 4 evenly-spaced signals given within 30 seconds. Repeat as required.

GLOSSARY

by Bill Chudd

Arroyo - A usually dry gully, at times containing a stream. After a rainstorm, or when there is a storm in nearby mountains, a dry arroyo may suddenly become a raging waterway.

Basalt - A dark igneous rock of volcanic origin, sometimes black and columnar.

Blaze - A mark on a tree made by chopping off a piece of bark. Blazes marking trails in the Santa Fe area generally consist of a short cut, with a longer cut below.

Blowdown - A tree or stand of timber that has been blown down by the wind.

Blowhole - Ancient volcanic gas vents.

Box canyon - A canyon with steep side walls terminating headwards in a vertical cliff.

Cairn - A heap of stones; specifically, a pile of stones placed as a landmark, or to indicate a specific site or trail.

Caja del Rio - *Box of the river.* The Caja del Rio Canyon, popularly called Diablo Canyon, is a narrow, not a box, canyon.

Caldera - A large volcanic crater.

Camino - Road.

Cañada - Canyon, *cañon*, ravine.

Cerro - Hill.

Chamisa - *Chrysothamnus spp.* The rabbitbrush, a ubiquitous gray-green bush whose odorous yellow flowers dominate the fall landscape of northern New Mexico.

Cholla - *Opuntia spp.* A tall, spiny, branching cactus with cylindrical stems.

Cornice - A mass of snow, ice, etc., projecting over a mountain ridge.

Cryptobiotic soil – Biological soil crusts made of mosses, lichens, fungi, bacteria and green algae which take many years to form and are very fragile.

Descanso - A roadside memorial from Spanish *descanso* "resting place (of a dead person)."

Desert hoodoos - A pillar of rock, usually of fantastic shape, left by erosion.

Diablo Canyon - *Devil Canyon* (see Caja del Rio).

Dike - A long, narrow cross-cutting mass of rock intruded into a fissure in older rock.

Divide - A ridge between two drainage areas.

Draw - A basin or ravine through which water drains.

Duff - Organic matter in various stages of decomposition on the floor of the forest.

Escarpment - A long, precipitous, clifflike ridge of land or rock, commonly formed by faulting or fracturing of the earth's crust.

Flume - An artificial channel, such as an inclined chute or trough, through which water is carried for irrigation or other purposes.

Frijoles - *Beans* (one of the crops cultivated by the ancestral Indians in Frijoles Canyon).

Mesa - Spanish for *table*; A small, high plateau with steep sides.

Petroglyph - A design cut or chipped into the patinated surface of a rock. Many interesting Indian petroglyphs may be seen in the Santa Fe area. Look, but please don't touch. Oils from your skin degrade the images.

Piñon – *Pinus edulis* A type of nut pine tree and the New Mexico State Tree. Santa Fe is in the piñon-juniper woodland zone.

Plug – Also known as a volcanic neck; the solidified lava or igneous rock filling a conduit leading to the vent of an extinct volcano.

Puerto Nambé - Spanish for *Gateway to the Nambé.*

Rio - River.

Rito - A small stream.

Saddle - A ridge between two peaks. Sometimes used loosely for any point where a trail or road tops a ridge.

Sangre de Cristo - *Blood of Christ.* The local mountain range was so named for the red color it reflects during some sunsets. Until the late 1800s the range was known by the name *Sierra Madre.*

Santa Fe - *Holy Faith.* The full name of the city is *La Villa Real de la Santa Fé de San Francisco de Asisi* - The Royal Village of the Holy Faith of St. Francis of Assisi.

Scat - Excrement, animal droppings.

Scoria - Porous cinderlike fragments of dark lava.

Scramble - To climb or descend using hands as well as feet.

Scree - Same as talus.

Talus - A sloping bank of rock debris at the base of a cliff.

Tarn - A high mountain lake or pond.

Tetilla - A small teat. Tetilla Peak was a landmark on the old Royal Road from Mexico, signaling the final approach to Santa Fe.

Tuff - A porous volcanic rock formed from compacted ash.

Yucca - *Yucca spp.* A plant of the lily family with sharply pointed, sword-shaped leaves.

TABLE OF ABBREVIATIONS

~	approximately
BLM	Bureau of Land Management
CDT	Continental Divide Trail
CR	County Road
FS	Forest Service
FR	Forest Road
ft	Foot / feet
hr	Hour
Hwy	Highway
NM	New Mexico Highway
Pk	Peak
RT	Round Trip
TH	Trailhead
Tr	Trail
US	United States Highway
USGS	United States Geological Survey

USEFUL ADDRESSES AND PHONE NUMBERS

In Case of Emergency

NM State Police Department:
505-827-9000
www.nmsp.com

Federal Agencies »» Bureau of Land Management

Bureau of Land Management (BLM)
1474 Rodeo Road, Santa Fe
505-471-1919
www.blm.gov

Rio Grande Gorge Visitor Center
US Hwy 64 West of Taos, NM
505-751-4899
www.nm.blm.gov/recreation/taos/rio_grande_wild_scenic_river.htm

Wild Rivers Recreation Area Visitor Center
1120 Cerro Road, Cerro, NM
505-770-1600
www.nm.blm.gov/recreation/taos/wild_rivers_rec_area.htm

»» Forest Service

Forest Service
1474 Rodeo Road, Santa Fe 87505
505-438-7840
www.fs.fed.us

Española Ranger Station.
505-753-7331 or 505-438-7801
www.fs.fed.us/r3/sfe/districts/

Jemez Ranger Station
505-829-3535
www.fs.fed.us/r3/sfe/districts/

Las Vegas Ranger Station
505-425-3534
www.fs.fed.us/r3/sfe/districts/

Pecos Ranger Station
505-757-6121
www.fs.fed.us/r3/sfe/districts/

Sandia Ranger Station
505-281-3304
www.fs.fed.us./r3/carson/html_main/general_welcome.html

Tres Piedras Ranger Station
505-758-8678
www.fs.fed.us/r3/carson/html_main/general_welcome.html

Valles Caldera Trust
18161 State Hwy 4, Jemez Springs, NM 87025
www.VallesCaldera.gov

»» National Park Service

National Park Service
1100 Old Santa Fe Trail, Santa Fe
505-988-6100
www.nps.gov

Bandelier National Monument
Los Alamos, NM
505-672-3861
www.nps.gov/band/

Pecos National Historical Park
Hwy 63, Pecos NM 87552
505-757-6414
www.nps.gov/peco/

Petroglyph National Monument Visitor Center
Jct. Unser & Western Trail, Albuquerque
505-899-0205
www.nps.gov/petr/

State and County Agencies

NM Department of Game and Fish.
505-827-7911
www.wildlife.state.nm.us

NM State Park & Recreation Division
2040 South Pacheco, Santa Fe.
505-827-7173

Santa Fe County Open Space and Trails Division
PO Box 276, Santa Fe, NM 87504
505-992-9868
www.co.santa-fe.nm.us/departments/pfmd/open_space.php

Medical Facilities

Pecos Valley Medical Center
30 Highway 50, Pecos
505-757-6482

St. Vincent Hospital - Emergency Services
455 St. Michael's Dr., Santa Fe 87505
505-995-3934 or 505-983-3361
www.StVin.org

Española Hospital
1010 Spruce St., Española, NM
505-753-7111
www.phs.org/facilities/espanola

Los Alamos Medical Center
3917 West Road, Los Alamos, NM
505-662-4201
www.LosAlamosMedicalCenter.com

Holy Cross Hospital
1397 Weimer Road, Taos, NM
505-758-8883
www.TaosHospital.org

St. Joseph Medical Center
601 Dr. Martin Luther King Jr. Ave. NE, Albuquerque
505-727-8000

Map Sources

Public Lands Bookstore
    1474 Rodeo Road, Santa Fe, NM 87505
    505-345-9498
    www.PublicLands.org

Travel Bug
    839 Paseo de Peralta, Santa Fe, NM 87501
    505-992-0418
    www.MapsOfNewMexico.com

Local Environmental Organizations

Northern New Mexico Group of the Sierra Club
    802 Early Street, Santa Fe, NM, 87505
    505-983-2703
    www.RioGrande.SierraClub.org/SantaFe/

Sangre de Cristo Audubon Society, Randall Davey Audubon Center
    1800 Upper Canyon Road, Santa Fe, NM 87501
    505-983-4609
    www.NewMexicoAudubon.org

Cerrillos Hills Park Coalition
    PO Box 191, Cerrillos, NM 87010
    505-438-3008
    www.CerrillosHills.org

Concerned Citizens for Nuclear Safety
    107 Cienega, Santa Fe, NM 87501
    505-986-1973
    www.NuclearActive.org

Forest Guardians
    312 Montezuma, Santa Fe, NM, 87501
    505-988-9126
    www.FGuardians.org

The Forest Guild / Forest Trust
    80 E. San Francisco, Santa Fe, NM, 87501
    505-983-8992
    www.ForestGuild.org

Leave No Trace Center for Outdoor Ethics
P.O. Box 997, Boulder, Colorado 80306
800-332-410
www.lnt.org/

Nature Conservancy
212 E. Marcy St., Suite 200, Santa Fe, NM 87501
505-988-3867
www.nature.org/wherewework/northamerica/states/newmexico

NM Environmental Law Center
1405 Luisa St., Suite 5, Santa Fe, NM, 87505
505-989-9022
www.NMEnviroLaw.org

New Mexico Heritage Preservation Alliance (Night Sky Program)
505-989-7745
www.NMHeritage.org/sky

Quivira Coalition
1413 Second Street, Santa Fe, NM 87505
505-820-2544
www.QuiviraCoalition.org

Santa Fe Watershed Association
1413 Second Street, Santa Fe, NM 87505
505-820-1696
www.SantaFeWatershed.org

Trust for Public Land
1600 Lena Street, Suite C, Santa Fe, NM 87505
505-988-5922
www.tpl.org

Valles Caldera Coalition, Randall Davey Audubon Center
1800 Upper Canyon Road, Santa Fe, NM 87501
505-983-4609, ext.25
e-mail: mpeale@vallescalderacoalition.org

Wildfire Information

Wildfire Information
877-971-F I R E
877-971-3473
www.NMFireInfo.com

ADDITIONAL READING

Hiking

Black Regnier, Linda, and Regnier, Katie. BEST EASY DAY HIKES SANTA FE. 2nd edition. Guilford, CT: Globe Pequot Press, 2006

Coltrin, Mike. SANDIA MOUNTAIN HIKING GUIDE. Albuquerque NM: University of New Mexico Press, 2004.

D'Antonio, Bob. SANTA FE - TAOS HIKING GUIDE. Englewood, CO: Westcliffe, 2004.

Hoard, Dorothy. A GUIDE TO BANDELIER NATIONAL MONUMENT. 3rd ed. Los Alamos, NM: Los Alamos Historical Society, 1995. **Out of print.**

Hoard, Dorothy. LOS ALAMOS OUTDOORS. 2nd ed., Los Alamos, NM: Los Alamos Historical Society, 1993. **Out of print.**

Julyan, Bob, and Till, Tom. NEW MEXICO'S WILDERNESS AREAS. Westcliffe, CO: Westcliffe, 1999.

Julyan, Bob. BEST HIKES WITH CHILDREN IN NEW MEXICO. 2nd ed., Seattle, WA: The Mountaineers Books, 2004.

Martin, Craig. 100 HIKES IN NEW MEXICO. 2nd ed., Seattle, WA: Mountaineers Books, Rev. 2001.

Maurer, Stephen. TRAIL GUIDE TO PECOS WILDERNESS, SANTA FE NATIONAL FOREST. Albuquerque, NM: Southwest Natural & Cultural Heritage Association, Revised edition, 1995.

Maurer, Stephen. VISITORS GUIDE TO SANDIA MOUNTAINS. Albuquerque, NM: Southwest Natural Cultural Heritage Assn., 1994.

Parent, Laurence. HIKING NEW MEXICO. Helena, MT: Falcon Press, 1998.

Salzman, Joan, and Salzman, Gary. HIKING ADVENTURES IN NORTHERN NEW MEXICO. Los Alamos, New Mexico: Aventuras Publishers, 2006.

Ungnade, Herbert E. GUIDE TO THE NEW MEXICO MOUNTAINS. 2nd rev. ed. Albuquerque, NM: UNM Press, 1972.

Wildlife

Alden, Peter, and Friedrici, Peter. AUDUBON FIELD GUIDE TO THE SOUTHWESTERN STATES. New York, NY: Alfred Knopf, 1999.

Cunningham, Richard L. 50 COMMON BIRDS OF THE SOUTHWEST. Globe, AZ: Southwest Parks & Monuments Association. 1990.

Hanson, Jonathan and Hanson, Roseann. 50 COMMON REPTILES & AMPHIBIANS OF THE SOUTHWEST. Globe, AZ: SWPMA, 1997.

Kavanaugh, James. POCKET NATURALIST: NEW MEXICO BIRDS. Waterford Press, 2002

Kavanaugh, James. POCKET NATURALIST: NEW MEXICO WILDLIFE. Waterford Press, 2005.

Kavanaugh, James. POCKET NATURALIST: SOUTHWESTERN DESERT BIRDS. Waterford Press, 2002.

Peterson, Roger Tory. A FIELD GUIDE TO WESTERN BIRDS. 4th ed. The Peterson Field Guide Series. Boston, MA: Houghton Mifflin, 1998.

Sibley, David Allen. THE SIBLEY FIELD GUIDE TO BIRDS OF WESTERN NORTH AMERICA. New York, NY. Alfred A. Knopf, 2005.

Sheldon, Ian. ANIMAL TRACKS OF ARIZONA AND NEW MEXICO. Renton, WA: Lone Pine Publishing, 1998.

Tekiela, Stan. BIRDS OF NEW MEXICO. Cambridge, Minnesota: Adventure Publications, 2004.

Geology

Baldwin, Brewster, and Kottlowski, Frank E. SANTA FE: SCENIC TRIPS TO THE GEOLOGIC PAST, NO. 1. 2nd ed. Socorro, NM: New Mexico Bureau of Mines and Mineral Resources, 1968. **Out of print.**

Bauer, Paul, *et al.* THE ENCHANTED CIRCLE. New Mexico Bureau of Mines and Mineral Resources. Socorro, NM.

Christiansen, Paige W., and Kottlowski, Frank E. MOSAIC OF NEW MEXICO'S SCENERY, ROCKS AND HISTORY: SCENIC TRIPS TO THE GEOLOGIC PAST, NO. 8. 3rd ed. Socorro, NM: New Mexico Bureau of Mines and Mineral Resources, 1972. **Out of print.**

Chronic, Halka. ROADSIDE GEOLOGY OF NEW MEXICO. Missoula, MT: Mountain Press, 1987.

Montgomery, Arthur, and Sutherland, Patrick K. TRAIL GUIDE TO THE GEOLOGY OF THE UPPER PECOS: SCENIC TRIPS TO THE GEOLOGIC PAST, NO. 6. 3rd ed. Socorro, NM: New Mexico Bureau of Mines and Mineral Resources, 1975. **Out of print.**

Muehlberger, W.R., and Muehlberger, Sally. ESPAÑOLA - CHAMA - TAOS: A CLIMB THROUGH TIME. SCENIC TRIPS TO THE GEOLOGIC PAST, NO. 13. Socorro, NM: NM Bureau of Mines and Mineral Resources, 1982. **Out of print.**

Mushrooms

Arora, David. MUSHROOMS DEMYSTIFIED: A COMPREHENSIVE GUIDE TO THE FLESHY FUNGI. Berkeley, CA: Ten Speed Press, 1990.

Smith, Alexander H. A FIELD GUIDE TO WESTERN MUSHROOMS. Ann Arbor, MI: University of Michigan, 1975.

Trees and Shrubs

Bowers, Janice E., and Wignall, Brian. SHRUBS & TREES OF THE SOUTHWEST DESERTS. Tucson, AZ: SWPMA, 1993.

Carter, Jack L. TREES AND SHRUBS OF NEW MEXICO. Boulder, CO: Mimbres Publishing, 1997.

Elmore, Francis H., and Janish, Jeanne R. SHRUBS AND TREES OF THE SOUTHWEST UPLANDS. 2nd ed. Popular Series, No. 19. Tucson, AZ: SWPMA, 1976.

Lamb, Samuel H. WOODY PLANTS OF THE SOUTHWEST. Santa Fe, NM: The Sunstone Press, 1977.

Little, Elbert L. NATIONAL AUDUBON SOCIETY FIELD GUIDE TO NORTH AMERICAN TREES, WESTERN REGION. New York, NY: Knopf, 1988.

Wildflowers

Arnberger, Leslie P. FLOWERS OF THE SOUTHWEST MOUNTAINS. Rev. ed. Globe, AZ: SWPMA, 1983.

Dodge, Natt N., *et al.* FLOWERS OF THE SOUTHWEST DESERTS. Rev. ed. Tucson, AZ: SWPMA, 1985.

Niehaus, Theodore F., et al. A FIELD GUIDE TO SOUTHWESTERN AND TEXAS WILDFLOWERS. The Peterson Field Guide Series. Boston, MA: Houghton Mifflin, 1998.

Spellenberg, Richard. THE AUDUBON SOCIETY FIELD GUIDE TO NORTH AMERICAN WILDFLOWERS, WESTERN REGION. New York, NY: Knopf, 2001.

Miscellaneous

Auerbach, Paul. MEDICINE FOR THE OUTDOORS: THE ESSENTIAL GUIDE TO EMERGENCY MEDICAL PROCEDURES AND FIRST AID. 3rd edition. Boston, MA: Lyons Press, 1999.

Bischoff, Matt. TOURING NEW MEXICO HOT SPRINGS. Guilford, CT: Globe-Pequot Press, 2001.

Butterfield, Mike and Greene, Peter. MIKE BUTTERFIELD'S GUIDE TO THE MOUNTAINS OF NEW MEXICO. Santa Fe, NM: New Mexico Magazine, 2006.

DeBuys, William. ENCHANTMENT AND EXPLOITATION: THE LIFE AND HARD TIMES OF A NEW MEXICO MOUNTAIN RANGE. Albuquerque, NM: UNM Press, 1985.

DeBuys, William and Don Usner, VALLES CALDERA, A VISION FOR NEW MEXICO'S NATIONAL PRESERVE. Santa Fe, NM: Museum of New Mexico Press, 2006.

Fleming, June. STAYING FOUND, COMPLETE MAP AND COMPASS HAND BOOK. 3rd ed. Seattle, WA: Mountaineers Books, 2001.

Julyan, Robert. PLACE NAMES OF NEW MEXICO. 2nd ed. Albuquerque, NM: UNM Press, 1998.

Julyan, Robert. THE MOUNTAINS OF NEW MEXICO. Albuquerque NM: University of New Mexico Press, 2006.
This book has geology, history, hiking, and more!

Letham, Lawrence. GPS MADE EASY. 4th edition. Seattle, WA: The Mountaneers, 2003.

Slifer, Dennis. ROCK ART IMAGES OF NORTHERN NEW MEXICO. Santa Fe, NM: High Desert Guides, 2006.

Wilkerson, James A., ed. MEDICINE FOR MOUNTAINEERING AND OTHER WILDERNESS ACTIVITIES. 5th ed. Seattle, WA: Mountaineers Books, 2001.

Note: Some of the books listed above may be out of print, but might be available from local libraries and bookstores, or on line.

USING GPS

Courtesy of the Travel Bug, Santa Fe

All of the maps in this book are shown with a UTM grid for use with all GPS receivers. The grid interval varies with the scale of the map, but the same standards are used throughout.

Datum	NAS 27 (North American Datum 1927)
Map Projection	UTM (Universal Transverse Mercator)

This standard is also the easiest to use on all USGS maps.

To use the grid you must have your GPS set up with the **SAME** parameters as the map. Typically, you need to find the SETUP menu in the GPS and then select UNITS wherein you should be able to find two fields:

1. Position or Location format (Name varies with the unit) and set it to the correct map projection. Typically UTM/UPS
2. Datum (there are many datums that you will never use) Typically NAD27(CONUS)

With these two parameters set you are ready to use your unit with the maps in this book. The larger number (known as the northing coordinate) will pertain to the north-south axis and is simply the number of meters from the equator. The smaller number (known as the easting coordinate) gives your east-west position in meters relative to the center of the Zone you are in. All of the hikes in the book will be in Zone 13S.

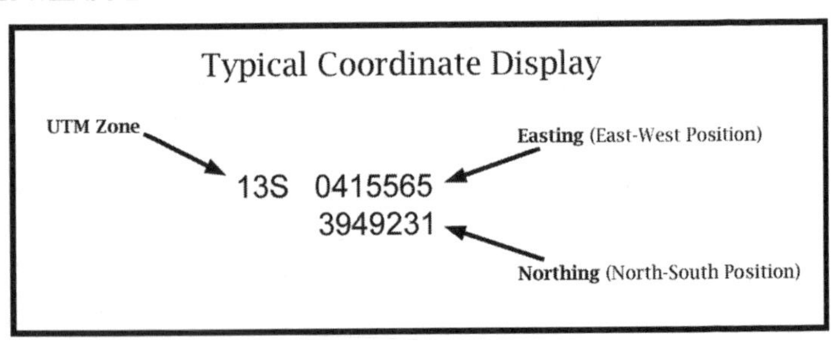

Drought, Heat, Dead Trees

by Norbert Sperlich

In recent years, the landscape of the Southwest and northern New Mexico has experienced dramatic changes. 1996 was the beginning of a severe drought, combined with warmer temperatures, which created conditions for forest fires and stressed many piñons in the piñon-juniper woodlands, making them unable to resist to bark beetles. The Dome Fire of 1996 and the Cerro Grande Fire of 2000 were two of the more notorious fires that sent their smoke plumes over Santa Fe. The Dome Fire ravaged the Dome Wilderness and part of Bandelier National Monument, and the Cerro Grande Fire reached parts of Los Alamos.

Massive tree die-off became evident in 2002 and continued through 2004. It slowed in 2005, when there was more precipitation and fewer trees left competing for the water. The winter of 2005–2006 was one of the warmest and driest on record. After a dry spring, the summer of 2006 turned out to be a very wet one. What's next?

The piñons in the 6,000-ft to 8,000-ft zone suffered the greatest damage from bark beetles, and in some areas most of them died. Junipers were affected, and ponderosas in the lower elevations also fell victim to the beetles. Even Douglas fir, usually found above the 8,000-ft level, were impacted.

Compared to the previous major drought (in the 1950s), this drought brought higher temperatures and was felt at higher elevations. Will the piñons come back as they have before, or are we dealing with the permanent effects of global warming?

Fire- or beetle-cleared slopes are much more susceptible to erosion, and hiking in the drought-stricken areas can be disconcerting, especially when one remembers the days when the trees were green and plentiful. Hiking through the piñon-juniper woodlands, you may have to negotiate fallen trees and eroded trails. But dead trees, too, are part of the cycle of nature, providing shelter for newly sprouting seeds and a variety of little critters. Learn about the current conditions before you go by calling the Forest Service or Bandelier National Monument.

	Summary of Hikes		Suitability				Hike		Time		
Hike No.	Hike Title	Rating	Spring	Summer	Fall	Winter	Hiking Miles, total	Elevation Gain, Cumulative, ft	Hiking Time, hrs	Driving Time, Round Trip, hrs	Comments *
1	Dale Ball Trails	E–S					2–5+	200–1000	2+	0.2	
2	Dorothy Stewart	E					3–4	440	2	0.3	
3	Atalaya	M					5.5–7	1600–1800	3–4	0.5	l,s
4	Rail Trail	E/M					4–10	2–300	2–3	0.5–1	
5	Hyde Park Circle	E–M					3.5	1100	3	0.7	f,l,s
6	Chamisa Trail	E					5	1240	2.5–3	0.5	w
7	Borrego/Bear Wallow Loop	E					4	900	2	0.7	w
8	Aspen Vista	E–S					11.5	2040	6	1	
9	Rio Nambe	S					10.5	2600	6	1.3	s
10	Deception/Lake/ Penitente Peaks	S					6–11	2500 3000	4–8	1.3	s,l
11	Nambé Lake	M					7	2100	5	1.3	l,s,w
12	La Vega	M					7	1500	3–4	1.3	w
13	Lake Katherine	S					14.5	3300	8	1.5	w
14	Santa Fe Baldy	S					14	3600	8	1.5	l,s
15	Tesuque Creek	E–M					3–7.5	500–1000	2–4	0.5	u,w
16	Rio En Medio/ La Junta Circuit	E S					5 14	800 2900	3 8	1	u,w
17	Rancho Viejo	S					13	2800	7	1	w
18	Tetilla Peak	E–M					3	950	2–3	2	h,l,s
19	Cerrillos Hills	E					4.5	363	2–3	1	u
20	Apache Canyon/ Glorieta Baldy	M S					6.5 13	800 2900	4 8	1.5	s,u
21	Glorieta Baldy	S					11.5	2800	6	1	l,s
22	Glor. Ghost Town	E–M					7	950	3–4	1	w
23	Holy Ghost/Spirit	S					14.5	2750	8	2.5	w
24	Stewart Lake	S					11	2100–2300	7	2.3	
25	Dockwiller Trail	M					8	1700	5	3	s,w
26	Cave Ck/ Horsethf Mdw/Lake Johnson	E–S					5–15	500–3000	2–8	2.5	f,w
27	Pecos Baldy Lk +East P.B. Peak	S					15 17	2600 3800	7.5 9	3.5	f,w
28	Beatty's Cabin/ Pecos Falls	S					10–20	1300–1640	5–8	3.5	f,h,w

***Comments** c = cliff (no dogs) d = dogs prohibited f = fee area
h = high clearance vehicle recommended l = loose footing
s = steep terrain u = unpaved access w = water plentiful

			Suitability				Hike		Time		
Hike No.	**Summary of Hikes** **Hike Title**	Rating	Spring	Summer	Fall	Winter	Hiking Miles, total	Elevation Gain, Cumulative, ft	Hiking Time, hrs	Driving Time, Round Trip, hrs	Comments *
29	Hermit Peak	S					8	2700	5	3.5	s
	+Porvenir Cyn						14	2800	7		w
30	Diablo Canyon	E					6	400	3	1.3	u
31	Buckman Mesa	M					5	1100	4	2	h,l,s,u
32	Blue Dot/Red Dot	M					7	800–1000	3–6	1.5	l,s
33	Ancho Rapids	M					6	1040	3	1.5	l,s
34	Cañada Bonita	E					3	650	2	2	
	+Guaje/Caballo Pk	S					15	3700	8		s
35	Upper Crossing	S					13	1600	7	2–2.5	d,f
36	Stone Lions Shrine	S					12.5	2700	8	2.5	d,f
37	Cerro Grande	M					4	1300	3	2.5	d
38	Valle Grande/ Coyote	E					2–3	4–500	1–2	2.5	d
39	Painted Cave	S					12.2	2400	8	4	d,h
40	East Fork Trl/Box	E–M					10	6/800	3–5	3	s,w
41	Los Griegos Ridge	M/S					7–8.5	1300–2000	4–6	3	
42	Tent Rocks	E					1.5–5	2–700	1.5	2	c,f,l,u
43	Tunnel Spring	S					15	3240	8–10	2.5	f,s,u
44	La Luz/Sandia Crest	S					9–16	3800–4200	5–10	2.5	f,l,s
45	Petroglyph N. Mon	E					1/3/2	100	1/2/2	2.5	f
46	Ojito Wilderness	M–S					6	600	5	3	l,u
47	Brazos Cabin	S					11.5	2550	7	2.5	h,w
48	Trampas Lakes +Hidden Lake	S					10.5 12.5	2450 2700	6 7.5	3	u,w
49	Santa Barbara	S					12	1100	7	3	u,w
50	Jicarita Peak	S					11	2452	7–8	4	s,u
51	Window Rock	M					7.5	1000	5	1.5	
52	Pedernal	S					9	1870	6–7	3.5	c,l,s,u
53	Kitchen Mesa	M					4.5	600	2.5	2.8	c,s,u
54	Rim Vista/Salazar	E/M					5.5/9	1700	3/5	3+	u
55	Ojo Caliente	E/M					3–6	700	2–4	2	
56	West Rim	E–M					7.5–9	200	4–6	3	
57	Lobo Peak	S					9–10	3500–3800	7	4	s
58	Wheeler Peak	S					15	4310	7–10	4	s
59	Gold Hill	S					10	3420	7	4	
60	Wild Rivers	M					4.5–9	800–1500	3–6	5	f,s,w

* **Comments** c = cliff (no dogs) d = dogs prohibited f = fee area
h = high clearance vehicle recommended l = loose footing
s = steep terrain u = unpaved access w = water plentiful

INDEX

FEATURED HIKES IN BOLD

NOTES

NOTES

MEMBERSHIP FORM

☐ ***Yes**, I want to be a member of the Sierra Club.*

☐ ***Yes**, I want to give a gift membership.*

MY NAME

ADDRESS

CITY/STATE ZIP

HOME PHONE NUMBER E-MAIL ADDRESS

I understand that a gift announcement card will be sent for my use. I've entered my name and address above and the recipient's name and address below.

GIFT RECIPIENT'S NAME

ADDRESS

CITY/STATE ZIP

Membership Categories

(CHECK ONE)	Individual	Joint
INTRODUCTORY	☐ $25	
REGULAR	☐ $39	☐ $47
SUPPORTING	☐ $75	☐ $100
STUDENT	☐ $24	☐ $32
SENIOR	☐ $24	☐ $32
LIMITED INCOME	☐ $24	☐ $32

Payment Method:

☐ Check ☐ MasterCard

☐ VISA ☐ AMEX

CARDHOLDER NAME

CARD NUMBER

EXPIRATION DATE

Contributions, gifts and dues to the Sierra Club are not tax-deductible; they support our effective, citizen-based advocacy and lobbying efforts. Your dues include $7.50 for a subscription to *Sierra* magazine and $1.00 for your Chapter newsletter.

F94QY 1704 2

Enclose payment information and mail to:

SIERRA CLUB

P.O. Box 52968, Boulder, CO 80322-2968

Explore, enjoy and protect the planet.

Membership Benefits

You'll Be Helping The Planet

You'll have the satisfaction of helping preserve irreplaceable wild lands and wildlife. Your voice will be heard through congressional lobbying and grassroots action. Your membership counts!

Sierra Magazine

You'll stay well-informed with a one-year subscription to award-winning Sierra magazine—featuring spectacular nature photography and in-depth reporting on the hottest environmental issues.

Discounts

Your membership entitles you to discounts on selected Sierra Club logo items. You'll also receive discounts on our distinguished books and celebrated nature calendars.

Worldwide Outings Program

Let us guide you, teach you, astound you. Sierra Club trips can take you to the far corners of the earth—paddling or pedaling, ski touring or trekking. We offer hundreds of exciting outings, from the tundra to the tropics. You can even build trails, preserve archeological sites and help clean up the environment on our exhilarating service trips!

Local Chapter Membership

As a member of your local Chapter, you'll receive up-to-date news on conservation issues, plus invitations to chapter events. You can also volunteer for local or national conservation campaigns.